Social psychology of exercise and sport

Applying social psychology
Series editor: Stephen Sutton

Published titles

Richard P. Bagozzi, Zeynep Gürhan-Canli and Joseph R. Priester: *The Social Psychology of Consumer Behaviour*

Mark Conner and Christopher J. Armitage: *The Social Psychology of Food*

Steve Sussman and Susan L. Ames: *The Social Psychology of Drug Abuse*

Social psychology of exercise and sport

Martin Hagger and Nikos Chatzisarantis

Open University Press

613,71019
H1455

Open University Press
McGraw-Hill Education
McGraw-Hill House
Shoppenhangers Road
Maidenhead
Berkshire
England
SL6 2QL

email: enquiries@openup.co.uk
world wide web: www.openup.co.uk

and Two Penn Plaza, New York, NY 10121-2289, USA

First published 2005 (twice)

A catalogue record of this book is available from the British Library

ISBN 0 335 21618 8 (pb)   0 335 21619 6 (hb)

Library of Congress Cataloging-in-Publication Data
CIP data applied for

Typeset by RefineCatch Limited, Bungay, Suffolk
Printed in UK by Bell & Bain Ltd., Glasgow

6/06

Contents

Series editor's foreword

Social psychology is sometimes criticized for not being sufficiently 'relevant' to everyday life. The Applying Social Psychology series challenges this criticism. It is organized around applied topics rather than theoretical issues, and is designed to complement the highly successful Mapping Social Psychology series edited by Tony Manstead. Social psychologists, and others who take a social psychological perspective, have conducted research on a wide range of interesting and important applied topics such as drug use, consumer behaviour, work, politics, the media, crime and environmental issues. Each book in the series takes a different applied topic and reviews relevant social psychological ideas and research. The books are texts rather than research monographs. They are pitched at final year undergraduate level, but will also be suitable for students on Masters level courses as well as researchers and practitioners working in the relevant fields. Although the series has an applied emphasis, theoretical issues are not neglected. Indeed, the series aims to demonstrate that theory-based applications of social psychology can contribute to our understanding of important applied topics.

This, the fourth, book in the series deals with exercise and sport. Both are topical issues. As the authors note, the profile of regular exercise and sport has risen in recent years, for different reasons: exercise, because of the links that have been observed in epidemiological studies between low levels of physical activity and risk of chronic diseases such as diabetes and heart disease; and sport, partly because televised sporting events have become a hugely popular form of entertainment. Social psychological research in the two domains has addressed somewhat different research questions. With regard to exercise, the key questions concern the psychological predictors and determinants of exercise behaviour and how such information can be used to inform interventions to increase physical activity. By contrast, social-psychological approaches to sport have attempted to explain individual and team perform-ance, again with implications for how performance can be enhanced. While research in the exercise domain has focused on the behaviour of individuals, work on performance in sport draws on the traditional social psychological area of intragroup processes to explain team performance. Although the book addresses the two topics separately, the final chapter provides an illuminating comparison between social psychological research in the two domains, in terms of themes, methods and theories. Both authors are active researchers in the fields of exercise and sport and have an intimate knowledge and obvious enthusiasm for their subject. In this book, they have succeeded in their aim of demonstrating the past and potential future contribution of social psychology to understanding exercise behaviour and sport performance.

Stephen Sutton

Acknowledgements

I dedicate this book to my parents, Mike and Elinor, and my brother Damian and his wife Mary-Jane for their inspiration and tolerance.

Martin Hagger

I would like to express my thanks to Professor Nikolas Karanikolas from the Anatolia College of Thessaloniki who kindled my creative instincts during my teenage years. Most importantly, I would like to extend my gratitude to my parents, Lazaros and Despoina Chatzisarantis, for support and encouragement.

Nikos Chatzisarantis

The authors would also like to express special thanks to Professor Stuart Biddle for his friendship, supervision, guidance, and encouragement. We would also like to thank Dr. Elaine Duncan, Professor Nannette Mutrie, Professor Stephen Sutton, Dr. Joanne Thatcher, and Dr. Mike Weed for their comments on earlier drafts of this book.

Finally, the author and the publisher would like to thank the following for granting permission to use material quoted in the text.

Figure 6.5: Source: Kerr (1985). Copyright © 1985 by Taylor and Francis Ltd, reprinted with permission.

Figure 7.1: Source: Carron and Hausenblas (1998). Copyright © 2002 by Fitness Information Technology, reprinted with permission.

Figure 7.2: Source: Carron (1992). Copyright © 1982 by Human Kinetics Publishers, adapted with permission.

Figure 7.3: Source: Carron, Widmeyer, and Brawley (1985). Copyright © 1985 by Human Kinetics Publishers, reprinted with permission.

Figure 7.5: Source: Beauchamp (2004). Adapted with permission.

Figure 7.6: Source: Aiello and Douthitt (2001). Copyright © 2001 by American Psychological Association, reprinted with permission.

Figure 8.1: Source: Silva (1980). Copyright © 1980 by Human Kinetics Publishers, reprinted with permission.

Introduction

The profile of regular exercise and sport in society has risen in recent years. The links between regular physical activity and physical and psychological health grow ever stronger and the role of competitive sport as entertainment and recreation is proliferating. Ever since Ralph Paffenbarger's seminal paper on the contribution of occupational physical activity to decreased mortality in Californian dock workers, epidemiological research has consistently reported a clear relationship between mortality rate and physical inactivity. Today, physical activity features high on the list of priority health behaviours for government campaigns aiming to improve health in industrialized nations. Sport, on the other hand, has always been a conduit for a nation to express its identity, but its increasing value for entertainment in the past two decades can be quantified not only by the observed rises in mass participation, but also in the earning power of and revenue generated by elite sporting individuals and teams. As exercise and sport are behaviours conducted in social contexts, social psychology has a significant role to play in understanding the **motivation** and behaviour of people involved in both recreational exercise for health and competitive sport. As social psychology is the study of human behaviour in social contexts, much of the investigation into the factors that contribute to examines exercise and sport behaviour, and the understanding of the relationships among these factors have been conducted by applying theoretical approaches from social psychology.

This book examines behaviour in sport and exercise from the point of view of social psychology. Principally, the text aims to devote considerable attention to key social psychological issues within the two disciplines: exercise behaviour for health reasons and the behaviour of competitive sport participants and the spectators of elite sport. Rather than presenting a broad, superficial overview of diverse areas in exercise and sport, the focus of the book is on a narrow range of selected topics and serves to provide a comprehensive, in-depth, analytical, and research-focused coverage using social psychology as a framework. The aim of the book is therefore to provide a thorough examination of how social psychological research and **intervention** have contributed to the understanding of key topics in exercise and sport behaviour.

Social psychology, like many disciplines in psychology, has many branches and sub-systems. This is not surprising, considering the multitude of questions and social problems that social psychologists try to address and the diverse methods of research inquiry that social psychologists adopt to investigate these problems. Social psychology can be considered even more diverse than other areas of applied psychology because it is informed by research from other areas of the social and behavioural sciences (Bagozzi *et al.* 2002). In the United Kingdom and the United States, social psychology has been treated as a science and tends to adopt a positivistic approach that is driven by both theory and hypothesis. The aim is to provide answers to research questions through quantitative empirical methods that are based on the principle of disconfirmation or falsification. This approach tends to be the dominant in the social psychological literature, mainly because many of the mainstream peer-reviewed journals are North American and tend to endorse this approach. This approach has been labelled **psychological social psychology** because it adopts the rigorous scientific approaches used by other sub-systems and disciplines in psychology. The *psychological* social psychology tradition is contrasted with an approach that focuses on the effects of the broader social context on social action. This *sociological* approach to social psychology examines the effects of personal experience, meanings, language, culture, ideology, and the material or physical environment on the 'lived experience' of individuals in those contexts and, in particular, their relationships with others. The key unit of analysis in this approach tends to be representations, stereotypes, and cultural images and how they relate to people's construction and interpretation of the meaning they attribute to themself and others on the basis of these broad social influences. **Sociological social psychology** tends to be predominant in Europe and adopts a relativist rather than absolute perspective towards truth and meaning.

The research presented in this book is derived primarily from the psychological social psychology tradition and the quantitative, hypothesis-testing methodological framework. This is primarily because it is the dominant tradition in applied research in exercise and sport psychology. However, we aim to provide a fair treatment of the various approaches and methods used in research in this area and have therefore included research from the sociological social psychology tradition that adopts a more grounded, theory-building approach rather than a theory-testing one and adopts qualitative methods to investigate research questions. We have excluded research from the skill acquisition literature including motor learning, motor control, and motor development perspective because most of the research in these areas has focused on perceptual and neurological explanations of movement far removed from social influences on human movement. Other exclusions include more sociolocal approaches to the explanation of exercise and sport behaviour. We have focused on the individual as the unit of analysis, as is the tendency in the psychological social psychological approach. While we recognize the influence of overarching social factors such as age, socio-economic status, culture, and ethnic background, these are treated as peripheral to the influence of personal variables such as personality, **beliefs**, emotions, expectations, and judgements on exercise and sport behaviour.

This book is divided into two parts: the social psychology of exercise (Part I) and the social psychology of sport behaviour (Part II). Part I consists of four chapters and will focus on the application of social psychological theory to the explanation of exercise and physical activity participation. The key issues covered in Part I include the links between exercise, and physical and psycho-logical health (Chapter 1), the social cognitive theories that have attempted to explain exercise behaviour (Chapter 2), the theories that aim to convert exer-cise intention and motivation into exercise behaviour (Chapter 3), and the role of the physical self in exercise behaviour and psychological disorders relat-ing to self-perceptions (Chapter 4). We have adopted a step-by-step approach to the understanding of social psychological theories and investigations in exercise and how they can lead to interventions to promote exercise behaviour in the general population. We initially introduce the prevailing theoretical approaches, the empirical research from the social psychological literature that has provided support for these theories, and provide a comprehensive overview on the basis of this research as to how interventions can be designed to change exercise behaviour in the general population.

Part II consists of four chapters and aims to provide coverage of key issues in sport-related behaviour. The key areas covered are social psychological approaches to motivation in sport (Chapter 5), the social psychology of emo-tion and anxiety in sport (Chapter 6), group processes and social influence on sport performance (Chapter 7), and aggressive behaviour and crowd violence in sport contexts (Chapter 8). Again, we aim to introduce the reader to the pertinent theories adopted by social psychologists to explain key social psy-chological behaviours in sport, particularly sport performance. At each stage we aim to provide a series of key target variables and highlight the strategies that sport psychologists and coaches can adopt to enhance performance in athletes and sports performers. In each chapter we provide an executive sum-mary of the pertinent points in the chapter along with some key annotated readings.

A common limitation of many books that cover psychological research in both the exercise and sport domains is that they fail to draw any conclusions on the commonalities between the two areas. This has the effect of reinforcing the notion that approaches to these areas are entirely different and exercise psychology and sport psychology should be rigorously compartmentalized into two entirely different disciplines. Chapter 9 aims to break this tradition and draws together the common themes and differences in the social psycho-logical approaches to exercise and sport behaviour. The aim of Chapter 9 is to point out to the reader that many of the approaches to exercise and sport from an applied social psychological perspective have as many similarities as they do contrasts. In this chapter similarities are covered in terms of themes, methods, and theories. In terms of themes, prediction of behaviour, affective outcomes, and social influences are common to both areas. The common methods adopted to investigate these predictions include cross-sectional studies, longitudinal, cross-lagged panel designs, experimental designs, and qualitative approaches. Theories of intention and motivation are common to social psychological research in both areas. Finally, to illustrate some of the contrasts inherent to social psychological approaches to exercise and sport, we review the potential conflict between sport for competition and sport for health purposes.

There is a glossary of key words and phrases at the back of the book. The first occurrence of each word in the glossary is shown in bold in the text.

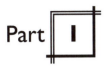

Part **I**

The social psychology of exercise

Social psychology, exercise, and health

This chapter will introduce some of the key concepts relating to physical activity and health and outline the problems faced by applied social psychologists in the field of physical activity and health. The aim is to provide sufficient background knowledge of the health, social, and economic problems presented by a sedentary population in industrialized nations. In addition, it will give an insight into research techniques such as descriptive epidemiology as a means to evaluate the extent of the epidemic of physical inactivity and obesity in industrialized countries. Subsequently, the focus will be on the importance of applied social psychology to inform and drive interventions to increase the levels of physical activity behaviour in sedentary populations. In addition, the different social psychological theoretical approaches to physical activity behaviour will be introduced.

What is physical activity?

People often talk about **sport**, **exercise**, and **physical activity** in an eclectic, unstructured manner, and occasionally use the terms synonymously. In everyday life, it seems, the understanding of the distinctions between these forms of physical endeavour is often unclear. It is therefore essential that these terms are formally defined before embarking on a discussion of the importance of physical activity to health and how social psychology can lend itself to an understanding of these behaviours. Physical activity is typically used to refer to all types of movement that expends energy, regardless of features such as type, location, mode, and intensity. Formally, Pate *et al.* define physical activity as 'any bodily movement produced by skeletal muscles that results in energy expenditure' (1995: 402). It can therefore be considered an umbrella term under which other more specific forms of physical activity fall. Exercise and sport are therefore subtypes of physical activity. Exercise generally refers to structured physical activity whose purpose is to incur a health benefit such as losing weight. Examples of these types of activity are jogging, cycling, swimming, rowing, and walking. Sport is another form of physical activity, but is far more structured than exercise, has specific sets of rules, and generally involves competition with other people. Exercise can, however, also be less structured such as that associated with certain occupations or for transport such as walking to work. Importantly, exercise has a number of properties that determine the degree of health benefit it can provide, namely, type, intensity, frequency, and duration. Exercise that involves and stresses large muscle groups (known as 'gross' motor tasks) over a long period of time and is of a vigorous intensity tends to be favoured by exercise promoters because this kind of exercise puts a high degree of stress on the cardiovascular system and has the potential to increase the daily energy expenditure of the individual. If undertaken frequently enough, such activity can assist in ameliorating risk from cardiovascular disease, can help promote skeletal and psychological health, and can reduce the risk of other illnesses such as cancer and type II diabetes, and may prevent other conditions that may compromise health such as obesity. Social psychological approaches to understanding exercise participation will be the subject of the first part of this book.

Evidence for the effect of physical activity on health

Physical activity and chronic disease in adults

Low levels of regular physical activity in the populations of industrialized nations have been implicated in a number of chronic diseases. These diseases include various forms of cardiovascular disease, obesity, type II diabetes, certain types of cancers, and hypertension. Cardiovascular disease, in particular, is a serious health issue. Recent statistics indicate that cardiovascular disease is the largest single cause of death in many industrialized nations. For example, cardiovascular disease accounts for approximately 931,000 deaths per year in the United States (CDC/NCHS 2001) and 238,000 deaths per year in the United Kingdom (Petersen *et al.* 2004). In addition, treatment for such diseases puts a substantial burden on public health services. For example, treatment for coronary heart disease, the most prevalent type of cardiovascular disease, costs the UK National Health Service £1.75 billion per year (Liu *et al.* 2002). Alongside cardiovascular disease, incidence of obesity, a clinical term for excess adipose or fat tissue, is increasing. Obesity also presents a health risk because it is implicated in many health problems such as cardiovascular disease, diabetes, colorectal cancer, and hypertension. Obesity is defined using a measurement that accounts for a person's height and weight, known as the body mass index (BMI). This is the ratio of a person's body mass to their height squared (weight/height^2) and a BMI greater than $30kg/m^2$ is considered obese. In the United States, 27.5 per cent of men and 33.4 per cent of women are considered obese (Centers for Disease Control and Prevention 2002), while in the United Kingdom 22 per cent of men and 23 per cent of women are classified as obese (National Health Service Health Development Agency 1996). This evidence indicates that cardiovascular disease and obesity are substantial problems to public health in industrialized nations.

There is a general consensus that multiple key risk factors contribute to the likelihood of an individual contracting cardiovascular disease, namely, age, gender, a family history or heredity of stress, tobacco smoking, elevated blood cholesterol (hypercholesterolemia) or more specifically a serum lipid profile that has a disproportionately high ratio of low density lipoproteins (LDL), hypertension or high blood pressure, obesity, type II diabetes, stress, and physical inactivity (American Heart Association 1999). Clearly, age, gender, and heredity are demographic variables that are unalterable. However, many of the other risk factors can be affected by behaviour change and research has indicated that regular physical activity of the relevant type, intensity, duration, and frequency can substantially alter the levels of these risk factors and thereby reduce the risk of cardiovascular disease (Wannamethee and Shaper 2001).

Physical inactivity has been isolated as a risk factor for cardiovascular disease (Wannamethee and Shaper 2001). Epidemiological studies have shown that low physical activity and fitness levels are related to all-cause mortality in the general population (e.g. Paffenbarger and Hale 1975), although physical fitness is controversial as a correlate of cardiovascular and other disease risk because it only indirectly relates to physical activity participation. Further epidemiological research has revealed some of the mechanisms behind these links. Research has shown that regular vigorous physical activity lowers blood cholesterol and produces a more favourable serum lipid profile, reduces hypertension, and can help control and reduce the severity of type II diabetes (Wannamethee and Shaper 2001). Physical activity, along with dietary manipulation, can also help maintain a healthy level of body fitness and has been shown to be effective in reducing obesity (Wannamethee and Shaper 2001). This evidence indicates that regular physical activity has profound effects on cardiovascular health and can reduce the risk factors associated with cardiovascular disease.

In addition to the ameliorating effect of physical activity on cardiovascular disease risk factors, research has also implicated physical activity in reducing the incidence of certain cancers. Recent evidence suggests that regular vigorous physical activity can reduce the risk of ovarian, breast, and colorectal cancer (Courneya and Friedenreich 1997). Although researchers are unsure as to the exact mechanism by which physical activity acts to reduce cancer risk, it is thought that it may be its efficacy in maintaining a healthy body weight and that exercisers tend to adopt more healthy behaviours such as eating foods high in antioxidants.

Regular physical activity has also been implicated in maintaining skeletal health, particularly in women (Branca 1999). Coupled with a diet that includes adequate calcium supplementation, regular weight-bearing physical activity can act as a preventive measure against osteoporosis – a chronic disease that results in the demineralization of bones and an increased susceptibility to fractures. Finally, an important effect of regular physical activity is its effect on psychological and mental health. Regular physical activity has been found to be an effective treatment for mental health and has been implicated in positive well-being and self-esteem in the general population (Fox 1999).

Physical activity and young people

Epidemiological and clinical studies have indicated that the occurrence of diseases such as cardiovascular disease and other illnesses linked with low levels of physical activity in adults is only a manifestation of behavioural patterns that have paediatric origins. Initial evidence that cardiovascular disease had paediatric origins was gleaned from autopsies on American infantrymen killed in action in the Vietnam War that showed the beginnings of atherosclerosis (a precursor of some forms of cardiovascular disease) in their arteries (McNamara *et al.* 1971). Research has shown that the risk factors associated with cardiovascular disease in adults are present among children and adolescents and that these risk factors tend to track into adulthood (Webber *et al.* 1983). In addition, rates of childhood or juvenile obesity are increasing with surveys indicating incidences of 20 per cent in the United States (Flegal 1999) and 9.2 per cent in the United Kingdom (Bundred *et al.* 2001), figures that represent substantial increases on previous years. The detrimental health effects of obesity are the same in adolescents as they are for adults such as hypertension, elevated blood lipids and high levels of LDLs, and increased risk of diabetes. Indeed, a study of obese children revealed that 97 per cent had three or more cardiovascular disease risk factors (Parker and Bar-Or 1991). Importantly, it seems that obese children and adolescents are likely to become obese adults and this highlights the need to control this through diet and exercise.

Indeed, research in the past two decades has established the importance of physical activity to children's cardiovascular health (Sallis and Patrick 1994). There is evidence to suggest that children who exhibit higher levels of physical activity and fitness are less likely to have high levels of cardiovascular risk factors, although there is only limited evidence that physical activity is related to hypertension and serum lipid profiles of young people (Raitakari *et al.* 1994). Aside from the amelioration of cardiovascular disease risk factors, increased physical activity in children is also associated with other health benefits. Higher levels of regular physical activity are associated with lower levels of juvenile obesity (Parker and Bar-Or 1991). Physical activity has been shown to promote skeletal health and aerobic fitness, have a positive effect on variables related to psychological health such as depression, anxiety, stress hostility, anger, and intellectual functioning and can also enhance self-esteem and overall well-being (Sallis and Patrick 1994). Such findings have compelled researchers in the behavioural sciences to further investigate the antecedents of children's physical activity behaviour.

Guidelines for physical activity

Converging evidence from these studies has highlighted the importance of physical activity to health and has forced exercise scientists to propose guidelines for physical activity and nutrition. National bodies and advisory groups have published position statements and guidelines to appropriate levels of physical activity to reduce risk of the diseases that are associated with low levels of activity and to maintain positive health and well-being. For adults, numerous guidelines have been issued stating the appropriate frequency, intensity, type, and duration of physical activity necessary for good health and these have been the focus of various campaigns to promote physical activity. The content of these guidelines is relatively uniform across nations and research bodies. The consensus drawn from these guidelines and recommendations from the United States (e.g. Byers *et al.* 2002) and the United Kingdom (e.g. Department of Health 1996) is that individuals should engage in continuous physical activity of at least moderate intensity for a period of 30 minutes on most days of the week, and preferably engage in bouts of higher-intensity vigorous physical activity on some days of the week. In addition, similar guidelines have been issued for special populations such as the elderly (American College of Sports Medicine 1998) and adolescents and children (Sallis and Patrick 1994).

The physical inactivity epidemic

Given the abundance of evidence to support the links between regular and vigorous physical activity and cardiovascular, skeletal, and mental health, research has also focused on the descriptive epidemiology of physical inactivity among populations in industrialized nations. Such an investigation aims to outline the extent to which people attain the recommended levels of physical activity associated with good health. Results from such studies have consistently indicated that there is an epidemic of inactivity among these populations. Evidence from national health surveys in the United States (Centers for Disease Control and Prevention 2003) and the United Kingdom (National Centre for Social Research 1999) show that approximately 30 per cent of people did not participate in any physical activity. In England, only 37 per cent of men and 25 per cent of women meet the recommended guidelines for physical activity (Joint Surveys Unit 1999). A survey of 15,339 consumers from the 14 European Union states (approximately 1,000 adults from each member state) found a large variation across national groups in the percentage of people who engaged in no physical activity, ranging from 1 per cent to 47.6 per cent (Institute of European Food Studies 1999). However, the percentage of people engaging in regular physical activity ranged from 92 per cent in Finland to 60 per cent in Greece. In addition, there is also evidence to suggest that the majority of children in the United States (Centers for Disease Control and Prevention 2003) and the United Kingdom (Cale and Almond 1992) do not engage in sufficient physical activity of the type, intensity, duration, and frequency likely to bring about health benefits.

Alongside these statistics that seem to indicate low levels of regular physical activity among many industrialized nations, surveys have also suggested that the majority of people believe that physical activity is important to health (UK Health Education Authority and Sports Council 1992) but only about 50 per cent of people surveyed agreed that they needed to do more physical activity than they currently did (Institute of European Food Studies 1999). Of great concern is the largely static percentage of physical inactivity over the past two decades. Population studies have shown that the level of physical inactivity remained largely unchanged between 1986 and 2002 (Centers for Disease Control and Prevention 2003). In summary, the majority of adults in industrialized nations do not engage in sufficient physical activity to gain the health benefits suggested by research, and levels of physical inactivity have remained relatively constant, while, paradoxically, the majority of people believe they do engage in sufficient physical activity.

Given this evidence, researchers have sought to examine the factors that affect physical activity behaviour. The importance of identifying these factors is paramount as they can tell on the basis of effective, theory-based interventions the factors that are most subject to change and will have the greatest influence on physical activity behaviour (Brawley 1993). Indeed, it is these kinds of social problems that have benefited from research in applied social psychological theory because these approaches aim to explain the problem, presenting both an identification of salient influences as well as an explanation of how those influences can affect behaviour. The next section will outline how research in social psychology can assist in identifying salient factors and help inform interventions to promote exercise among predominately sedentary populations.

The role of social psychology

One way to promote exercise participation is to consult theories of social behaviour that identify the salient antecedent variables and mechanisms underpinning the motivation of social behaviour, and then test these theories in the domain of physical activity (Brawley 1993). Theories provide an explanatory system as to *how* the antecedents of physical activity behaviour affect behaviour and provide a general guide as to how physical activity behaviour can be promoted. For example, if a theory identifies **attitudes** as an important determinant of behaviour, then it can be suggested that physical activity behaviour can be promoted by changing attitudes.

However, it is important to realize that theories from social psychology can guide promotion of physical activity participation only if they explain physical activity participation satisfactorily (Brawley 1993). Unfortunately, empirical evidence suggests that theories from social psychology cannot explain more than 50 per cent of variance in physical activity behaviour (Hagger *et al.* 2002b). Such levels of prediction obtained by social psychological models are far below the levels of prediction obtained by models in the pure sciences, and suggest that it would be naïve to expect psychological interventions to be entirely effective in promoting physical activity participation. Therefore, from the perspective of social psychology, the promotion of physical activity participation should be viewed as an ongoing process that consists of identification of antecedents of physical activity participation (**formative research**) and of **applied research** that evaluates utility of interventions in promoting physical activity behaviour.

Formative research aims at the identification of the most important psychological variables that underline exercise participation (Ajzen 1991). Social psychologists can contribute a great deal to the development of formative research through a variety of different study designs such as cross-sectional, longitudinal, panel, and experimental studies. Such studies aim to quantitatively evaluate the extended, modified, or refined versions of existing social psychological models in predicting exercise participation (Hagger *et al.* 2002b) through the principle of converging evidence. However, it is important to distinguish between variables and psychological models that only *predict* exercise participation and those that *predict and explain* exercise participation (Ajzen and Fishbein 1980). Variables and theories that predict participation in physical activities are only useful in identifying those who exercise and those who do not. While such information is important in identifying sub-populations who are at risk, they may not help explain why some people exercise and others do not. Explanation of exercise participation is only achieved when exercise participation is predicted by variables that can be manipulated. For example, it is widely accepted that **attitudes** can change (Eagly and Chaiken 1993), and therefore predictions obtained by attitudes provide information about behavioural change. Therefore, development of models of exercise participation should focus on the identification of variables that both predict and explain exercise participation. In addition to formative research, promotion of exercise participation can ultimately benefit from applied social psychological research that evaluates interventions in promoting active lifestyles (Brawley 1993; Hardeman *et al.* 2002). Intervention studies have the potential to evaluate whether manipulations of social psychological variables actually can change exercise habits.

Part I of this book reviews some leading social psychological theories applied to the explanation of volitional behaviours such as exercise. It also focuses on the limitations of these theories and the measures taken to address these limitations. This is important because these potential solutions to resolve these limitations can produce modified versions of the existing theories to strengthen the efficacy of the theory to explain and promote exercise participation.

Suggested reading

Brawley, L.R. (1993) The practicality of using psychological theories for exercise and health research and intervention, *Journal of Applied Sport Psychology*, 5, 99–115. Provides an introductory insight into the utility of social cognitive approaches to change exercise behaviour.

Cale, L. and Almond, L. (1992) Physical activity levels of school-aged children: a review, *Health Education Journal*, 51, 192–7. Provides details on the research suggesting an epidemic of physical inactivity among young people.

Pate, R.R. (1995) Recent statements and initiatives on physical activity and health, *American Academy of Kinesiology and Physical Education*, 47, 304–10. An overview of the guidelines offered by health campaigns to promote exercise and physical activity for health.

Summary

- Physical activity refers to all bodily movement that expends energy. Exercise is formal physical activity expressly to expend energy for health reasons and sport often involves some form of physical activity, but is engaged in for a number of different reasons such as competition and demonstration of competence.
- Physical inactivity is a risk factor for cardiovascular disease and has numerous psychological and health benefits for adults and young people. Exercise scientists recommend people engage in at least 30 minutes of moderate physical activity per day, accompanied by some bouts of vigorous physical activity.
- Formative research in social psychology can provide useful insight into the mechanisms behind the antecedents of physical activity and can help inform interventions applied to physical activity behaviour.

2

Social cognitive theories of exercise behaviour

Understanding regular participation in exercise requires an understanding of the psychological constructs that predict and explain exercise behaviour (Ajzen and Fishbein 1980). This chapter aims to introduce and review the formative and applied research in social psychology on theories of **social cognition** and exercise behaviour. Common to these theories is the inclusion of belief-based constructs such as attitudes and motivational constructs such as intentions that are learned from previous experience. Another important feature of these models is that they focus on the *formation* of motivation and the processes that lead to intentions. They do not contend with the more automatic processes that give rise to intentions nor do they aim to explain the mechanisms by which intentions are converted into behaviour. These will be dealt with in Chapter 3. Finally, the chapter will outline some of the practical guidelines that arise from research with these models.

Intentions and social cognitive models of exercise behaviour

Many important social psychological theories of human motivation incorporate the construct of **intention**. Such theories propose that people are rational decision-makers who choose to engage in the target behaviour by processing the available information relating to the advantages and disadvantages associated with that behaviour. Theories of intentional behaviour also share the view that human motivation is unidimensional (Deci and Ryan 1985) and that the construct of intentions, which represents motivation, is the most immediate determinant of human action (Ajzen 1991). Importantly, these theories tend to focus on intention formation and do not offer any explanation for the processes that underpin the enactment of previously formed intentions (Ajzen 2002b). **Volitional theories**, which are reviewed in the next chapter, detail the processes by which intentions are translated into actions (Gollwitzer 1999). In the next section, theories of intentional behaviour are introduced, and their implications for future research and for practice in the exercise domain are discussed.

The health belief model

The **health belief model** proposes that an individual's readiness (intention) to perform a health behaviour is a function of his or her perceived vulnerability to a health condition and the probable severity of that condition (Rosenstock 1974). The model posits that readiness is determined by a person's beliefs about the benefits to be gained by a particular behaviour such as exercise, weighted by their perceived barriers to doing that behaviour. Finally, the model predicts that readiness may not result in overt action unless some instigating event occurs to set the action process in motion. Rosenstock called such instigating events cues to action. Overall, the health belief model predicts that if a person feels vulnerable to an illness, and if it is perceived to be severe, and if he or she believes that a particular health behaviour will reduce the health threat associated with that illness, then he or she will have a high degree of readiness to engage in the health behaviour. For example, individuals may feel susceptible to cardiovascular disease because they have a poor diet and have been told by their doctor that they have hypertension. They may also believe that regular exercise will reduce the threat of cardiovascular disease. According to the model, these perceptions are likely to motivate the individual to participate in exercise behaviours. The health belief model is summarized in Figure 2.1.

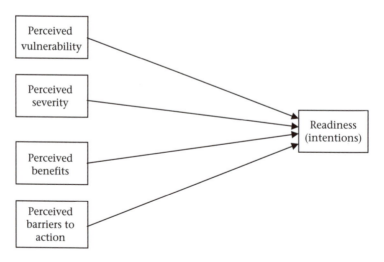

Figure 2.1   The health belief model

Formative research has shown that perceived severity and beliefs about the benefits of a health behaviour exert strong influences on readiness to engage in that behaviour, while perceived severity and barriers have smaller roles (Quine *et al.* 1998; Abraham *et al.* 1999). In addition, evidence suggests that the direct effects of perceived vulnerability, severity, susceptibility, benefits, and barriers on health behaviours are small and are mediated by readiness (Abraham *et al.* 1999). There is also evidence to suggest that the health belief model does not sufficiently capture all the psychological determinants of social behaviour and that the model might benefit from considering the effects of other constructs such as **self-efficacy** on intentions and behaviour.

One limitation of the health belief model is that it does not offer clear operational definitions of its psychological constructs such as perceived vulnerability, nor does it specify how different variables can combine in influencing intentions and behaviour (Quine *et al.* 1998). For example, it is unclear which particular behaviours are facilitated by perceived vulnerability to an illness. In the case of a perceived vulnerability to cardiovascular disease, the model does not explicitly state whether vulnerability would facilitate exercise or dieting behaviour, given that both behaviours would be effective in ameliorating cardiovascular disease risk. As a result, empirical evidence related to the health belief model varies greatly across studies because different studies have used different operational definitions for psychological constructs (Harrison *et al.* 1992).

Protection motivation theory

The **protection motivation theory** (Rogers 1983) is similar to the health belief model and advocates that the performance of health behaviour is a function of two distinct appraisals: threat appraisals and coping appraisals with respect to an illness that poses a health threat (see Figure 2.2). As in the health belief model, threat appraisals are derived from two sets of beliefs: perceived vulnerability and perceived severity. Perceived vulnerability is the person's belief that they are vulnerable to the health threat and perceived severity is the person's belief that the occurrence of the disease will have severe consequences. Coping appraisals comprise beliefs that a given behaviour will be effective in reducing the health threat, known as response efficacy, beliefs that one possesses the necessary capabilities to perform the health behaviour, called self-efficacy beliefs, and beliefs regarding the perceived costs associated with performing the health behaviour (Rogers 1983). Overall, protection motivation theory predicts that individuals will adopt a health behaviour: (1) if they believe a disease to be severe and likely to occur; and (2) if they perceive that health behaviour is effective in reducing the health threat, something that they feel capable of doing, and if it does not cost a lot.

Formative research has documented the utility of threat appraisals and coping appraisals such as self-efficacy in predicting health-related intentions and behaviours (Hodgkins and Orbell 1998; Milne *et al.* 2000). In addition,

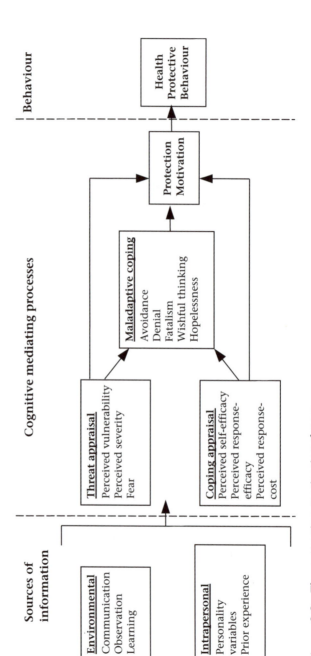

Figure 2.2 The protection motivation theory

there is evidence that corroborates the view that threat appraisals can facilitate maladaptive coping responses (Hodgkins and Orbell 1998). In the exercise domain, formative research has also documented the utility of self-efficacy, response efficacy, and perceived vulnerability in influencing exercise intentions (Milne *et al.* 2002). Most important, intervention studies have found effects from coping appraisals and threat appraisals on intentions (Milne *et al.* 2002). However, it is important to note that effects of coping appraisal and threat appraisal on intentions and behaviour have been modest (Milne *et al.* 2000).

Designing interventions based on the health belief model and the protection motivation theory

As previously noted, an important function of formative research is to provide information about the content of interventions. Generally speaking, the greater the relative importance of a factor in predicting intentions, the more likely it is that changing that factor will influence intentions and ultimately behaviour. Given that studies adopting the health belief model and the protection motivation theory have shown that appraisals related to the health threat such as perceived vulnerability and perceived severity, and appraisals related to coping strategies such as self-efficacy and response efficacy, can influence intentions to exercise, it is suggested that attempts to change exercise behaviour should try to manipulate threat appraisals and coping appraisals (Milne *et al.* 2000). An important question, therefore, is how health appraisals and coping appraisals can be influenced.

Threat appraisals can be manipulated through fear-arousing communications emphasizing (1) the painful and debilitating effects of an illness, i.e. its perceived severity; and (2) that people who do not exercise regularly are vulnerable to heart disease, i.e. perceived vulnerability. Coping responses can be manipulated by providing people with information that explains the effectiveness of exercise in preventing the disease, that presents an intervention to change response efficacy, and by prompting people to choose to perform types of exercise that are relatively easy to execute that will alter self-efficacy. One caveat of interventions based on the health belief model and the protection motivation theory is that, although they may be successful in strengthening intentions, they may not always bring substantial changes in exercise behaviour (Milne *et al.* 2000). Therefore, it cannot be expected automatically that application of these theories will have a strong effect on exercise behaviour. Instead, the effectiveness of the protection motivation theory in changing exercise behaviour may be enhanced through the implementation of volitional techniques that can help people translate intentions into actions. Another limitation of the health belief model and the protection motivation theory is that the threatening messages can sometimes undermine rather than enhance intentions (Hodgkins and Orbell 1998). Therefore, fear-arousing communications should be designed and applied with caution.

The theory of reasoned action

The **theory of reasoned action** (Ajzen and Fishbein 1980) is one of the most influential and oft-cited models of intentional behaviour (Sheppard *et al.* 1988). According to this theory, the performance of volitional behaviours such as exercise can be best predicted from a person's stated intention to participate in the behaviour. Ajzen and Fishbein (1980) hypothesized that intention indicates the degree of planning a person puts into their future behaviour and represents how hard people are willing to try and how much effort they expect to exert in the performance of behaviour. It is therefore a construct that is motivational in nature and function, much like traditional conceptualizations of intention (Meiland 1970). Intention is assumed to be the most immediate or *proximal* antecedent of behaviour (Ajzen and Fishbein 1980). Intention is in turn a function of a set of personal and normative perceptions regarding the performance of the behaviour, the attitudes and the subjective norms, respectively. Attitudes represent an overall positive or negative evaluation towards the target behaviour. Subjective norms represent perceived influences that significant others may exert on the execution of the behaviour. Generally speaking, the theory of reasoned action predicts that the more favourable an individual's attitude and **subjective norm**, the stronger his or her intentions to perform the behaviour. Finally, intentions are hypothesized to lead directly to behavioural engagement and intentions are proposed to mediate the effects of attitudes and subjective norms on behaviour. This means that intentions explain the attitude–behaviour and subjective norm–behaviour relationships. Intentions are therefore necessary to convert attitudes and subjective norms into behaviour.

The theory also deals with the antecedents of attitudes and subjective norms. The theory proposes that attitudes arise out of a combination or composite of the actor's beliefs that behaviour will lead to certain outcomes, known as **behavioural beliefs**, and their evaluation of these outcomes, termed **outcome evaluations** (Ajzen and Fishbein 1980). Similarly, the origins of subjective norms can be traced to corresponding belief-based judgements that include **normative beliefs** and **motivation to comply**. Normative beliefs refer to behavioural expectations that important referent individuals or groups will approve or disapprove of the behaviour (Ajzen and Fishbein 1980) and motivation to comply is the actor's general tendency to go along with the wishes of the salient referents. This relationship between behavioural and normative beliefs and their respective evaluations is grounded in the expectancy × value model, and the belief-based measures of attitudes and subjective norms are considered *antecedents* of the directly measured attitude and subjective norm constructs. The theory of reasoned action is shown in Figure 2.3.

The major hypothesises of the theory of reasoned action have been supported in numerous studies of a number of different behaviours (Sheppard *et al.* 1988), including exercise (e.g. Hausenblas *et al.* 1997; Hagger *et al.* 2002b)

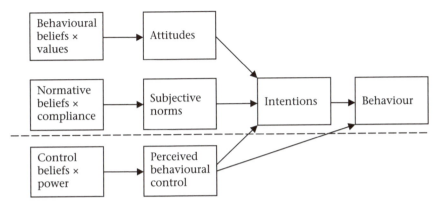

Figure 2.3　Theories of reasoned action and planned behaviours
Note: Constructs and relationships above the broken line represent the theory of reasoned action. Constructs above and below the broken line together represent the theory of planned behaviour.

and sports training (Theodorakis *et al.* 1991b). In the exercise domain, tests of the theory of reasoned action have provided strong evidence for the overall predictive value of intentions and have shown that attitudes have a pervasive effect on intentions with a lesser role for subjective norms (Hausenblas *et al.* 1997; Hagger *et al.* 2002b). Formative research adopting the theory of reasoned action in the exercise domain has also shown that the typically large effect of attitudes and small effect of subjective norms on intentions are not influenced by whether belief-based or direct measures of attitudes and subjective norms have been used (Theodorakis *et al.* 1991a). Moreover, panel studies have indicated that the strong effects of attitudes on intentions remain stable over time (Chatzisarantis *et al.*, in press a; Hagger *et al.* 2001).

Equally important have been applications of the theory of reasoned action that reveal a number of salient behavioural and normative beliefs related to exercise. The beliefs are typically elicited from open-ended questionnaires administered to a pilot sample prior to the development of standard questionnaires to measure the belief-based constructs of theory of reasoned action (Ajzen and Fishbein 1980). Behavioural beliefs identified in this research include: 'good companionship', 'weight control', 'benefit my overall health', 'take too much time', 'fun', 'get fit', 'stay in shape', 'improve skills', 'get an injury', and 'makes you hot and sweaty' (Hagger *et al.* 2001). Important referents for the normative beliefs and motivation to comply measures tend to be family members such as parents, grandparents, and siblings along with friends and schoolteachers (Hagger *et al.* 2001). However, these beliefs have not been shown to unequivocally account for unique variance in the directly measured attitude and subjective norm constructs and alternative subsets of beliefs may exist (Hagger *et al.* 2001).

Boundary conditions of the theory of reasoned action

Although research has consistently supported the validity of the theory of reasoned action (Sheppard *et al.* 1988), three conditions, outlined by Ajzen and Fishbein (1980), limit the utility of the theory of reasoned action in predicting and explaining behaviour. These are the conditions of **correspondence**, *stability*, and *volitional control*. The boundary condition of correspondence states that the predictive efficacy of the theory of reasoned action variables such as intention is improved when measures of intentions and measures of behaviour are phrased in a way that correspond in four key ways: action (e.g. exercise); target at which action is directed (e.g. four times per week); time at which the behaviour is performed (e.g. over the next three months); and context in which the action is performed (e.g. during leisure time). If the measures of constructs such as intentions do not correspond to the behaviour in one or more of these elements, then, according to the principle of correspondence, the predictive validity of intentions will decrease. The second boundary condition states that intentions will predict behaviour provided that intentions have not changed before the behaviour is observed. However, intentions are more likely to change the longer the time interval between assessments of intentions and behaviour. This is due to the increased likelihood that new information will be made available to the individual which would be likely to change or modify intentions. The third boundary condition outlined by the theory of reasoned action is also related to predictive validity of intentions. This condition proposes that intentions will only effectively predict behaviours that are under the *complete* volitional control of the individual (Ajzen and Fishbein 1980). Generally speaking, behaviours are under complete volitional control when they can be performed at will, and are not facilitated or impeded at all by personal (e.g. low ability) and/or environmental (e.g. lack of time) factors (Ajzen and Fishbein 1980; Ajzen 1985). When other factors influence the performance of a behaviour and the individual cannot control the impact of those other factors on behaviour, intentions may be less effective as predictors of behaviour.

The theory of planned behaviour

Although the theory of reasoned action has been successful in predicting and explaining participation in physical activities, the boundary condition of *complete* volitional control was considered unrealistic and a major limitation of the theory (e.g. Ajzen 1985). To counter this criticism, Ajzen proposed a **theory of planned behaviour** to account for behaviours that are not under complete volitional control. As in the original theory of reasoned action, the theory of planned behaviour proposes that intention is a central determinant of social behaviour and that intention is a function of attitudes and subjective norms with corresponding behavioural beliefs and normative beliefs respectively. Further, as in the reasoned action theory, the theory of planned behaviour acknowledges that intentions explain behaviour only when it is under complete volitional control. However, the theory of planned behaviour also proposes that when perceived control over behaviour is problematic, an additional factor, termed **perceived behavioural control**, can influence performance of behaviour (Ajzen 1985).

For Ajzen (1991), the construct of perceived behavioural control refers to general perceptions of control. He compared it to Bandura's (1977) construct of self-efficacy that captures judgements of how well one can execute volitional behaviours required to produce important outcomes. The construct of perceived behavioural control is also underpinned by a set of **control beliefs** and the **perceived power** of these beliefs (Ajzen and Fishbein 1980). Control beliefs refer to the perceived presence of factors that may facilitate or impede performance of behaviour, and perceived power refers to the perceived impact that facilitative or inhibiting factors may have on performance of behaviour (Ajzen 1991). In the same way that an expectancy × value model is used to form indirect antecedents of attitudes and subjective norm, an indirect measure of perceived behavioural control can be formed from the composite of each control belief multiplied by its corresponding perceived power rating (Ajzen 1991).

The inclusion of perceived behavioural control in the theory of reasoned action is important because it reveals the personal and environmental factors that affect performance of behaviour (Ajzen 1985). To the extent that perceived behavioural control influences intentions and behaviour, the researcher can evaluate which behaviours are under the volitional control of the individual and the degree to which the behaviour is impeded by personal and/or environmental factors. Ajzen (1991) hypothesized that when control over the behaviour was problematic, perceived behavioural control would exert two types of effects within the theory of planned behaviour. First, perceived behavioural control would influence intentions alongside attitudes and subjective norms. This additive effect reflects the *motivational* influence of perceived control on decisions to exercise. For example, an individual expressing positive attitudes and subjective norms toward exercise but low perceived behavioural control is unlikely to report stronger intentions to exercise than an individual reporting the same positive attitudes and subjective norms but higher levels of perceived behavioural control. Second, perceived behavioural control may predict behaviour directly especially when perceptions of behavioural control are realistic. This reflects the effect of actual, real constraints or barriers to doing the behaviour. In this case perceived behavioural control is a proxy measure of actual control over the behaviour (Ajzen 1991). These relationships are shown in Figure 2.3.

A number of studies have shown the theory of planned behaviour to be superior to the theory of reasoned action in predicting and explaining volitional behaviour (Armitage and Conner 2001). For example, meta-analytic studies (Armitage and Conner 2001) and narrative review studies (Conner and Armitage 1998) have supported the consistent effect of perceived behavioural control on behavioural intentions. In addition, it has been shown that the effect of perceived behavioural control on intentions is robust and that it is not influenced by questionnaire format or social desirability (Armitage and Conner 1999a). Further, formative research has shown that the effect of perceived behavioural control on intentions is particularly pronounced for behaviours that are difficult to implement, are not under the control of volitional processes and for participants who do not believe that they have the ability to control behaviour and outcomes (e.g. Sheeran 2002). Finally, a number of researchers have shown that the effects of perceived behavioural control on intentions remain stable over time (Chatzisarantis *et al.* in press a; Hagger *et al.* 2001). Notwithstanding this corroborating evidence, a number of studies have demonstrated that, in comparison to the effect of perceived behavioural control on intentions, the direct effect of perceived behavioural control on behaviour is small (Armitage and Conner 2001), and statistically non-significant when belief-based measures of behavioural control are used and when perceptions of control are not realistic (Notani 1998).

In the exercise domain, studies have supported the hypotheses of the theory of planned behaviour in a variety of exercise contexts (Hagger *et al.* 2002b). Evidence suggests that the theory of planned behaviour has a greater predictive value than the health belief model and protection motivation theory (Quine *et al.* 1998). In addition, a number of studies have shown that perceived behavioural control predicts both intentions and behaviour equally well (Hagger *et al.* 2002a). Formative research has demonstrated that perceived behavioural control moderates the attitude–intention relationship so that attitudes predict intentions only among individuals who report high levels of perceived behavioural control (Ajzen 1991).

A number of studies have also identified certain control beliefs including barriers and facilitating factors related to exercise such as 'bad weather', 'age', 'heart pain', 'costs', 'fatigue', 'no time' (e.g. Godin *et al.* 1991). As with behavioural and normative beliefs, studies have demonstrated that control beliefs vary considerably across different populations and behaviours. For example, studies in the exercise domain have identified 'age' and 'fear of having a heart attack' among the control beliefs for older and clinical populations (Godin *et al.* 1991), but these beliefs do not feature among the control beliefs of younger populations.

Designing interventions based on the theories of reasoned action and planned behaviour

Empirical research findings from studies adopting the theories of reasoned action and planned behaviour have informed the development of interventions to promote exercise behaviour (Brawley 1993; Hardeman *et al.* 2002). Considering that formative research has shown that the theory of planned behaviour is superior to other models of social cognition such as the health belief model, protection motivation theory, and the theory of reasoned action

(Hausenblas *et al.* 1997; Quine *et al.* 1998; Hagger *et al.* 2002b), it can be suggested that exercise interventions should target attitudes and perceived behavioural control. Interventions should not target subjective norms or psychological variables espoused by the health belief model and protection motivation theory because these constructs have minimal impact on intention and behaviour.

The theories of reasoned action and planned behaviour propose that attitudes and perceived behavioural control can change by modifying their underlying belief systems. According to Ajzen (1991), changes in beliefs are most likely to produce demonstrable changes in attitudes, subjective norms, and/or perceptions of control only when the modal salient beliefs are targeted. Modal beliefs are the most frequently cited beliefs regarding the behaviour elicited from the target population. Modal salient beliefs can be identified by using open-ended questionnaire techniques that require individuals to recall and list beliefs about the target behaviour (Ajzen and Fishbein 1980).

Once salient beliefs have been identified, the theories of reasoned action and planned behaviour propose persuasive communications in the form of pamphlets, face-to-face discussion, observational modelling, or any other applicable method that can be gainfully employed in designing interventions (Ajzen and Fishbein 1980). Persuasive communications are appeals that involve arguments endorsing the positive aspects and outcomes of the target behaviour while at the same time downplaying the negative aspects. One of the key contributions of research adopting the theory of planned behaviour is concerned with the proposition that arguments are most persuasive when they are centred on accessible beliefs rather than non-accessible beliefs.[1] For example, a persuasive appeal that aims to change the attitudes of adolescents towards exercise may take the form of the following text that highlights the advantages and downplays disadvantages of exercise:

> Participating in regular exercise has many benefits. You might learn how to play a new game or sport as well as improving your general level of fitness and well-being at the same time. Exercise can be a great fun. It does not necessarily cause injuries or make you feel uncomfortably hot and sweaty if you exercise at an intensity you feel comfortable with.

This persuasive appeal should be effective in changing young people's attitudes because it targets the accessible behavioural beliefs of young people identified in formative research. Unfortunately, in the exercise domain, few studies have examined the utility of the theory of planned behaviour in promoting participation in physical activities and many have produced inconsistent results with significant limitations. For example, Rodgers and Brawley (1993) administered an intervention to produce changes in the affective attitudes and self-efficacy and this resulted in concomitant increases in participation in an exercise programme. Smith and Biddle (1999), on the other hand, reported that an intervention targeting salient beliefs was not successful in changing attitudes, subjective norms, perception of control, and intentions (see also Courneya *et al.* 2002). Such inconsistent results may be due to interventions targeting non-accessible behavioural beliefs. Therefore, one important avenue for future research is to examine the utility of intervention programmes that target accessible versus non-accessible beliefs in promoting exercise behaviour.

However, persuasive appeals may not be effective in changing intentions if mean scores of the predictors such as attitudes and perceived behavioural control are very high (Ajzen 1991). For example, an intervention that targets attitudes in a population that already tends to have very high levels of attitudes is unlikely to influence intentions simply because there is not much room for change. Ideally, therefore, research applications of the planned behaviour should target important predictor variables that do not display very high mean scores.

Although the theories of reasoned action and planned behaviour provide general guidance on how to change intentions and behaviour, they do not indicate how persuasive messages should be structured so that maximum effects can be obtained. Practitioners need to consult theories of persuasion in optimizing the effectiveness of persuasive messages. The elaboration likelihood model is a very popular model of persuasion that has been extensively used in studies of attitude change (Petty and Cacioppo 1986). The elaboration likelihood model posits that there are two routes to attitude change. First, there is a central route in which attitude changes as a result of thoughtful elaboration processes. Elaboration refers to the extent to which individuals are motivated to think carefully about the arguments contained in a persuasive communication. Elaboration can be identified by counting the number of thought processes that a person generates during information processing and/ or by evaluating the quality of arguments presented in the persuasive communication (Petty and Cacioppo 1986). Second, there is a peripheral route to attitude change, which occurs as a result of non-thoughtful processes such as inference, associative, and heuristic approaches. The elaboration likelihood model predicts that attitude change that arises from the central route demonstrates greater temporal persistence and resistance to persuasion than attitude change that arises from the peripheral route.

The elaboration likelihood model has been extensively used in studies of social attitudes (Petty and Cacioppo 1986) but very few studies have used it in conjunction with the theory of planned behaviour. Recently, Quine, Rutter, and Arnold (2001) showed that a series of persuasive messages that motivate young cyclists to elaborate accessible beliefs was successful in changing behavioural beliefs and normative beliefs but not control beliefs related to wearing a helmet. Therefore, an interesting avenue for future research is to design exercise interventions that take into consideration assumptions underlying the elaboration likelihood model and assumptions underlying the theory of planned behaviour. The elaboration likelihood model complements the theory of planned behaviour: the theory of planned behaviour helps identify accessible beliefs and the elaboration likelihood model indicates how arguments that are based on accessible belief can be structured and communicated so that maximum and more lasting effects on attitude change can be achieved.

Another limitation of interventions that are based on the theories of reasoned action and planned behaviour is that they can only be directed at individuals who do not intend to perform a behaviour rather than at those who have already formed intentions. For example, interventions based on these theories can produce positive intentions among non-intenders by changing behavioural beliefs, normative beliefs, and/or control beliefs but cannot help people convert an already strong intention into behaviour. This is because the theories are *motivational theories* that can only facilitate the formation of intentions. In contrast, *volitional theories* of intention are most efficacious in facilitating the enactment of behavioural intentions and can be gainfully applied alongside interventions based on the theories of reasoned action and planned behaviour. These theories will be discussed in Chapter 3.

In summary, the development of interventions based on the theory of planned behaviour should therefore comprise three interrelated stages. First, formative research studies should be conducted to identify the most important determinants of intentions. Second, further research should aim to identify the salient modal beliefs that underpin these determinants. Third, persuasive messages that target the salient beliefs should be developed and their efficacy in changing intentions evaluated.

Sufficiency of the theory of planned behaviour

The theory of planned behaviour focuses mainly on the immediate determinants of intentions and behaviour, but more distal determinants may exist (Ajzen 1991). Ajzen (1985, 1991) claims that the theory can account for the most immediate determinants of volitional behaviour, and that more distal determinants of behaviour are background factors that influence intentions and behaviour by their impact on behavioural, normative, and control beliefs. For example, the theory supposes that more generalized constructs such as personality and other trait-like constructs can influence intentions and behaviour, but only indirectly via attitudes, subjective norms, and perceived behavioural control (Ajzen 1991). The immediate, proximal determinants of intention will therefore *mediate* the influence of these more distal variables on intention.

However, formative research has found that these proximal constructs do not account for all the determinants of intentions and behaviour and researchers have proposed extensions and modifications to the theory to further explain variance in intentions and behaviour (Conner and Armitage 1998; Armitage and Conner 2001). Such suggestions are not new. Ajzen (1991) insists that the theory is open to additional predictors if it is shown that they capture a significant portion of *unique* variance in intentions or behaviour. As a consequence, a number of constructs have been introduced into the framework of the theory of planned behaviour. These additional constructs and the modification of the theory will be discussed next.

Frequency of past behaviour and habit

One criticism of the theories of reasoned action and planned behaviour is that they focus exclusively on deliberative processes and ignore the effect of automatic mental processes on behaviour (Fazio 1990). In general, deliberative processes are characterized by considerable cognitive work and effort. They involve the deliberation on the available information and an analysis of costs and benefits. In contrast, automatic processes facilitate fast decisions and non-intentional behaviours that are based on simple rules or *heuristics* that individuals develop through past experience and observation (Chaiken 1980; Bargh 1994). Recognizing the possible influence of these non-deliberative and automatic mental processes on volitional behaviour, researchers have attempted to control for these effects within the deliberative paradigm of the theory of planned behaviour. As a consequence, studies have included a *habit* measure in the theory of planned behaviour as a means to control for such influences because habitual behavioural engagement is largely determined by these automatic mental processes (Ajzen 2002b).

Habit refers to frequently performed acts that are done so often that the advent of situational cues is sufficient to trigger the behavioural response automatically without any deliberation or information processing (Bargh 1994). The *frequency* and *consistency* of performance of behaviour in the past are the main ingredients that result in the development of habits. As a consequence, several applications of the theory of planned behaviour have used self-reported frequency of past behaviour as an indicator of habit (e.g. Godin *et al.* 1991; Chatzisarantis *et al.* 2002; Hagger *et al.* 2002a, 2002b). These research applications have shown that past behaviour captures a significant portion of variance in intentions and behaviour after the theory's current variables have been taken into account (for reviews, see Hagger *et al.* 2002b). This research evidence therefore corroborates the view that regular exercise is a function of both deliberative and automatic processes, and that the theory of planned behaviour is insufficient in capturing these automatic processes. However, several researchers have questioned the use of past behaviour to control for these automatic effects as it is very limited as an index of habit (Ajzen 2002b).

Overall, although research evidence has consistently supported strong effects of frequency of past behaviour on intentions, the nature of this relationship remains elusive because frequency of past behaviour does not sufficiently represent habit (Bargh 1994; Ajzen 2002b). Some researchers claim that past behaviour may reflect the influences of other unmeasured variables on intention (Ajzen 2002b; Hagger *et al.* 2002b). The effects of past behaviour on intention may also reflect recent performance of the behaviour. This is because recent occurrences of an event are more available and accessible in memory than earlier occurrences (Ajzen 2002b). Past behaviour may also not be a very precise measure of habit because the consistency with which behaviour is performed across situations contributes to the development of habit, and measures of frequency of past behaviour do not take into consideration such cross-situational consistency (Verplanken and Orbell 2003). Therefore, measures of habit that take into consideration both frequency and consistency of performance of past behaviour are urgently needed so that more precise conclusions about the nature of past behaviour effects can be reached. However, it is important to acknowledge that inclusion of past behaviour in the theory of planned behaviour is important because it tests the sufficiency of the theory of planned behaviour. The consistent effect of past behaviour on exercise intentions and behaviour suggests that the theory of planned behaviour does not offer a complete explanation of volitional behaviour (Chatzisarantis and Biddle 1998).

Personality traits

Another key extension of the theory of planned behaviour is the inclusion of **personality** traits to predict intentions and behaviour. In general, personality traits are generalized dimensions of individual differences in tendencies to show stable patterns of thoughts, feelings, and actions (McCrae and Costa 1996). Recent research in the exercise domain has indicated that personality traits, such as those identified by McCrae and Costa, can influence exercise intentions and behaviour (e.g. Conner and Abraham 2001; Courneya *et al.* 2002; Rhodes *et al.* 2002a). Although considerable evidence corroborates the link between personality traits and social behaviour in the general social psychology literature (e.g. Sherman and Fazio 1983), little is known about the processes by which personality traits influence behaviour.

Sherman and Fazio proposed that there are at least two processes through which personality traits can influence social behaviour. The first process is deliberative (Fazio 1990) or systematic (Chaiken 1980). The deliberative model proposes that people engage in an analysis of costs and benefits of behaviour and may base their descision-making on whether the behaviour is congruent with their global tendencies. For example, the indirect effects of extroversion on exercise via the mediation of attitudes and intentions in the theory of planned behaviour implies that personality traits motivate people to compare various behavioural outcomes in order to decide whether or not a behaviour is appropriate and suitable (Sherman and Fazio 1983). The second process by which traits can influence social behaviour is through activation of automatic pathways (Sherman and Fazio 1983). Research on automaticity in social psychology literature suggests that traits can be activated spontaneously by the presence of trait-relevant behavioural cues and results in behaviour consistent with these personality traits (Bargh 1994). Some studies have shown that personality traits can facilitate non-intentional behaviour in the theory of planned behaviour. For example, Rhodes and co-workers (Courneya *et al.* 2002, 2002) illustrated how the activity facet of extroversion predicted exercise participation over and above intentions. This evidence therefore supports the view that active individuals engage in unplanned behaviour perhaps because they are more likely to notice unplanned situations where the opportunity to be active presents itself. Despite this evidence, it has to be acknowledged that in comparison to the effects of intentions on exercise behaviour, the direct effects of traits on exercise behaviour are small (Rhodes *et al.* 2002a). However, little is known about how traits influence exercise behaviour and future research needs to explore the processes through which values and personality traits influence exercise behaviour.

Attitude-based modifications of the theory of planned behaviour

Attitude strength
The role of **attitude strength** has been the subject of recent investigations in the theory of planned behaviour. The general approach suggests that the predictive efficacy of the attitude construct is limited by the strength of the attitude in the individual's memory. The strength of an attitude in memory is determined by several attitudinal properties such as extremity, consistency, ambivalence, frequency, polarization, and consensus (Eagly and Chaiken 1993). In support of the attitude strength model, several studies have found that the attitude–behaviour relationship increases in proportion to the amount of behavioural information available to the individual and the degree of past experience an individual has with the attitude object or behaviour (Nederhof 1989). Further, research suggests that the attitude–behaviour relationship decreases as **attitudinal ambivalence** increases (Conner *et al.* 2003). Nederhof (1989) has demonstrated that attitudes are strong predictors of intentions and behaviour when people consider the attitude object or behaviour to be important to them. More recently, studies in the exercise domain have included an attitude strength construct in the theory of planned behaviour. Attitude strength was found to mediate the effects of subjective norms and attitudes on intentions (e.g. Theodorakis 1994). Overall, these data suggest that the stronger the attitude, the more effective the prediction of intentions and behaviour.

Affective and cognitive attitudes
Research has examined the importance of the emotional or **affective attitudes** and instrumental or **cognitive attitudes** within the theory of planned behaviour. Trafimow and Sheeran (1998) have argued in favour of a multi-dimensional conceptualization of attitudes on the grounds that the unidimensional model ignores the unique effects of the instrumental and emotional aspects of attitude on behaviour (Eagly and Chaiken 1993). Indeed, studies

have shown that this distinction can be made on the basis of the belief systems that underpin attitudes (Trafimow and Sheeran 1998). Studies have found that affective attitudes exert unique effects on intentions for a number of health behaviours including exercise (Lowe *et al.* 2002). Interestingly, Lowe *et al.* have shown that the affective component exerts a direct effect on exercise behaviour after controlling for intentions and past behaviour. This evidence suggests that the affective component of attitudes facilitates spontaneous or unplanned behaviour (Fazio 1990), and reinforces the necessity of testing both the affective and instrumental components of attitudes within the theory of planned behaviour.

Although the conceptual and empirical distinction between affective and instrumental attitudes appears sound, there has been a recent resurgence of interest in the conceptualization of the attitude construct within the theory of planned behaviour, particularly in its constituent components. Hagger and Chatzisarantis (in press) argue that a major problem is that affective and instrumental attitudes are not always consistent. When the affective and instrumental components are highly consistent, such as in exercise behaviour, they should be typically measured as indicators of a global attitude component, rather than distinct constructs. In contrast, when affective and instrumental components are inconsistent, they should be considered distinct and permitted to exert independent effects on intentions. The basic argument then seems to be that while a model that acknowledges independence between affective and instrumental attitudes cannot be rejected on statistical or theoretical grounds, a second-order model can be favoured in the exercise domain in that it gives the most parsimonious account of the attitude influences on intention.

Normative extensions of the theory of planned behaviour

Normatively controlled individuals
Research applications of the theory of planned behaviour have frequently cited a lesser role for the subjective norms construct in the prediction of intentions when compared with the variance explained by the attitude and perceived behavioural control constructs (e.g. Conner and Armitage 1998; Armitage and Conner 2001). This may be because only a minority of individuals form intentions on the basis of norms, so-called normatively controlled individuals (Trafimow and Finlay 1996). Studies using within- and between-participants designs have found that subjective norms are particularly important in the health domain and that normatively controlled people are likely to perform more health behaviours than individuals who form intentions on the basis of attitudes (Finlay *et al.* 2002). However, Finlay *et al.* also found that normatively controlled individuals were less likely to enact their intentions across a number of behaviours within the exercise domain. It seems that exercise behaviour may be enacted more if a person has a tendency to be attitudinally biased in their decision-making.

Descriptive norms
One reason why studies have not *always* observed moderating effects of subjective norms on the attitude–intention relationship may be the fact that subjective norms insufficiently capture social influences. Several studies have made the distinction between subjective or *injunctive norms* as the perceived pressure from significant others to engage in the target behaviour and **descriptive norms**, a construct that taps the extent to which significant others engage in the target behaviour (Rivis and Sheeran 2003). Research has found injunctive and descriptive norms to be conceptually and empirically distinct constructs (Hagger and Chatzisarantis, in press), and that descriptive norms have a unique effect on intentions independent of the traditional subjective norms (e.g. Rivis and Sheeran 2003). Indeed, Rivis and Sheeran's recent **meta-analysis** across studies adopting the descriptive norms construct within the framework of the theory of planned behaviour found a medium-to-strong sample-weighted average correlation between descriptive norms and intentions ($r_c = 0.44$). The analysis also revealed that descriptive norms increased the variance explained in intention by 5 per cent after controlling for attitudes, injunctive norms, and perceived behavioural control. The significant effect of descriptive norms on intentions has also been supported in the exercise domain (Baker *et al.* 2003). However, Conner, Sherlock, and Orbell (1998) have shown that descriptive norms and subjective norms may possess discriminant validity for some behaviours and there is little evidence for the moderation of the intention–behaviour relationship by descriptive norms. Indeed, studies often report strong correlations between descriptive norms and subjective norms that may question their discriminant validity (Hagger and Chatzisarantis, in press). Therefore, studies have not consistently found main and moderating effects of descriptive norms on intentions.

Social support
The logic behind incorporating descriptive norms in the theory of planned behaviour is based on learning theories that posit that modelling or observing others' behaviour is an important source of influence (Bandura 1977, 1997). However, some researchers have argued that descriptive norms may not sufficiently capture all the types of influence that social factors exert on intentions. Courneya *et al.* (2000) have argued that social support, a construct that indicates the extent to which significant others are perceived to assist performance of behaviour, can also exert unique effects on intentions (see also Rhodes *et al.* 2002b). The logic behind incorporating measures of social support in the theory of planned behaviour is that for behaviours that are difficult to execute, assistance provides additional impetus towards forming intentions beyond beliefs that the behaviour is beneficial, that the actor has the capacity to do it, and that significant others want them to do it (Courneya *et al.* 2000).

Several studies have shown that social support and subjective norms tap conceptually distinct constructs (Rhodes *et al.* 2002b), and that social support predicts intentions (Courneya *et al.* 2000) particularly among individuals who perceive that behaviour is difficult to execute (Povey *et al.* 2000). Further, in accordance with the contingent consistency hypothesis, Povey *et al.* have demonstrated that social support moderates effects of attitudes on intentions so that attitudes predict intentions only when participants perceive that significant others support their performance of the behaviour. Nevertheless, it is important to realize that studies have reported strong correlations between social support and descriptive norms, and small effects of social support on intentions relative to the effects that attitudes exert on intentions (Courneya *et al.* 2000).

Control-related extensions of the theory of planned behaviour

Self-efficacy
Recent studies have indicated that it is possible to distinguish two sub-components of Ajzen's (1991) perceived behavioural control construct: *perceived controllability*, defined as the extent that an individual has access to the means to exert control over the target behaviour (Ajzen 2002a), and *self-efficacy*, defined as an individual's estimate of ability and personal capacity to engage in the behaviour (Terry and O'Leary 1995). Measures of perceived controllability have often focused on statements regarding the degree of *subjective control* an individual has over the target behaviour, while self-efficacy is often tapped using items referring to the perceived *abilities* and *capacities* of the actor in participating in the target behaviour. Studies have made the explicit distinction between perceived controllability and self-efficacy and provided conceptual and empirical evidence in support of the distinction in a number of behavioural domains (Armitage and Conner 1999b, 2001), including exercise (Terry and O'Leary 1995). In addition, strong support for the distinction between attitudes and perceived behavioural control has been made experimentally on the basis of the belief systems that underlie these constructs (Trafimow *et al.* 2002). Notwithstanding the increasing body of evidence in support of this distinction, there is little conclusive evidence to support a clear, unambiguous pattern of predictions for perceived behavioural control and self-efficacy within the theory of planned behaviour (Ajzen 2002a).

Anticipated regret and moral norms[2]

Although, in principle, all possible outcomes can be reflected by the different types of beliefs in the theory of planned behaviour, some theorists suggest that personal beliefs about whether a behaviour is morally right or wrong, termed moral norms, and **anticipated regret** for behaving in a certain way may not be adequately represented in the theory (Conner and Armitage 1998). The concept of anticipated regret is featured in regret theory (Loomes and Sugden 1982) which proposes that people's decisions in certain situations can be based on feelings and emotions that they expect to experience from rejecting alternative behavioural courses, rather than a rational analysis of the costs and benefits associated with behavioural engagement. Regret theory proposed that an attractive behavioural option like eating a tasty ice-cream is likely to be rejected if people believe that they will experience regret and guilt after choosing that option because they are on a diet. Therefore, people familiar with post-behavioural feelings of regret and guilt are likely to reject alternatives that will make them feel regretful because they are motivated to avoid feelings of regret.

The construct of anticipated regret is closely related to moral norms and for this reason several studies have considered anticipated regret and moral norms to constitute indicators of a general construct that is termed personal norms. Moral norms and anticipated regret are interrelated because often feelings of regret and guilt arise from breaking a moral rule. For example, individuals are likely to feel guilty if they harm an important other or when they contravene a social rule that is highly valued. Therefore, anticipated regret and moral norms are closely linked because anticipated emotions are contingent on the breaking of an internalized moral rule. Given this conceptual distinction, however, there is no conclusive evidence in support of the conceptual distinction between moral norms and anticipated regret. Therefore, an important avenue for future research is to examine the conceptual distinction between moral norms and anticipated affect.

Several studies have supported the inclusion of moral norms and anticipated regret in the theory of planned behaviour (e.g. Parker *et al.* 1995; Bozionelos and Bennett 1999). In the exercise domain, Bozionelos and Bennett revealed that personal norms did not contribute to the prediction of exercise intentions or behaviour. This may be because exercise behaviour is unlikely to have moral or ethical connotations. However, due to the competitive nature of some types of exercise such as sports, it is not difficult to envisage situations in which moral norms may influence intentions to behave in a dishonest way. Therefore, an important avenue for research is to investigate the types of exercise intentions influenced by moral norms. Research has also demonstrated the importance of anticipated regret in understanding the intention–behaviour relationship. Abraham and Sheeran (2003) have shown that anticipated regret moderates the intention–behaviour relationship so that participants are most likely to exercise if they both intend to exercise and report high levels of anticipated regret if they fail to exercise. In addition, Abraham and Sheeran (2004) also demonstrated that manipulations of anticipated regret that prompt people to focus on negative emotions that follow decisions not to exercise can strengthen exercise intentions.

Summary of theoretical extensions and recommendations for practice

One clear conclusion that emerges from the research that has extended and modified the theory of planned behaviour is that a host of other variables can be incorporated into the framework of the theory and account for *unique* variance in intentions and behaviour. This suggests that the theory does not sufficiently capture the psychological determinants of volitional behaviour, but is both versatile and flexible. However, it is important to acknowledge that the contribution of these additional variables to the prediction of exercise intentions and behaviour has been relatively modest (Conner and Armitage 1998; Hagger *et al.* 2002b; Hagger and Chatzisarantis, in press). Furthermore, these modifications must be evaluated alongside the original theory's parsimony in accounting for a large amount of variance in intentions and behaviour.

Another conclusion that emerges from this research is the practical value of the extensions and modifications of the theory. Formative research that evaluates extended versions of the theory can provide useful information about the content of interventions. For example, the contribution of personality traits to the prediction of exercise behaviour suggests that exercise programmes should take into consideration the personality characteristics of participants. Exercise programmes that are tailored around personality characteristics are likely to be more successful than those that focus solely on the proximal predictors of intention (Courneya *et al.* 2002). Another example is the distinction made between affective and instrumental attitudes as this can help identify whether affective or cognitive means of persuasion are more appropriate to a particular behavioural domain (Hagger and Chatzisarantis, in press). However, it must be recognized that not all additional variables can be manipulated, such as **past behaviour**. Interventions in the exercise domain have not attempted to manipulate the additional variables identified in this research. Therefore, interventions that evaluate the utility of the extended theory in promoting exercise behaviour are urgently needed.

One issue that deserves future research attention is the conceptual overlap between additional variables. Obviously, some psychological variables that have been incorporated into the theory of planned behaviour are defined and measured in similar, if not identical, ways. For example, the constructs of anticipated affect and anticipated regret are very similar, given that both constructs describe post-behavioural affective reactions (Parker *et al.* 1995). Conceptual overlap between the theory constructs was also evident in a recent study conducted by Hagger and Chatzisarantis (in press) that found higher-order constructs could satisfactorily model the common content of these additional variables and could successfully represent influences from these additional variables on intentions. Such commonalities between the psychological constructs from the theory give rise to an important practical question: to what extent are the manipulations implied by different psychological constructs redundant? Research that investigates commonalities and differences between additional variables is urgently needed. Trafimow et al.'s (2002) study of perceived behavioural control is an excellent example of a series of experimental studies that have pointed out conceptual differences between perceived controllability and perceived difficulty.

Finally, it is important to investigate conceptual similarities and differences between the psychological constructs in models like the theory of planned behaviour in order to arrive at realistic and practical frameworks to understand exercise behaviour. Clearly, people cannot process a great deal of information simultaneously. As a consequence, the practice of adding new variables within the theory of planned behaviour may provide an unrealistic picture of the decision-making process because such extended models imply that people can deal with lots of different information at the same time. In addition, extended models may not be very helpful in promoting exercise behaviour because interventions based on such models provide greater amounts of information that may over-complicate the issue of behaviour change for the recipients of the message. One way to address the problem of limited processing capacity is to point out redundancies between psychological constructs. Redundant variables should be excluded from intervention programmes because they provide little or no additional information about behavioural change.

Other leading theories of social behaviour

The model of goal-directed behaviour

One limitation of the social cognitive theories such as the theories of reasoned action and planned behaviour is that they focus on behavioural appraisals in lieu of goal appraisals. The model of goal-directed behaviour extends previous theories of intentional behaviour by explicitly considering the broader goal-context in which behaviour is enacted (Perugini and Conner 2000; Perugini and Bagozzi 2001). The model therefore views the fundamental components of the theory of planned behaviour with respect to goals rather than behaviours. For example, attitudes are defined as the extent to which people think that performing a behaviour x in order to achieve a goal y is beneficial versus harmful. In addition, the model of goal-directed behaviour also includes the influence of anticipated emotional reactions toward goal achievement. Again, the model defines positive and negative anticipated emotions with respect to goal achievement and failure. That is, instead of measuring the extent to which performing behaviour x will make people feel excited or happy, the model refers to how the achievement of goal z will make people feel. For example, individuals are asked how they would feel if they succeeded in achieving goal z.

The **model of goal-directed behaviour** maintains that **desires** are the most proximal determinant of intentions. Desires aim to reflect the motivational aspects of attitude that are not captured by traditional intentions. In the model, measures of desires are focused on goals rather than behaviours. Furthermore, desires are hypothesized to mediate the effects of attitudes, anticipated affect, subjective norms, and perceived behavioural control on intentions. Another key feature of the model is concerned with the conceptualization of intentions. Perugini and Conner (2000) have argued that the conceptualization of intentions in the theory of planned behaviour does take the goals of the intended behaviour into consideration. The concept of intentions in the model of goal-directed behaviour resolves this issue by including three aspects of volition: (1) a direct expression of intentions (e.g. 'I will try to perform a behaviour x in order to achieve a goal z'); (2) a statement of plans to perform acts that are instrumental to the achievement of a goal (e.g. 'I intend to perform a behaviour x in order to achieve a goal z'); and (3) an expression of volition and effort needed to enact the behaviour (e.g. 'I will expend effort to perform a behaviour x in order to achieve a goal z'). Finally, the model of goal-directed behaviour specifies effects from past behaviour on behaviour, volitions, and desires. Effects of past behaviour are considered to represent effects from automatic mental processes on motivational and volitional variables. The model is depicted in Figure 2.4.

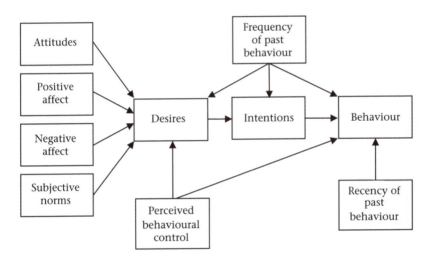

Figure 2.4   The model of goal-directed behaviour

Studies of a number of health behaviours including exercise have suggested that the model of goal-directed behaviour has a greater predictive value than the theory of planned behaviour (Perugini and Conner 2000; Perugini and Bagozzi 2001). Empirical studies have also shown that attitudes, subjective norms, perceived behavioural control, and positive and negative anticipated emotions predict desires and that desires predict intention. Perugini and Bagozzi have also shown that desires mediate the effects of attitude, subjective norms, perceived behavioural control, and anticipated emotions on intentions. However, there are as yet no intervention studies that have tested utility of the model in promoting exercise behaviour.

The transtheoretical model

In the context of alcohol addiction and smoking behaviour, Prochaska and DiClemente (1982) developed a model that incorporated behaviour change along with social cognitive constructs to identify the progression that people undergo when changing unhealthy behaviours. At the core of the model is the premise that people pass through stages towards making a behaviour change and each stage is characterized by a particular pattern of psycho-social and behavioural variables. These *stages of change* are the most widely adopted aspects of the model, although there are also *levels of change* and *processes of change*. The stages are: pre-contemplation, contemplation, preparation, action, and maintenance. At the *pre-contemplation* stage people have no conceptualization of the need to change unhealthy behaviours or lifestyle, let alone enacting any change. *Contemplators*, however, have realized the need for change and are thinking about doing so but have no idea or inclination to make the change. People who are in the *preparation* stage want to change and are making the necessary personal and social moves and commitment towards changing behaviour. In the *action* stage, people are beginning to make successful and unsuccessful attempts to change their behaviour and their behavioural change may be inconsistent and could possibly relapse to a previous behavioural pattern more akin to their former unhealthy lifestyle. Finally, the *maintenance* stage is characterized by a continuity of successful and consistent behavioural change.

In terms of the processes involved with moving people from one stage to another in the transtheoretical model, Prochaska and DiClemente (1982) suggested that *self-efficacy* and *decisional balance* are key intrapersonal variables that are responsible for such change. It is the incorporation of such social cognitive constructs and behavioural constructs as well as the dynamic nature of the model that inspired the name of the theory because it is proposed to straddle theories of intention and theories of enactment of intentions. Self-efficacy in the context of the transtheoretical model refers to an individual's beliefs in their ability to make desired behavioural changes to gain desirable outcomes. Research adopting the transtheoretical model has supported differences in the level of self-efficacy across the stages of change, with the highest coinciding with people in the maintenance stage and the lowest for those in the pre-contemplation stage (Armitage and Arden 2002).

Decisional balance reflects people's overt beliefs about the advantages and disadvantages, or the *pros* and *cons*, of performing the behaviour, with the hypothesis that the balance of pros and cons determines when a person begins to make behavioural changes. Therefore, it is hypothesized that when the pros just begin to outweigh the cons the person will be in the preparation stage. Research has supported this hypothesis in a number of behavioural contexts including exercise, such that the decisional balance is largely in favour of pros in actors and maintainers, roughly equal in people at the preparation stage (Prochaska *et al.* 1994). In summary, the research testing the efficacy of self-efficacy and decisional balance to change stage in the transtheoretical model has supported theory hypotheses across a number of studies and a recent meta-analysis has supported this view in the exercise domain (Marshall and Biddle 2001).

The transtheoretical model has also been investigated within the framework of other social cognitive models in an attempt to further examine the processes that expedite transfer from one stage to another. Indeed, researchers have drawn some parallels between the core antecedents of intention in the theory of planned behaviour and the decisional balance and self-efficacy constructs in Prochaska and DiClemente's exposition of the transtheoretical model (Armitage and Arden 2002; Armitage *et al.* 2003). For example, the belief-based measures of attitude are proposed to reflect the advantages and disadvantages (behavioural beliefs) relating to behavioural engagement, and could therefore be considered akin to decisional balance. In addition, the perceived behavioural control variable has been overtly compared with the self-efficacy construct so that perceived behavioural control is considered, at least in part, to reflect levels of self-efficacy. A number of studies across different health behaviours (e.g. Armitage and Arden 2002; Armitage *et al.* 2003), including exercise (Courneya 1995) have found linear increases in these theory of planned behaviour constructs across the stages of change.

While the transtheoretical model has demonstrated concurrent and predictive validity alongside other intention models of social cognition, it is not without its critics. Some have questioned its validity because it represents a less than coherent mix of cognitive and behavioural constructs with no clear notion of the exact nature of each stage (Davidson 1992). Furthermore, some have claimed that it is not a genuine stage model, but only a 'pseudo-stage' model because the boundaries of the stages are not distinct and cannot be discriminated empirically (Sutton 2000; Armitage and Arden 2002; Armitage *et al.* 2003). This is supported by the linear trends for all of the social cognitive constructs from other theories across the transtheoretical model stages. In some respects, the stages of change adhere very closely to measures of intention and in this respect the stages themselves are merely a reflection of the different levels of intention toward engaging in the behaviour. Thus, in theory, any number of stages could be identified across the continuum of low to high intention (Armitage and Arden 2002).

Sutton (2000) suggests that for the transtheoretical model to exhibit the characteristics of a true discrete stage model, discontinuity patterns in key social psychological variables would have to be observed across the stages. In other words, the differences in key variables thought to be responsible for moving a person from on stage to another would have to exhibit a non-linear change. An example of a discontinuity pattern might be that attitudes may exhibit an increase across the contemplation and preparation stages but no increase across the subsequent stages of preparation and action or action and maintenance. In this example, interventions targeting attitudes would be efficacious in progressing individuals from the contemplation stage to the

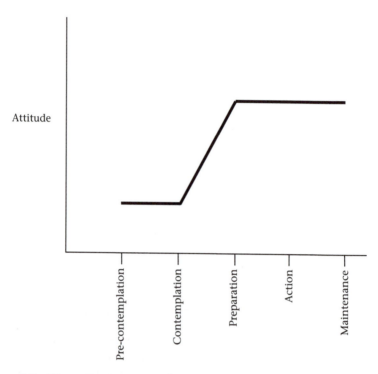

Figure 2.5 Discontinuity pattern for intention in the context of the transtheoretical model

preparation stage, but would not progress people already in the preparation stage. This is illustrated in Figure 2.5. There have, however, been few empirical tests to corroborate these discontinuity patterns.

Recently, another feature of attitudes, that of attitudinal ambivalence, has been viewed as an important process variable in changing transtheoretical model stages and has been shown to exhibit the discontinuity patterns suggested by Sutton (2000). Ambivalence suggests that individuals may hold both positive and negative evaluations of a behaviour simultaneously and this may result in conflict when decisions are made. Ambivalence has been shown to be a moderator of the attitude–intention relationship, so that high levels of ambivalence compromise the motivational efficacy of attitudes (Armitage and Conner 2000). In the context of the transtheoretical model, Armitage *et al.* (2003) found that while the theory of planned behaviour variables exhibited linear relationships across stages of change, the relationship was non-linear (quadratic) with attitudinal ambivalence. The data showed that the highest levels of ambivalence were seen in the contemplation, preparation, and action stages, and the lowest levels in the pre-contemplation and maintenance stages. The authors suggested that changing ambivalence may encourage pre-contemplators into contemplation, preparation, or action stage, but not across these stages while resolving ambivalence may prevent those in the maintenance stage from relapsing. These findings need further replication in an exercise context and would be useful in characterizing the transtheoretical model as a bona fide stage model.

Suggested reading

Conner, M. and Armitage, C.J. (1998) Extending the theory of planned behavior: a review and avenues for further research. *Journal of Applied Social Psychology*, 28: 1429–64. Covers many of the theoretical issues associated with the theory of planned behaviour and modifications of this theory.

Conner, M. and Norman, P. (1996) *Predicting Health Behaviour: Research Practice with Social Cognition Models*. Buckingham: Open University Press. Highly recommended review of the theoretical and practical issues related to the health belief model, protection motivation theory, and the theory of planned behaviour.

Hagger, M.S., Chatzisarantis, N. and Biddle, S.J.H. (2002) A meta-analytic review of the theories of reasoned action and planned behaviour in physical activity: predictive validity and the contribution of additional variables. *Journal of Sport and Exercise Psychology*, 24: 3–32. The most recent and comprehensive review of research on this key social cognitive model in exercise contexts.

Marshall, S.J. and Biddle, S.J.H. (2001) The transtheoretical model of behavior change: a meta-analysis of applications to physical activity and exercise. *Annals of Behavioral Medicine*, 23: 229–46. State-of-the-art cumulative review of research using the transtheoretical model in the exercise domain.

Perugini, M. and Conner, M. (2000) Predicting and understanding behavioral volitions: the interplay between goals and behaviors. *European Journal of Social Psychology*, 30: 705–31. Showcase research publication for the model of goal directed behaviour.

Summary

- Social cognitive theories aim to identify the social psychological factors that explain variance in exercise behaviour. Intention is a central motivational construct to many of these theories.
- The *health belief model* and the *protection motivation theory* examine the effects of cognitive appraisals of perceived threat (e.g. severity, vulnerability) and perceived health benefits of behaviours such as exercise on intentions and behaviour. Meta-analyses have supported the relationships among these variables in health behaviours. Interventions based on these theories using fear-arousing communications have had limited success in changing intentions but not behaviour.
- The *theories of reasoned action* and *planned behaviour* are parsimonious and effective social cognitive models of intention and behaviour and have

received considerable attention in the exercise literature. The belief-based constructs of attitudes and subjective norms in the theory of reasoned action with the perceived behavioural control construct in the theory of planned behaviour are strong and consistent predictors of exercise intentions, and intentions have been shown to mediate these distal constructs on exercise behaviour.

- The theory of planned behaviour is a versatile and flexible theory as it has often been modified to incorporate numerous additional constructs that explain unique variance in exercise intention and behaviour. Modifications have been made to include past behaviour, personality, attitude-based constructs (e.g. attitude strength, affective and cognitive attitudes), normatively-based constructs (e.g. normatively controlled individuals, descriptive norms, social support), control-related modifications (e.g. self-efficacy), anticipated regret, and moral norms.
- The *model of goal-directed behaviour* is an alternative theory of intentional behaviour. The theory aims to explain the concept of desires as the most proximal predictor of behaviour and focuses on behavioural goals rather than behavioural enactment *per se*. The model has been shown to have some utility among health behaviours.
- The transtheoretical model is a stage model of behaviour change. The theory proposes that people move systematically through five stages when changing behaviour: pre-contemplation, contemplation, preparation, action, and maintenance. The theory has intuitive appeal and has been linked to decisional balance and intention. Recent support has come from discontinuity patterns with respect to social cognitive constructs like attitude.

Notes

1 The concept of *accessibility* was initially introduced by Higgins *et al.* (1982) and Haddock and Zanna (1998) whose research showed that models that take accessible beliefs into consideration provide a more realistic representation of the processes underlying attitude formation compared with models that do not account for accessibility.

2 Some authors have used the terms personal normative beliefs and moral obligation with reference to the constructs of moral norms and personal norms (Sparkes and Shepherd 1995; Triandis 1980; Godin *et al.* 1996). However, the items used to measure all these constructs are virtually identical.

3

From exercise intention to exercise behaviour and beyond

The social cognitive theories discussed in Chapter 2 are motivational theories in that they indicate how intentions are formed and change (Gollwitzer 1999). However, these theories do not provide an explanation of how people carry out their previously formed intentions. This is highlighted by the boundary condition of intentional stability in the theory of planned behaviour that states that intentions predict behaviour only to the extent that intentions remain stable over time. For example, several studies have documented that stable intentions are more predictive of future behaviour than unstable intentions (Sheeran *et al.* 1999; Conner *et al.* 2000). As a consequence, researchers have developed alternative theories of volition to understand how people carry out their previously formed intentions (e.g. Gollwitzer 1999). In addition, the social cognitive theories of intention propose that the key predictor variables such as attitudes and subjective norms are formed through specific sets of beliefs and evaluations. However, little has been proposed as to the origins of these beliefs. Theories of psychological needs such as self-determination theory may provide a theoretical basis for belief formation. This chapter will review these theories and examine how volitional theories complement the motivational social cognitive theories covered in Chapter 2 to explain exercise behaviour. In addition, self-determination theory is introduced and its efficacy in explaining the origins of the social cognitive constructs from theories of intention reviewed. Multi-theory approaches that combine hypotheses from these theories to explain exercise behaviour will also be proposed.[1]

Limitations of social cognitive theories and introduction to volitional processes

Intention stability

Ajzen (1985) originally downplayed the theoretical importance of the boundary condition of **intention stability** by arguing that the issue of stability is largely a technical problem and does not challenge the assumption that intentions influence behaviour. Reduced predictive accuracy of intentions may merely reflect reduced accuracy of measures of intentions available to the investigator (Ajzen 1985). This can occur when there is a large delay between assessments of intentions and behaviour (Sheeran *et al.* 1999b). The greater the delay, the greater the opportunities for intentional change, and hence the predictive accuracy of intentions is reduced (Ajzen 1985). For this reason, Ajzen (1991) has proposed that, ideally, intentions should be measured as close as possible to the incidence of behaviour. Research has corroborated Ajzen's proposition by showing that short-range intentions and stable intentions are stronger predictors of exercise behaviour than long-range intentions and unstable intentions (Sheeran *et al.* 1999b; Conner *et al.* 2000).

However, it can be argued that the issues of stability and predictive validity are not mere technical problems but do pose important theoretical and practical questions about the utility of the theory of planned behaviour in predicting and explaining volitional behaviour. First, the boundary condition of stability can be considered unrealistic because the construct of intention is state-like and likely to change over time. Therefore, intentional change is unavoidable because change is integral to the nature of intentions (Hagger *et al.* 2001; Chatzisarantis *et al.*, in press a). In addition, stable intentions predict behaviour more accurately than unstable intentions because theories of intention have not been designed to explain the psychological processes underlying intention *change*. Indeed, research has shown that the theory of planned behaviour does not predict adherence to, relapse from, and delayed participation in health behaviours (Orbell and Sheeran 1998). Having described the factors that may facilitate changes in intentions, theories of intentional behaviour should predict behaviour even when intentions are unstable (Ajzen and Fishbein 1980; Ajzen 1991). Further, from an applied perspective, it can be argued that the relatively modest levels of behavioural prediction obtained by social cognitive theories of intentional behaviour substantially undermine the practicality of these theories. Therefore, the boundary condition of stability is a theoretical and practical limitation of the theory of planned behaviour and other theories of intention because they do not provide a realistic view of the way intentions operate.

Scale correspondence

One reason why intentions may not predict behaviour very well is that measures of intentions and behaviour do not correspond in terms of action, target, context, and time (Ajzen 1985). For example, participation in exercise behaviour during leisure time is predicted more accurately and precisely from measures of intentions to exercise during leisure time than from measures of intentions to engage in another context, such as physical education classes. Courneya and co-workers (Courneya and McAuley 1994) argue that the relationship between intentions and exercise behaviour in previous research is modest and highly variable because studies use different types of scales in measuring intentions and behaviour. However, although improving scale and measurement correspondence strengthens the intention–behaviour relationship, research has shown the principle of correspondence does not fully explain variations in the intention–behaviour relationship (Courneya and McAuley 1994). Studies in the exercise domain have shown that a great deal of variance in exercise behaviour remains unexplained even when measures adhere to the correspondence rule (Hagger *et al.* 2002b).

Intention formation

Bagozzi and Yi (1989) argued that when an individual has given much consideration to a behaviour and has well-formed intentions, the intention–behaviour relationship will be strengthened. They suggested that poorly formed intentions are more vulnerable to change due to differential retrieval or forgetting of information on which the intentions are based. This suggests that poorly formed intentions are more unstable and will be less effective in accounting for variance in behaviour. Bagozzi and Yi demonstrated empirically that the intention–behaviour relationship is stronger for well-formed intentions than for ill-formed intentions. Future studies should examine the issue of intention formation in an exercise context.

Self-schema

Self-schema is another variable that has been shown to affect the intention–behaviour relationship. Self-schemas are cognitive generalizations about the self that are derived from past experience. Self-schemas are typically measured by participants' self-ratings of the descriptiveness and importance of traits relevant to a domain (Sheeran and Orbell 2000). For example, a person who rates domain relevant traits as highly self-descriptive and important to their self-image are considered to be *schematics*. *Non-schematics* are people who rate such traits as not descriptive of their self but important. *Aschematics* are people whose ratings of domain-relevant traits are moderately self-descriptive but unimportant. The rationale behind the argument that self-schema moderates the intention–behaviour relationship is that schematics have a greater number of strategies for acting intentions and will therefore exhibit greater consistency between intentions and behaviour than non-schematics. In accordance with this hypothesis, Sheeran and Orbell have shown that schematics display stronger relationships between exercise intentions and behaviour than non-schematics. However, once again self-schema does not fully explain why intentions do not always translate into actions.

Volitional and forced intentions

Building upon the work of Meiland (1970), Chatzisarantis and Biddle (1998) have argued that one reason why the long-term predictive efficacy of intentions is relatively low is because intentions do not necessarily reflect a willingness to perform a behaviour as originally assumed by Ajzen (1985). This assumption may be untenable considering that previous research has differentiated between volition and intentions, and demonstrated deferential effects from volitional and forced decisions on behaviour. Specifically, more than four decades of experimental work on cognitive dissonance theory have shown that decisions can be either volitional or forced and that volitional decisions exert greater effects on attitudes and overt behaviour than forced decisions (Festinger and Carlsmith 1958). Further studies have shown that volitional decisions are associated with effort and persistence in health-related behaviours whereas this is not always the case for forced decisions (Deci et al. 1999a). This evidence suggests that making the distinction between volitional-forced intentions in the theory of planned behaviour may assist in further explaining how intentions are translated into actions.

Chatzisarantis, Biddle, and Meek (1997) developed a simple measure of volitional and forced intentions in order to examine the contribution of these two types of intentions to the prediction of exercise behaviour. Participants are considered to hold volitional intentions if they described their intentions as something that they want to execute by themselves. In contrast, participants are considered to hold forced intentions when they describe their intentions as something that they are obliged to do. Chatzisarantis et al. found that volitional and forced intentions added to the prediction of exercise behaviour after controlling for traditional measures of intentions, but the effects of volitional and forced intentions on exercise behaviour were small. On balance, the distinction between volition and intentions does not fully explain the intention–behaviour relationship and has not been shown to have a major impact on the explanation of exercise behaviour.

Implementation intentions

One reason why theories of intentional behaviour do not fully explain the processes by which intentions translate into actions is that people often forget to carry out their intentions (Orbell et al. 1997; Gollwitzer 1999; Sheeran and Orbell 1999). Alternatively, people's execution of their intentions may be interrupted because other competing goal-directed behaviours take priority over the original intended behaviour (Verplanken and Faes 1999). Motivational theories do not address these difficulties associated with enactment of intentions, and for this reason they may not fully explain the intention–behaviour relationship.

One approach that has been put forward to resolve the inadequacies of the intention–behaviour relationship in the theory of planned behaviour is **implementation intentions**. Implementation intentions are self-regulatory strategies that involve the formulation of specific plans that specify when, how, and where performance of behaviour will take place. Experimental paradigms have been used to initiate implementation intentions and require research participants to explicitly specify *when, where,* and *how* they will engage in an intended behaviour to achieve their behavioural goals. According to Gollwitzer (1999), implementation intentions are powerful self-regulatory strategies that help people move from a motivational phase to a volitional phase and they ensure that their intentions are converted into action. In accordance with this hypothesis, research has indicated that forming implementation intentions decreases the probability of people forgetting to initiate their goal-directed action at the point of initiation (Orbell *et al.* 1997; Sheeran and Orbell 1999). This is because planning *when* and *where* to initiate a prospective action strengthens the mental association between representations of situations and representations of actions. Research has also shown that increased accessibility of situational representations in memory increases the probability of action opportunities getting noticed, and of action initiation occurring, given that the mere perception of action opportunities can automatically trigger a behavioural response (Bargh 1994; Orbell *et al.* 1997; Gollwitzer 1999; Sheeran and Orbell 1999; Koestner *et al.* 2002). Importantly, implementation intentions increase behavioural engagement through these post-decisional, automatic mechanisms, and not by concomitant increases in motivation or intention (Orbell *et al.* 1997).

Recent research has evaluated the effectiveness of interventions that *combine* motivational techniques with volitional techniques such as implementation intentions in influencing the performance of social behaviour (Koestner *et al.* 2002; Milne *et al.* 2002; Prestwich *et al.* 2003; Sheeran and Silverman 2003). The rationale behind this combined approach is that motivational strategies focus on increasing intention levels but do not facilitate the enactment of intentions, while volitional strategies such as implementation intentions increase the probability that these strong intentions will be converted into action but not on changing intentions. Research has corroborated the utility of these combined techniques in increasing exercise behaviour. For example, Milne *et al.* (2002) demonstrated that implementation exercises strengthen the ability of protection motivation theory constructs. Similarly, Sheeran and Silverman (2003) found that an intervention that combined an application of the theory of planned behaviour and implementation intentions is more effective in promoting attendance at health and training courses than an intervention that is based on the theory of planned behaviour alone. In addition, Prestwich *et al.* (2003) have demonstrated that an intervention with a combination of a rational decision-making strategy, or *decisional balance* sheet, and implementation intentions was more effective in promoting exercise behaviour than either of the strategies alone. Koestner *et al.* (2002) also found an interaction between a motivational strategy to enhance self-concordant goals and implementation intentions in goal attainment and persistence. These results support the existence of two distinct phases of motivation: a motivational or pre-decisional phase during which people decide whether or not to perform a behaviour and a volitional, post-decisional, or implemental phase during which people plan when and where they will convert their intentions into behaviour. In addition, research evidence suggests that the combination of motivational and volitional techniques is most effective in promoting exercise behaviour.

Continuation intentions

One final reason why intentions change over time and consequently do not always translate into actions is that people tend to devalue the behaviours and outcomes as they get closer to achieving them (Chatzisarantis *et al.*, in press c). Consider for example the relationship between exercise behaviour and body weight. Initially, people may be highly motivated to participate in exercise because they expect doing so will help them to lose weight. However, people may start losing interest in the goal of losing weight once they do start to lose weight. According to Lewin, this is because outcome evaluations such as the value attached to losing weight are inversely proportional to the psychological distance between the self and the outcome like actual weight loss. This means that the greater the distance between the person's current state and the actual outcome, the higher their belief that they need to lose weight. Given that intentions are associated with outcome evaluations (Ajzen and Fishbein 1980), it is hypothesized that intentions will decline over time and may be less effective in predicting behaviour in the long run.

Chatzisarantis *et al.* (in press c) have proposed that the long-term intention–behaviour relationship can be improved if the theory of planned behaviour can be modified to account for the decline in interest in the behavioural outcome as the attainment of that outcome approaches. These authors proposed that to account for the changes that occur in intentions as the achievement of a long-term outcome nears, theories need to account for people's intentions to continue the performance of the target behaviour after they have achieved or failed to achieve the outcome. Chatzisarantis *et al.* (in press c) defined two constructs: **continuation intentions** *of success* and *continuation intentions of failure*. Continuation intentions of success were defined as an individual's intent to continue engaging in a behaviour when presented with a hypothetical situation in which the individual is successful in attaining their behavioural outcomes. Continuation intentions of failure refer to intentions to continue the performance of the behaviour when presented with a hypothetical situation that signifies unsuccessful progress toward the behavioural outcome. Their study showed that these continuation intentions contributed to the prediction of exercise behaviour after traditional components of the theory of planned behaviour were taken into consideration.

Recommendations for future research and practice in volitional strategies

A trend clearly evident in the literature is that motivational techniques do not necessarily facilitate successful enactment of behavioural intention (Ajzen 1991) and volitional techniques do not effect changes in intentions (Orbell 2003). The theoretical and practical implication of these findings is that interventions that combine motivational techniques with volitional strategies are more effective in promoting exercise behaviour than motivational techniques alone (Koestner *et al.* 2002; Sheeran and Silverman 2003). These results provide strong evidence that human motivation consists of two phases: a motivational or pre-decisional phase and a volitional, implemental, or post-decisional phase (Gollwitzer 1999). In the motivational phase people deliberate over advantages and disadvantages of behaviour and this culminates in the formation of intentions. The theories of reasoned action and planned behaviour (Ajzen and Fishbein 1980; Ajzen 1985) and protection motivation theory (Rogers 1975) are examples of motivational theories that explain intention formation. In the volitional phase, people decide when, where, and how to implement their intention (Gollwitzer 1999).

One caveat is that it is not yet known whether interventions that facilitate continuation intentions and implementation intentions improve the utility of motivational interventions in promoting exercise behaviour. There is some preliminary evidence to support the supplementation of the motivational strategies based on the theory of planned behaviour with volitional strategies such as implementation intentions (Koestner *et al.* 2002; Prestwich *et al.* 2003). Further, the different volitional techniques have not been combined or compared in terms of their effectiveness in promoting exercise behaviour. It is possible that while implementation intentions promote initiation of exercise behaviour by enhancing memory of action initiation, continuation intentions may promote a more sustained participation in exercise behaviour by strengthening motivation to persist under adversity. Therefore, one important avenue for future research is to examine the differential processes by which different volitional techniques such as implementation intentions and continuation intentions facilitate participation in exercise behaviour.

Self-determination theory

Self-determination theory is a theory of human motivation that has been applied extensively to the understanding of exercise behaviour (Deci and Ryan 1985, 2000). It comprises three sub-theories: **cognitive evaluation theory**, causality orientation theory, and **organismic integration theory**.[1] In general, self-determination theory argues that theories of intentional behaviour are too simplistic and mechanistic to provide a complete picture of human motivation (Deci and Ryan 1985). For example, the two-phase conceptualization of motivation advocated by social cognitive theories of intentional behaviour does not account for the motivational factors that give rise to these social cognitive predictors in intentional theories. Self-determination theory proposes that the three *essential* and *innate* psychological needs for self-determination, competence, and relatedness form the basis of motivation. Self-determination refers to the need to experience oneself as initiator and regulator of one's actions. Competence refers to the need to be able to produce behavioural outcomes. Relatedness refers to the need to experience satisfactory relationships with significant others (Deci and Ryan 2000).

These three psychological needs are considered to be *essential* for optimal psychological development, well-being, and growth (Deci and Ryan 2000). Just as humans have biological needs such as thirst and hunger, people also have the universal need to seek out and obtain experiences of self-determination, competence, and relatedness (Deci and Ryan 2000; Sheldon *et al.* 2001). In addition to addressing issues related to the energization of human motivation by psychological needs, self-determination theory also places importance on the social contexts that can affect motivated behaviour (Deci and Ryan 2000). According to Deci and Ryan, psychological need satisfaction is a necessary but not sufficient condition for optimal psychological development, well-being, and growth. Psychological needs must also be supported by the social context because otherwise individuals will feel alienated and will not experience need satisfaction (Deci and Ryan 1985). It is evident therefore that self-determination theory is a *dialectic* theory that views the environment as nurturing need-satisfaction and motivation.

Another important difference between theories of intentional behaviour and self-determination theory is concerned with *form* or quality of motivation. Unlike theories of intentional behaviour that view motivation as varying in strength alone, self-determination theory proposes the interplay between the environment and the individual gives rise to different types of motivation (Deci and Ryan 1985). Self-determination theory distinguishes between two forms of motivated behaviour. **Intrinsic motivation** refers to doing an activity for its inherent satisfaction rather than for some tangible or extrinsic outcome, while *extrinsic motivation* refers to doing an activity for external outcomes that are separable from the activity itself (Deci and Ryan 1985, 2000). In addition, organismic integration theory, a sub-theory of self-determination theory, distinguishes between five different forms of extrinsic motivation, *external* *regulation, introjected regulation, identified regulation, integrated regulation,* and *intrinsic motivation.*

The specification of these different types of motivation permits the study of individual differences in the quality of motivation toward volitional behaviours. Deci and Ryan (2000) argue that the intensity or level of motivation of two people may be equivalent and can lead to behavioural performance that is quantitatively comparable, but if the form of motivation is different, the quality of performance may differ. For example, self-determined or intrinsic motivation may lead to better performance on creative tasks but controlling or extrinsic motivation may facilitate performance on more mundane, mechanistic tasks. Furthermore, a person may be either intrinsically or extrinsically motivated towards certain behaviours, but, from the point of view of an external observer, their level of behavioural engagement is the same. However, when it comes to persistence with that behaviour, the observed behaviour may differ depending on the type or form of the motivation, suggesting that the quality of motivation may explain variance in behaviour across different situations. Therefore, acknowledging different forms of motivation is important because it provides a means of explaining behavioural persistence. Finally, unlike theories of intentional behaviour that consider many different short- and long-term consequences of behaviour, self-determination theory addresses the *ultimate* or *universal* reasons for motivation and behaviour (Sheldon *et al.* 2001). These reasons or motives are more distal than the social cognitive predictors in theory of intention such as attitudes and intentions in the theory of planned behaviour.

However, it is important to realize that self-determination theory does share some similarities with social cognitive theories of intentional behaviour. For example, it considers both internal events such as attitudes and intentions and social environments to be important determinants of behaviour. Therefore, self-determination theory and theories of intentional behaviour are not antithetical but may be able to complement each other. The differences lie in the proximity and origin of the constructs that influence behaviour. While theories of intention deal with more specific cognitive and affective determinants of action, self-determination theory focuses on the more general, organismic conditions that give rise to motivation and behaviour. Deci and Ryan (1985) recognize the potential for such a theoretical union: 'Cognitive theories begin their analysis with . . . a cognitive representation of some future desired state. What is missing, of course, is a consideration of the conditions of the organism that make these future states desired' (1985: 228). Self-determination theory therefore offers reasons why such social cognitive variables exist. In the next sections, cognitive evaluation theory and organismic integration theory will be introduced and their application to the explanation of exercise behaviour discussed.

Cognitive evaluation theory

Cognitive evaluation theory is a sub-theory of self-determination theory that was developed to explain the effects of intrinsic motivation on behaviours and how social contexts affect intrinsic motivation (Deci and Ryan 1985). Intrinsic motivation can be measured or indicated in two ways. First, time spent engaged in a target task during a free choice period in which several attractive alternatives other than the target task are available constitutes a behavioural measure of intrinsic motivation. To the extent that people freely choose and persist with the target task, the researcher has a strong indication of the degree on intrinsic motivation towards that task. Therefore, the longer the time spent in the task, the more the person is assumed to enjoy the task and the higher their inferred level of intrinsic motivation. Second, self-reports of the degree of interest a person derives from the target task during the free choice period is an alternative measure of intrinsic motivation.

Cognitive evaluation theory aims to explain variance in intrinsic motivation. It proposes that intrinsic motivation is engendered when external and internal events relevant to the initiation and regulation of behaviour support a person's innate psychological needs for self-determination and competence (Deci and Ryan 1985). In addition, the theory proposes that there are three general processes by which external events such as tangible rewards and internal events such as goals can influence intrinsic motivation. The first process is through perceived locus of causality. The construct of perceived locus of causality indicates whether people perceive their behaviour as emanating from their self, and is therefore volitional and self-determined, or whether their behaviour is regulated by some external force such as a significant other. With regards to perceived locus of causality, Deci and Ryan have predicted that events relevant to initiation and regulation of behaviour that promote a more internal perceived locus of causality will promote intrinsic motivation, whereas events that promote a more external perceived locus of causality are likely to undermine intrinsic motivation.

The second process by which external events influence intrinsic motivation is via perceived competence. Events that affirm personal competence are likely to maintain intrinsic motivation, while events that diminish perceived competence undermine intrinsic motivation. The third process of influencing intrinsic motivation relates to how people construe events relevant to initiation and regulation of behaviour. Deci and Ryan suggest that external events can be viewed as having *informational*, *controlling*, or *amotivating* aspects with respect to motivation. A social context can be considered as supporting one of these aspects and this is likely to affect an individual's perceived competence and intrinsic motivation. The informational aspect provides competence-relevant information in the context of choice. When this aspect is salient, it is likely to promote intrinsic motivation. The controlling aspect undermines feelings of self-determination by pressuring people to behave, think, and feel in particular ways. When the controlling aspect is salient, intrinsic motivation is undermined. The amotivating aspect signifies that a sense of competence cannot be attained by participating in the behaviour. When the amotivating aspect of an external event is salient, people feel amotivated and they do not intend to engage in the behaviour (Wild and Enzle 2002).

Applications of cognitive evaluation theory

Cognitive evaluation theory has important ramifications for practice because predictions can be made about the impact that various environmental and internal events exert on intrinsic motivation (Deci and Ryan 1985, 2000). For example, cognitive evaluation theory predicts that external events such as rewards and feedback that do not support competence and promote an external perceived locus of causality will undermine intrinsic motivation, whereas events that affirm competence and support an internal perceived locus of causality will enhance intrinsic motivation. A number of experimental studies have examined effects of various external events such as tangible rewards, verbal rewards, and interpersonal context on intrinsic motivation. A meta-analysis of experimental studies adopting cognitive evaluation theory found strong effects of tangible rewards on intrinsic motivation and behaviour (Deci *et al.* 1999a). Specifically, the analysis showed that the expectation of tangible rewards such as money, trophies, and scholarships resulted in a decrease in intrinsic motivation. In addition, the analysis found that the effects of expected rewards on intrinsic motivation varied as a function of how rewards are introduced or communicated (Deci *et al.* 1999a). When rewards are expected and given for being present at an experimental session, called *task-noncontingent rewards*, then intrinsic motivation will not be undermined. This is because expected rewards that are not contingent on doing the task do not pressure people to behave in particular ways, and therefore are less likely to influence intrinsic motivation. Task-noncontingent rewards are likened to real-life situations in which people are paid for their occupation.

Research has also shown that *task completion rewards* that are given for completing a task undermine intrinsic motivation because people feel obliged to complete the task to gain the reward. In such cases the reward is experienced as controlling and results in a shift in the perceived locus of causality from internal to external (Deci *et al.* 1999a). In addition, *engagement contingent rewards*, which are given for engaging in a task but not completing it, are also experienced as controlling, and therefore undermine intrinsic motivation. This is because people have to work on the task to get the reward (Deci *et al.* 1999a; Deci and Ryan 2000). Further, *performance contingent rewards*, which are given for performing an activity well by matching some standard of excellence or surpassing some criterion, undermine intrinsic motivation because people have to meet some standard in order to receive the reward. However, when performance contingent rewards convey competence-affirming information such as when people meet the standard implied by the reward, they may have a diminished negative effect on intrinsic motivation. This is because competence-affirming information offsets some of the negative controlling effects that performance contingent rewards exert on intrinsic motivation (Deci and Ryan 1985, 2000).

In addition, research has shown that *competitively contingent rewards*, which are given to people competing directly with others for a limited number of rewards undermine intrinsic motivation (Reeve 2002). Competitively contingent rewards and face-to-face competitive situations are highly controlling because winning is instrumental to attaining the reward (Deci and Ryan 1985; Reeve 2002). In the domain of exercise, the effects of reward contingencies on intrinsic motivation have not been examined thoroughly. However, there have been a number of studies examining the effects of rewards on intrinsic motivation in sports competitors and these will be reviewed in Chapter 5 (McAuley and Tammen 1989; Vansteenkiste and Deci 2003).

In addition to examining effects of tangible rewards on intrinsic motivation, several studies have examined the effects of verbal rewards on intrinsic motivation. Positive feedback that is administered immediately after completion of a task is an example of a verbal reward. Research has shown that verbal rewards usually enhance intrinsic motivation because they tend to affirm personal competence (Deci *et al.* 1999a). For example, positive feedback that indicates a person has done well on a task is likely to enhance intrinsic motivation by increasing their sense of competence. This is in accordance with cognitive evaluation theory that hypothesizes that perceived competence enhances intrinsic motivation in the context of self-determination (Deci and Ryan 1985). Therefore, it is important to realize that the effect of a verbal reward on intrinsic motivation can vary as a function of the context in which the reward is communicated. If rewards are communicated in a controlling way or imply evaluation then they are likely to undermine intrinsic motivation (Deci and Ryan 1985, 2000). For example, if positive feedback is reported in a controlling manner (e.g. 'you have done as well as you *should*'), then intrinsic motivation is likely to be undermined because the modal operator of 'should' facilitates a sense of being controlled (Deci *et al.* 1994).

In addition, verbal rewards will only enhance intrinsic motivation if they are communicated in the context of self-determination (Deci and Ryan 1985). This can be achieved by simply informing people about their performance avoiding the use of pressuring language, by instructing people how to self-administer informational feedback, and by structuring feedback in way that does not imply evaluation (Deci and Ryan 1985, 2000). In the exercise domain, Whitehead and Corbin's (1991) experimental study found that positive feedback enhanced intrinsic motivation in a physical task. Further, longitudinal studies have supported the effect of perceived positive feedback on intrinsic motivation (Koka and Hein, in press).

Although cognitive evaluation theory and the concept of intrinsic motivation have attracted a great deal of scientific interest and debate (Deci *et al.* 1999a), it is important to realize that cognitive evaluation theory applies only to behaviours and tasks that are highly interesting, such as puzzles and prob-lems. The theory does not apply to mundane tasks that are monotonous and boring and unlikely to be intrinsically motivated such as brushing one's teeth or wearing a seat belt. As a consequence, cognitive evaluation theory does not explain how interest develops or how a boring task can be transformed into an interesting task. Another limitation of cognitive evaluation theory is that it does not account for the psychological need for relatedness, despite evidence that relatedness is an essential and fundamental psychological need (Sheldon *et al.* 2001). In fact, Deci and Ryan (2000) have flagged the psychological need for relatedness as important because it explains why people perform mundane tasks that are important for personal development and growth but are unlikely to be intrinsically motivated.

Organismic integration theory

Organismic integration theory is a second sub-theory of self-determination theory that explains the motivation of non-intrinsically motivating behaviours on the basis of all three of the psychological needs identified by Deci and Ryan (2000). The theory proposes that people engage in behaviours that are unlikely to be intrinsically motivated because of the need for related-ness. That is, because people are intrinsically motivated to experience satisfac-tory relationships with others, they engage in non-intrinsically motivated behaviour in order to function effectively in the social world (Deci and Ryan 1985, 2000). Central to organismic integration theory is the hypothesis that people engage in non-intrinsically motivated behaviours for the attainment of extrinsic outcomes such as praise, but it also recognizes that people can *internalize* such extrinsically motivated behaviours and eventually accept them as emanating from the self. Thus, the theory proposes that some extrinsically motivated behaviours can eventually become self-determined through the process of *internalization* (Deci *et al.* 1994; Deci and Ryan 2000).

A model describing internalization and human motivation from an organ-ismic integration theory perspective is presented in Figure 3.1. On the right-hand side of the model is amotivation, referring to a person's lack of inten-tionality and sense of personal causation (Ntoumanis *et al.*, in press). Lack of perceived competence and beliefs that behaviour cannot reliably lead to desired outcomes can precipitate amotivation. Adjacent to amotivation on the continuum are the four different forms of extrinsic motivation, namely, external regulation, introjected regulation, identified regulation, and inte-grated regulation. Each of these forms of regulation reflects the pursuit of behaviours to attain external outcomes that are separate from doing the behaviour for its own sake. However, they do reflect varying degrees of internalization and self-determination. Internalization of an action is depend-ent upon receiving praise or positive feedback from significant others to whom individuals feel attached or related (Deci and Ryan 2000). Behaviours that are externally reinforced are characterized as externally regulated. Introjected regulation lies alongside external regulation and it refers to behaviours that are performed to avoid the pressuring emotions of guilt or shame. External regulation and introjected regulation, therefore, describe less internalized and more controlling forms of behaviour because they refer to behaviours that are performed under some form of internal or external pressure.

A less controlling and more self-determined form of external regulation is identified regulation, which refers to a behaviour that is performed to achieve personally relevant and valued outcomes. Identified behaviours are therefore characterized as being more internalized and self-determined. The most autonomous and least controlling form of externally regulated behaviour is integrated regulation which refers to identified behaviours that are brought into congruence with other behaviours and roles that are enacted in life. Finally, adjacent to integrated regulation lies intrinsic motivation, which refers to behaviours that are performed for their own sake and not for the attainment of external outcomes that are independent of the activity itself. Intrinsically motivated behaviours display many similarities with identified regulation and integrated regulation. For example, intrinsically motivated, integrated, and identified behaviours all are characterized by high levels of enjoyment. However, integrated and identified behaviours imply that people derive enjoyment from the attainment of the valued outcome rather than the activity itself. In contrast, the construct of intrinsic motivation implies that people derive enjoyment from the activity itself and not from the attainment of valued outcomes.

Organismic integration theory also places great emphasis on the effect of context on the types of motivation. Contexts that support psychological needs are hypothesized to promote more self-determined forms of extrinsic motivation such as identified regulation and integrated regulation, while contexts that frustrate psychological needs promote less self-determined forms of extrinsic motivation such as external regulation and introjected regulation (Deci and Ryan 2000). In general, the theory differentiates between two types of interpersonal context that can either support or frustrate psychological needs. Interpersonal contexts, in which significant others encourage choice and participation in decision-making, provide a meaningful rationale for doing the behaviour, use neutral language (e.g. use of 'may', 'could' and not 'should', 'must') during interpersonal communication, and acknowledge people's feelings and perspectives support self determined forms of motivation (Deci *et al.* 1994). Conversely, interpersonal contexts in which significant others do not explain why performance of the behaviour may be important, use pressuring language during interpersonal communication (e.g. use of 'should' and 'must'), and do not acknowledge difficulties associated with performance of behaviour tend to frustrate psychological needs.

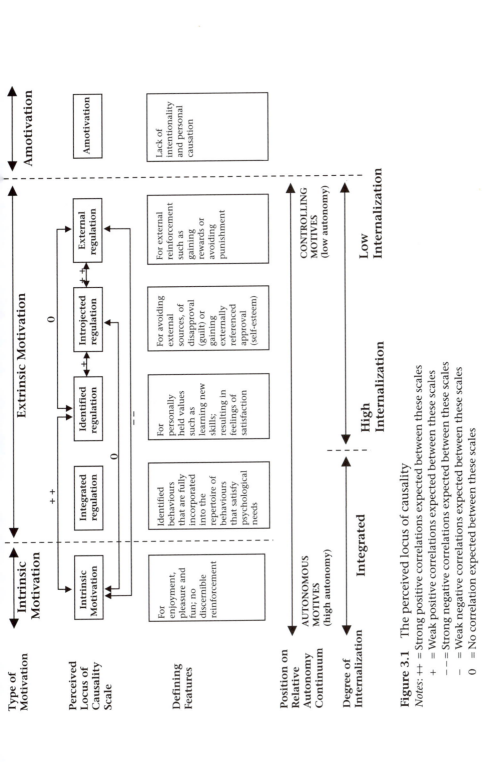

Figure 3.1 The perceived locus of causality

Notes: ++ = Strong positive correlations expected between these scales
+ = Weak positive correlations expected between these scales
– – = Strong negative correlations expected between these scales
– = Weak negative correlations expected between these scales
0 = No correlation expected between these scales

Applications of organismic integration theory

A measure of the different forms of motivation in organismic integration theory was developed by Ryan and Connell (1989), termed the **perceived locus of causality** (PLOC) scale.[2] The PLOC measures external regulation, introjected regulation, identified regulation, and intrinsic motivation. In a preliminary study, the intercorrelations among these scales were found to conform to a *simplex-ordered* structure. A simplex-ordered structure is evident when the correlation between scales measuring adjacent types of motivation such as external regulation and introjected regulation is higher than the correlation between dimensions that lie further apart such as external regulation and identified regulation (see Figure 3.1). Such a pattern indicates the presence of a continuum which Deci and Ryan (2000) describe as a developmental continuum of self-determination. However, Deci and Ryan also suggest that support of a continuum does not preclude the possibility for individuals to internalize a new behaviour at any point along this continuum depending on prior experience and current situational factors.

Several studies in a number of contexts have corroborated the importance of the distinction between self-determined and controlling forms of extrinsic motivation in understanding behaviour (e.g. Williams *et al*. 1998; Williams *et al*. 2002). In particular, intervention, prospective, and longitudinal panel design studies have shown that forms of extrinsic motivation such as external regulation and introjected regulation influence health behaviours and outcomes directly or indirectly via perceived competence (Williams *et al*. 1998; Williams *et al*. 2002). In addition, **perceived autonomy support** has been shown to influence behaviour mediated by self-determined forms of extrinsic motivation such as identified regulation and perceived competence (Guay *et al*. 2001; Hagger *et al*., 2003b; Hagger *et al*., in press b).

A number of valid and reliable measures of intrinsic motivation and the perceived locus of causality have also been developed in the exercise domain. Most prominent of these is the behavioural regulation in exercise questionnaire (BREQ) developed by Markland and colleagues (2004). Other nongeneric measures have been adopted such as Goudas, Biddle, and Fox's (1994) and Hagger et al.'s (2003b) adaptation of items from Ryan and Connell's (1989) self-regulation questionnaire for use in physical education contexts. These instruments have measured external regulation, introjected regulation, identified regulation, and intrinsic motivation but not integrated regulation. Despite marginal differences in the items used by these inventories, these scales have been shown to conform to the simplex-ordered structure as hypothesized by organismic integration theory (e.g. Chatzisarantis *et al*. 2003).

Research in an exercise context has also examined utility of self-determined forms of motivation in the prediction of exercise behaviour. Several studies have shown that the types of motivation from the PLOC influence exercise behaviour directly (Ntoumanis 2001; Chatzisarantis *et al*. 2002; Chatzisarantis *et al.* 2003) and indirectly via the mediation of intentions (Hagger *et al.* 2003b) and attitudes (Hagger *et al.* 2002a). However, the direct effects of self-determined forms of motivation on intentions and behaviours are generally small (Chatzisarantis *et al.* 1997; Chatzisarantis *et al.* 2002; Chatzisarantis *et al.*, in press d; Hagger *et al.* 2002a).

In exercise and physical education contexts, research has investigated the influence of self-determined forms of extrinsic motivation and intrinsic motivation on some key motivational determinants of exercise behaviour. Goudas *et al.* (1994) found that perceived competence mediated the effects of self-determined forms of extrinsic motivation on intentions. These results are consistent with studies conducted in health psychology that found perceived competence to partially mediate the effects of self-determined forms of extrinsic motivation on health outcomes (Williams *et al.* 2002). Conversely, several other studies have found that self-determined forms of extrinsic motivation mediate the effects of perceived competence on exercise intentions and behaviour (Ntoumanis, 2001; Sarrazin *et al.* 2002; Hagger *et al.* 2003b; Standage *et al.* 2003). Hence, the role of self-determined forms of extrinsic motivation in predicting and explaining exercise intentions and behaviour is complex and there has not been complete convergence in the exact pattern of influence of these variables on intentions and behaviour.

The trans-contextual model

The **trans-contextual model** builds upon previous applications of self-determination theory and aims to explain how motivation in one context, namely physical education, facilitates motivation, intentions, and behaviour in a different but related context, namely exercise behaviour during leisure time. From its outset, research on intrinsic motivation and self-determination theory has demonstrated the importance of context in influencing perceived locus of causality (Deci and Ryan 1985). Contextual factors such as presentation of tasks and support of choice with a clear rationale, acknowledgement of conflict, and informational feedback have been shown to enhance intrinsic motivation (Deci *et al.* 1994), while rewards, threats, evaluation, and deadlines have been shown to undermine intrinsic motivation (Deci and Ryan 1985). The results of this research have led to recommendations suggesting that quality and quantity of motivation can be enhanced by environments that support psychological needs and an internal perceived locus of causality (Deci and Ryan 2000). Following this, research has supported these premises in naturalistic settings, demonstrating that perceived autonomy support influences behaviour in a motivational sequence (Chatzisarantis et al., in press b). The sequence dictates that perceived autonomy support affects perceived locus of causality, which in turn influences motivation and behaviour. The trans-contextual model builds upon this evidence and postulates that the teaching styles of physical educators influence the forms of motivation that pupils endorse in physical education classes. Specifically, it is suggested that autonomous supportive physical education teachers facilitate intrinsic motivation or self-determined forms of extrinsic motivation whereas teachers whose teaching style is not autonomy-supportive facilitate controlling forms of extrinsic motivation (Figure 3.2).

The trans-contextual model also proposes a cross-contextual interplay between motives, such that intrinsic motivation in one context such as physical education can lead to intrinsic motivation in another, such as leisure time. In turn, this increased motivation can lead to participation in related activities in a different context such as leisure-time exercise behaviour (Vallerand 1997). The trans-contextual model therefore proposes that intrinsic motivation and self-determined forms of extrinsic motivation in physical education classes is more likely to facilitate intrinsic motivation with regard to leisure-time exercise behaviour than controlling forms of extrinsic motivation. This is because people tend to search for opportunities to re-enact intrinsically motivating behaviours in relevant contexts (Chaiken 1980).

Recent research on intentional behaviour has also indicated that the integration of constructs from self-determination theory and the theory of planned behaviour provide complementary explanations of the unexplained processes within each theory. The inclusion of self-determination theory in social cognitive models has helped researchers to explain the quality of the relationships in the theory of planned behaviour (Chatzisarantis *et al.* 1997; Chatzisarantis and Biddle 1998; Sheeran *et al.* 1999a) and the antecedents of the theory of planned behaviour variables (Chatzisarantis *et al.* 2002; Hagger *et al.* 2002a). For example, Chatzisarantis *et al.* (1998, 1997) have demonstrated that the predictive utility of the theory of planned behaviour in an exercise context can be increased by the inclusion of volitional intentions. Similarly, Hagger *et al.* (2002a) have shown that an internal perceived locus of causality has a pervasive impact on attitudes and perceived behavioural control with respect to exercise behaviour. However, the strong correlation between intrinsic motivation and intentions to participate in exercise behaviour was completely mediated by attitude and, to a lesser extent, by perceived behavioural control. These results were replicated by Chatzisarantis and co-workers (2002), who also demonstrated that an internal perceived locus of causality determined the effort people invested in pursuing exercise behaviour. Such research acknowledges the role of different types of motivation in explaining the bases for intentions, attitudes, subjective norms, and perceived behavioural control. It also recognizes that the theory of planned behaviour has utility in providing a basis for the translation of general motives from the perceived locus of causality into intentional action (Chatzisarantis *et al.* 2002; Hagger *et al.* 2002a).

In congruence with the findings of these studies examining the impact of perceived locus of causality on intentions and behaviour within the theory of planned behaviour (Chatzisarantis *et al.* 1997; Chatzisarantis and Biddle 1998; Sheeran *et al.* 1999a; Chatzisarantis *et al.* 2002; Hagger *et al.* 2002a), the trans-contextual model predicts that motives of perceived locus of causality in

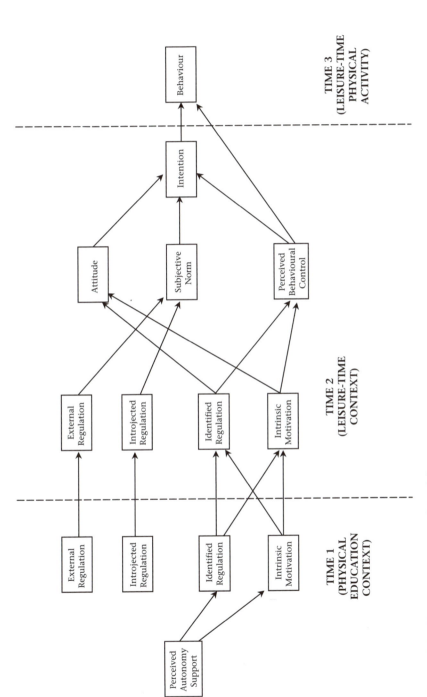

Figure 3.2 The trans-contextual model

a leisure-time context will influence exercise intentions and behaviour only via the mediation of the belief-based constructs of attitude, subjective norms, and perceived behavioural control. Thus the perceived locus of causality is presumed to act as a source of information for the formation of attitudes, subjective norms and perceived behavioural control, and, indirectly, intentions.

Thus far, research has shown that the autonomy-supportive teaching styles of physical educators influence participation in exercise behaviour during leisure time via the mediating role of intrinsic motivation, attitudes, perceived behavioural control, and intentions. In addition, evidence has shown that perceived autonomy support in physical education influences exercise behaviour during leisure time even after effects of past behaviour are taken into consideration (Hagger et al. 2003b). Further, preliminary results suggest that the effects of the trans-contextual model have been replicated across four cultures in Europe and Asia (Hagger et al., in press b). However, it is important to note that there are no intervention studies or large-scale studies that examine the impact that teaching styles have on motivation for exercise behaviour. Further, little is known about the influence that peer groups and parents exert on exercise behaviour. Therefore, one direction for future research is to evaluate effectiveness interventions based on the trans-contextual model in promoting exercise behaviour.

Practical recommendations based on self-determination theory

Perceived autonomy support

In terms of practical recommendations, Reeve (2002) identifies the specific behaviours exhibited by those involved in the promotion of exercise behaviour that are likely to support autonomy in individuals seeking to increase their exercise levels. One way is to avoid the use of external incentives and controlling, non-informational forms of feedback as the only contingency for doing the activity (Deci and Ryan 1985). Clearly, however, this is only a small aspect of the provision of an autonomy supportive environment. Behavioural strategies exist that enhance motivation such as providing the individual with opportunities to choose and express themselves in exercise contexts (Chatzisarantis et al., in press a), fostering an environment focusing on activities involving task or mastery rather than the ego (Ames 1992), and avoiding competition and external rationales for participation (Ryan et al. 1984). Furthermore, providing appropriate feedback that is informational and competence-related is important in terms of monitoring progress (Deci et al. 1994).

Motivational interviewing

One technique that has been shown to be efficacious in changing people's exercise motivation and behaviour is **motivational interviewing** (Rollnick and Miller 1995; Miller 1999), and this has recently been linked with self-determination theory approaches to motivation (Markland 2004). Motivational interviewing is a clinically developed intervention that aims to alter problem behaviours by investigating the nature of the problem with the 'client' and assisting them in self-directed behavioural change. Rollnick and Miller, the central proponents of motivational interviewing, define it as,

> a directive, client-centered counselling style for eliciting behavior change by helping clients to explore and resolve ambivalence. Compared with nondirective counselling, it is more focused and goal-directed. The examination and resolution of ambivalence are its central purpose, and the counselor is intentionally directive in pursuing this goal. (1995: 325)

Originally developed in the context of alcoholics and problem drinkers, motivational interviewing should not, according to Rollnick and Miller, be confused with a set of techniques that are applied to the client or person with a problem, but an 'interpersonal style' that is adopted by a clinician or interviewer in the pursuit of directing a client-centred programme of cognitive and behavioural change. Importantly, this set of styles should not be considered as confined to clinical settings, but can be applied to interventions and contexts wherever behaviour change is salient.

 According to Rollnick and Miller, motivational interviewing contrasts with traditional approaches to clinical interventions for behaviour change because it removes the conflict caused by the confrontational styles, argumentation, and direct persuasion often seen in other clinical approaches. Rather, it adopts an approach that is directed by the interviewer, but the focus is primarily on conflict resolution and behaviour change that is based upon the client or individual's own personal suggestions. As such, the traditional resistance and scepticism often expressed by individuals undergoing traditional confrontational means of behaviour change are allayed and the client is much more empowered to pursue changes to his/her own problem behaviour that are suggested by they themselves. Furthermore, there are no direct suggestions made by the clinician or interviewer, and thus no direct persuasion 'techniques' are used as with interventions and campaigns based on the theory of planned behaviour covered in the previous chapter. Motivational interviewing does not therefore involve dictating changes to individuals or involve pointing a finger at their unhealthy lifestyle, instead it should be viewed as a partnership between the clinician or interviewer and patient or person undergoing change.

 The starting point of motivational interviewing is investigating and resolving the ambivalence that surrounds the problem behaviour. The ambivalence is characterized by conflicts between the problem behaviour and other, usually healthier, courses of action. The client's task in motivational interviewing is therefore to elicit their own reasons for change, not those suggested by the interviewer. It is therefore the role of the client to express personally relevant benefits (pros) and costs (cons) of changing the difficult behaviour. For example, a client may make statements like: 'I actually do like exercising, it makes me feel good, and I know it's good for me losing weight, but it's far too much effort when you have kids and I just can't seem to fit it in.' It is the role of the interviewer to help the client investigate both sides of this and direct them toward a resolution that may lead to motivation and sustained action toward changing behaviour. Therefore, ambivalence is viewed by the motivational interviewing approach as the primary obstacle toward changing people's behaviour, and once this is overcome, behaviour change will follow, provided the information and skills are given to the individual undergoing change.

In addition, there are four other core principles that must be adhered to at all times by the interviewer when conducting a motivational interview: (1) express empathy; (2) support self-efficacy; (3) roll with resistance; and (4) develop discrepancy. The client expects to be told in the interview that their behaviour is unhealthy and needs to change, instead principles of motivating interviewing compel the interviewer to acknowledge their understanding of or *empathy* with the difficulties that the interviewee encounters with the problem behaviour and trying to change. There is also no single manner to change behaviour and the interviewer should provide support to the client in terms of supporting their confidence or *self-efficacy* towards the strategies that they adopt. In addition, the interviewer should not counter any resistance with arguments or by challenging the views of the client, this may only create more resistance, instead the interviewer *'rolls' with the resistance* by acknowledging the conflict in the individual and using the momentum to investigate the conflict and possible means for resolution. Finally, motivational interviewers aim to direct the client into highlighting discrepancy between their current behavioural status and their ideal situation. Together these principles underlie the motivational interviewing approach and assist in preventing relapse or resistance often associated with other approaches.

Motivational interviewing is conducted via a 'menu of strategies' that is adopted by the interviewer to direct the client towards their investigation of ambivalence. The menu is varied according to the state of readiness expressed by the client and verified by the interviewer prior to the interview. Importantly, in keeping with the ethos of the approach, any resistance, defensive manoeuvres, or scepticism expressed by the client is not viewed as a failure by the client to comply with the wishes of the interviewer, but is viewed as a failure of the interviewer in estimating a state of readiness to change that is more advanced than the interviewee's current status. An example of the menu of strategies, a summary of the general approach and aims of each strategy, and example statements likely to be evoked from the client for each strategy is given in Table 3.1. The menu of strategies is adopted alongside the core

Table 3.1 Menu of strategies for motivational interviewing

Strategy	Purpose	Type of comments from interviewer
Reviewing a typical day	Builds rapport and focuses on entire lifestyle not specific problem behaviours	*'Can we spend the next 5–10 minutes going through a day from beginning to end. What happened, and how did you feel? Is there any time you could have fitted in exercise? Let's start at the beginning.'*
Looking back	Explores what life was like before they experienced health problems like obesity, low activity	*'So things have really changed. Tell me a little more about what life was like back then.'*
Good things and less good things	Explores the pros and the cons of the problem behaviour i.e. lack of activity	*'You said that your weight has affected your self-confidence. Tell me about a time when that happened.'*
Discussing the stages of change	Interviewer introduces stages of change and enters into a discussion with client, client encouraged to provide ways of moving/ changing stage	*'Can you think of any ways that you could change from being someone who is aware of the need for change (contemplator) and someone who is getting ready to make a change (preparer)?'*
Assessment feedback	Interviewer provides client with a summary of their achievements so far	*'Would it be okay if I offered a little information to you based on what we've talked about so far? Correct me if I'm wrong about anything . . .'*
Values exploration	Clients encouraged to explore their 'ideal self' and compare it to their 'current self' to reveal their values	*'Think about the amount of exercise you do now, how much would you have to change so that you were doing the amount of exercise that is ideal for you?'*
Looking forward	Asks the client to explore two different futures: one in which they made changes to their unhealthy behaviour and the other if they did not.	*'What do you think would happen in future if you made the changes you have said to your exercise? Compare that to what would happen if you didn't make those changes.'*
Exploring importance and confidence	Asks clients to explore the importance of each change they have proposed and how confident they are at achieving the change	*'Thinking about the changes you have said to your exercise habits, how confident do you think you are in making those changes?'*

Table 3.1 (*cont'd*)

Strategy	Purpose	Type of comments from interviewer
Decisional balance	Client is asked to list the pros and cons of making behavioural change – similar to good things and less good things	*'Can you list all of the pros and cons of doing exercise behaviour in future?'*
Change planning	Used if a client is at advanced stage of readiness, interviewer explores possible actions that could change behaviour in future	*'What are the possible things you could do in the next month to increase your current level of exercise? Try to come up with as many as you can.'*

principles in the pursuit of client-centred change. Importantly, the change does not have to be actual behaviour change. Instead, successful change is often established on the basis of movement from one stage of change to another. Thus increases on readiness to change is considered a successful outcome rather than actual behaviour change. This can often be reflected using assessments such as a decisional balance sheet. These changes are expected to be progressive over a series of interview sessions in which readiness for change is evaluated. Motivational interview sessions are expected to last about 40 minutes with several sessions (up to 6), but recent research has resulted in the development of brief motivational interviewing that last approximately 20 minutes and with single sessions (Rollnick and Miller 1995).

Research with motivational interviewing has generally supported its effectiveness in a number of behavioural domains, including exercise. Research in an exercise context has reported motivational interviewing as having applicability to this behaviour in primary care settings, however, few randomized control studies have used motivational interviewing as an intervention technique to promote exercise behaviour. For example, Harland *et al.* (1999) conducted a randomized control trial that examined the effectiveness of an intensive motivational interviewing intervention (6 interviews over 12 weeks), a brief interviewing session (1 interview), and a financial incentive (vouchers) on participants' exercise behaviour. The intensive interview intervention group exhibited 55 per cent more exercise behaviour than control after 6 weeks but the vouchers and brief interviewing patients did not exhibit a significant increase, suggesting that intensive motivational interviewing is the most effective in sustained exercise change.

While motivational interviewing seems to be efficacious, it seems to be based on limited theoretical evidence and testable hypotheses and evidence for the mechanisms for its effectiveness are limited. Miller admitted not devoting sufficient attention to the provision of a comprehensive theoretical background to motivational interviewing and agrees that 'we do not have, in my view, a satisfactory explanation of why and how motivational interviewing works' (1999: 2). Motivational interviewing has been only loosely allied with the trans-theoretical model, particularly the stages of change, self-efficacy theory, cognitive dissonance theory, and client-centred therapy (Miller 1999). Recently, Markland (2004) has drawn parallels between the processes adopted by motivational interviewing and self-determination theory. His suggestion is that motivational interviewing may alter motivation and behaviour by changing the key constructs from the theory. Markland suggests that motivational interviewing creates an interpersonal environment likely to foster a sense of self-determination and support the autonomy of individuals trying to change their behaviour. It does this by supporting autonomy through means such as providing positive feedback that is competence related, by the provision of an appropriate structure to enhance intrinsic motivation through the identified regulation of personally relevant goals and the presentation of clear contingencies between behaviour and outcome, and by the involvement of the individual in the process of determining goals, courses of action, and planning for change. Markland summarizes these parallels in Figure 3.3.

Further parallels can be drawn between self-determination theory and items from the guiding principles and menu of strategies in motivational interviewing. These parallels, in particular, arise from the types of feedback put forward by Deci *et al.* (1994) likely to facilitate the internalization of externally regulated behaviours in the repertoire of behaviours that would be important to personal functioning and an autonomous existence. These types of feedback were provision of a clear rationale, acknowledgement of conflict, and the provision of informational feedback. In the core principles of motivational interviewing, the development of discrepancy provides informational feedback that is self-directed regarding the relationship between personal behaviour (e.g. doing exercise) and personally relevant goals (e.g. losing weight). In the menu of strategies, the examination of the 'good things and the bad things' and the exploration of value items provide a self-directed rationale for doing the behaviour. Finally, the setting of personally relevant goals that address these values may shift the locus of causality for the behaviour towards identified regulation – because the behaviour is related to a specific value. Furthermore, expressing empathy is akin to acknowledging conflict because the interviewer provides some understanding of the aspects of the behaviour that the interviewee does not want to do and the conflict that leads to ambivalence. In summary, it seems that motivational interviewing is an effective strategy to change exercise behaviour, provided it is sustained, and it may be that motivational interviewing changes self-determination theory constructs that may be responsible for sustained behavioural change.

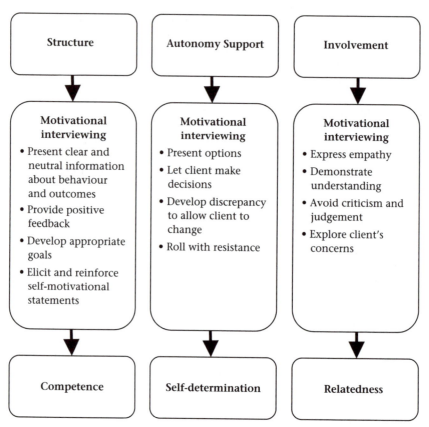

Figure 3.3   Relations between psychological needs and motivational styles from self-determination theory and the core principles from motivational interviewing
Source: Markland (2004)

Suggested reading

Deci, E.L. and Ryan, R.M. (2002) *Handbook of Self-Determination Research*. Rochester, NY: University of Rochester Press. The most comprehensive reader of self-determination theory to date with contributions from many of the influential authors in the area.

Gollwitzer, P.M. (1999) Implementation intentions: strong effects of simple plans, *American Psychologist*, 54: 493–503. Gollwitzer's lucid review of his own work on implementation intentions.

Hagger, M.S., Chatzisarantis, N., Culverhouse, T. and Biddle, S.J.H. (2003) The processes by which perceived autonomy support in physical education promotes leisure-time physical activity intentions and behavior: a trans-contextual model, *Journal of Educational Psychology*, 95: 784–95. A review of our own work on self-determination theory and the theory of planned behaviour and introduction to the trans-contextual model.

Summary

- Social cognitive theories of intention explain how intentions to exercise are formed, but are inadequate in explaining how exercise intentions are converted into behaviour.
- Several properties of intention likely to enhance the relationship between exercise intentions and behaviour have been identified including intention stability, scale correspondence, intention formation, self-schema, and volitional versus forced intentions.
- The formation of an implementation intention in which an actor specifies when, where, and how they are going to exercise has been shown to enhance the intention–behaviour relationship. This is because the statement of such cues serve to enhance the link between intention and behaviour and reduce the likelihood of an exerciser forgetting to carry out their intentions.
- Self-determination theory is a theory of motivation that aims to explain motivation on the basis of psychological need satisfaction. The theory has two influential sub-theories: cognitive evaluation theory and organismic integration theory.
- Cognitive evaluation theory hypothesizes that context will affect the quality of motivation experienced by exercisers. The quality of motivation is characterized by a perceived locus of causality, a continuum of different forms of motivation ranging from intrinsic to extrinsic. Informational contexts tend to enhance intrinsic motivation, a sense that exercise is performed through a sense of choice, enjoyment, and interest. Controlling contexts tend to undermine intrinsic motivation and behaviours are viewed to be controlled by others and performed out of a sense of obligation.
- Organismic integration theory explains how intrinsic motivation is developed and how extrinsically motivated behaviours can become internalized or integrated and viewed as emanating from the self with a locus of causality closer to intrinsic forms of motivation.
- Perceived autonomy support is a means to enhance intrinsic motivation through key autonomy-supportive behaviours of teachers and instructors such as non-contingent positive feedback.
- Motivational interviewing is a client-centred counselling approach to changing exercise behaviour and adopts the basic principles of expressing empathy, supporting self-efficacy, rolling with resistance, developing discrepancy, and a menu of strategies to change interviewee's readiness to change. Parallels with this approach have been drawn with self-determination theory in that it supports autonomy, provides an appropriate

structure for self-determined change in exercise behaviour, and involves the client in the process of change.

Notes

1 This chapter will focus on cognitive evaluation theory and organismic integration theory because these have been applied most frequently to explaining behaviour in a physical activity context.
2 Cognitive evaluation theory has also used the construct of perceived locus of causality to explain effects of external events on intrinsic motivation. The difference between perceived locus of causality as conceptualized by cognitive evaluation theory and organismic integration theory is that organismic integration theory considers perceived locus of causality to comprise four dimensions (external regulation, introjection, identification and intrinsic motivation). In contrast, cognitive evaluation theory considers perceived locus of causality to comprise two dimensions (extrinsic versus intrinsic).

4

Exercise and the physical self

The self is one of the most widely researched and focal concepts in social, educational, and personality psychology. According to Oyserman, 'Self-concept and identity provide answers to the basic questions "Who am I?", "Where do I belong", and "How do I fit (or fit in)"' (2004: 5). The self is therefore considered to be of high importance as it is implicated in a person's decision-making, motivation, and behaviour. It is also intrinsically implicated in our choices, such as the behaviours we choose to pursue and the groups we choose to affiliate with (Deci and Ryan 2000). As a consequence, the self is an integral part of volition. This considered, it is not surprising that the self is prominent in many theories that aim to explain variance in human behaviour and motivation, such as self-efficacy theory (Bandura 1997), and self-determination theory (Deci and Ryan 1985). Such theories suggest that social cognitive variables related to the self are integral to self-regulatory behaviour. Researchers have identified both personal and social identities, and these strongly affect people's behaviour, particularly in private and public domains. Indeed, theories aimed at explaining **group dynamics** and inter-group behaviour such as **social identity theory**, view the self and the self-esteem paramount. This is because the way in which we view ourselves is also tied in with the groups to which we belong. Self-categorization theory, a sub-theory of social-identity theory, suggests that people are motivated to preserve in-group consistency and be less tolerant or favourable towards outgroup members when the self is vulnerable. Suffice to say, the self, like attitude, is an essential and important construct in social psychology.

Similarly, the self is an essential construct in theories of motivation and behaviour in exercise and sport contexts. Along with dieting, exercise is the only means available other than invasive surgery, for an individual to modify their physical appearance in terms of body fat content and muscle tone. Physical appearance is an important aspect of the self and plays an important role in determining self-perception. As a result, aspects of the self associated with physical appearance are likely to be implicated in the decision-making processes related to engage in exercise behaviour. In addition, self-esteem may be an important psychological outcome of exercise behaviour. We have already noted that participation in regular exercise is a determinant of a number of psychological variables, such as positive affect and well-being. Self-esteem or a positive self-regard is also likely to be affected by regular exercise participation, particularly if that participation is accompanied by the achievement of positive outcomes such as the attainment of personal goals and positive affect. Self-esteem may also be part of the process by which exercise behaviour determines positive outcomes. For example, psychological well-being may arise from exercise behaviour providing increased positive self-regard, in which case self-esteem may mediate the influence of exercise behaviour on psychological well-being. This chapter will review and evaluate the contribution that the physical self has made to social psychological explanations of exercise behaviour. The theoretical structure and effects of self-esteem in the physical domain will be covered, as well as behavioural phenomena related to the self and exercise such as eating disorders and exercise addiction.

Defining self-esteem

What is self-esteem?

A perusal of the social psychology literature will reveal that self-related terminology is both multitudinous, varied, and, at times, inconsistent. A variety of terms have been introduced that refer to the same or similar constructs, and tend to be used interchangeably: self-esteem, self-worth, self-concept, self-description, self-regard, self-perceptions, and self-image. All these terms have been used at one time or another to refer to the construct of self-esteem. Early researchers adopted the term self-concept and defined the construct as statements about the self such as 'I have brown hair' or 'I am an athlete' (Rosenberg 1979). However, recent theories have made the distinction between purely descriptive statements such as those listed previously and more evaluative statements about the self 'I like Italian food' or 'I am good at tennis' (Harter 1996). The latter statements therefore not only describe attributes of the self, as the individual sees himself or herself, but qualify it with opinions of 'worthiness'. Often this distinction is encapsulated in the adoption of the term 'self-description' to refer to the purely descriptive, non-evaluative statements about the self, and 'self-esteem' or 'self-concept' to refer to statements that contain evaluative information, although this distinction is not always clear. Among contemporary theorists there is a general consensus that self-esteem comprises the perceptions that individuals have regarding themselves, incorporating both descriptive and evaluative content (Harter 1996). This has not, however, stemmed the tide of indiscriminate adoption and use of the various self-related terms, and has introduced some degree of ambiguity in the self-esteem literature. Suffice to say, the use of self-esteem terms in the design, investigation, and discussion of research on the self should be treated with caution and with close attention to the meaning of the terminology adopted. We will therefore operationally define self-esteem as both descriptive and evaluative self-related statements.

As a social psychological construct, self-esteem is attractive because researchers have conceptualized it as an influential predictor of pertinent outcomes, such as academic achievement (Marsh 1990) or exercise behaviour (Hagger *et al.* 1998). In addition, self-esteem has also been treated as an important outcome in itself due to its close ties with psychological well-being (Marsh 1989), and self-esteem may also predict motivational tendencies as people seek behaviours in areas of competence in order to maintain or enhance self-perceptions. Indeed, one key assumption in research on self-esteem is that it represents the virtuous, ideal, and generally positive elements of an individual's personality, and by implication this means that the enhancement of self-esteem is a desirable, adaptive outcome. Therefore, self-esteem has evaluative and descriptive components, and has efficacy both as an independent and dependent variable in social psychological models that aim to explain behaviour. Further, it has been implicated in the mechanisms of such models in the prediction of behaviour. Accordingly, self-esteem has been 'variously conceptualized as a dependent, independent, mediator, moderator construct' (Oyserman 2004: 5).

However, two notes of caution should be heeded at this juncture. First, we have generally focused on self-esteem as an adaptive, or positive outcome or influential construct. While this may be true, there is evidence to suggest that high levels of self-esteem could be accompanied by maladaptive outcomes and behaviours (Sedikides and Gregg 2003). Theorists suggest that it is non-contingent self-esteem, i.e. high self-regard that is not dependent upon clearly defined goals or outcomes and self-esteem striving without intrinsic goals that may be implicated in such social ills (Crocker and Luhtanen 2003). This issue will be visited in greater detail in the next section. Second, self-esteem has thus far been proposed to be implicated in a number of social psychological processes that underlie motivation. However, some researchers have argued that the influence of self-esteem on behavioural and psycho-logical outcomes may be spurious and its effect may fall away with the inclusion of other motivation-related constructs (Miller and Downey 1999). Furthermore, if the observed effects are present between self-esteem and psychological and behavioural outcomes, the direction of causality cannot be inferred, so studies with sophisticated longitudinal, panel designs may be necessary to establish the true role of self-esteem in an exercise context (Sedikides and Gregg 2003).

Models of self-esteem

When self-esteem research was in its infancy, self-esteem was largely regarded as a dispositional, unitary construct, much like the way in which global self-esteem is viewed in more contemporary models of self-esteem (Rosenberg 1979). Self-esteem was therefore viewed as a global, all-encompassing construct that comprised all self-related statements made by an individual. This conceptualization was limited because it was global; self-esteem constructs were too general and distal from the specific behaviours they were proposed to predict to account for a large amount of variance. However, these early models represented pioneering research into the self and represented a groundbreaking attempt to define, conceptualize, and quantify self-esteem.

Another major criticism of the unidimensional conceptualization of self-esteem was that it did not account for multiple dimensions of self-esteem (Marsh and Shavelson 1985). Self-esteem researchers therefore proposed a global or overarching conceptualization of self-esteem comprising a number of self-esteem evaluations made by individuals based on their experiences and reinforcements in a variety of behavioural domains and contexts (Shavelson *et al.* 1976; Marsh and Shavelson 1985). This instigated the possibility that self-esteem could be relatively high in one context or domain, but low or compromised in another. This made conceptual, empirical, and intuitive sense, individuals demonstrate competency or lack of competence in a variety of domains, and a person's sense of self draws on experiences and engagement in behaviours in each of these domains. The multidimensional model proposed that overall or global self-esteem comprised self-esteem in areas like academic, social, physical, and occupational domains (Marsh and Shavelson 1985). It was an important advancement because it permitted the estimation of the relative contribution of self-esteem statements to global or overall self-esteem. In addition, it also permitted the examination of each of the domain-levels self-esteem statements with respect to each other i.e. inter-domain relationships.

Shavelson, Hubner, and Stanton (1976) adapted the multidimensional model to account for the issue of generality, proposing that self-esteem was organized hierarchically with global self-esteem sitting at the apex of a hierarchy governing domain-level constructs that, in turn, determined self-esteem in the different contexts. A schematic representation of the model is given in Figure 4.1. The self-esteem domains are one level removed from the global self-esteem construct in terms of generality, and are therefore more specific, less enduring, less stable, and more subject to change from external constructs. It was proposed, however, that the hierarchy further operated within the domains, so that the domains could be further subdivided into more subordinate constructs that reflected more specific self-esteem evaluations within each context. For example, academic self-esteem would comprise self-esteem evaluations in the subdomain areas of mathematics, English, science, and so on. In addition, within each subdomain, further subordinate facets could be

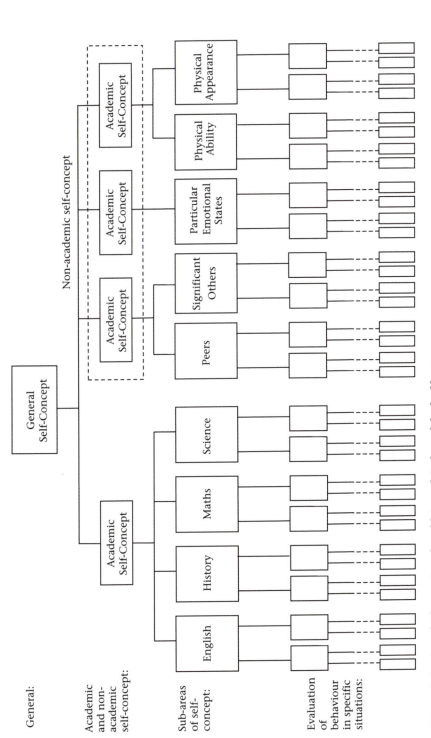

Figure 4.1 A multidimensional and hierarchical model of self-esteem
Source: Shavelson *et al.* (1976: 408)

identified until, theoretically, the level of specificity could be traced to individual perceptions of competence at the situational level, that are constantly subject to change, relatively unstable, and highly dependent on context. Therefore, the different levels of the hierarchy of self-esteem are distinct on the basis of generality and stability. Global self-esteem is regarded as relatively stable and enduring compared with domain and subdomain-level self-evaluations. Subdomain level and further sub-divisions reflect situational, more transient, and less stable evaluations of the self.

Nearly two decades of research into the structure of self-esteem have provided considerable support for the multi-faceted and hierarchically organized model proposed by Shavelson, Hubner, and Stanton (1976). This model has considerable advantages over other unidimensional approaches (Rosenberg 1979) because it recognizes that self-esteem arises from multiple sources and operates in a variety of contexts. The multidimensional, **hierarchical model** is advocated by leading researchers and has received support in many domains, especially educational settings (e.g. Marsh and Shavelson 1985; Harter 1988; Marsh 1989). Marsh and co-workers have provided strong evidence for the validity of a broadly stated self-esteem model that incorporates many domains (e.g. Marsh and Shavelson 1985; Marsh 1990). This research has led to the development of a series of rigorously tested psychometric instruments to test this model, known as the Self-Description Questionnaire (SDQ) series (Marsh and O'Niell 1984). The latest version, SDQ-III, measures self-esteem in 13 different areas: physical abilities, physical appearance, opposite-sex relationships, same-sex relationships, parent relationships, honesty/trustworthiness, spiritual values/religion, emotional stability, verbal/reading, mathematics, problem solving, general school, and general self-esteem. The SDQ series has demonstrated construct, discriminant, and cross-cultural validity (Marsh and O'Niell 1984; Marsh 1990). The multidimensional, hierarchical model has also been adopted by researchers using a divergent approach in their research to examine the effects of self-esteem on numerous dependent variables such as academic performance, academic achievement, psychological well-being (Marsh 1990), and perceived competence (Harter 1996). Such studies reinforce the predictive validity of a multidimensional, hierarchically organized model of self-esteem. In addition, researchers adopting a convergent style of research have shown enhanced self-esteem to be the outcome of a number of psychological processes such as competence (Harter 1996), perceived ability (Marsh 1990), and perceived autonomy support (Reeve 2002). In sum, the proposed model of self-esteem has been supported and rigorous testing of self-description questionnaires has provided self-esteem measurement instruments yielding valid and reliable scores.

One key advantage of the Shavelson *et al.* (1976) model is that it permits the detailed study of self-esteem in a single domain while simultaneously maintaining the relevance of the domain to global self-esteem. Adopting the model for this purpose enables the study of the organization and predictive validity of domain-relevant self-esteem statements but does not isolate the domain-level self-perception from global self-esteem. Instead, the relative contribution of the domain to global self-esteem and the mediation of the sub-domain facets by the domain-level construct as implied by the hierarchy are explicitly modelled. This makes the multidimensional and hierarchical model of self-esteem a versatile and adaptable model for the examination of the structure of self-esteem in the physical domain. Once validated, it also permits the study of the effects of a number of motivational process variables on self-esteem as an outcome and the effect of self-esteem, as an independent variable, on a number of salient outcome variables in the physical domain. The next section will outline the application of multidimensional, hierarchical models of self-esteem in the physical domain.

Multidimensional and hierarchical models of self-esteem in exercise and physical activity

While the SDQs measured physical self-esteem as part of the elaborate multidimensional and hierarchical model of self-esteem proposed by Marsh *et al.* (1985), specific sub-facets of the physical domain were not examined. This is in contrast to the inclusion of specific mathematics and English sub-facets identified as part of the general school or general academic domain in the SDQ-III (e.g. Marsh and O'Niell 1984). As a result, researchers interested in self-esteem in the physical domain have adopted the Marsh *et al.* model to study the structure of sub-facets specific to this domain (Fox and Corbin 1989; Marsh *et al.* 1994) and the impact of self-esteem on health-related behaviours such as exercise behaviour (Sonstroem *et al.* 1994) and physical fitness components (Marsh and Redmayne 1994). Fox and Corbin (1989) were the first to propose an elaborated model in this regard, and introduced a multidimensional, hierarchical model of physical self-esteem. They adopted the proposed structure of Shavelson *et al.* (1976) and Marsh *et al.* (1985) and the profile approach of Harter (1988) to develop the accompanying measure, the Physical Self-Perception Profile (PSPP).

Fox and Corbin (1989) proposed that a general **physical self-esteem** was superordinate to four subdomain factors: *sports competence, physical conditioning, body attractiveness,* and *physical strength*. In keeping with the Shavelson model, general physical self-esteem mediated relations between the subdomains and global self-esteem at the apex of the hierarchy (see Figure 4.2). Conceptually, global self-esteem is the most general, enduring, and stable construct and is least likely to change; it is, in effect, trait-like in nature. The subdomains are more changeable, less stable, and less enduring, they are therefore considered more state-like in their outlook. This is congruent with the original Shavelson *et al.* (1976) model that proposed top-down and bottom-up effects in the hierarchy, so that specific situational experiences of competence in the difference subdomains areas effect change in the upper levels, while the upper levels are used as a source of information for motivational decisions in specific exercise experiences (see also Sonstroem and Morgan 1989). A

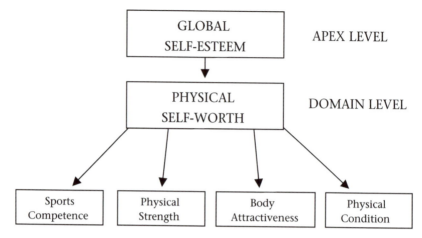

Figure 4.2   Fox and Corbin's (1989) multidimensional and hierarchical model of physical self-esteem
Source: Fox and Corbin (1989: 14)

schematic diagram of these effects is given in Figure 4.3 with examples from the sports competence and body attractiveness PSPP domains. The factor structure of the proposed model was supported in a number of studies using both exploratory and confirmatory factor analytic methods (Fox and Corbin 1989; Marsh *et al.* 1994; Sonstroem *et al.* 1994), and has been shown to be cross-culturally invariant (Asçi *et al.* 1999). In addition, the predictive validity of the model has been supported (Kowalski *et al.* 2001) and components of the model have been shown to be important outcomes of exercise behaviour (Fox 2000).

Marsh and Redmayne (1994) elaborated on Fox and Corbin's initial model and rigorously tested an alternative instrument that adopted the same multi-dimensional, hierarchical approach. The Physical Self-Description Question-naire (PSDQ, Marsh and Redmayne 1994; Marsh *et al.* 1994) comprised nine subdomain scales, four of which were proposed to be equivalent to the PSPP subdomains. The strength, appearance, condition/endurance, and sport scales of the PSDQ were equivalent to the physical strength, body attractiveness, physical condition, and sports competence scales from the PSPP, respectively. Additional subdomain scales in the PSDQ generally referred to aspects of phys-ical fitness: *flexibility, health, coordination, activity,* and *body fat* (see Figure 4.4). The scale demonstrated excellent factorial validity on the basis of several confirmatory factor analyses (Marsh and Redmayne 1994; Marsh *et al.* 1994). Furthermore, concurrent and predictive validity of the additional scales was confirmed alongside objective measures of children's physical fitness

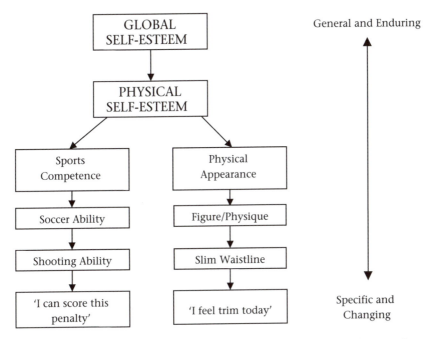

Figure 4.3 Examples of specific sub-facets of two subdomains of Fox and Corbin's model of self-esteem
Source: Adapted from Fox (1990: 4)

components (Marsh and Redmayne 1994). Marsh *et al.* (1994) also provided some concurrent validity for the PSDQ in relation to competing instruments adopting the same theoretical model, namely the PSPP and the physical self-esteem scale proposed by Richards (1988) using multi-trait, multi-method (MTMM) analyses.

While Fox and Corbin's (1989) and Marsh and Redmayne's (1994) models have exhibited satisfactory validity in terms of both the multidimensional nature and hierarchical arrangement of the factors, recent research has questioned the hierarchical nature of the model (Marsh and Yeung 1998; Kowalski *et al.* 2003). While cross-sectional data supports the existence of the hierarchical model, and has even rejected competing models that break the hierarchy with direct effects from the subdomain level to global self-esteem (Hagger et al., in press a; Sonstroem *et al.* 1994), when tested longitudinally there is only very weak support for the hierarchy. Using the physical and academic domains from the SDQ, Marsh and Yeung (1998) adopted a one-year cross-lagged panel design and found little support for top-down (global self-esteem predicting domain and subdomain-level self-esteem over time) or bottom-up (subdomain-level self-esteem predicting domain-level and global

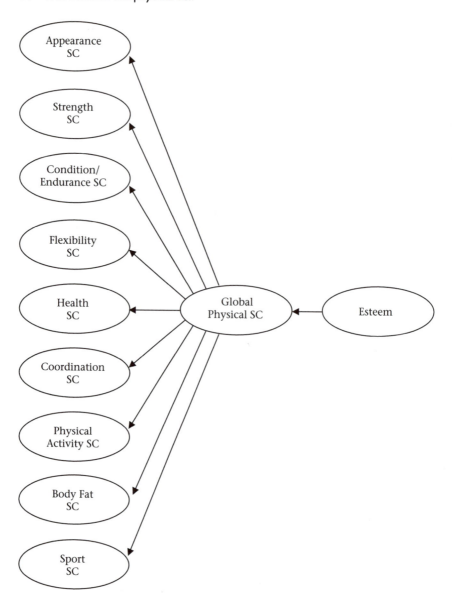

Figure 4.4 Marsh and Redmayne's (1994) multidimensional and hierarchical model of physical self-esteem, including additional scales introduced in subsequent revisions of the model by Marsh *et al.* (1994)

self-esteem over time) effects. This supported the notion of multidimensionality, but did not support the hierarchy. Adopting a similar design, Kowalski *et al.* (2003) examined top-down, bottom-up, and longitudinal effects using the PSPP physical self-esteem constructs over a one-year period, and their results again supported a horizontal rather than hierarchical model. Future studies would examine these effects in the hierarchical physical self-esteem constructs over variable time periods.

The effect of physical self-esteem on exercise behaviour

Both Fox and Corbin's (1989) and Marsh and Redmayne's (1994) models of physical self-esteem have been used to predict exercise behaviour. Theoretically, physical self-esteem may act as an antecedent of exercise behaviour because perceptions of competence in a given domain, or how confident they feel that exercise will enhance their sense of self, will compel a person to perpetuate those sensations of competence. A number of studies have found that the PSPP subscales could adequately distinguish between active and non-active individuals, with physical conditioning and sports competence accounting for the most variance (Hagger *et al.* 1998). Strong relationships have been found between the PSPP subdomains and prospective exercise behaviour. For example, Marsh and Redmayne (1994) found significant correlations between the activity PSDQ subdomain and self-reported exercise behaviour, but self-reported exercise behaviour was also significantly related to the endurance, strength, flexibility, coordination, sport ability, and general physical self-esteem. It is evident that these results suggest that a multitude of physical self-esteem components may be implicated in participation in physical exercise. However, the processes behind the relationship are not easily understood without motivational models to explain the pattern of influence (Biddle 1997), and a process model of self-esteem and exercise behaviour will be presented in subsequent sections (Sonstroem and Morgan 1989; Sonstroem *et al.* 1994).

Studies of self-esteem in an exercise context

Physical self-esteem in children and young people

Recently, there has been increased interest in the importance of physical self-esteem in young people, particularly in the light of guidelines recommending the promotion of exercise behaviour in young people (Sallis and Patrick 1994). The Fox and Corbin model of physical self-perceptions has demonstrated adequate validity in young people and shown considerable utility in the prediction of exercise behaviour. Whitehead (1995) introduced a children's version of Fox and Corbin's physical self-perception profile (C-PSPP) and subsequent validation studies have supported the proposed structure in young people (Hagger, Biddle et al., in press a). Furthermore, physical self-esteem components have been positively related to exercise behaviour. For example, Hagger *et al.* (1998) and Raudsepp, Liblik, and Hannus (2002) showed the subscales of body attractiveness, physical strength, and sports competence to be positively related to exercise behaviour in children. These data support the structure of the Fox and Corbin model of physical self-esteem in young people and indicate that physical self-perceptions are an important influence on exercise participation in young people in leisure-time and physical education contexts. There may also be important developmental changes in physical self-esteem components, and perhaps an effect for Shavelson et al.'s (1976) proposed differentiation, or increased diversity in self-esteem with increasing age and experience, within the physical domain. These issues will be visited in the next section.

Age and gender differences in physical self-esteem

Examining the effects of age and gender in physical self-esteem, Whitehead and Corbin (1997) found that C-PSPP scale scores were typically one-half point lower in female adolescents than males in research with Fox and Corbin's (1989) model. Hagger, Biddle, and Wang (in press a) conducted a meta-analysis of the original data from these studies and found that these differences equated to medium effect sizes across subdomains in the studies by Whitehead (1995) (median Cohen's $d = 0.34$) and Marsh *et al.* (1994) (median Cohen's $d = 0.38$). These findings support the notion that adolescent males tend to have higher physical self-esteem ratings than their female counterparts. One problem with these studies is that they do not support the multidimensional, hierarchical structure of the self-esteem constructs in the samples they were testing. Marsh and co-workers (1989) provided support for the structure of self-esteem across age and gender groups before examining the main and interactive effects of age and gender on self-esteem levels, and cited this as a necessary condition to confirm that the differences were true differences and not just artefacts of structural change such as increased self-esteem differentiation (Shavelson *et al.* 1976; Marsh 1989).

In the physical domain, a recent study adopting a representative sample of 2949 school children aged 12 to 14 years supported the structure of Fox and Corbin's model (1989) within the age and gender groups (Hagger, Biddle *et al.*, in press a). Tests of difference in the levels of the constructs revealed significant gender differences, with boys scoring significantly higher than girls in all of the physical self-esteem subdomains, and in global self-esteem. There were also significant age effects, with eighth-grade children scoring higher on the body attractiveness, physical strength, and general physical self-esteem C-PSPP scales. In summary, research trends suggest that there are significant gender and grade differences in physical self-esteem with boys and younger children tending to score higher in the PSPP subdomains. Gender differences may be explained by the fact that competence in the physical domain is stereotypically masculine in nature, while age differences may reflect self-esteem differentiation (Shavelson *et al.* 1976) but more likely indicate more realistic impressions of self-esteem with increasing age (Marsh 1990).

Elite athletes and self-esteem

Elite and high-level athletes represent a specific sub-population whose pursuit of achievement in sport may well result in this being manifested in significantly higher perceptions of physical ability or sports competence than those in the normal population. Marsh *et al.* (1995) examined SDQ-III scores in representative samples of mixed-gender and female athletes and non-athletes. They found that athletes scored significantly higher on a number of the PSDQ subdomains, but most markedly for the physical ability scale. Other sub-domains that exhibited significantly higher levels in athletes included same sex, opposite sex, and parent relationships and global (Marsh *et al.* 1995). Given these differences, one can speculate that high-level athletic participation has a positive effect on physical ability scores. Future research is needed to identify the level of sports participation required to produce this effect or whether the effect is a linear one. In addition, future research will differentiate between sport type to examine whether these demographic variables affect the perception of physical ability. For example, one hypothesis might be that perceived physical ability may be different across sports with gross-muscle movements compared with those requiring more fine motor skills.

Exercise and physical self-esteem model

Sonstroem and Morgan (1989) proposed a conceptual model aimed at explaining the process by which exercise experience affects physical competence and self-esteem. Sonstroem proposed that the effects of situational experiences of competence in sport and exercise settings affected global self-esteem in a bottom-up fashion. The proposed exercise and self-esteem model hypothesized that situation-specific estimates of competence, or self-efficacy (Bandura 1977, 1997), influenced self-esteem in the physical domain mediated by physical competence. A schematic diagram of the model is given in Figure 4.5. In the model, physical competence is closely related to self-esteem in the physical domain, while global self-esteem is included because it acts as an indirect measure of psychological well-being. In addition, the model also includes physical self-acceptance, a variable proposed to influence physical self-esteem along with self-competence (Sonstroem and Morgan 1989). Physical acceptance is an individual's subjective personal regard for themselves in a given domain, regardless of levels of physical competence. In Figure 4.5, the pre-intervention state of the model reflects baseline correlations among the study constructs, and the directional relationships in the post-intervention section of the model reflects the pattern of influence among the study variables after experiences of competence in an activity in the physical domain. In this

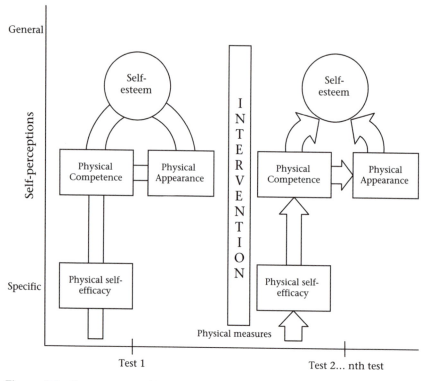

Figure 4.5 Sonstroem and Morgan's (1989) exercise and self-esteem model
Source: Sonstroem and Morgan (1989: 333)

respect the model is dynamic and implies continued modification of self-esteem, the outcome variable. Finally, an additional premise of the model is that global self-esteem affects exercise behaviour in a top-down fashion, such that the impact of global self-esteem on exercise behaviour is mediated by the competence and self-efficacy paths.

The model has been tested in a number of studies and results have generally supported its major propositions. Sonstroem *et al.* (1991) used confirmatory factor analysis and structural equation modelling to test the proposed model on cross-sectional data. The factor analysis supported the construct and factorial validity of the measures and factors adopted, and significant structural relations were found between self-efficacy and physical competence constructs, and between physical competence and global self-esteem as measured by Rosenberg's (1979) self-esteem scale. There was no direct effect of self-efficacy on self-esteem, as predicted. In addition, the dynamic premises of the model were tested longitudinally across a competitive swim season (Sonstroem *et al.* 1993). Results indicated significant increases in self-esteem, perceived competence, and skill level over the season. However, an autoregressive path analysis indicated that changes in skill level were not caused by self-esteem or perceived competence. Additional tests of the model have been proposed to examine its ability to account for variance in exercise behaviour. It was expected that the expanded exercise and self-esteem model would operate in a top-down fashion in the prediction of exercise behaviour (Sonstroem *et al.* 1994). Results indicated that self-efficacy was the most proximal predictor of exercise behaviour, and mediated the impact of the physical self-esteem subdomains of physical condition and body attractiveness on exercise behaviour.

Cross-cultural developments in physical self-esteem

Many of the studies conducted on physical self-esteem are undertaken in Western European contexts with high individualist and moderate-to-low collectivist cultural orientations. In cultures with a predominantly collectivist cultural norm, individuals have a greater tendency to view their self as interdependent with other members of society, while in cultures with a largely individualist cultural norm individuals tend to regard their self as independent of others (Triandis 1995). This is particularly relevant for self-esteem research, given findings that suggest that people's self-esteem may be organized into private and collective views of the self (Trafimow *et al.* 1991). Furthermore, some researchers have argued that self-esteem is a largely individualist phenomenon, and may not be relevant to cultures that have a collectivist notion of the self (see Triandis 1995).

Researchers have therefore sought to examine the cross-cultural validity of the physical self-esteem constructs, particularly in nations that generally endorse a high collectivist cultural norm. While some studies have replicated the multidimensional and hierarchical model of physical self-perception in individual samples from different cultures (e.g. Asçi *et al.* 1999), true cross-cultural evaluation should involve comparisons across at least three cultures (Marsh *et al.* 2002). Marsh and co-workers (2002) and Hagger, Lindwall, and Asçi (2004) have examined the cross-cultural validity of the two most prevalent measures of a multidimensional and hierarchical model of physical self-esteem in the literature, the PSDQ and the PSPP respectively. Marsh *et al.* (2002) examined the feasibility of the factor structure of the PSDQ in two different European cultures, Australia and Spain, and a Middle Eastern culture, Turkey. Results indicated that the factor structure, i.e. the same number and arrangement of factors and questionnaire items, was invariant across cultures, supporting the generalizability of the model in these cultures. Further, in a recent study Hagger *et al.* (2004) examined both the factor structure and mean differences in the levels of the PSPP constructs across three diverse cultures in Northern Europe (Sweden), the Middle East (Turkey), and Western Europe (Great Britain). Results supported the replicability and generalizability of the factor structure in all three cultures, but, most importantly the PSPP scales tended to be rated more highly in the British sample. Cross-cultural studies have also evaluated the cross-cultural validity of Fox and Corbin's (1989) model of physical self-esteem in children and results have corroborated findings in adult studies (Raudsepp *et al.* 2002; Hagger *et al.* 2003a; Hagger, Biddle et al., in press a) and supporting the hypothesis that individualist cultures to endorse the physical self more than collectivist cultures.

Eating disorders in exercise and sport and exercise dependency

While regular exercise yields positive health benefits, particularly with respect to healthy weight management, individuals who participate in regular exercise for the control of body weight may be vulnerable to psychological disorders that are manifested in compulsive dietary and exercise patterns. Among these disorders are anorexia nervosa and bulimic nervosa. In addition, disorders relating to excessive and compulsive exercise participation may also arise among exercisers. Given that diet and exercise are the primary means available to individuals to modify their weight and body image, it is not surprising that some have argued that both dieting and activity-related disorders arise, sometimes concurrently, in exercisers, and have similar aetiology. Furthermore, there is evidence to suggest that a compromised body image or physical self-esteem may be a risk factor for these conditions to arise. This section will define these conditions, outline their prevalence, identify their causes, and propose potential interventions to ameliorate their incidence.

Eating disorders and exercise

Anorexia nervosa and bulimia nervosa are considered psychological disorders classified by the *Diagnostic and Statistical Manual of Mental Disorders* (DSM-IV, American Psychiatric Association 1994) and occur in a relatively small number of people among both athletic and non-athletic populations. The vast majority of eating disordered people are female; only an estimated 5 to 15 per cent of eating disordered people are male (Andersen 1995). Anorexia nervosa occurs in between 0.50 and 1.50 per cent of the population in the United States (American Psychiatric Association Work Group on Eating Disorders 2000) and between 0.00 and 0.90 per cent in the countries of Europe (Institute of Psychiatry 2004). Clinical definitions of anorexia in the DSM-IV make reference to a refusal or inability to maintain a body weight that is within 85 per cent of the expected weight of the person for a given height (American Psychiatric Association 1994). In young people, anorexics are classed as unable to reach an expected increase in weight during a period of growth, which is particularly relevant to athletic at-risk groups such as gymnasts. It is also characterized as an intense fear of becoming fat or overweight, even when clearly underweight, and extreme distortions in perceived body image and low physical self-esteem. Anorexics develop unusual eating habits, such as avoiding food and eating small quantities, and avoiding social situations centred about food like restaurants. Anorexic people may repeatedly check their body weight and engage in other behaviours to control their body weight and composition, such as intense and compulsive exercise, or purging by means of vomiting and abuse of laxatives, enemas, and diuretics. Girls with anorexia often experience a delayed onset of their first menstrual period, which is often the case of young gymnasts.

Bulimia nervosa occurs in between 1.10 and 4.20 per cent of the population in the United States (American Psychiatric Association Work Group on Eating Disorders 2000) and in between 0.00 and 3.90 per cent of European populations (Institute of Psychiatry 2004). Bulimia is defined by the DSM-IV as a condition in which an individual consumes excessive amounts of food in a short space of time with a concomitant sensation of loss of control and follows this by compensatory behaviour to prevent weight gain such as purging (vomiting), misuse of laxatives and diuretics, enemas, excessive exercise, and fasting. The frequency of the binge–purge cycle should be of the order of at least twice a week for three months for a clinical diagnosis. In some bulimics no purging occurs, but other compensatory behaviours are adopted, known as the non-purging type. Similar to anorexics, body image tends to be distorted and mainly focused about body shape and weight. Often anorexia and bulimia tend to coincide and up to 50 per cent of anorexics develop a binge–purge cycle similar to that in bulimics (National Institute of Mental Health 1993). Bulimics, in terms of diagnostic criteria, do not have the clinically defined low body weight exhibited by anorexics.

While the incidence of these eating disorders in the general population is relatively small, their profile in the media is exceptionally high, and this has been attributed to links made between the portrayal of the body, particularly the female body, in magazines, television, film, and other media, especially in advertising (Kalodner and DeLucia-Waack 2003). One reason for this might be the exceptionally young average age for the onset of eating disorders, between 16 and 18 years. Ironically, those portrayed in the media have an increased tendency to succumb to eating disorders in order to perpetuate the prevalent waif-like images among fashion models in the media and advertising. However, these eating disorders have a complex aetiology, and their development may be the result of the prevalence of a number of risk factors. Further, there may be factors unique to sport and exercise that result in the development of eating disorders among athletes and exercisers.

The potential health risks of anorexia and bulimia are serious and have the potential to result in mortality. In anorexics, the health risks are consistent with severe malnutrition such as extreme muscle wastage, not only in the skeletal muscle but also in respiratory and cardiac muscle, amenorrhea in females, anaemia, and loss of bone mineral leading to conditions such as osteoarthritis (Becker *et al.* 1999). The physical symptoms of anorexia nervosa are excessive weight loss and skeletal muscle wastage, loss of hair, fatigue, and low energy. Psychologically, eating disorders can lead to depressed mood and depression. Mortality in anorexic people and, in fewer cases, bulimic people is often due to complications from the condition such as cardiac arrest or electrolyte imbalance. In athletes, there is also enhanced potential for injury due to fatigue and overuse injury as well as increased potential for bone fractures if bone mineralization is limited (Yates 1999; Golden 2002). In addition, female athletes with low body fat tend to have intermittent periods of amenorrhoea which makes it difficult to detect the amenorrhoea that results from an eating disorder (Golden 2002).

Numerous factors, biological, demographic, cultural, and social psychological have been identified as contributing to the development of eating disorders. Research suggests that the development of eating disorders may have a genetic component and that a complex combination of inherited traits and environmental situations may give rise to the development of eating disorders (Walters and Kendler 1995). As introduced earlier, such environmental factors may be the culture of 'thinness' observed in media images in the Western world. Globalization, the increase of media access in developed nations, and the trend toward thin, waif-like physiques for females has been attributed to the increased incidence of eating disorders in the past century (Toro *et al.* 1994). In terms of psychological factors, low self-esteem and body image (Ackard *et al.* 2002), high trait anxiety (Lehoux *et al.* 2000), elevated anger and depression (Breaux and Moreno 1994), high levels of social anxiety (Hinrichsen *et al.* 2003), and a compulsive/dependency personality type (Bornstein 2001) may also contribute to the development of an eating disorder.

In athletes, there may be additional factors that lead to the development of eating disorders. There is evidence to suggest that athletes with eating disorders may differ from eating disordered people from a normal population. For example, Madison and Ruma (2003) found that athletes have a lower correlation between the severity of their eating disorder and psychopathy with level of exercise, suggesting that activity level is less associated with a disordered psychological profile in athletes. In addition, Martin and Hausenblas (1998) indicated that among aerobic instructors, levels of eating disordered symptoms were low, and much lower than other athletic populations, suggesting that it may be competitive aspects of sport that could lead to eating disorders in athletes. It may therefore be that exercise *per se* is not an essential aspect of the eating disorder for athletes, possibly because they were exercisers before they developed their condition. Furthermore, the focus of athletes' eating behaviour modification may not be linked to appearance *per se*. Instead, an emphasis on a lean physique and the association with such a physique to performance may result in an athlete developing eating and associated behavioural patterns that, over time, become disordered. Halley and Hill (2001), for example, found that eating-disordered elite runners had much lower self-esteem, mental health, and placed considerable emphasis on a lean physique compared with runners who did not have an eating disorder.

Furthermore, social factors may be important influential factors on an athlete's development of disordered eating patterns. Although perhaps unintentional, coaches, managers and parents, particularly those of young athletes, may convey an impression to the athletes that their performance is contingent on appearance (Griffin and Harris 1996). In some cases, this message is very overt and coaches have been known to be very critical of athletes' weight and appearance, which can at best undermine the confidence of the performer and at worst can contribute to the development of disordered patterns of eating and exercise. Furthermore, in sports such as gymnastics, figure-skating, ice-dance, and diving there is external judging criteria which may provide additional external pressures on the need for the athlete's appearance to conform to an ideal-performer stereotype. In addition, like non-athletic populations of eating disordered individuals, low self-esteem has been implicated as a risk factor for the development of eating disorders in athletes, as at-risk groups tend to have low self-esteem as eating disordered athletes (Yates 1999). All these criteria are external to the athlete and, coupled with compulsive personality traits, may result in the development of eating disorders.

Treatment for eating disorders in athletes often has additional complications because often weight loss *per se* is not the sole reason for the manipulation of the diet. Furthermore, the detection of eating disorders in athletes may be difficult given that athletes that do not have eating disorders share the same personality traits as those that do (Thompson and Sherman 1999). One of the main challenges is raising the awareness of the problem with the athlete, with the secondary problem of getting them to curtail their training regime or give it up altogether (Yates 1999). Since sport and competition are central to the athlete's self-esteem and may also be the focus of their disordered eating behaviour, it is not easy to convince them to stop and show that their activity is compromising their health, a likely paradox in the mind of an athlete. Regular screening of athletes, early detection, and counselling have been shown to be efficacious in raising awareness and curtailing the disorder (Golden 2002). Once detected and awareness raised, the treatment methods adopted are often similar to those in non-athletes. Athletes are often referred to counselling and clinicians, depending on the severity of the disorder, particularly if weight loss is substantial and life-threatening. Much emphasis is placed on support from coaches and family members (Ryan 1992). Furthermore, there are education programmes to raise coaches' awareness of potential problems and to educate them to adopt appropriate language and behaviours that do not give messages to athletes that could be misinterpreted and lead to psychological profiles matching those of eating disordered individuals and result in persistent dietary modification (Ryan 1992). Specific recommendations for coaches are to seek specialist help if a case of an eating disorder in an athlete is suspected, avoiding comments about physique and weight, make referrals, and to provide information about nutrition, diet, and eating disorders. Importantly, coaches are advised to be open in their approach to eating disorders, but to encourage athletes to talk confidentially about their weight and diet concerns if they feel the need.

Exercise addiction, exercise dependence, and activity disorders

In the first four chapters of this book, the weight of research evidence seems to favour the view that regular exercise is beneficial to health with a vast array of positive physiological and psychological outcomes. This is clearly not the case for the individuals who exercise to the extreme, which can lead to damaging outcomes such as injury, maladaptive motivational profiles, and negative affective states. This section will outline the issues relating to excessive exercise, establish whether excessive and persistent exercising is an 'addiction', outline the clinical basis of such disorders, highlight the effects and psychological antecedents of these disorders, and introduce strategies that have been proposed to treat the disordered individual.

The term 'exercise addiction' refers to the condition in which individuals develop disordered patterns of exercise characterized by extreme levels of exercise and this has largely been abandoned in favour of terms like **activity disorders** (Yates 1991) or exercise dependence (Cockerill and Riddington 1996). Exercise dependence is defined as 'a craving for leisure-time physical activity that results in uncontrollable excessive exercise behaviour and that manifests in physiological and/or psychological symptoms' (Hausenblas and Symons-Downs 2002a: 90). Such a broad definition of activity disorders based on clinical observation and psychological constructs has been favoured because evidence to support a biological basis for such disorders and align them with other clinical addictions has been limited (Cockerill and Riddington 1996). For example, evidence that exercise dependence is based on an 'addiction' to endogenous opiates like β-endorphins has not conclusively been linked to exercise dependency (Pierce *et al.* 1993). Instead, the condition has been more associated with personality and psychological constructs that are thought to influence this pattern of exercise behaviour (Cockerill and Riddington 1996). It is difficult to reconcile exactly the level or extent of participation in exercise with the existence of an activity disorder. In other words, exercise dependence makes reference to the *experience* of the excessive patterns of exercise rather than the extent of the exercise *per se*. Therefore, an excessive level of exercise is a necessary but not sufficient condition for exercise dependence to arise. The example given previously regarding the high-level athlete illustrates this point. Often athletes who compete at a high level may exhibit levels of activity that are indicative of an activity disorder, but exhibit none of the characteristic patterns of psychological disturbance that are associated with such a disorder. It is therefore the manner in which the exercise is experienced by an individual and how it impacts on their lifestyle that are indicative of an activity disorder.

Some researchers have made the distinction between a primary form of exercise dependence that is independent of dietary manipulation and secondary exercise dependence that arises concurrent with an eating disorder (Veale 1995), although research findings have subsequently questioned this distinction. However, Yates (1991) claims that the development of eating disorders shares a similar aetiology with the development of compulsive and disordered patterns of exercise and physical activity. Yates identified a group that had developed these unusual patterns of exercise behaviour among male runners. Yates *et al.* interviewed a number of male runners who covered more than 50 miles per week in training. The majority of those interviewed were high achievers who participated in running because it gave them a sense of achievement and felt it contributed to their psychological well-being and their emotional stability. For these runners, their exercise patterns were considered adaptive and contributing to overall psychological functioning. However, a small percentage of the runners for whom their sport 'instead of . . . *contributing* to their adaptation, running had *become* their adaptation. They seemed locked into and controlled by the activity. These men were dubbed the "obligatory" runners' (1991: 26). The obligatory runners were characterized by very high running mileage (up to 70 or 80 miles per week), but most importantly, their patterns of behaviour were consistent with the obsessive and compulsive behavioural patterns of anorexic or bulimic patients. Their lifestyle revolved about their running and was characterized by its disciplined, well-ordered, and inflexible routine. The obligatory runners maintained a strict, regimented running programme and often subordinated other aspects of their life such as diet, occupation, and socializing to their running. Indeed, dieting and exercise, Yates argues, are 'interrelated methods of managing the body' (1991: 49), and therefore obligatory runners are often subject to obligatory dieting, particularly among females.

The detrimental effects of obligatory or compulsive exercise are numerous. There is risk of over-use injury, potential for excessive weight loss which results in similar health difficulties as anorexics, psychological burnout, mood disturbance, depression, eating disorders, and low level of psychological well-being (Hausenblas and Symons-Downs 2002a, 2002b). As a group, compulsive exercisers like Yates' obligatory runners tend to claim that they are content and happy with their life when they are running, and become depressed and frustrated when they become injured and cannot run. However, a different picture emerges when obligatory runners are interviewed several months after an injury that has forced them to stop running. They often cite that their running was 'a chore they forced themselves to engage for reasons they did not completely understand' (Yates 1991: 59). Thus, an obligatory runner exhibits a maladaptive pattern of motivation, consistent with what Ryan and Deci (1989) call an introjected locus of causality. Such a motivational orientation suggests that although the activity has been partially integrated into the person's repertoire of behaviours, it still remains outside a sense of true self. Importantly, individuals with these conditions participate for largely extrinsic reasons and tend to be afflicted by guilt and shame when they do not complete their daily routine. Therefore, individuals with 'activity disorders' tend to exhibit low levels of psychological well-being and a maladaptive pattern of motivation. Furthermore, they have the potential to result in serious harm to themselves due to injury and excessive weight loss.

The obligatory runners are exemplars of activity-disordered individuals whose exercise and dieting behaviours are defined as clinically compulsive. Yates (1991) argues that activity disordered individuals, like anorexics and bulimics, are compulsive rather than 'addictive' disorders like drug and alcohol addictions. Activity disorders may appear on the surface to be 'addictive' because activity disordered individuals obsessively engage in exercise and seem unable to moderate their participation, just as a drug addict or alcoholic finds themselves unable to moderate their intake of their drug (Griffiths 1999). Furthermore, some theorists argue that activity disordered individuals do gain a physiological 'reward' through their disordered behaviour such as increased levels of β-endorphins, linked to the blood–brain reward system (Yates 1991), although there is little evidence that levels of β-endorphins are related to degree of exercise dependence (Pierce *et al.* 1993). Moreover, this is an oversimplification of the disorder, as addictive or obsessive behaviours are fundamentally different to compulsive behaviours. Drug addicts and alcoholics enjoy their behaviours and the euphoric state they achieve as the result of their behaviour, their behaviour is termed ego-syntonic, and therapy seeks to motivate individuals to cease their damaging *impulsive* behaviour. Addicts are content to relinquish self-control over their addiction. However, as noted earlier, activity disordered individuals do not enjoy their exercise or sport, are introjected-oriented towards their actions, but engage in their behaviour because they feel that they should. Their compulsive behaviour is driven by an intense desire to exert self-control over their life and behaviour, and their behaviour is called ego-dystonic. Their behaviour is motivated by negative affective states such as fear of losing control, guilt, and shame, even though they may wish to stop their pattern of behaviour. Therapy therefore focuses on helping compulsive individuals to moderate their behaviour and demonstrate that they can exert control over their lives without the need for compulsive behaviours. Yates claims that activity disorders share their compulsions with anorexics and bulimics, in that these individuals exert similar control over their behaviour and physical appearance, and feel compelled to diet, binge, and purge in order to maintain their control.

The complex pattern of behaviour observed in exercise-dependent individuals develops as a result of multiple risk factors and antecedents. These are related to theoretical explanations of the disorders. As stated previously, biological bases of activity disorders such as β-endorphin and arousal from the sympathetic nervous system have not been supported (Pierce *et al.* 1993), and current research suggests that personality characteristics along with situational factors may predispose individuals to becoming activity disordered (Hausenblas and Giacobbi 2004). Furthermore, the pathology of the development of activity disorders is similar, Yates argues, to those that result in conditions like anorexia and bulimia. This is corroborated by research that has associated the diagnosis of an activity disorder with measures of disordered eating patterns (Keski-Rahkonen 2001). A number of personality factors have been linked to the development of activity disorders, such as an obsessive-compulsive tendency (Davis 1999), extroversion (Yates 1991), trait anxiety (Spano 2001), and perfectionism (Hausenblas and Symons-Downs 2002b). Research has also shown that parents of anorexics and bulimics emphasize independent achievement and outcome-oriented success in school and occupation (Yates 1991). Some researchers suggest that failure to succeed under these pressures can result in the development of disordered eating patterns like anorexia to exert control over themselves and 'achieve' in the outcome of losing weight, and a high achievement or outcome orientation may be implicated in the development of activity disorders, as well (Yates 1991). In addition, family or parents who attach a great deal of value to the control of weight, appearance, and exercise may also serve as risk factors for the development of an activity disorder. Finally, compromised self-image and appearance self-esteem are implicated in the development of exercise dependence (Hausenblas and Symons-Downs 2002a).

Detection of exercise dependence or activity disorder can be achieved using validated questionnaire methods and also by adopting an appropriate diagnostic framework from clinical guidelines (Ogden *et al.* 1997; Hausenblas and Symons-Downs 2002b). Adams, Miller and Kraus (2003) have proposed the criteria for inclusion of exercise dependence in accepted clinical diagnostic manuals such as the DSM-IV (American Psychiatric Association 1994). A recognized pattern of observed and self-reported symptoms of exercise dependence has been put forward, supported by evidence from the development of exercise dependence diagnostic tools. Converging evidence has identified the following characteristic symptoms of exercise dependence: tolerance or increased requirement of exercise to gain desired effect, withdrawal symptoms, an *intention* effect or taking more exercise than intended, lack of control, time spent in activity, reduction of other activities, activity viewed as an end rather than a means to an end, and continuance even in the face of persistent injury (Ogden *et al.* 1997; Hausenblas and Symons-Downs 2002a, 2002b). The exercise dependence questionnaire (EDQ, Ogden *et al.* 1997) and the exercise dependence scales (EDS, Hausenblas and Symons-Downs 2002b) are psychometrically sound inventories that adhere to the DSM-IV criteria for the classification of a clinical disorder and have been validated in clinically diagnosed populations.

Interventions and therapy to address exercise dependence and activity disorders are drawn from both the psychological and clinical literature. Yates (1991) advocates the use of cognitive behavioural therapy which is a combination of the two most effective clinical techniques for the treatment of psychological disorders: behaviour therapy and cognitive therapy. Behaviour therapy aims to intervene and break the cycle of situational cues to action and the conditioned maladaptive behavioural responses to those cues. Examples of this are social situations such as drinking in a bar or public house coupled with the habitual response of lighting a cigarette. Cognitive therapy aims to identify and change the thought patterns or beliefs that underpin the maladaptive behaviour. This is usually achieved through the investigation of the thought processes that often accompany situations that evoke the undesired behavioural response and produce rational alternatives. Yates (1991) suggests that the substitution of alternatives activities for the disordered behaviours during therapy is a useful means of correcting the behavioural response to the situational cues that give rise to the maladaptive behavioural pattern. Therapists adopting cognitive behavioural therapy initially focus on behavioural means to control the disordered behaviour, and this is then followed by the investigation and substitution techniques to modify the dysfunctional beliefs, and thereafter focus on maintaining both the behavioural and cognitive changes.

Other intervention techniques include information giving and educational programmes and are suitable for mild activity-disordered individuals as their behaviour is often perpetuated by misconceptions and fallacies regarding exercise and its physiological and psychological effects (Sundgot-Borgen 2000). Educational sessions with an activity-disordered individual should be followed up with goal setting with reasonable targets focused on optimal health. For example, activity-disordered individuals are likely to have persistent injuries and a goal could be to reduce the incidence of these injuries (Carnes and Sachs 2002). Goals could also involve activity substitution such that the activity disordered individual is encouraged to substitute exercise with other engaging and rewarding activities such as socializing or going for a walk. Role models or self-help groups may be of assistance in this regard. Although exercise dependence is a relatively rare condition, the inclusion of self-help groups where activity-disordered individuals can discuss and share their experiences may have positive effects on the success of changes made towards reducing dependence upon exercise (Carnes and Sachs 2002).

Suggested reading

Fox, K.R. (1997) *The Physical Self*. Champaign, IL: Human Kinetics. A recent compendium of research on self-esteem and exercise with a heavy focus on hierarchical models.

Yates, A.B. (1991) *Compulsive Exercise and the Eating Disorders*. New York: Brunner/Mazel. A readable clinical text on social psychological aspects of exercise and eating disorders.

Summary

- Physical self-esteem is the descriptive and evaluative perceptions about the self in physical contexts.
- Physical self-esteem is often viewed in the context of multidimensional and hierarchical models of physical self-esteem, with general or global self-esteem at the apex, physical self-esteem at the domain level and more specific facets of self-esteem such as physical appearance, physical strength,

sports competence, coordination, flexibility, and physical conditioning at the subdomain level.

- Physical self-esteem is a modest predictor of exercise behaviour and research has suggested that physical self-esteem tends to be higher in males and elite-athletes.
- Anorexia nervosa and bulimia nervosa are clinical psychological disorders that result in severely altered eating patterns and pose a risk to health. These occasionally occur in athletes and exercisers with risk factors including portrayal of body images by the media, association of performance with lean physique, and judging criteria.
- Interventions to assist eating-disordered individuals include hospitalization, cognitive behavioural therapy, counselling and psychotherapy, and drug therapy, and coaches of at-risk athletes are required to refer athletes with suspected eating disorders for professional assistance.
- A tendency to engage in exercise and physical activity in an obsessive manner with a lack of control, increased tolerance for exercise, withdrawal symptoms, a tendency to take more exercise than intended, a reduction of other activities, and persistence when injured are indications of an activity disorder.
- Intervention strategies to help activity-disordered individuals include cognitive behavioural therapy and information giving/educational strategies.

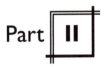

Part **II**

The social psychology of sport

5

Social psychology and motivation in sport

Motivation is central to many theories that aim to explain the complex processes involved in people's goal striving and attainment in achievement contexts such as school or university (e.g. Reeve 2002), the workplace (e.g. Stajkovic and Luthans 1998), and sport (e.g. Duda 1993). In sport, motivation is recognized as an important and necessary ingredient for success, and has been a focal construct since the outset of social psychological investigations into sport behaviour. As is often the case in applied social psychology, everyday use of the word 'motivation' is usually unstructured with little consensus or consistency in its meaning. For example, when a person describes another as 'highly motivated' it could mean that through continuous observation that person has displayed behaviour in a number of different contexts that is goal-directed and persistent. Conversely, it could be that in a given situation a person exhibits high persistence and puts in a lot of effort to their behaviour to achieve their goals and outcomes in that situation. The study of motivation in sport contexts must therefore begin with a clear definition of the construct.

The assumptions and thought processes that underpin the previous example reveal some interesting properties of motivation and the way information in the social context such as a behavioural observation reveals these properties in others. First, motivation is a social psychological construct, therefore it operates in social contexts, determines behaviour, and, in the social cognitive tradition, is determined by the processing of contextual and intrapersonal information regarding behavioural contingencies and outcomes. Second, motivation can be global or contextual, generalized or specific, and stable or unstable – motivation can therefore be trait-like or state-like in its characteristics depending on the situation and context. Third, motivation is influenced by a number of internal (e.g. needs, drives, effort, goals) and external (e.g. relationships, rewards, social influence) sources of information. Formal definitions of motivation will clarify and expand on the above properties. These definitions are a prologue to studying the main theoretical explanations of motivation in social psychology in sport contexts covered in this chapter.

Defining motivation and motivational theories

At the most basic level, motivation is defined as an internal state that activates, energizes, or drives action or behaviour and determines its intensity and direction. In addition, motivation is also thought to encompass the arousal and persistence of action or behaviour. This definition tends to account for both biologically based motives that serve to satiate physiological needs such as hunger, thirst, and sex, as well as psychological or higher-order needs such as fulfilment and self-actualization. Biological and emotion-based theories view motivation as arising from an organism's need to satisfy biological requirements in a drive reduction hypothesis, derived from behaviourist principles of arousal and reinforcement. Approaches that have focused on so-called higher needs tend to view humans as having innate psychological requirements such as the need for achievement or to demonstrate competence (White 1959; Deci and Ryan 1985). The latter are derived from humanistic approaches to motivation such as those put forward by Maslow (1943) in which biological need satisfaction precede the satisfaction of higher-order needs towards a complete satisfaction of a person's needs repertoire in a hierarchical fashion.

In social psychology, recent approaches to the study of motivation adopt a social cognitive perspective, stressing informational processing, volition, and explicit motivational constructs as the important processes that give rise to goal-directed behaviour. Theories of intention (e.g. Meiland 1970; Ajzen and Fishbein 1980) and self-efficacy theory (Bandura 1997) are influential **social cognitive theories** to motivation (cf. Chapter 2). In such theories motivation is viewed in terms of the pursuit of target behaviours to achieve a particular goal. In sport and other achievement situations like academic and occupational performance, goals are often essential to functioning and instrumental in fostering motivation. For example, **attribution theory** (Heider 1958) and **achievement goal theory** (Nicholls 1989) are two goal-oriented social cognitive approaches to motivation and behaviour in sport. Such social cognitive models of motivation are often criticized for not being explicit enough in explaining the origins or formative antecedents of motivation. Theories based on psychological needs such as self-determination theory (Deci and Ryan 1985, 2000) are attractive in this regard as they provide the basis on which motives toward specific behaviours arise. Need theories therefore address the 'why' questions related to motivation. As Deci and Ryan state: 'cognitive theories begin their analysis with a cognitive representation of some future desired state (outcomes). What is missing, of course, is the consideration of the conditions of the organism that makes these states desired' (1985: 228). Therefore, need theories complement the social cognitive approaches because they suggest that human behaviour in a multitude of contexts is underpinned by psychological needs.

In summary, motivation is the driving force behind behaviour and is characterized by its focus (selection and direction) and valence (intensity and duration). Social psychological theories of motivation in sport have typically adopted a social-cognitive perspective and assume that motivation is based on the processing of social information. Some models have adopted a needs-based approach in which psychological needs explain the origin or formation of the social cognitive antecedents of situated action. The next sections will critically evaluate the different social psychological theories of motivation applied to the sport context, with a focus on social cognitive and needs-based approaches.

Attribution theory

Sports participants and athletes are always striving to make sense of the causes of good and bad performances. Sometimes they make excuses for not making the right decisions or not living up to expectations. Other times they are bashful or magnanimous in the face of success or failure, citing good luck rather than good judgement as reasons for their accomplishment. Some blame themselves or others for the misfortune of losing. Others brashly state that they knew that they would be successful and expect to be successful again. In all these scenarios, athletes are making attributions for their successes and failures. They are assigning perceived causes to the outcomes they have experienced as a result of their performance or behaviour in sport. Attribution theory is the study of the processes that underlie these attributions and how they affect subsequent motivation and behaviour.

Weiner's (Weiner *et al.* 1972) theory of attribution focused on understanding the nature, causes, and consequences of attributions of success and failure in achievement situations. He adopted Heider's (1958) proposal that attributions could be internal or external and extended them to account for the range of attributions possible in achievement situations. Weiner hypothesized that people's attributions for success or failure could be characterized by three bipolar dimensions: locus of causality (internal or external), the stability of the cause (stable or unstable), and whether the cause is controllable by the individual making the attribution (controllable or uncontrollable). In terms of mechanisms, it was theorized that after an achievement event, an individual assesses whether they have succeeded or failed and they experience a general positive or negative emotional response, respectively. The attribution is then ascribed following the experience of more specific affective responses based on specific performance outcomes (e.g. pride if success is attributed to ability, or hopelessness if failure is attributed to luck). On the basis of these attributions, expectations of future success regarding prospective behavioural engagement are formed. This model resulted in the development of a three-dimensional taxonomy of attributions in achievement situations, illustrated in Figure 5.1.

Weiner initially focused on the locus of causality and stability dimensions and illustrated how attributions of success or failure could be internal and stable (ability), internal and unstable (effort), external and stable (task

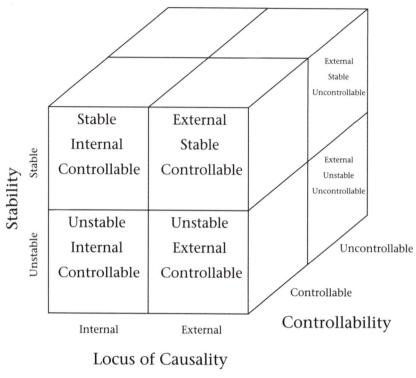

Figure 5.1   Weiner's (1972) three dimensions of attribution

difficulty), or external and unstable (luck). It was hypothesized that most attributions would be characterized by this 2×2 conceptualization (see front face of Figure 5.1). The model was viewed as dynamic and changing such that attributions and expectancies of success varied according to the available information regarding performance. It was also expected that attributions would influence motivation and persistence (approach) or desistence (avoidance) with respect to future participation in the behaviour, depending on the type of attribution generated by past experience. An adaptive attribution pattern likely to contribute to heightened motivation and persistence would be to attribute success to internal factors (e.g. ability or effort) and failure to external factors (e.g. task difficulty or luck). For example, if an athlete is successful in achieving his or her goal when performing a sports skill, he or she would feel confident and efficacious towards that task if they attributed it to their own skill or effort, and this would result in a positive expectation of future success. Analogously, the athlete's confidence would not be undermined if they attributed an unsuccessful performance to external factors. However, this attribution profile may be problematic if the attribution of success to internal and stable (i.e. ability) causes is followed by a failure on the next attempt. This may lead to an attribution of the failure to ability as well, which will result in a maladaptive attributional profile. Beliefs about control over future task performance are important in this regard. Ability tends to be relatively fixed and uncontrollable, and therefore an attribution of success to a more controllable form of cause (i.e. effort) may result in a more adaptive motivational pattern in subsequent performance.

In sport, a large body of research has examined the efficacy of attribution theory to explain the attributions that athletes make regarding their success and failure, and also whether those attributions have implications for future motivation (Biddle et al. 2001; McAuley and Blissmer 2002). Early research in attribution theory examined the prevalence and nature of attributions according to Weiner's (Weiner et al. 1972) conceptualization. These studies demonstrated that the attributions did not fall into the neat taxonomy offered by Weiner and found that certain attributions were interpreted differently under success and failure. For example, Iso-Ahola (1977) found that effort was related to ability in a win situation but to luck and task difficulty in a lose situation in young baseball players. This suggested a flexibility in the children's attributions such that effort was treated as an internal attribution in successful circumstances, and as external in conditions of failure. Further, different types of attribution were found in sports participants, for example, lack of practice or training was an important external attribution under failure conditions (Iso-Ahola 1977). Similarly, Roberts and Pascuzzi (1979) found that the attributions made by undergraduate sports students regarding sport situations could not be adequately categorized as ability, effort, luck, and task difficulty. However, the attributions could be adequately categorized into Weiner's 2 × 2 (locus of causality × stability) contingency of attributions. These findings suggest that while Weiner's dimensions were applicable to attributions in sport, the rigid classification of the type of attributions, i.e. ability, effort, task difficulty, and luck did not hold.

Studies have also investigated whether a self-serving bias exists when individuals make attributions for their success and failure in sport contexts. Self-serving biases are observed in many areas in social psychology, and reflect an individual actively trying to maintain their self-esteem or a positive and consistent view of themselves. In attribution research, individuals have been shown to generally attribute success to internal causes and failure to external causes (Weiner et al. 1972). This self-serving bias was supported by a meta-analysis of 91 studies conducted by Mullen and Riordan (1988). They found moderate effect sizes for a general internal/external and ability dimensions and low effect sizes for effort, luck, and task difficulty. This seemed to point to a deliberate bias towards internal attributions, however, group size also affected the size of the bias leading the authors to conclude that the attribution profile was more a function of information processing than intentional bias towards the self. Similarly, research has suggested that athletes may have dispositional tendencies to report certain types of attributions, known as attributional style, although little evidence of a clear pattern in attributional style is evident (Biddle *et al.* 2001). Taken together, this evidence does not unequivocally support a self-serving bias in attributions in sport.

In terms of outcomes, attributions have been shown to be related to motivational and emotional outcomes, as predicted by Weiner's theory. Weiner anticipated that individual expectancy of success in subsequent behavioural engagement would be influenced by an attribution to stable causes. This provides greater certainty in the expectation that future outcomes could be repeated in future, an unstable attribution would suggest that future expected outcomes were uncertain. Research examining attributions in high-school athletes indicated that positive expectancies of success occurred more frequently after success than failure and due to stable attributions (Singer and McCaughan 1978). Further, Rudisill (1989) showed that future expectancies of success and adherence to a balancing task with a stabliometer were predicted by controllable and internal attributions and with high competence, but, against predictions revealed that unstable attributions were more influential than stable ones. Finally, Grove and Pargman (1986) found that effort rather than ability attributions were associated with positive future expectancies of success, and, given that effort is not a stable construct, this indicates that unstable but controllable attributions are implicated in future expectancies of success. In addition, internal attributional profiles have been associated with positive emotional profiles in sport (Biddle *et al.* 2001). Research has indicated that attributions tend to account for significant variance in emotional outcomes after controlling for appraisals in models examining cognitive-motivational-relational models of emotion (Vlachopoulos *et al.* 1997). These findings suggest that encouraging athletes to make controllable and internal attributions for success are likely to give rise to positive future expectancies of behaviour.

Biddle outlines the problems with attribution theory in sport and exercise. He notes a decline in the productivity of researchers in this area suggesting that interest in attribution theory as an explanation of motivation in sport may be waning. He suggests that a possible reason for this is that attribution research has focused on too narrow a set of constructs and further research incorporating dispositional constructs from other motivational theories is necessary for research in the area to progress. Specifically, he stresses that the incorporation of constructs relating to perceived control, competence, and achievement goals (see section on achievement goals in sport, this chapter) in models of sport motivation will answer important attribution-related questions an athlete might ask themselves in sport, such as 'Why did I fail at this task?' (Biddle *et al.* 2001).

Social cognitive theory and self-efficacy

Self-efficacy is an important social psychological construct derived from Bandura's (1977, 1997) influential social cognitive theory. Self-efficacy has established itself as a key variable in many social psychological theories and models of motivation and in a number of applied contexts such as educational, health, occupational, and sport settings. Bandura's work has been extremely influential and enduring. To appreciate the measure of the importance of Bandura's theories to the study of motivation, one need only consider his place in the psychology canon. For example, Hagbloom et al.'s (2002) research on the citation records of psychologists over the past century ranks Bandura fifth on the list of the most frequently cited psychologists in the professional literature and on the American Psychological Association's Members' list of the most eminent. Further, nearly 30 years of research in sport psychology has established self-efficacy as one of the most potent and consistent constructs relevant to performance and motivation. Literally hundreds of sport-related studies have included self-efficacy as an antecedent, outcome, or process (mediator or moderator) variable. The main reason for its longevity is that it is a powerful predictor of behaviour and unequivocally implicates the role of perceived rather than actual ability in sport behaviour and performance. This section will define self-efficacy, outline the important tenets of social cognitive theory, and examine the important effects and processes related to self-efficacy and sport performance.

Definition of self-efficacy

Self-efficacy is an individual's personal estimate of confidence in his or her capability to accomplish a certain level of performance. According to Bandura, 'Perceived self-efficacy is defined as people's beliefs about their capabilities to produce designated levels of performance that exercise influence over events that affect their lives' (1994: 71). Unpacking this rather dense definition, self-efficacy is a set of beliefs held by an individual regarding his or her capacity or ability regarding their performance of an upcoming behaviour or action. It also comprises beliefs related to their ability that doing the behaviour will result in salient outcomes. Self-efficacy beliefs are a function of a number of different experiential and situational factors as determined by social cognitive theory. An important property of self-efficacy is that it is situation-specific and reflects judgements or expectations in a given context directed towards personally-defined outcomes. It has therefore been defined by some authors as 'situation-specific self-confidence' (Feltz and Chase 1998: 60). Indeed, as with many other theories that adopt a correspondence rule or boundary condition (e.g. Ajzen 1985), self-efficacy generally has most potency in predicting outcomes such as performance and behaviour when it is specific to that behaviour. In addition, due to its situated specificity, self-efficacy is also modifiable. As will be seen later, an individual's level of self-efficacy is dependent on a number of interpersonal and external variables that serve as sources of information for the formation of self-efficacy judgements. Self-efficacy can therefore be considered a state-like construct that can be manipulated and changed.

Self-efficacy has been shown to have a profound influence on self-regulation. It affects cognition (e.g. interpretation of information), motivation (e.g. intentions to perform a behaviour), affect (e.g. satisfaction), and behaviour (e.g. performing a motor task) (Biddle *et al.* 2001). Self-efficacy is implicated in human achievement motivation and subjective well-being processes (Weiner *et al.* 1972). A person reporting high self-efficacy towards a task in a given situation is able to have influence over their environment, persist in the face of difficulty and failure, put a great deal of effort into the task to attain desirable goals, solve problems more effectively, be more interested in the task and immerse themselves in it more deeply, have a conceptualization of ability as changeable, attain satisfaction from their endeavours toward the task, and have an approach rather than avoidant orientation towards the task. Given the pervasive effects of high levels of self-efficacy it is easy to see the importance of the construct and why it has a role in a number of theories on motivation, in both exercise (see Chapter 2) and sport (see sections on self-determination theory and achievement goal theory, this chapter).

Social cognitive theory

Social cognitive theory was developed as an offshoot of Bandura's (1977, 1997) **social learning theory** and the effects of observational learning in the treatment of anxiety, phobias, and other behaviours. Social learning theory examines the effect of vicarious experience and familiarization with a task on subsequent approach motivation and confidence towards that behaviour. Bandura was a profound believer in the powerful effects that models, or people demonstrating a task to be learned, had on behaviour and supported this through behaviourist theories of reinforcement but also through observational learning. The importance of observational learning and vicarious experience has been supported in numerous experiments (see Bandura 1977). However, it was the presence of situation-specific self-confidence or 'self-efficacy' that was proposed to have the most pervasive effect in these experiments, such as snake phobics overcoming their phobias.

In social cognitive theory, self-efficacy was deemed to arise from several sources of information about a person's confidence or subjective beliefs in their skills or ability to affect outcomes by performing a given behaviour or action. These sources of confidence information are previous performance accomplishments, vicarious experience, verbal persuasion, and physiological states. The relations between self-efficacy beliefs and these sources of information are outlined in Figure 5.2. There are two broad categories of information sources, previous experience and current influences. *Performance accomplishment* reflects previous successful personal experiences with the action or the behaviour. Importantly, it is not necessarily past experience *per se* but the *mastery* of the performance that is important in influencing self-efficacy beliefs. Performance accomplishments are viewed as the single most important influence on self-efficacy beliefs in social cognitive theory (Bandura 1977). As another source of confidence information, *vicarious experiences* have strong, albeit less potent, effects on self-efficacy beliefs. It is assumed in social cognitive theory that the correct execution of a behaviour is reinforced when an individual observes another performing the behaviour. Observational learning is assumed to be a potent source of confidence. For example, an intermediate-level athlete may watch a skilled professional performing a sports skill and their confidence may be positively enhanced because their own execution of the skill is reinforced by the act of observation. The features of the model and the matching of the characteristics of the model to the observer are important contributory factors in the effectiveness of vicarious experiences in influencing efficacy beliefs.

Self-efficacy beliefs are also affected by sources of information from the current behavioural context. *Verbal persuasion* represents task-related information available from coaches and other team members or personal. This can be in form of positive feedback and technical commentary or person-centred

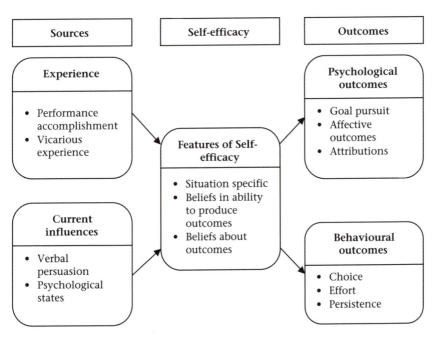

Figure 5.2   Relationships between information sources, self-efficacy, and psychological and behavioural outcomes in Bandura's (1977) social cognitive theory

information such as the use of imagery or self-talk. These sources of information reinforce expectancies of success. Finally, *physiological states* such as
autonomic arousal, negative emotional states associated with threat in
achievement contexts such as anxiety and worry, or positive emotional states
associated with approach motivation such as state self-confidence also affect
self-efficacy beliefs. These can also refer to other physiological states such as
fatigue and fitness level. In sport, these physiological states are likely to have a
profound effect on self-efficacy beliefs because of the elevated physiological
arousal associated with the stress of exercise and the inherent involvement
of emotional states in sport performance, such as competitive state anxiety
(see Chapter 6). The effects of persuasion, vicarious learning, and physiological states on self-efficacy are hypothesized to be less salient than performance accomplishments. Together these sources of information contribute
synergistically to efficacy expectations.

Just as self-efficacy has several antecedent variables, it also acts as predictor
of a number of salient psychological and behavioural outcomes (Figure 5.2). In
terms of psychological outcomes, self-efficacy is deemed to act on social cognitive thought processes and affective outcomes such as the choice of goals set,
psychological well-being or worry, and the attribution of behaviour to a given
cause. The higher an individual's self-efficacy towards a given behavioural
pattern, the more likely they are to set challenging goals, cite positive well-
being, and attribute causality to internal, stable sources (Bandura 1977). In
addition to psychological outcomes, self-efficacy is also hypothesized to influence a person's choice, effort, and persistence towards a given behaviour.
Choice is likely to reflect whether a person decides to approach or avoid a
behaviour, in other words, the direction of the behaviour, while effort and
persistence indicate the valence and prolonged nature of their behavioural
application.

Self-efficacy and outcome expectations

Bandura (1977, 1997) also proposed that people not only hold beliefs about
their ability to perform a given behaviour, but also that the behaviour will
result in certain outcomes. Feltz and Chase make the distinction between the
two constructs in terms of the nature of their beliefs: 'In essence, outcome
expectations are concerned with beliefs about one's environment, and efficacy
expectations are concerned with beliefs about one's competence' (1998: 66).
Bandura (1977, 1997: 511) argues that both sets of beliefs interact in determining a behavioural response, so that high levels of self-efficacy towards
engaging in a particular task or action to produce a desirable outcome will
predict behaviour when the person also has high expectations that the
behaviour will result in desired outcomes. These action-outcome links are
therefore implicated in a synergistic process that results in approach
behaviours, effort, and persistence. Pragmatically, in achievement contexts, it
is often assumed that an individual holds positive outcome expectations with

regard to propensity of the behaviour to produce outcomes. Further, it is also assumed that the outcome is deemed to be salient to the individual. Further, self-efficacy is generally assumed to have a more pervasive effect on behaviour than outcome expectations (Feltz and Chase 1998). However, when it comes to goal setting, it is important to consider the role of outcome expectancies because the outcome or goal needs to have personal value to the individual.

Self-efficacy in sport

Self-efficacy and social cognitive theory have been the subject of intensive and prolonged research in a number of applied social psychology areas, including educational psychology, health psychology, occupational psychology, and sport and exercise psychology. Meta-analyses of research with self-efficacy have indicated a significant relationship of moderate effect size between self-efficacy and behaviour such as work-related performance (e.g. Stajkovic and Luthans 1998). To date, there is no meta-analysis of the effects of self-efficacy on the salient outcome variables from Bandura's social cognitive theory in sport, which is surprising considering the number of studies that have been conducted in the area. There are, however, a number of narrative reviews of the effect of self-efficacy in sport that have supported the important tenets of social cognitive theory (e.g. Feltz and Chase 1998; McAuley and Blissmer 2002). These reviews unanimously acknowledge the pervasive effect of self-efficacy beliefs on sport performance. Feltz and Chase, for example, cited 11 studies with 29 tests of the explicit relationship between level of self-efficacy and overt performance and revealed that 25 of these tests were significant. Reviews have also noted trends in relationships between self-efficacy and other salient relationships from social cognitive theory, such as the large effect that performance accomplishment has on self-efficacy above the other antecedent variables and the effect of self-efficacy on intention and motivation (Feltz and Chase 1998). The consensus from these reviews is that self-efficacy is an important and influential construct in sport psychology and motivation, mirroring the support for self-efficacy in meta-analyses in other domains. Future researchers in the field should seek to conduct the first meta-analysis of self-efficacy in the sport domain to quantify the relationships identified in the narrative reviews.

Self-efficacy and sport performance

There is a large body of experimental and cross-sectional research that supports the effect of self-efficacy on sport performance. In experimental studies, the classic technique to manipulate self-efficacy beliefs involves using misleading or 'bogus' feedback about performance in a pre-trial task. In these experiments, high and low self-efficacy groups of participants are created by having participants perform the desired task in an ostensible familiarization test before the 'main' trial. The performer is then given feedback that they have performed better or worse than expected compared to normative results or a confederate (e.g. Weinberg *et al.* 1980). Self-reported self-efficacy beliefs and subsequent performance of the task in a main trial then form the core independent and dependent variables of the experiment respectively. Using this paradigm, studies have shown that high self-efficacy participants performed better than low self-efficacy performers (Weinberg *et al.* 1980), and did so under conditions of failure alone (Weinberg *et al.* 1980) and under failure when a cognitive strategy to enhance self-efficacy was used (Weinberg 1986). The experimental manipulation of self-efficacy has also been shown to result in superior sport performance compared to other manipulations designed to enhance intrinsic motivation and attentional focus (Lohasz and Leith 1997). These studies support hypotheses relating to self-efficacy and sport performance in social cognitive theory.

Several studies have adopted cross-sectional and longitudinal designs to examine the effects of self-efficacy on performance. Self-efficacy has been shown to be strong predictor of objectively measured performance in basketball free throw shooting performance (Kavussanu *et al.* 1998), a tennis service task (Theodorakis 1995), gymnastics performance (Weiss *et al.* 1989), and placing in distance running races (Martin and Gill 1995). Studies have also examined the effect of competition on the self-efficacy-performance relationship. For example, Kane *et al.* (1996) found that self-efficacy was related to performance in high-school wrestlers, especially in competitive conditions. Similarly, studies have shown that self-efficacy predicted performance in high-avoidance tasks such as difficult routines in platform diving (for review, see Feltz and Chase 1998). This is consistent with Bandura's (1977) hypothesis that situational self-confidence towards performing a task that is feared is highly predictive of engagement. Overall, these studies support the self-efficacy–sport performance relationship in keeping with social cognitive theory, the narrative reviews of self-efficacy in sport, and the meta-analytic reviews of self-efficacy in other domains.

Outcome expectancies

Another salient variable in social cognitive theory is outcome expectancies. Bandura (1977, 1997) viewed these as beliefs regarding the potency of the behaviour rather than beliefs about personal skill and ability. It was proposed that both sets of beliefs will affect behavioural and psychological outcomes, but in achievement situations, self-efficacy will have a stronger influence on sport performance and persistence. Lee provided some evidence to support the higher validity of personal evaluations of outcome compared with objective evaluations based on previous performance in gymnasts. It was found that outcome expectancies were a more accurate predictor of gymnasts' scores than previous scores, supporting the importance of subjective judgements regarding the behaviour. Interestingly, Martin and Gill (1991) found a stronger influence of what they called outcome self-efficacy on the performance of a fine motor task compared with performance self-efficacy. However, the definition of outcome self-efficacy was not in terms of outcome expectancies, but rather a different focus of the self-efficacy variable. Other studies have indicated that outcome expectancies moderate the influence of self-efficacy beliefs on behaviour and outcome, but only in the exercise domain and not in sport (Williams and Bond 2002), and this seems to be an area where research is lacking.

Antecedents of self-efficacy

Research in sport and exercise has examined the effect of each of the four key sources of information: performance accomplishments, vicarious experience, verbal persuasion, and physiological states (see Figure 5.2) on self-efficacy beliefs. Previous experience, although a slightly crude proxy for performance accomplishment, has been shown to predict self-efficacy in a number of studies (e.g. George 1994; Feltz and Chase 1998). In terms of vicarious experience, studies have indicated that models have a pervasive effect on self-efficacy (Gould and Weiss 1981; McAuley 1985). The effects of self-modelling on self-efficacy have been inconclusive, although Starek and McCullagh (1999) found no differences in novice swimmers' self-efficacy levels when either self or other models were used. Carnahan, Shea, and Davis (1990) demonstrated that participants completing a bench-press exercise reported higher self-efficacy when their 'spotter' provided visual and verbal cues compared with no cues, indicating that verbal persuasion can affect self-efficacy. Finally, physiological states such as cognitive and somatic anxiety have been implicated in predicting self-efficacy (e.g. Martin and Gill 1991), although some studies have examined anxiety from a trait perspective (e.g. George 1994; Martin and Gill 1995) which does influence self-efficacy but is not strictly a physiological state but a tendency to be in that state in threatening situations.

A limited number of studies have investigated the impact of multiple sources of information on self-efficacy simultaneously. Gould and Weiss (1981) examined the effects of similar and dissimilar models that gave varying levels of verbal persuasion (they called it 'self-efficacy talk') on participants' performance of a muscular endurance task. Model similarity had the strongest effect on performance, with participants given a model similar to themselves performing better on the motor task than participants given a dissimilar model. Participants receiving positive 'self-efficacy talk' and no-talk conditions performed better than those receiving negative talk and 'irrelevant' talk models. Wise and Trunnell (2001) studied the effects of three types of information on bench-press exercise performance: performance accomplishment, use of a model, and verbal message. Results demonstrated that performance accomplishment resulted in the highest levels of self-efficacy, followed by modelling and use of a verbal message. This is supported by Feltz and Chase (1998) who report that previous performance is a better predictor of self-efficacy than autonomic (physiological) perception. Previous performance accomplishment seems to be a major source of information from which athletes draw their self-efficacy beliefs.

Self-efficacy and outcomes

Self-efficacy is also hypothesized to influence psychological and behavioural outcomes, according to social cognitive theory (see Figure 5.2). Other than performance of the task, these key outcomes are grouped into psychological processes, e.g. goals, affective states, and attributions, and behavioural outcomes, e.g. task choice, effort, and persistence. In terms of psychological processes, Duncan and McAuley (1987) found that self-efficacy did affect the pattern of post-performance attribution of outcome in basketball players performing a free-throw task, but Gernigon and Delloye (2003) found that self-efficacy mediated the influence of performance-related feedback on causal attributions and some research has suggested that attributions may be a source of information for self-efficacy (Bond *et al.* 2001). Turning now to affective outcomes, Hall and Kerr (1998) and George (1994) found that high levels of self-efficacy coincided with low levels of cognitive and somatic anxiety in competitive fencers and baseball players respectively. With respect to behavioural outcomes, a vast number of studies have supported the prediction of sport behaviour in terms of task performance, but few have examined effort. George (1994) showed that self-efficacy beliefs were associated with effort across a six-game period in a longitudinal study of baseball games across a season. These results lend some support to the proposed effects of self-efficacy on outcomes.

Self-efficacy, goal setting, and imagery

In sport, goal setting is often mooted as an important means to enhance the motivation of athletes. One of the mechanisms by which goal setting might affect performance, adherence, and persistence in sport is through enhanced self-efficacy. This is because goal setting is likely to provide salient information about the task, particularly when such a task has been performed successfully in the past, is valued by the performer, and is likely to demonstrate competence. Furthermore, goals must be of the optimal level of difficulty to permit the performer to be confident in their ability to achieve it, but not so difficult as to be unreachable or so easy as to be unchallenging. For example, Miller and McAuley (1987) showed that basketballers who received training to set appropriate goals and targets had a stronger relationship between self-efficacy and basketball free-throw performance compared with those that did not receive goal training. In addition, studies have demonstrated that goal setting mediates the relationship between self-efficacy and performance (Theodorakis 1995). These results suggest that variations in performance due to self-efficacy are accounted for by changes in personal goal setting. The role of goal setting may determine the self-efficacy–performance relationship (a moderation effect) but it may also explain why self-efficacy influences performance (a mediation effect).

Given the effectiveness of modelling on self-efficacy, sports psychologists have adopted interventions to replicate the modelling effect through the use of imagery and examine whether it alters self-efficacy levels. Many of these interventions use multiple strategies so it is difficult to disentangle the effects of imagery from other elements of the intervention. Studies using these composite intervention techniques have shown significant increases in self-efficacy levels, but they have used other techniques alongside imagery such as relaxation and coping skills (e.g. Meyers *et al.* 1982). However, other than training and conditioning drills, Gould *et al.* (1990) found that athletes rated imagery among the most effective strategies to enhance self-efficacy. Several intervention studies examining imagery alone have indicated that it positively affects self-efficacy levels in rock climbers (Jones *et al.* 2002) and participants performing a laboratory muscular endurance task (Feltz and Chase 1998). Recently, Short *et al.* (2002) have examined the effect of imagery type and direction (facilitative or debilitative) of imagery on self-efficacy and performance of a golf-putting task. Results indicated that imagery that had a motivational rather than cognitive function and was facilitative in direction enhanced self-efficacy, suggesting that interventions should consider both the function and interpretation of the imagery when attempting to enhance self-efficacy through these means.

Achievement goal theory

Achievement goal theory is a prominent approach that aims to explain motivation and behaviour in sports settings (Duda 2001). Theories of achievement goals have been put forward by a number of theorists and have common elements and some subtle differences (Nicholls 1989; Ames 1992; Dweck 1992). Common to these theories is the hypothesis that individuals focus on demonstrating competence in achievement situations. Thus, the way an individual views their ability or success in an achievement context will result in their persistence or desistance in competence-demonstrating behaviours. These theories suggest that two distinct motivational tendencies or achievement goal perspectives prevail in achievement situations and influence the way competence information is interpreted: (1) a *task* or *mastery* orientation; and (2) an *ego* or *performance* orientation. The theories propose that these goal orientations define the way people tend to view their ability in a given context. If that person's view tends to be more personal or self-referent, then he or she will be motivated to persist, even under failure, while if his or her view leans towards being normative or other-referenced, he or she may persist but generally only under conditions of success.

In terms of motivation in competitive situations, an individual who adopts a predominantly task-oriented approach, i.e. a high-level of task orientation, is likely to view success as demonstrating competence by achieving task-related successes. For example, a soccer player may view their success in terms of the number of passes they complete relative to their own personal target or a basketball player may view success in the number of rebounds they take relative to their previous match. An individual who adopts a predominantly ego orientation will view success in competitive situations by demonstrating competence through beating others, winning, and achieving a high rank compared to others. Thus, finishing first in a 100m race, topping the leaderboard in a golf tournament, or being on the winning side in a hockey match are all examples of ego-oriented demonstrations of competence. It is important to note, of course, that although task and ego orientations are considered orthogonal (independent) constructs, it is possible to hold high levels of both task and ego orientations simultaneously so that competence can be demonstrated from both a self-referenced and other-referenced perspective.

However, it is under conditions of failure or losing where the theory makes its most influential predictions with respect to motivation. An individual in an achievement situation who has a predominantly ego orientation and has a low task orientation is likely to view success only in terms of demonstrating competence through winning. In this case, the individual will be unable to demonstrate competence if they lose or experience failure which is likely to undermine motivation to engage in that behaviour again. If, however, they are task-oriented as well (or task-oriented alone, with low ego orientation), then they will be able to demonstrate competence through the achievement of task-related goals that are personally relevant and have meaning to themselves, regardless of success or failure. They may have lost the match, for example, but at least they played well and were able to demonstrate competence though their own goals independent of the win–lose outcome. In this respect, a task orientation alone or in conjunction with an ego orientation is motivationally adaptive in terms of persistence and effort on subsequent occasions (Goudas *et al.* 1994). Importantly, it can be seen that goal orientations may determine a number of psychological processes that lead to persistence in motivation. For example, task orientation reflects the demonstration of personally relevant goals internal to the individual and is likely to predict the type of motivation associated with persistence and satisfaction, namely intrinsic motivation (Butler 1987; Ryan and Deci 1989). Further, a person with a high-task orientation is likely to make an attribution of success to high ability and internal reasons regardless of objective outcome. Thus, achievement goal theory may influence motivational constructs from self-determination theory and attribution theory respectively.

Research adopting achievement goal theories in sport have been dominated by Nicholls' (1989) approach to achievement goals, mainly because early research and development of valid instrumentation have focused on this version of the theory. Two instruments have been developed for the measurement of achievement goal orientations in sport settings. The task and ego orientation in sport questionnaire (TEOSQ, Duda and Nicholls 1992) and the perceptions of success in questionnaire (POSQ, Roberts *et al.* 1998) contain items measuring task orientation (e.g. 'I feel successful in sport when I learn new skills') and ego orientation (e.g. 'I feel most successful in sport when others can't do as well as me'). Exploratory and confirmatory factor analytic studies have supported the factor structure, internal consistency, and test–retest reliability of these instruments (e.g. Duda and Nicholls 1992; Roberts *et al.* 1998). Studies have also confirmed the criterion validity of these instruments with high and significant correlations between the two traits across the different methods (Fonseca and Balague 1996), although no multi-trait, multi-method study has been conducted to compare these instruments. Together these instruments have been adopted for almost all of the research using achievement goal theory in sport contexts.

To date there is no meta-analysis that has tested the hypothesized relationships between achievement goal orientations and motivational constructs. However, there are a number of good narrative reviews of the area (e.g. Biddle 1999; Ntoumanis and Biddle 1999; Duda 2001). Research has indicated that achievement goals predict a number of motivation-related constructs such as beliefs about causes of success (Duda and Nicholls 1992), self-motivation (Biddle *et al.* 1996), and effort (Williams and Gill 1995), sources of competence information (Williams 1994), competitive state anxiety (Newton and Duda 1995), enjoyment and satisfaction (Allen 2003), and motivation-related behaviours (Boyd *et al.* 2002). Overall, the general pattern of results suggests that a task-orientation tends to be more strongly related to adaptive motivational constructs such as self-confidence from the CSAI-2 (Newton and Duda 1995), self-referenced sources of competence information like goal attainment (Williams 1994), experiences of learning and improvement (Williams 1994) and incremental beliefs about ability (Sarrazin *et al.* 1996), personally controllable attributions of success/failure (Vlachopolous and Biddle 1997), intrinsic motivation (Kavussanu and Roberts 1996), perceived control (Pensgaard 1999), self-esteem (Boyd *et al.* 2002), effort (Williams and Gill 1995), and enjoyment (Allen 2003). An ego orientation has been shown to be significantly and positively related to other-referenced and motivationally maladaptive outcomes such as cognitive and somatic anxiety (Newton and Duda 1995), indices of moral functioning in sport such as moral judgement, intentions, and behaviour (Kavussanu and Roberts 2001), and personally uncontrollable attributions of success/failure (Vlachopolous and Biddle 1997).

Goal involvement

Much of the research on achievement goal theory in sport and exercise has focused on the effects of the dispositional and trait-like task and ego orientations on motivation-related constructs and behaviour. This research has tended to emphasize the importance of a task orientation, alone or in conjunction with ego orientation, to foster motivationally-adaptive psychological profiles in athletes. However, recent research has questioned the heavy focus on task *orientation* as the individual difference that makes motivation in sport, particularly competitive sport, adaptive (Hodge and Petlichkoff 2000). Researchers are recognizing the need to account for the effects of situational factors such as **motivational climate** (Seifriz *et al.* 1992) and involved achievement goal *states* of an individual in achievement contexts (Harwood 2002). A distinction between situational, involved achievement goal perspectives and the more traditional dispositional goal orientation has been proposed. Consequently, there has been a shift towards a profile approach to goal orientations and a more individual, ideographic basis (Harwood 2002). Harwood has criticized the focus of the majority of research adopting achievement goal theory on nomothetic methods and individual difference data on achievement goals from groups of athletes. While it is recognized that this has offered some useful recommendations in terms of the coaching styles and motivational climates afforded by coaches for their athletes, such approaches are limited because much of the data is cross-sectional, which limits causality inferences, but, more importantly, it neglects the importance of goal involvement at the situational level which are state-like and changeable over time.

Harwood supports this argument with data gained from involved measures of task and ego orientation compared with dispositional data. For example, Harwood used involved competition-specific measures of achievement goal orientations to show that involved goal state profiles were markedly different to goal orientations at the dispositional level as measured by the TEOSQ. Athletes tended to report higher levels of involved ego orientation in competition than their levels on dispositional ego orientation towards their sport in general. Results indicate the importance of over-reliance on dispositional measures and the importance of taking into account individualized levels of psychological constructs. Together these findings suggest that interventions to change motivational orientation should target goal involvement at a contextual or even situational level. It may be that goal orientations in sport are arranged hierarchically in keeping with other social cognitive theories of motivation (cf. Vallerand 1997).

Motivational climate

One of the key contributions made by Ames' (1992) research on achievement goal theory is the role that situational factors, particularly the prevailing goal structure operating in the achievement context, have on the situational goal states observed in a given achievement situation. Ames (1992) and Nicholls (1989) hypothesized that the motivational orientation experienced by an individual performing a task in an achievement context was a function of their dispositional goal orientation and the situational goal structure or *motivational climate* operating in the context. Motivational climate reflects how competence is typically evaluated with respect to tasks in a given environment and is viewed as a function of the goals to be achieved, the role of competition or relationships between individuals in that context, and the reward structure in that environment. Ames created a mastery-oriented motivational climate by presenting tasks so that effort was rewarded and the primary criterion for success and found elevated levels of effort and persistence among school children operating in such a climate.

In sport, motivational climate has been investigated alongside dispositional goal orientations to examine the effects of personal dispositions and situational factors on motivational constructs. Seifriz, Duda, and Chi (1992) examined the effects of motivational climate and dispositional achievement goal orientations on motivational constructs from the intrinsic motivation inventory and beliefs about success. They developed an inventory, the perceived motivational climate in sport questionnaire (PMCSQ, Seifriz *et al.* 1992) based on items from Ames's (1992) achievement goals questionnaire, and administered it with the TEOSQ to high-school male basketball players. Results showed that motivational climate positively predicted enjoyment and negatively predicted tension in basketball players, but beliefs about success, competence, and effort were accounted for by dispositional goal orientations alone.

Subsequent research has shown that a mastery-oriented motivational climate predicts adaptive motivational and outcome variables in athletes such as enjoyment and satisfaction (Boyd *et al.* 1995), attribution of success to effort (Treasure and Roberts 1998), self-referenced sources of competence information such as goal attainment (Halliburton and Weiss 2002), intrinsic motivation (Kavussanu and Roberts 1996; Petherick and Weigand 2002), perceived competence (Sarrazin *et al.* 2002), self-efficacy (Kavussanu and Roberts 1996), and problem-focused coping (Ntoumanis *et al.* 1999). Analogously, an ego-oriented motivational climate tends to influence negative outcomes and be related to maladaptive achievement pattern such as worry and stress (Pensgaard and Roberts 1995), attribution of success to ability (Treasure and Roberts 1998), other-referenced sources of competence information such as peer comparison and competition performance (Treasure and Roberts 1998; Halliburton and Weiss 2002), extrinsic motivation (Petherick and Weigand 2002), and emotion-focused coping (Ntoumanis *et al.* 1999). In terms of mechanisms, Newton and Duda (1999) found a significant interaction between mastery climate and a task orientation on satisfaction and effort. These findings indicated that a situational goal structure that supports a task orientation results in individuals reporting that they put in a great deal of effort and attribute their success to effort.

Self-determination theory

Self-determination theory, particularly the sub-theory of cognitive evaluation theory, has much to offer in the explanation of motivation in achievement tasks as well as exercise. As seen in Chapter 3, cognitive evaluation theory aims to explain variance in intrinsic motivation, most principally the environmental contingencies that either promote or thwart intrinsically motivated behaviour. In sport, just as in education and other achievement contexts, these contingencies have to do with the nature of presentation of rewards and the feedback given to individuals about their performance. This is particularly relevant to those involved in the motivation of athletes in training and competition such as coaches, managers, and parents as well as those promoting exercise for health. This is because they are often in a situation where they have the opportunity to foster the appropriate motivational context to promote athletes' intrinsic motivation. Intrinsic motivation is especially relevant to athletes in achievement situations. Not only are the outcome psychological states of intrinsic motivation congruent with many athletes' original motives for participating in sport such as for enjoyment or pleasure, for competence, and for affiliation (Ashford *et al.* 1993), but they are also relevant for adherence and continued participation. Getting an athlete to self-regulate and perform training behaviours and practices on their own without any external reinforcement is essential for a coach, particularly for those who have limited time to spend with athletes or who coach from a distance. Therefore strategies to enhance intrinsic motivation are essential to a coach and these will be reviewed later in this section.

The central premise of cognitive evaluation theory is concerned with how rewards can potentially undermine intrinsic motivation, and how the nature of the presentation of the reward and information regarding the reward through interpersonal context may promote or enhance intrinsic motivation (Deci and Ryan 1985). Interpersonal context refers to the manner in which rewards are presented, usually through informational (autonomy supportive) or controlling (autonomy thwarting) feedback. Rewards take a number of different forms; they can be tangible such as money, trophies, medals, distance and proficiency badges, and certificates or intangible such as recognition, praise, encouragement, enjoyment, satisfaction, and pride. Clearly, the set of intangible rewards can be considered internal to the individual such as satisfaction and enjoyment or external to the individual such as praise and recognition. At the opposite pole to rewards are punishments and these can also be either tangible, e.g. fines and withdrawal or removal of bonuses or intangible, e.g. being dropped from the team, being dismissed from training, criticism, guilt, and shame. All these rewards and punishments are types of reinforcements that can be used to induce persistence in some sort of behaviour. Furthermore, tangible rewards and punishments are very effective in maintaining compliance and persistence in behaviour, but only to the extent that the reinforcer remains omnipresent (Deci and Ryan 1985). Withdrawal of the reward is likely to result in a decrease in motivation and reduced adherence to the behaviour. This is particularly the case if the behaviour is made solely contingent on gaining the reward. Cognitive evaluation theory maps how non-contingent rewards may help motivate behaviour and maintain intrinsic motivation (Deci and Ryan 1985).

Cognitive evaluation theory states that if the role of a reward has an informational function with respect to behavioural performance rather than the behaviour being performed for the reward itself, then it will not undermine intrinsic motivation (Deci and Ryan 1985). However, if a person engages in the behaviour for the reward itself, the intrinsically motivating properties of the behaviour will be lost to the individual and they will feel that their engagement in the behaviour is outside their personal sphere of effectance or 'locus of causality'. This has been labelled the undermining effect (Deci et al. 1999b) because the reward represents an additional reason for doing the behaviour that is without explanation and above and beyond the intrinsic reasons. Studies examining individuals solving interesting puzzles have supported this effect on a number of occasions. For example, Deci and Ryan (1985) report a series of experiments in which participants solving a novel puzzle were presented with a monetary reward. Half of the subjects were given controlling feedback about their performance being told that they did as well as they should according to the normative standard. The other half given informational feedback about their performance; they were told that they did well according to their own standards and the money was presented to acknowledge their success. The group that received the controlling feedback exhibited significantly lower levels of intrinsic motivation than the participants receiving the informational feedback, as indicated by free choice engagement in the puzzle when the experimenter left the room. In addition to the undermining effect, perceived competence also plays an important role in cognitive evaluation theory. As reviewed in Chapter 3, feedback that supports competence and is informational regarding performance (e.g. positive feedback, verbal praise) will enhance intrinsic motivation while feedback that compromises competence and is controlling with respect to performance (e.g. negative feedback, criticism) will reduce intrinsic motivation.

The undermining effect of rewards and other external contingencies such as deadlines and feedback has been the subject of a large number of studies in a number of achievement domains, but mostly in educational contexts. A number of meta-analytic studies have been conducted to examine robustness of the findings for this effect across studies (e.g. Cameron and Pierce 1994; Deci et al. 1999a). Cameron and Pierce conducted a meta-analysis on 96 experimental studies and found that verbal praise increased intrinsic motivation in rewarded participants, but intrinsic motivation was not substantially undermined by the presence of a reward. They suggested that the undermining effect is an exaggerated phenomenon only seen in certain contingencies, such as when the reward was given for a behaviour with no prior expectation. They also found that praise undermined intrinsic motivation when an extrinsic reward was given. The authors concluded that the 'negative effects of rewards are limited and easily avoidable' (1994: 29). However, Cameron and Pierce's analysis was criticized as confounding some interaction effects for rewards and small effect sizes (Deci et al. 1999a). Deci et al. conducted another meta-analysis of 128 experiments on the undermining effect and found significant effect sizes for all types of reward contingencies (e.g. task-contingent, task-completion, engagement contingent, and performance contingent, see Chapter 3) for the undermining of intrinsic motivation. A strong effect was also found for verbal praise on intrinsic motivation. The authors concluded that these data provided strong support across a number of contexts for the undermining effect. On reflection, it seems that the balance falls in favour of cognitive evaluation theory and that the undermining effect may be a real one, and this may be especially so if the reward communicates controlling contingencies.

In sport, cognitive evaluation theory has been investigated primarily with respect to the effects of feedback on performers (Ryan et al. 1984). Self-determination theory constructs in sport context have typically been measured largely by the sport motivation scale (SMS, Pelletier et al. 1995), which has constructs common to measures of the perceived locus of causality in other contexts and exhibits adequate construct validity and internal reliability (Sarrazin et al. 2002). A number of studies have indicated significant effects of positive feedback and verbal praise on athletes' intrinsic motivation and competence (e.g. Vallerand and Reid 1984; Whitehead and Corbin 1991). These studies used intervention and control groups of athletes with the intervention groups receiving varying levels of feedback from coaches or experimenters about their performance of sport-related tasks. Furthermore, in these studies, perceived competence seemed to be a mediator of the influence of intrinsic motivation of sports performance, consistent with the notion that needs for competence and self-determination are complementary, as has been shown in research in other contexts such as education (Reeve 2002). However, to date, no sports-related study has replicated the findings of Deci and colleagues in terms of the effect of feedback on free-choice sport behaviour and interest, a study that would unequivocally support self-determination theory in sport contexts. Further, although many authors have cited the role that cognitive evaluation theory has to play in examining the effects of rewards on sport behaviour, few studies have examined the effect of a tangible reward on sports performance.

Research in sport has also examined associations between perceived locus of causality and other motivational variables. Pelletier et al. (1995) found positive correlations between identified regulation and other hypothesized determinants of sport behaviour such as perceived autonomy and competence and outcome variables such as effort, intentions, and behaviour. Self-determined forms of extrinsic motivation was found to influence persistence among competitive swimmers over a 22-month period. Studies have also pointed out positive relationships between perceived relatedness, autonomy, and locus of causality (e.g. Ntoumanis 2001). This empirical evidence supports the construct validity of the perceived locus of causality in a sport context and suggests that the motivational constructs in the sport motivation scales have a significant effect on key determinant and outcome variables.

Self-determination theory and competition

Of supreme relevance to motivation in sport contexts is the application of intrinsic motivation and cognitive evaluation theory to competition. In particular, theorists are interested under what conditions intrinsic motivation is maintained in competitive situations regardless of objective outcome. For example, is it possible to maintain intrinsic motivation in sports performers whose performance outcome was a loss rather than a win? Deci and Ryan (1985) have hypothesized that, consistent with cognitive evaluation theory, competition would have the same undermining effect on intrinsic motivation as extrinsic rewards because competition tends to make externally referenced criteria for success salient to the individual. It was, however, also anticipated that the undermining effect could be allayed by the presentation of the competition as informational (e.g. gaining positive feedback about one's own performance) rather than controlling (e.g. trying to beat the others in the competition). Experimental research in education (Reeve *et al.* 1985) and sports contexts (Vallerand and Reid 1984) has suggested that participants for whom the outcome of their behavioural engagement is failure or losing, generally report lower intrinsic motivation than those who are successful or win. This suggests that competition may be inherently controlling. This conclusion was supported by Deci *et al.* (1981) who found that participants solving puzzles together had significantly lower intrinsic motivation if they were told they should try to beat the other person than when they were told to try to do their best. Reeve and Deci (1996) attributed the inherently controlling and undermining nature of competition to the contingency of positive feedback on winning and the negative competence feedback associated with losing.

However, it can be seen that it is the individual's personal interpretation of success and failure and the interpersonal context in which the competition is presented that may also explain the undermining effect of competition on intrinsic motivation. For example, McAuley and Tammen (1989) found that basketball players who rated their perceived success highly had significantly higher levels of perceived competence and intrinsic motivation compared with those who reported lower ratings of perceived success. Importantly, there were no differences in objective measures of winning or losing, suggesting that it is the interpretation of the outcome that is important. The interpretation of the competition outcome is likely to be dependent upon the degree to which the structure of the competition was able to provide information about the person's performance that supported competence rather than being controlling and fostering a dependence on external cues. Vallerand and co-workers (1986) found that participants in a competitive situation who were told they would be compared to their other competitors exhibited lower intrinsic motivation than those who were in a non-competitive situation and were encouraged to do as well as they could on the task. Reeve and Deci (1996) also found that when participants won a competition solving puzzles in an interpersonal context that was non-pressuring, i.e. the participant was not told to beat the other competitors, their intrinsic motivation was not undermined but under pressuring conditions the undermining effect occurred. Importantly, comparing these finding with a control group that had no competition and no pressuring/non-pressuring feedback, Reeve and Deci found that the winning/non-pressuring group participants had higher levels of intrinsic motivation than the control group and the winning/pressuring group participants had lower levels of intrinsic motivation.

The issue of competition becomes more complex when rewards are introduced in conjunction with competition. However, the tenets of cognitive evaluation theory are able to explain the effects of interactions between competition, rewards, and interpersonal context on intrinsic motivation. In competition, there are two types of rewards, competitively contingent rewards and performance-contingent rewards. Competitively contingent rewards are rewards that are attained for beating an opponent in direct competition, while performance-contingent rewards are given when a normative standard is reached. Thus, a performance-contingent reward can be attained by a number of individuals while a competitively contingent reward can only be given to the winner. In experiments studying competition and rewards, the effect of three independent variables on intrinsic motivation can be seen: (1) the type of the reward (competitive contingent or performance-contingent); (2) the competitive outcome (winning or losing); and (3) the interpersonal context in which the competitive task is presented (controlling or informational feedback). These groups are typically compared with groups that perform the task in the absence of competition, receive no feedback, and receive no reward. Research in this area has been limited, but findings suggest that when considered together, winners and losers receiving competitively contingent rewards have lower levels of intrinsic motivation compared to a no-competition/no-feedback/no-reward condition (Prichard et al. 1977).

Vansteenkiste and Deci (2003) investigated the effects of winning or losing on intrinsic motivation in competitors who received competitive and performance-contingent rewards. Winners were more intrinsically motivated than losers, which partially reaffirms the premise that competition is inherently controlling. However, it was found that among losers in competitive situations positive feedback for meeting a specified standard (performance-contingent feedback) went a long way to allay the negative effects of losing on intrinsic motivation, while losers who received a reward for achieving a specified standard of performance (performance-contingent feedback) exhibited reduced intrinsic motivation but their enjoyment of the task was unaffected. The authors concluded that:

> a focus on winning may indeed be counter-productive . . . with respect to intrinsic motivation . . . If, instead of emphasizing winning above all else, participants in activities and observers of the activities focused more on good performance than on winning, the results for the participants' motivation is likely to be far more positive. (2003: 298)

Thus, coaches would.do well to help their athletes instill performance-related goals that are personally relevant and informative about performance rather than attending to goals relating to winning relative to others *per se*. Furthermore, a coaching style that emphasizes the informational aspects of competition and focuses on presenting competition as a means of measuring performance against set criteria rather than against others is important.

Autonomy support in sport settings

Previously, in Chapter 3, the effect of perceived autonomy support of significant others on the intrinsic motivation of students in a leisure-time exercise context was discussed, particularly in the recently developed trans-contextual model (Hagger *et al.* 2003b). Perceived autonomy support has also been found to be a strong predictor of intrinsic motivation in educational (e.g. Koestner *et al.* 1984; Reeve *et al.* 1999) and health (Williams *et al.* 1998; Williams *et al.* 2002) settings. Further, perceived autonomy support has been validated against 20 core autonomy supportive behaviours in teachers in educational settings (Reeve 2002). Given these findings and the research introduced in the previous section on 'the importance of informative goals and feedback in the maintenance of intrinsic motivation, the autonomy supportive behaviours suggested by Reeve and colleagues (2002) are likely to have important effects on intrinsic motivation and persistence in sport performance in training and competition. This is because coaches' autonomy supportive behaviours are likely to promote intrinsic motives and enhance the informative nature of the competition to their athletes. For example, Gagné, Ryan, and Bargmann (2003) conducted a longitudinal diary-based study of the effect of perceived autonomy support on the well-being of young gymnasts. They found that the gymnasts' subjective well-being was determined by the relative satisfaction of psychological needs by the autonomy support gained from parents and coaches. This preliminary evidence suggests that coaches' autonomy-supportive behaviours are strongly recommended because they tend to produce the desirable motivational orientations likely to maintain intrinsic motivation and persistence in athletes.

Authoritarian and democratic styles

Legendary English soccer coach Brian Clough was notorious for his regimented, authoritarian, and controlling coaching style and exhibited behaviours on the training ground that exemplified those that would undermine intrinsic motivation. Yet on the pitch his players were among the most committed, hard-working, and cohesive teams in the English league and Clough steered them to successive European cup titles in 1979 and 1980. How did the adoption of such an autocratic style, which seemed to go against many of the predictions and recommendations of self-determination theory, engender such seemingly intrinsically motivated behaviours in the team?

According to Iyengar and DeVoe (2003), the answer may lie in the structure or underlying norms of the group and its effect on the way free choice and the causality of behaviour is viewed, an explanation that is consistent with self-determination theory.

Iyengar and DeVoe present evidence to suggest that people in collectivist cultures tend to take into account the considerations of significant others when making choices and decisions. As a consequence, people in collectivist cultures tend to report higher intrinsic motivation when their choices are consistent with the wishes of significant others or the cultural norm than when making choices on their own. This may have a pervasive effect on how choice and intrinsic motivation operate in a team context in which the pervading environment is autocratic and no autonomy-supportive behaviours are displayed by the coach. Iyengar and DeVoe report experiments that examined the effects of a collectivist culture on the intrinsic motivation. They used two groups of children: European-Americans who had a predominantly individualist cultural norm and endorsed personal choice and an independent view of the self; and Asian-Americans whose prevailing cultural norm was collectivist with an interdependent notion of self. Participants from each group were presented with the opportunity to solve a series of anagrams of equal difficulty presented under three conditions. One group of children was told that the anagrams had been chosen by an adult unknown to them (an experimenter) while another was told that a significant other (their mothers) had chosen for them. A third group was allowed to choose for themselves. In the experimenter choice condition, Asian-American and European-American reported identical levels of intrinsic motivation. Most telling though was the finding that European-American children reported significantly higher intrinsic motivation than Asian-Americans children when personal choice was granted, while Asian-Americans reported significantly higher intrinsic motivation when they were told the significant other chose the anagram.

To explain these findings, it was proposed that the significant other choice was more appealing to the preferences of children from the collectivist culture because it reflected their tendency to respectfully account for significant others' views when making decisions. According to self-determination theory, the participants from the collectivist group had internalized the group norm to respect and accept the choices of other important members of the in-group, and that is considered more important than personal choice. Thus, the choices of others and those of the in-group are more salient to intrinsic motivation in a collectivist culture than personal choice. Recent research suggests that differences in collectivist and individualist group norms also operate in social contexts not just in cultural groups (McAuliffe et al. 2003). Therefore, it is possible that a collectivist group norm operated in Clough's teams and they were prepared to forego personal choice and volition because the group respected and had internalized the instructions and autocratic style of the coach. In such a context it is possible for intrinsic motivation to flourish in a team where autonomy support is not evident and controlling leadership styles pervade. However, it is always important for athletes to be given a choice when working in an autocratic environment. If athletes are forced into accepting authoritarian styles, then intrinsic motivation is likely to be undermined.

A hierarchical model of motivation

Vallerand (1997) proposed a hierarchical model of motivation that aimed to integrate global, trait-like constructs related to motivation, such as psychological need satisfaction, with context- and situation-level motivation. Vallerand's model is an extension of self-determination theory that explicitly hypothesizes links between the global, contextual, and situational aspects of differing motivational styles adopted in the perceived locus of causality (see Chapter 3). It also specifies links between social factors or interpersonal context, motivational styles, and the consequences and outcomes of behavioural engagement. In this model, global motivational constructs affect motivation in specific situations via the mediation of context-level motivation (see Figure 5.3). Other than the proposal of three levels of generality, Vallerand states that a complete model of motivation needs to account for intrinsic motivation (IM), extrinsic motivation (EM), and amotivation (AM), the absence of intentionality or goal-directed striving, and that motivation in a given context is determined by situational factors and top-down effects from motivation at the most proximal level. This model explicitly states that overarching motives that reflect need satisfaction have wide-ranging and generalized effects across contexts and situations. However, having stated these hypotheses, the complexity of the model has resulted in researchers seeking to support specific hypotheses relating to its important postulates rather than testing the whole model simultaneously.

One of the most comprehensive tests of the hierarchical model was provided by Guay, Mageau, and Vallerand (2003). They aimed to examine the top-down, bottom-up, and horizontal effects of some of the key constructs in the model. Adopting a longitudinal design, the authors measured intrinsic motivation at the two levels of generality in two samples of school children at two time points: one and five years apart respectively. They employed a cross-lagged panel design, a powerful research design that enables the researcher to better infer causality that cannot be done with data measured at a single time point. The relationships tested are illustrated by the arrows in Figure 5.4. The design permitted the researchers to establish whether global motivation influenced situational motivation in a top-down fashion (arrow a in Figure 5.4), whether situational motivation caused global motivation (arrow b in Figure 5.4), whether the relationships were reciprocal (arrows a and b in Figure 5.4), or whether the majority of the variance in global and situational intrinsic motivation was explained by the same variable measured at the previous timepoint (arrows c and d in Figure 5.4). Results across both studies showed that global motivation exhibited the greatest stability supporting the proposition of the model that this construct reflects more generalized, less

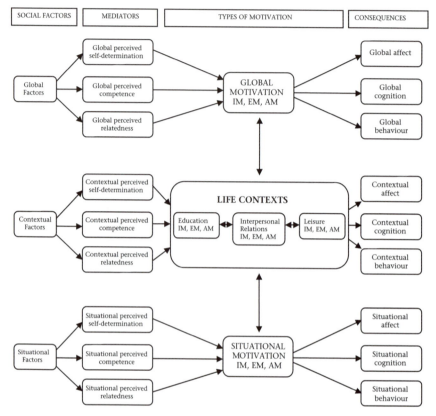

Figure 5.3 Vallerand and Ratelle's (2002) hierarchical model of intrinsic and extrinsic motivation
Source: Vallerand and Ratelle (2002: 41)

changeable perceptions of motivation. Furthermore, a reciprocal effects model best fit the data in both samples, suggesting that motivation at any level of generality is caused partly by the stability of the motivation and perceived motivation at the most proximal level.

In a sport context, Sarazin *et al.* (2002) provided a longitudinal test of the hierarchical model in female handball players. In particular, they focused on the proposed motivational sequence that determines behavioural consequences: social factors→psychological mediators→type of motivation→consequences (Vallerand 1997). The authors aimed to test whether global motives reflecting players' psychological needs for autonomy, competence, and relatedness (psychological mediators) influenced intrinsic motivation (type of motivation) and dropout intentions and behaviour (consequences). They found that the contextual needs-related variables influenced contextual intrinsic motivation

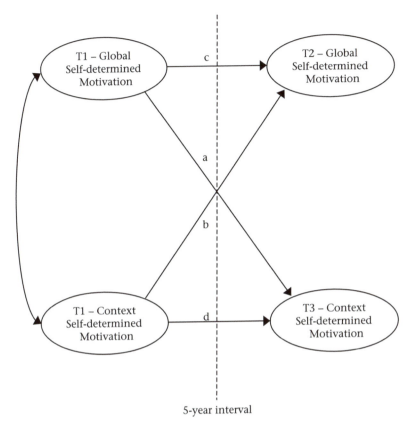

Figure 5.4 Guay et al.'s (2003) hierarchical model of motivation, showing top-down, bottom-up, horizontal, and reciprocal effects of global and context-level motivation over time
Source: Guay et al. (2003: 994)

in keeping with the theory. Intrinsic motivation negatively predicted intentions to drop out of handball participation and intentions to drop out significantly predicted behaviour. This means that high levels of intrinsic motivation offered a protective effect against specific intentions to drop out at the end of the season. This study also examined the influence of social context on the contextual motivation (Vallerand 1997). This provided a further test of Vallerand's hypothesis that an interpersonal context that promoted intrinsic motives would have a positive effect on intrinsic motivation. In a leisure-time context, this has been studied with respect to perceived autonomy support (Hagger et al. 2003), but Sarrazin et al. (2002) capitalized on recent evidence that a task-involving motivational climate (see previous section on achievement goals) would enhance intrinsic motives. Indeed, the authors found support for the sequence proposed by Vallerand (1997) from social context (task-orientated motivational climate), to motivational styles (perceived autonomy, relatedness, and competence), to intrinsic motivation, and situational decisions and behaviour (dropout intentions and behaviour). This provides support for some major tenets of the hierarchical model in a sport context.

Suggested reading

Biddle, S.J.H. (1999) Motivation and perceptions of control: tracing its development and plotting its future in exercise and sport psychology, *Journal of Sport and Exercise Psychology*, 21: 1–23. Award-winning review of motivational theories in sport and exercise and control-related social cognitive constructs.

Biddle, S.J.H., Hanrahan, S.J. and Sellars, C.N. (2001) Attributions: Past, present, and future, in R.N. Singer, H.A. Hausenblas and C.M. Janelle (eds), *Handbook of Sport Psychology* (pp. 444–71). New York: Wiley. A review of attribution theory and its contribution to exercise and sport psychology.

Chatzisarantis, N.L.D., Hagger, M.S., Biddle, S.J.H., Smith, B. and Wang, J.C.K. (2003) A meta-analysis of perceived locus of causality in exercise, sport, and physical education contexts, *Journal of Sport and Exercise Psychology*, 25: 284–306. Summarizes the contribution of self-determination theory to sport.

Duda, J.L. and Hall, H. (2001) Achievement goal theory in sport: recent extensions and future directions, in R.N. Singer, H.A. Hausenblas and C. Janelle (eds), *Handbook of Sport Psychology* (pp. 417–43). New York: Wiley. Recent update of the role of achievement goal theory in sport.

Feltz, D.L. and Chase, M.A. (1998) The measurement of self-efficacy and confidence in sport, in J.L. Duda (ed.), *Advances in Sport and Exercise Psychology Measurement* (pp. 65–80). Morgantown, WV: Fitness Information Technology. A very informative overview of self-efficacy theory in sport psychology.

Summary

- Motivation is a social cognitive construct that describes the intensity and direction of an athlete's activation or readiness to engage in a sports skill or behaviour.
- The purpose of Heider (1958) and Weiner's (1972) attribution theory was to explain how athletes attribute the cause of their success or failure to various sources. The sources are characterized according to three bipolar continua: internal-external locus of causality, stable-unstable, and controllable-uncontrollable.
- Social cognitive theory (Bandura 1977, 1997) has had a substantial impact on sport psychology research and motivation. The theory proposes that self-efficacy, as situation-specific self-confidence, is a strong predictor of sport performance and salient outcomes. Self-efficacy is sourced from

performance accomplishment, vicarious experiences, verbal persuasion, and physiological states.

- Achievement goal theory (Nicholls 1989) is one of the most frequently cited theoretical approaches in sport psychology. The theory's main premise is that athletes view their ability or success as either ego-oriented (success is viewed as achieving performance outcomes like winning) or task-oriented (success is viewed as achieving personal outcomes like learning new skills). Achievement goal orientations have been found to influence motivational constructs like intention, effort, and self-efficacy as well as behavioural constructs like persistence, adherence, and sport performance.

- Self-determination theory (Deci and Ryan 1985) aims to examine the events that foster and maintain intrinsic motivation. Cognitive evaluation theory, a sub-theory of self-determination theory, proposes that an athlete's intrinsic motivation is a function of whether their behaviour or performance is contingent on an extrinsic reward (e.g. money, verbal praise) and whether the reward is interpreted as informational or controlling. External rewards and controlling feedback/competition tend to undermine intrinsic motivation while rewards and competition that are presented so as to give informational feedback on personal success promote intrinsic motivation.

6

Athletes are emotional, too

In achievement contexts, considerable demands are placed on an individual who has the potential to challenge their ability to cope and evoke a substantial emotional response. Sport is an excellent example of such a context. Theories of motivation in sport often cite positive **affect** – a positive emotional state – as both an *adaptive* outcome of sport participation and a source of information for future motivation to engage in the sport. However, the competitive nature of sport also has the ability to evoke more negative or *maladaptive* affective or emotional states. Sport, especially at the elite level, exerts considerable stress on the athlete or performer. This is because at the highest level of performance the stakes are very high; for example, professional sports performers depend on success to earn their salary, prize monies, and win bonuses, as well as attain intrinsic rewards such as personal satisfaction and self-esteem, rewards and outcomes common to competitive athletes at all levels of sport. If there is a mismatch between the demands placed on an athlete or sport performer by their environment and their ability to cope with the concomitant emotive states that arise from that demand, then it may interfere with their ability to perform what Zajonc (1965) called the 'dominant response', i.e. the well practised or trained movements and skills involved in sport performance. This can often, catastrophically, manifest itself in sometimes embarrassingly poor performances relative to performances in practice and training, even among the most highly skilled athletes. This is a phenomenon often referred to as 'choking' (Baumeister 1984).

Many of us can think of occasions when this has happened in elite sport. Think of France's soccer team, the reigning World and European Champions and tournament favourites at the 2002 FIFA World Cup in Japan, leaving the championship after the first round in disgrace after an abysmal series of performances in which they failed to win a match or score a goal. Think of Jean van der Velde's slump in the 1999 British Open golf championship when he triple bogeyed the last hole after leading by five shots into the last. He needed only a six to win, and he took seven in what is acknowledged as one of the greatest 'chokes' of all time. There are other examples, Martina Hingis resorting to serving underarm against Steffi Graf in the 2000 French Open tennis final after being unable to get any serve in and John Aldridge's penalty miss that handed the English FA cup to Wimbledon in 1988. Why should these acknowledged champions fail to perform to anywhere near the high standards they and others expect of them in high pressure situations? **Anxiety**, the set of negative affective states associated with an inability to cope with stress placed on an individual by environmental demands, is often the culprit. Elite and professional athletes are schooled in the negative effects of anxiety and so-called 'negative' emotional states on sport performance and many athletes seek the help of sport psychologists for assistance with anxiety control. Indeed, the majority of sport psychology consultations involve anxiety management (Crocker *et al.* 1988). This chapter aims to evaluate social psychological research into the role of **emotion** in sport and describe the relationships between emotional states, psychological constructs, and sports performance.

Why social psychological approaches to emotion and anxiety?

On the surface, research in cognition and emotion may not seem entirely relevant to social psychological investigations into sport performance. However, an examination of the components of social cognitive theories will stand as testament to the importance of emotion constructs in social psychology. For example, as we saw in Chapter 2, affect has been shown to be an integral component of the attitude construct in extensions of the theory of planned behaviour (Hagger and Chatzisarantis, in press). Moreover, while models of social cognition acknowledge that social information from the environment (stimuli) and learnt personal belief systems are processed and serve as a basis for motives, decisions, intentions, and behavioural responses, this does not happen in a vacuum, devoid of feeling states or emotions (Eagly and Chaiken 1993; Perugini and Conner 2000). Emotions can also operate as response or outcome states as well as sources of information for attributions, judgements, beliefs, expectations, desires, intentions, and other social cognitive constructs. Therefore, the study of *social* cognition and emotion in applied settings such as sport is necessary, given the clearly complementary nature of these constructs, in order to explain the complex set of behavioural responses observed in intense emotive sport situations, such as 'choking'.

Defining affect, emotion, anxiety, arousal, and mood

Before embarking on a discussion of the role of emotions in social psychological research applied to sport performance, a prerequisite step is to define emotion and emotion-related terms such as affect, emotion, arousal, mood, and anxiety. These terms are often used in a non-systematic manner and interchangeably making the interpretation and the exact nature of the explanations offered by social psychological approaches of the role of affect-related constructs in sports performance difficult. That stated, full agreement among researchers in social cognition and emotion as to the distinction between affect, emotion, and emotion-related terms is lacking and researchers state that formal working definitions of these terms may be unclear due to substantial overlaps between the concepts (Smith *et al.* 1993). Therefore, any definitions of affect-related concepts must indicate the boundaries, limitations, and potential confounds.

Affect is a general or 'umbrella' term that encompasses all 'mental feeling processes' (Bagozzi *et al.* 2002: 37), and therefore can account for the 'felt' aspects of emotion as well as the directive and motivational aspects, such as the case of affective attitudes. A number of authors have suggested that affect reflects 'valenced feeling states', a term that implies both directionality and a number of specific emotion-related terms such as emotion and **mood**. Therefore, emotion and mood can be considered as specific types of affective states with anger, anxiety, guilt, and shame being specific examples of these emotion types.

Formal definitions of emotion usually incorporate not only feeling states, but also make reference to a 'mental state or readiness' arising from cognitive interpretation of psychological and physiological states such as heightened arousal (Smith *et al.* 1993). Furthermore, emotions are considered to have direction towards a given object, person, or behaviour, much like attitudes, particularly according to appraisal theorists (Smith *et al.* 1993). In addition, emotion can also be described as having a behavioural or response function in that it affects behaviour, such as facial expression of emotion and cognitive and behavioural means to cope with the emotion (Bagozzi *et al.* 2002). Emotions therefore have 'action tendencies'. A vast array of emotions have been identified in the social psychology literature, but ethological and cross-cultural psychology research has identified six basic or core emotions: anger, fear, sadness, happiness, surprise, and disgust (Ekman 1992). However, as we shall see later, although not considered a core emotion, anxiety is recognized as an important emotion in sport.

Mood is, by convention, considered different from emotion as it usually comprises a profile of different affective states, is less intense, more prolonged, and with no action tendency. Mood is therefore less transient than emotion and does not usually arise from the appraisal of specific events. However, the boundary is sometimes less clear and both mood and specific emotions have been implicated in sports performance. Indeed, some theorists claim that temporal stability as a defining property of mood with respect to emotion is not valid given moods and emotions can be both transient and prolonged (Frijda 1994). Despite this lack of a clear distinction, mood is generally considered by emotion theorists as different from emotion in its reduced ability to produce an action tendency, its lower intensity, and its prolonged rather than transient nature.

Defining anxiety and arousal

More than any other single emotion, anxiety has been the focus of the vast majority of research on emotion and social cognition in sports performance (Gould *et al.* 2002). Anxiety is a specific emotion that has been described as an unpleasant feeling of apprehension and distress, and is usually accompanied by unpleasant physiological responses (Martens *et al.* 1990). Sensations such as 'sweaty palms' (also known as 'galvanic skin response') and 'butterflies in the stomach' (this may be the result of the shunting of blood from the stomach due to the effect of catecholamines) are common physiological or 'somatic' symptoms of anxiety. Anxious athletes report these symptoms as well as thoughts of negative performance expectations, a fear of failure, and inability to concentrate (Jones and Hardy 1990). Modern theorists make the distinction between state and trait anxiety. It follows that anxiety can be both a tendency to respond with anxious symptoms in situations evaluated as being competitive (trait-like) and a psychological state determined by environmental factors such as competition and audience presence, as well as intrapersonal variables such as the appraisal of the event as being important (state-like). In either case, appraisal and cognitive-motivational-relational theories of emotion propose that anxiety is a specific emotion with a specific pathology and characterizing features.

Theorists also make the distinction between anxiety and **arousal**. Anxiety is classed as having a somatic component (symptoms experienced physically e.g. 'sweaty palms', 'butterflies in stomach') and a cognitive component (symptoms felt psychologically e.g. 'worry', 'inability to concentrate') (Martens *et al.* 1990). Somatic anxiety is concurrent with some forms of physiological arousal caused by changes in the sympathetic nervous system, and cognitive anxiety is linked to the somatic form through the interpretive system that gives rise to that heightened state of arousal. Of course, arousal itself is not anxiety, but it is implicated in the anxiety process (Bagozzi *et al.* 2002). Somatic anxiety, for example, is not physiological arousal but a person's *awareness* of the symptoms of arousal. Arousal is often considered a heightened state of activation in a person's physiological and psychological state. It is defined as a unidimensional, 'motivational construct' (Landers 1980) and can be considered to operate on a continuum from *very deep sleep* to *extreme excitement*. Arousal is manifested physiologically through changes in the autonomic nervous system and hormones in the bloodstream that give rise to elevated heart rate, blood pressure, perspiration rate, and muscle tension. A state of anxiety is often accompanied by increased arousal, and, according to appraisal and cognitive-motivational-relational theories of emotion, it is the interpretation of the arousal that gives rise to specific emotions. Importantly, arousal is an intrapersonal variable that is likely to give rise to anxiety, but not all aroused individuals become anxious, and the pathology of the arousal is such that it may be a necessary but not sufficient condition for an anxiety response. Arousal may therefore not always be accompanied by an anxiety response, and early psychophysiology research showed that the interpretation of the arousal could give rise to different interpretations of the accompanying emotions (e.g. Schacter and Singer 1962). Recent appraisal theorists believe that arousal is implicated in emotional responses such as anxiety, but there are specific patterns of emotional responses according to the way in which the arousing situation is appraised.

Trait versus state distinction

Early research with measures of anxiety considered only the trait aspect of anxiety. Anxiety was viewed as a stable facet of personality and therefore considered trait-like in nature. In this view, anxiety was not directly like personality in the strictest sense because anxiety tendencies were considered to have both an innate and learnt component. Early researchers such as Sarason *et al.* (1960) produced scales that tapped anxiety as a general disposition that determined anxiety responses in a variety of situations. It was thought that individuals would exhibit characteristic behavioural patterns according to their levels of trait anxiety (see Frijda 1994).

However, Spielberger, Gorusch, and Lushene (1970) noted that the explanations provided by the conceptualization of anxiety as a trait did not yield particularly satisfactory results. Spielberger *et al.* contended that anxiety should have both state-like and trait-like properties. State anxiety was defined as feelings of apprehensiveness and tension that were usually paired with arousal of the autonomic nervous system (Spielberger *et al.* 1970). It was contended that while trait anxiety may explain some variance in anxiety states in given situations, it could not explain all the variance in the state level of anxiety because such states were determined by more proximal situational factors and the individual's interpretation of them. It is clear that such a premise is a precursor of appraisal theories in cognition and emotion. Trait anxiety therefore served as an indicator of an individual's tendency to interpret ambiguous situations as threatening (Frijda 1994). State anxiety, on the other hand, is the actual level of anxiety in a given situation, all dispositional and situational factors considered. Spielberger *et al.* subsequently developed an inventory to measure both components; the State–Trait Anxiety Inventory (STAI). Subsequent tests of anxiety appeared in the sport psychology literature measuring both the trait (Sport Competition Anxiety Test; SCAT) and state components of anxiety for competitive sport (Competitive State Anxiety Inventory; CSAI) (Martens *et al.* 1990). The CSAI is particularly interesting and important in this regard because it distinguishes between the somatic and cognitive components of anxiety but also introduces a third element, *self-confidence* to account for the 'positive' aspects of anxiety extracted in factor analytic studies of emotion-related scales in sports performance. A more in-depth review of the CSAI and its revisions is provided later in this chapter.

Applying social psychology research on anxiety to sport

The academic study of anxiety in sport has undergone a series of evolutions since Martens *et al.* (1990) introduced the first formal means of measuring the construct. This evolution has mirrored the development of emotion research in the general social and personality psychology literature. Theories of anxiety in competitive sport were founded in early research in personality psychology (Gould *et al.* 2002) and considered anxiety as a trait, or at least a trait-like construct. However, such generalized theories had limited explanatory power in predicting behaviour, a limitation attributed to the fact that such inventories were too far removed in their generality to have any bearing on action and performance in specific situations. Spielberger and colleagues pioneered the hypothesis that anxiety should be segregated into trait and state forms and developed the SCAI for this purpose, and modern sport psychologists adhere to this model of anxiety.

The state–trait distinction in anxiety research in sport psychology was mirrored in the development of inventories to measure both components. Martens developed the SCAT to measure trait anxiety which was defined as a tendency to interpret competitive situations as threatening with concomitant feelings of apprehension and tension (Martens *et al.* 1990). As a result of Spielberger et al.'s distinction between state and trait anxiety, Martens *et al.* developed the CSAI, and state anxiety was defined as an immediate, transient feeling of tension and apprehension in a specific competitive sport situation. The CSAI adopted the approach set out by Spielberger *et al.* and used many items from the original STAI, but adopted items that had relevance to competitive situations. Extensive development and validity research supported the validity and reliability of the CSAI as a unidimensional measure of competitive state anxiety. However, psychophysiological research and trends in test anxiety indicated that in competitive situations a distinction should be made between the felt or experienced symptoms of an anxious state or *somatic* anxiety, often associated with heightened arousal interpreted as an anxiety response, and the psychological disruption, tension, and worry termed *cognitive* anxiety. In addition, seminal work by Burton (1988) suggested that for a comprehensive evaluation of the anxiety–performance relationship, researchers needed to adopt a multidimensional model incorporating the cognitive-somatic distinction.

This compelled Martens and co-workers (1990) to develop a state anxiety inventory that explicitly made this distinction. The CSAI-2 was therefore proposed and researchers adopted a rigorous classical test theory approach to the development of the inventory content. Martens *et al.* also aimed to tap other components specific to sports-related distress such as physical harm and generalized anxiety. Exploratory factor analyses of the initial pool of items extracted three factors. One factor clearly contained items reflecting the *somatic* component of anxiety (e.g. 'my body feels tense', 'I feel jittery'). However, the items purportedly measuring *cognitive* anxiety loaded on two different factors. The content of the items loading on the first of these factors reflected negative aspects of the cognitive anxiety pool of items (e.g. 'I am concerned about performing poorly', 'I am concerned about choking under pressure') while the item content of the remaining factor reflected positively worded items from the cognitive anxiety item pool (e.g. 'I feel self-confident', 'I am confident of coming through under pressure'). These factors were labelled *cognitive anxiety* and *self-confidence*, respectively. The structure and content of the resulting 27-item inventory representing Burton (1988) and Martens et al.'s (1990) multidimensional model of anxiety have received much attention in the literature (Burton 1998; Gould *et al.* 2002; Craft *et al.* 2003). However, while in the initial validity studies the use of the CSAI-2 supported its construct and factorial validity, discriminant validity, test–retest reliability, internal consistency, and predictive validity in terms of levels of the cognitive and somatic components prior to competition (Martens *et al.* 1990), recent research has questioned some of these initial analyses.

The CSAI-2 has been further developed using confirmatory factor analysis that has a number of advantages over the exploratory model used in the initial development of the inventory (Cox *et al.* 2003). These analyses have revealed that the inventory had a problematic structure that was mainly attributed to the inclusion of items that displayed high residual variance, that is, items that were not adequately representative of their hypothesized latent factor. Cox systematically eliminated 10 items from the original inventory to produce a more parsimonious 17-item revised CSAI-2 that exhibited good fit with multiple samples in subsequent confirmatory factor analyses (Cox *et al.* 2003).

In addition to questions surrounding the construct validity of the CSAI-2, studies have also indicated that the relationships between its components are highly variable. The correlations between somatic and cognitive anxiety components and self-confidence usually reflect a theoretically predictable pattern with negative relations between self-confidence and the two anxiety components and positive relationships observed between the two anxiety components. Schwenkmezger and Steffgen (1989) meta-analysed a series of studies examining these interrelations and suggested that the corrected correlations were in the predicted direction and were significantly different from zero. However, more recent meta-analytic studies on the CSAI-2 have indicated that the relationships between the components of anxiety are significant, relatively strong, and in the predicted direction (Craft *et al.* 2003). These results lend support to the notion that the multiple components of competitive anxiety exhibit discriminant validity. In summary, despite problems with the factor structure that have been resolved through the modification of the inventory by confirmatory factor analysis, the CSAI-2 appears to have adequate conceptual and measurement properties. The next section will review the efficacy of research examining the anxiety-sport performance relationship.

Anxiety and the prediction of sport performance

Anxiety–performance hypothesis

One of the key criteria for the validation of the CSAI-2 and an important hypothesis of multidimensional anxiety theory is the anxiety–performance hypothesis. Martens *et al.* (1990) and Burton (1998) suggested that as competition approached, the three components of anxiety would exhibit a characteristic pattern in terms of level and influence on performance. It was proposed that self-confidence ratings would increase prior to competition and then be subject to changes within competition. It was hypothesized that somatic anxiety levels would be relatively low until shortly before competition, would rapidly increase immediately prior to competition, and then rapidly decrease thereafter. It was expected that cognitive anxiety would be at an elevated state prior to competition and decrease at the onset of competition, but be subject to changes during competition, particularly for open skills. Research has generally supported the predicted temporal fluctuations in anxiety levels prior to performance and has shown the detrimental effects of these levels of anxiety on sport-related cognitive and motor tasks as competition approaches (Martens *et al.* 1990). In addition, research has suggested that self-confidence ratings tend to remain stable leading up to competition, but tend to decrease just prior to and during competition (Martens *et al.* 1990).

Martens *et al.* also expected the strength of relationships between the different components of somatic, cognitive, and self-confidence and performance to vary prior to competition. They report a study examining relationships between sport performance and cognitive and somatic anxiety in elite golfers in non-competition (1–2 days before competition), pre-competition (1 hour before), and mid-competition (after first 9 holes) indicated that non-competition and pre-competition cognitive and somatic anxiety levels did not determine initial performance (first 9 holes) but significantly predicted later performance (last 9 holes). Mid-competition scores for both cognitive and somatic anxiety did predict later performance. This provides some empirical support that pre-competition state anxiety only interferes with subsequent performance, which is contrary to anecdotal observations that elevated anxiety just prior to an event may hinder immediate performance. Furthermore, findings from this study did not support the differential effects of cognitive and somatic anxiety on performance, the effects were similar for both anxiety components. However, subsequent follow-up studies showed stronger negative relationships between cognitive anxiety and sport performance for competitive swimmers and a positive relationship between self-confidence and performance and a curvilinear relationship with somatic anxiety (Burton 1988). These results have been supported in other studies, although the temporal patterning of the correlations has not received consistent support, as indicated by Martens *et al.* (1990).

Meta-analysis of the anxiety–performance relationship

A large number of studies have examined the anxiety–performance relationship, and the vast majority have adopted the CSAI-2 to measure anxiety (Burton 1998) and the multidimensional model of anxiety (Burton 1988; Martens *et al.* 1990). Initial results from the validation studies were promising, acknowledging the influence of cognitive anxiety on performance was negative, the impact of self-confidence on performance was positive, and that somatic anxiety exhibited a curvilinear relationship on performance (Burton 1988). Interestingly, the role of task complexity and duration on the somatic anxiety–performance relationship did not yield consistent results. In addition, results of subsequent studies have yielded inconsistent findings for the anxiety–performance relationship for the three components of anxiety.

In an attempt to resolve these inconclusive findings, Craft *et al.* (2003) conducted a meta-analysis of 29 studies examining relationships between the multiple components of the CSAI-2 and sport performance. The authors reported strong and significant intercorrelations among the somatic, cognitive, and self-confidence anxiety subcomponents supporting their discriminant validity. Using the attenuation-corrected correlations in a multivariate regression of the dependent variable of performance on the three anxiety components permitted the authors to evaluate the unique effect of each component on sport performance across all of the studies. Significant attenuation-corrected beta-weights (β_c) were observed between performance and cognitive anxiety ($\beta_c = 0.13$, $p < 0.05$), somatic anxiety ($\beta_c = 0.09$, $p < 0.05$), and self-confidence ($\beta_c = 0.36$, $p < 0.05$). However, homogeneity tests for these corrected correlations indicated that the relationships were heterogeneous in all cases, indicating a significant proportion of the error variance in the relationships remained unexplained after correcting for sampling error. This indicated that these relationships were affected by moderator variables.

Craft *et al.* also examined the impact of several moderator variables: type of sport (team/individual), skill type (open/closed), type of athlete (elite/European/college athlete/college PE student), and time of CSAI-2 administration (< 15 mins/16–30 min/31–59 min/1–4 hours prior to performance). It was hypothesized that individual sports performers would report higher levels of anxiety (Beedie *et al.* 2000), that performance-based open skills such as team sports would be affected more by anxiety levels due to greater interaction with other competitors and a changing environment than closed skills like golf or rowing (Terry and Youngs 1996), that elite level athletes may experience stronger effects of anxiety on sport performance even though they may be more accustomed to it than recreational athletes (Kliene 1990), and that anxiety would be a better predictor of sport performance the closer to competition it was measured (Martens *et al.* 1990). Results revealed significant attenuation-corrected beta-weights for all anxiety components on performance level for studies on athletes in individual sports and for open skilled sports. These findings support a previous theory that a continuously changing environment and interactions with others perhaps place more demands on the performer and therefore increase performance-related anxiety responses. Although, analogously, individual sports performers seem to demonstrate a greater anxiety–performance relationship, particularly for self-confidence, this is probably because there are no teammates to moderate levels of anxiety and pressure is greater when competing alone.

Anxiety levels and self-confidence ratings in elite level athletes, particularly European club-level athletes, had the strongest impact on performance than any other athlete group. Interestingly, at this level, cognitive anxiety and somatic anxiety had a positive effect on performance, which has implications for the facilitative anxiety model that will be reviewed later (see Jones *et al.* 1994). Paradoxically, the anxiety levels from the CSAI-2 seemed to have the strongest influence at an intermediate time-point prior to competition (31–59 min) compared with longer and much shorter time intervals. The authors suggested that proximal levels of anxiety have a time lag before they have an impact on performance, possibly because self-reported anxiety levels are unrealistic or inaccurately reported, while distal measures of anxiety are not as relevant because the competition is a long way off. In summary, the meta-analysis suggests that although cognitive and somatic anxiety are related to sports performance, and moderated by type of sport, type of skill, athlete level, and time prior to competition, they have only weak influences on performance. Self-confidence levels have a stronger impact on performance and are much more consistently related to performance than the other anxiety components. These results therefore point to the importance of the self-confidence variable, corroborate a cognitive approach to the study of anxiety, and suggest that means to promote more positive cognitive-affective states would be most efficacious in improving sport performance.

The inverted-U hypothesis

From the outset it was stated that arousal is not an equivalent term for anxiety. Indeed, some cognitive theories of emotion suggest that physiological changes such as arousal are unnecessary for the expression of emotion and such arousal states are artefacts of that felt emotion (Smith *et al.* 1993). However, psychophysiological theories and studies have implicated arousal in the expression of emotions such as anxiety (e.g. Schacter and Singer 1962). The multidimensional model of anxiety explicitly states that the symptoms of arousal are separate from the cognitive component of the anxiety construct, and called somatic anxiety. Therefore these theories imply that physiological arousal is expected to accompany the performance situations that give rise to competitive anxiety in an individual. The role of arousal in anxiety-evoking competitive situations cannot be denied and an evaluation of the role of arousal is essential to the understanding of the anxiety process in competitive sport situations.

Early theories of arousal in sport drew on Yerkes and Dodson's (1908) proposed simple linear relationship between arousal and performance. This was derived from experiments with mice that Yerkes and Dodson observed were superior at negotiating complex mazes when more physiologically aroused. They hypothesized that the heightened state of physiological arousal triggered an increased intensity to satisfy innate physiological needs such as thirst and hunger, hence it was termed 'drive' theory. In competitive sport, it was hypothesized that heightened physiological arousal would increase psychological and physical preparedness for competition, and the theory suggested that the higher the arousal, the better the preparedness and hence the better the performance (see Figure 6.1, broken line). However, observations that very low or very high levels of arousal resulted in inferior performance of fine motor skills and complex cognitive tasks when compared to intermediate arousal levels in competitive sport led to several researchers proposing that an optimal level of arousal was the most effective for performance (Oxendine 1970; Landers 1980). This relationship was referred to as optimal arousal theory or the **inverted-U hypothesis**, named because of the shape of the curve representing the relationship on arousal–performance axes (see Figure 6.1, solid lines). Indeed, Oxendine (1970) suggested that for sports involving gross motor activities and large muscle groups (e.g. boxing, athletics, weightlifting), a high level of arousal was considered necessary for optimal performance. However, in sports where very fine motor skills were prevalent (e.g. golf, snooker, darts), a much lower level of arousal was deemed vital for optimal performance, such that a level of arousal that may be associated with optimal performance for a 100m sprinter would be debilitative to performance for a table pool player. Thus different inverted-U relationships would exist for performers of different sports, dependent on the demand characteristics of the sport in terms of the gross or fine nature of the movements (see Figure 6.1, solid lines for sprinter and table pool player).

While the inverted-U hypothesis is attractive because of its neat and clear set of predictions, it has been criticized because of its over-simplification of the role of arousal and the nature of skills within a variety of different sports (Jones 1990). Indeed, Landers (1980) suggested that optimal arousal theory did not account for the complex blend of fine and gross motor skills that combine most sports. For example, soccer comprises gross movements in terms of multiple sprints and sustained running required for movement about the pitch, as well as fine skills involved in ball control, dribbling, and turning. Sports such as this are therefore difficult to classify on a bipolar continuum of motor skills ranging from gross to fine. Further criticisms of the optimal arousal theory were levelled at the purely descriptive relationship between performance and anxiety that did not offer an explanation as to *why* performance is sub-optimal at lower and higher levels of arousal. Multidimensional anxiety theory has attempted to provide a better explanation of the relationships between anxiety and arousal by incorporating somatic anxiety as a measure of the 'felt' symptoms of heightened arousal (Burton 1988). In addition, the shape of the curve in the arousal–performance relationship was criticized as being

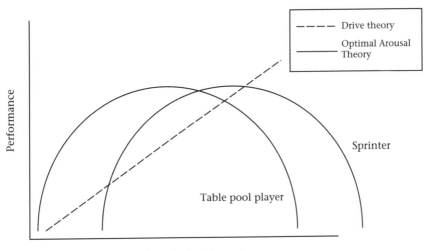

Figure 6.1   Optimal arousal and drive theories

inadequate and a more complex relationship has been proposed by Hardy and co-workers (Hardy 1990; Hardy and Parfitt 1991) (see catastrophe theory, this chapter). In summary, while arousal has been implicated in emotional responses such as anxiety in competitive situations, and optimal arousal theory provided an early theoretical basis for the arousal–performance relationship, limitations of these theories have demanded the development of more sophisticated explanations of the arousal–performance relationship embedded in cognitive theories of anxiety.

Antecedents of anxiety in sport: theoretical approaches

Thus far the focus of this chapter has been on examining the role of anxiety on sport performance. However, just as anxiety is an antecedent of sports performance, social psychological theories have identified a number of constructs that give rise to elevated anxiety in competitive situations. Such antecedents are particularly relevant for targeting key variables for intervention. For example, if the reduction of cognitive anxiety will result in a concomitant increase in performance as the hypotheses of multidimensional anxiety theory predict, then the psychological variables that reduce cognitive anxiety would be useful targets for intervention. In this respect such psychological constructs would have an indirect effect on sports performance mediated by anxiety (see Figure 6.2). Therefore, distal, trait-like constructs (such as competitive trait anxiety, or goal orientations) would determine more proximal, state-like

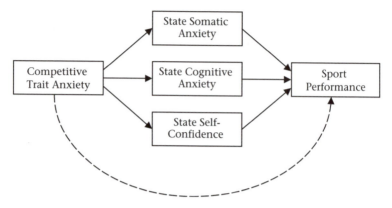

Figure 6.2   Mediational model of hierarchical anxiety and performance

anxiety constructs, which would predict sport performance, as proposed by authors of mediational models in the social psychology literature.

Trait anxiety

As mentioned previously, one of the means cited by Martens *et al.* (1990) in multidimensional anxiety theory to account for baseline or 'typical' anxiety in athletes would be to control for trait anxiety. Partialling out trait anxiety would serve to control (statistically set all individuals in an interindividual test of the anxiety–performance relationship to the same level of trait anxiety) the effect of a general tendency to be anxious in competitive situations and permit the examination of the unique effects of situated, state anxiety on performance. It is therefore of interest to researchers concerned with predicting performance whether trait anxiety explains variance in state anxiety, and more importantly if trait anxiety accounts for variance in sports performance and whether the trait anxiety–performance relationship is accounted for by state anxiety. This would give rise to a top-down, hierarchical model of anxiety from a generalized, global construct to more specific situational judgements in keeping with other hierarchical social cognitive models of behaviour (e.g. Vallerand 1997), as shown in Figure 6.2.

Research has indicated significant relationships between trait anxiety and the components from the CSAI-2 (Gould *et al.* 1984; Yan Lan and Gill 1984; Crocker *et al.* 1988). In terms of the specific components, differential predictions of cognitive and somatic anxiety are inconclusive with some researchers finding strong correlations for trait anxiety with both cognitive and somatic components (Gould *et al.* 1984), and some with either cognitive (Crocker *et al.* 1988) or somatic (Yan Lan and Gill 1984) components alone. In addition, trait measures of self-confidence have predicted state measures of self-confidence (Vealey 1986). However, few studies have controlled for trait levels of anxiety when predicting sport performance from state anxiety levels, and this remains a useful avenue for further research.

Goals and motivational orientations

Social cognitive theories of intention and behaviour in sport have recognized the importance of social cognitive variables as antecedents of competitive anxiety. Swain and Jones (1992) and Hall and Kerr (1998) adopted approaches from competitive orientations and goal orientations pioneered by Gill and co-workers (Gill and Deeter 1988) and Duda and Nicholls (1992, see Chapter 5) respectively to explain the interpersonal antecedents of competitive state anxiety. Swain and Jones (1992) measured the different competitive orientations and related them to the three components of competitive anxiety from the CSAI-2. The Sport Orientation Questionnaire (Gill and Deeter 1988) was used to measure track and field athletes' levels of competitive and win orientation. It was expected that a win orientation and competitiveness would be most strongly related to anxiety levels. Results showed that competitiveness was strongly related to all three components of anxiety, but a win orientation was not. Importantly, the relationships between competitiveness and the somatic and cognitive components were negative, suggesting that athletes who perceived themselves to be least competitive exhibited the greatest levels of anxiety. Athletes who viewed themselves as being more competitive were more self-confident and therefore more able to handle competitive situations, as indicated by the positive correlation between competitiveness and self-confidence.

These findings have been bolstered by significant correlations between goal orientation and competitive state anxiety, although relationships have been inconsistent. For example, Duda et al. (1995) found that an ego orientation determined the degree of cognitive anxiety in athletes across a number of competitive sport contexts, while Ommundsen and Pedersen (1999) found no relationship between ego orientation and cognitive anxiety. Instead they found that a task orientation and perceived competence significantly and negatively predicted cognitive anxiety, and perceived competence negatively predicted somatic anxiety. Finally, Newton and Duda (1995) found that expectations of performance outcome were the best predictors of cognitive anxiety and self-confidence, rather than goal orientations. These results suggest that the role of goal orientations may be inconsistent and that performance expectations in the form of perceived ability and competence better account for variance in competitive anxiety levels.

The adoption of cognitive-motivational-relational theories of motivation has provided more comprehensive mediational models of the appraisal and coping processes implicated in the role of social cognitive variables such as goal orientations on anxiety and emotion. Gaudreau, Blondin, and Lapierre (2002) examined the role of coping potential in accounting for the relationship between goal orientations and negative affect (including anxiety) in sport performers two hours prior, one hour after, and 24 hours after competition. Results indicated that the discrepancy between task and ego goal orientations, a relative measure of how personal or performance-related an individual's goal orientation is, was significantly related to positive and negative affect. Importantly, active coping strategies like planning mediated the goal orientation discrepancy–positive affect relationship, while behavioural disengagement mediated the relationship between goal orientation discrepancy and negative affect. This suggests that adaptive coping strategies tend to account for cognitive appraisals of the situation as relevant to personal goals and positive affective responses, and passive coping strategies account for the negative relationship between goal orientation and negative affect. This suggests that active coping strategies, like planning, have an adaptive function (Gaudreau *et al.* 2002).

Goal orientations, motivational climate, and anxiety

Given the evidence that motivational orientations are predictive of competitive state anxiety, researchers have also examined the characteristics of the perceived competitive environment or motivational climate in giving rise to anxiety responses. Since there is research to support the influence of motivational climate on goal orientations and motivational states (Duda 1993; Seifriz *et al.* 1992, see Chapter 5), it has been hypothesized that goal orientations may mediate the effect of perceived motivational climate on anxiety states in sport performers. Ntoumanis and Biddle (1998) supported this hypothesis and illustrated no direct effects of motivational climate on the components of state anxiety in team-sport athletes. Instead, the positive effects of a perceived performance- or ego-oriented motivational climate on cognitive and somatic anxiety were exerted through ego orientation and self-confidence. Again the role of self-confidence is pervasive in the effect of achievement goal orientations on anxiety.

In a further test of this hypothesis, White (1998) examined the role of achievement goal orientations and perceived parent-initiated motivational climate on competitive trait anxiety in adolescent athletes. Results indicated that athletes who scored low on task orientation and high on ego orientation viewed the motivational climate endorsed by their parents as one that fostered low effort-contingent success and worry over making mistakes. This group exhibited the highest competitive trait anxiety, indicating that athletes with low-task, high-ego motivational orientations viewed the climate engendered by their parents as performance-focused and were more likely to interpret competitive situations as anxiety-provoking. Future directions of research will examine the causal nature of these relationships and establish whether a performance-involved motivational climate induces a motivational orientation that is low-task and leads to a tendency to be more highly anxious in competition.

In terms of interventions, a recent study by Yoo (2003) introduced an intervention to change goal orientations and competitive anxiety levels in adolescents attending tennis classes. Participants were assigned to a class that had a pervading task-involving or performance- or ego-involving motivational climate for six weeks. Performance levels significantly increased and cognitive and somatic anxiety levels were significantly decreased for participants acting in a task-involved motivational climate while anxiety did not change and performance significantly decreased in participants receiving an ego-involving motivational climate. These preliminary results support relations between perceived motivational climate, achievement goal orientations, and levels of anxiety in athletes and suggest that interventions can attenuate anxiety levels if a mastery climate is engendered.

Recent theories of anxiety in sport

Intensity versus direction distinction

The previous section discussed the social cognitive antecedents of the sub-components of anxiety, with a focus on climates and interventions that would reduce the effects of the cognitive and somatic constructs. This assumes that anxiety, particularly the cognitive component, has a detrimental or *debilitative* effect on performance, and focuses solely on the level or intensity of athletes' anxiety response. However, a recent branch of research has examined the potential of heightened cognitive and somatic anxiety to have a positive or *facilitative* effect on performance. Jones and co-workers (Jones et al.1993; Jones *et al.* 1994; Jones and Swain 1995) hypothesized that it is not the intensity of the athlete's anxiety response *per se* that has a debilitative effect on perform-ance, rather, it is the interpretation or direction of the anxiety response that will determine its impact. They proposed that the appraisal of the competitive situation as threatening as well as a secondary appraisal of coping ability, or control over resources to cope with the threatening situation, would deter-mine whether the anxiety response would be interpreted as facilitative or debilitative.

Research support for the debilitative-facilitative conceptualization of anx-iety has focused first of all on whether the directional component of anxiety predicted performance and, second, whether control-related constructs would moderate the directional component of the anxiety response. If the theory is correct and in keeping with cognitive-motivational-relational theories of motivation, then sports performers with high control and self-efficacy would interpret anxiety as facilitative and demonstrate stronger relationships between directional anxiety scores and sport performance. Jones *et al.* (Jones et al. 1993, 1994; Jones and Swain 1995) developed a measure of competitive state anxiety direction that was administered concurrently with the CSAI-2 which has become known as the Directional Modification of the Competitive State Anxiety Inventory-2 (DM-CSAI-2, Burton 1998). The measure asks respondents to label or interpret the anxiety symptoms on the CSAI-2 as facilitative or debilitative, and research has shown that the intensity and directional components for cognitive and somatic anxiety exhibit discriminant and predictive validity (Jones et al. 1993; Jones et al. 1996). Jones, Swain, and Harwood (1996) found that sports performers who reported high positive affect interpreted their anxiety as more facilitative, but a concomitant pattern was not found for negative affect and debilitative anxiety. Mellalieu, Hanton, and Jones (2003) found that athletes with a facilitative interpretation of their anxiety or 'facilitators' labelled their pre-competitive affective states as positive compared with 'debilitators' who interpreted their pre-competitive affective experiences as negative.

Research examining the influence of anxiety direction on performance has typically split groups of athletes into high and low anxiety on the direction subscales. These studies have consistently indicated that the intensity of the anxiety response for both the cognitive and somatic anxiety subscales is consistent in performers regardless of their direction, highlighting the importance of accounting for direction scores. Importantly, direction scores are strongly correlated with performance, such that better performers report their anxiety as more facilitative. For example, Jones et al. (1993) demonstrated that gymnasts reporting 'good' performances on a balance beam trial reported their anxiety to be facilitative while poorer performers reported their anxiety to be debilitative. In addition, research has shown that a direct linear relationship exists between cognitive anxiety direction scores and performance in basketballers, while the intensity components cognitive anxiety and self-confidence reflected an inverted-U relationship (Swain and Harwood 1996). This indicates that interventions to positively affect sport performers' anxiety direction scores are likely to have a concomitant positive effect on performance. Thus, the first premise of the theory, that performers reporting high facilitative anxiety will influence performance, has been supported and has shown discriminant and predictive validity in sports with gross and fine motor skills.

Subsequent research has also focused on the effects of competence-related variables such as ability, goal attainment, and self-confidence on the relationship between the directional component of anxiety and performance. For example, elite swimmers and cricketers were found to interpret their anxiety as more facilitative than their non-elite counterparts, even though the intensity levels of anxiety did not differ across the groups (Jones et al. 1994). In addition, Jones and Hanton (1996) found that swimmers with positive expectancies of goal attainment reported higher levels of facilitative anxiety than swimmers with vague or low expectancies of goal attainment. Self-confidence, another competence-related variable, has been shown to be higher in athletes with a facilitative interpretation of their anxiety (Jones et al. 1993, 1994; Edwards and Hardy 1996). One possibility is that the self-confidence component may be the mechanism by which facilitative anxiety direction scores predict performance and there may be an interaction effect. Future research will further examine the interaction between self-confidence and performance. Such a study may test the hypothesis, based on previous findings, that a sports performer reporting a facilitative anxiety interpretation and high self-confidence anxiety pattern would exhibit the most optimal level of performance.

The question of how to promote a facilitative interpretation of anxiety symptoms has been the subject of recent research. Researchers have attempted to identify the strategies adopted by athletes with an adaptive anxiety direction profile and designed interventions based on these findings (Hanton and Jones 1999a, 1999b). Hanton and Jones (1999a) followed up their empirical work supporting the effect of facilitative interpretations of cognitive and somatic anxiety in sports performers by qualitatively analysing interviews with elite swimmers who consistently reported facilitative anxiety interpretations. Results of a content analysis of the transcripts revealed that the elite swimmers had acquired a number of key strategies, either intuitively or through formal psychological skills training, that were implicated in their facilitative interpretation of anxiety symptoms including goal setting, imagery, and self-talk. Based on this research, Hanton and Jones (1999b) developed an intervention strategy to engender a more facilitative interpretation of anxiety in elite swimmers that consistently reported debilitative interpretations prior to competition. Using an idiographic, single-participant approach across a series of 10 competitions, three of the four swimmers involved in the intervention reported facilitative interpretations, and this change was still evident in a post-intervention follow-up. These results support the use of cognitive interventions to change the interpretation of the anxiety response, and are congruent with problem-focused and emotion-focused coping strategies from cognitive-motivational-relational theories of emotion.

In summary, Jones' (1995) control model of anxiety has advanced research on the anxiety-performance relationship and has illustrated that the effects of anxiety on performance may not be one of mere negative affect on performance. However, the theory has been criticized by a number of researchers. Some have questioned the validity of the DM-CSAI-2, suggesting that the directional measures have not received much formal validation in a manner commensurate with the rigorous development of the CSAI-2 (Burton 1998). Researchers have also questioned the concept of the directional measure, that it may, instead be a measure of positive affect or 'excitement' that has been noted by Jones (1995). Research is needed to further validate the directional component, particularly with respect to measures of positive affect. Furthermore, given that the directional component of anxiety in the DM-CSAI-2 is measured alongside measures of state and trait anxiety, some researchers believe that the directional scale should interact with the intensity scale given the large inter-individual variation of intensity scores (Burton 1998). In this way, the directional component would moderate the effect of the intensity component on performance, although this hypothesis has not been supported by empirical evidence (Edwards and Hardy 1996).

Catastrophe theory

One additional limitation that has been levelled at Jones' (1995) control theory of facilitative-debilitative anxiety is that it does not explicitly account for the level of arousal experienced by an individual. Indeed, Edwards and Hardy (1996) have noted that anxiety intensity can have a facilitative effect on performance when levels of physiological arousal are low and debilitative effects when physiological arousal levels are high. These findings suggest a more complex pattern of relationships between anxiety intensity, direction, and performance, and imply that physiological arousal needs to be implicated in any complete model of the anxiety process in sport performance. Following Zeeman's (1976) adoption of catastrophe models that aimed to explain the discontinuous relationships evident in normally linear or continuous functions, Hardy (1990) adopted the most common of the 'catastrophe' models – the 'cusp' catastrophe – to model discontinuities in performance due to the influence of physiological arousal and cognitive anxiety (Figure 6.3), i.e. **catastrophe theory.**

The essential premise of the 'cusp' catastrophe model of anxiety and sport performance is that at low levels of cognitive anxiety, the relationship between physiological arousal and performance will follow an inverted-U relationship – the continuous predictable relationship proposed by optimal arousal theory. Conversely, at high levels of cognitive anxiety, the performance–

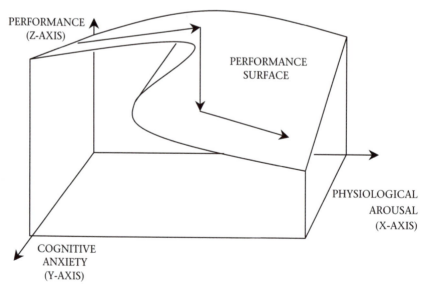

Figure 6.3 Hardy's (1990) catastrophe theory
Source: Jones and Hardy (1990: 88)

physiological arousal relationship will increase in keeping with the inverted-U relationship until optimal arousal is reached. However, an increase in physiological arousal above the optimal point will result in a steep, 'catastrophic' drop in performance. The model is best illustrated using a set of three-dimensional Cartesian co-ordinates (see Figure 6.3). In Figure 6.3, physiological arousal, cognitive anxiety, and performance levels are expressed by the x, y, and z axes, respectively. At low levels of cognitive anxiety, the arousal–performance relationship follows a flattened inverted-U relationship, as reflected by the far face of the graph. However, if cognitive anxiety is elevated and arousal is increased performance will only follow the inverted-U relationship until optimal arousal is reached, and this is illustrated by the arrowed line on the upper part of the performance surface. The 'fold' in the performance surface illustrates the catastrophic decline in performance once optimal arousal is exceeded under conditions of high cognitive anxiety. The catastrophe theory is unique in that it is the only model that explicitly states that cognitive anxiety and physiological arousal interact in their effect on performance. Moreover, the hypotheses from other theories, such as Jones' control model of anxiety can be incorporated in the model. For example, cognitive anxiety does not always have a debilitative effect on performance, but can actually facilitate performance at optimal levels of arousal, such that under high levels of cognitive anxiety, performance will be substantially better than low levels of cognitive anxiety provided arousal is at an optimal level (Edwards and Hardy 1996). If arousal is too great, however, performances under high levels of cognitive anxiety will be substantially worse than performances under low levels of cognitive anxiety.

Importantly, once the performance catastrophe has occurred, the performer cannot recover their performance until their physiological arousal and cognitive anxiety state levels have returned to baseline levels, this is known as the *hysteresis* hypothesis. This is illustrated in Figure 6.3. Under hysteresis, performance will follow a different path when physiological arousal is increasing compared to when it is decreasing. In this case, if, after the catastrophe, arousal continues to increase, performance will not increase, and may continue to decline, but at a slower rate. If arousal is decreasing, then performance may start to recover, but will only do so once physiological arousal has decreased to a much lower level than when the catastrophe occurred.

Although the original catastrophe models were notoriously difficult to test using experimental designs (Zeeman 1976), the advent of specific catastrophes, like the cusp catastrophe, permitted the testing of specific hypotheses relating to the cusp catastrophe model of anxiety and performance (L. Hardy 1990). Hardy reports a series of studies in the initial development of the theory to test its corollaries. For example, Hardy and Parfitt (1991) tested the interaction of physiological arousal and cognitive anxiety on performance and the hysteresis hypothesis in female basketball players. An experimental manipulation of the three components of the catastrophe model – physiological arousal, cognitive anxiety, and performance – was adopted.

Physiological arousal was manipulated by increasing the heart rate of an individual by exercise to a given target zone. Cognitive anxiety was manipulated using the time-to-event paradigm based on research that has shown high levels of cognitive anxiety one-day prior to competition and low levels of cognitive anxiety one-day after competition. Performance was tested using a free-throw basketball test, an ecologically valid test of performance for the participant-group. Results supported the catastrophe in performance under high levels of cognitive anxiety and high-arousal. Findings also indicated that performance under high cognitive anxiety was different for participants whose level of arousal was increasing compared to when it was decreasing, supporting the hysteresis hypothesis. Subsequent studies have also provided support for the facilitative effect of high cognitive anxiety on performance under conditions of low or intermediate levels of physiological arousal and a debilitative effect under levels of high physiological arousal (Edwards and Hardy 1996).

Hardy (1996) clarified the corollaries of catastrophe theory and presented statistical procedures to provide an omnibus test of the theory. Hardy tested the model with experienced golfers using self-reports of anxiety from the CSAI-2, heart rate as a measure of physiological arousal, and golf putting as an objective measure of performance. Hardy used direct differences methods to test the fit of the catastrophe curves to the data and provided some evidence in support of the cusp curve. Importantly, the inclusion of self-confidence as an independent variable in the model increased the predictive efficacy of the model, suggesting that self-confidence should still be implicated in any interactive effect of cognitive anxiety and arousal on performance (Gould et al. 2002). Recently, some qualitative support for the catastrophe model has been promulgated. Edwards, Kingston, Hardy, and Gould (2002) conducted a hierarchical content analysis of interviews on performances from eight elite athletes about phenomenological experiences of 'catastrophic' drops in performance during competition. Two themes emerged, one representing a sudden drop in performance and the other continued performance deterioration. The sudden, steep decrease in performance followed by a shallow continued decrease was characteristic of the catastrophe predicted by Hardy's (1990, 1996) theory and the hysteresis hypothesis. Suffice to say that catastrophe theory is an important addition to the literature, but tests of the model have been limited, perhaps due to its complexity, and further investigation is required, particularly with respect to omnibus tests of the model.

Individual zones of optimal functioning (IZOF)

Many of the approaches thus far have adopted quantitative, empirical investigations into the social psychological approach to anxiety and emotion in sport. The focus of these has been the examination of inter-individual differences in social psychological constructs and emotion variables. These investigations have been predominantly nomothetic (group-oriented) in approach with the advantage that findings are assumed to be generalizable across athletes within the confines of the validity of the methodology and the homogeneity or representitiveness of the sample. Hanin (1995, 2000) proposed the **individualized zones of optimal functioning (IZOF)** model, an alternative approach to the study of emotion in sport performance. The model offers an integrated perspective on emotional experience and sport performance that adopts hypotheses from person–environment interactions theory, appraisal theories of emotion, idiographic versus nomothetic views of personality, general systems theory, trait–state distinctions, and psychological readiness for competition. This approach is largely from an individualized or idiographic approach, but also attempts to generalize to athletes on the basis of trends in intra-individual and inter-individual emotional experiences of successful and poor performances.

The aim of the IZOF model is to provide a holistic view of the emotion–performance relationship in sport and it includes a number of specific hypotheses (Hanin 2000). First, emotions arise from the cognitive appraisal of the probability that individual goals will be achieved in a given sport context. Second, athletes learn specific emotional responses to given competitive situations over time. Third, emotional responses are specific to the individual, the context, and time frame of the competitive event. Fourth, there is a reciprocal relationship between emotion and performance. And finally, different emotions exert optimal or dysfunctional effects on performance. In summary, the IZOF model focuses on the effect of an individual's personal emotional responses to a given competitive situation on performance and the effect of performance on emotional responses.

Much of the research on the IZOF model has focused on pre-competitive anxiety because it has provided useful descriptions, particularly in an individual setting, of the relationship between multiple dimensions of emotion, including anxiety, and sport performance (Hanin 2000). Key principles of the IZOF with respect to anxiety, and indeed other emotional states related to sport, is that every athlete has an optimal level or range of emotional intensity (high, medium, or low), such as anxiety and other emotional states, that will lead to successful performance in sport. An emotional profile that falls out with this range, i.e. above or below the optimized levels, will be debilitative towards performance. This is known as the *in-out of zone principle*. An individual's optimal level of anxiety is established using recall methods of successful ('best ever') and poor ('worst ever') performances to establish the optimal zones of anxiety necessary for successful performance. Hanin (1995) found that participants were surprisingly accurate in recalling their pre-competition anxiety levels even after a substantial time lag of up to four months. These studies supported the IZOF model indicating performance decrements when sports performers' anxiety levels fell outside their recalled optimal zones.

However, the cognitive-somatic anxiety distinction was not clearly met in early work with the IZOF model, and researchers found they have had equal success in using somatic anxiety measures to identify optimal zones of functioning (Morgan *et al.* 1988). Hanin's (2000) reconceptualization of the model to include a full complement of emotional responses in competition addressed the multidimensionality of competitive state anxiety and subsequent studies have illustrated that separate zones could be established for the cognitive and somatic aspects of competitive state anxiety. Studies have supported the basic premises of the IZOF model, indicating that a wide variability in performance is exhibited at given levels of pre-competitive state anxiety (Hanin 1995). A more sophisticated model was adopted by Gould *et al.* (1993) using the interactive effects of both cognitive and somatic anxiety to produce a unitary optimal zone. This research found strong support for the IZOF model, stronger than studies that have used the cognitive or somatic anxiety dimensions alone.

Narrative and meta-analytic reviews have also supported the basic premises of the IZOF model for the anxiety–performance relationship (Gould and Tuffey 1996; Jokela and Hanin 1999). Gould and Tuffy (1996) conducted a critical review of IZOF model research and concluded that performance on the basis of the in-out of zone principle was generally supported, although the authors had some theoretical and methodological reservations. Jokela and Hanin (1999) conducted a meta-analysis of 19 empirical studies of the IZOF model with 146 effect sizes and found fairly good support for the in-out of zone principle such that athletes in their optimal zone performed significantly better than athletes out of their zone with a medium effect size (Cohen's d = 0.44). In addition, the study also provided additional support for athletes' ability to recall and anticipate their levels of competitive state anxiety. The authors concluded that the IZOF model was efficacious in discriminating between high and low performing athletes, and claimed that the specific optimal levels of anxiety were superior in the prediction of performance than individually unspecified levels of anxiety intensity from other models using a nomothetic approach (e.g. Kliene 1990).

One advantage of the IZOF model is that it has intuitive or face validity, which is useful for sports psychologists who typically adopt measures such as performance profiling to gauge the success of their interventions. It is one of the few theories in sport psychology that has been developed with specific recommendations for intervention in naturalistic settings in mind. In addition, most applied sports psychologists work using an individualized or idiographic approach, so a model developed in a naturalistic setting is advantageous because it is supremely relevant to practitioners. This makes intuitive sense for sports psychologists focusing on the pragmatic issues of resolving maladaptive anxiety patterns in their performers.

However, the model is not without its critics. One criticism levelled by Gould and Tuffey (1996) is that the theoretical underpinning of the IZOF model is questionable because it does not explain the antecedents or predictors of optimal anxiety, but instead focuses on the individual nature of the anxiety–performance relationship. Moreover, many of the studies have adopted small sample sizes and methodological inadequacies such as lack of objective measures of performance and longitudinal measures (Gould and

Tuffey 1996). In addition, Hanin (2000) claims that the model is able to generate further hypotheses through an inductive, grounded-theory approach. While such an approach has its advantages, the co-existence of a hypothesis-driven, quantitative, deductive framework with an inductive, data-driven, qualitative approach does not make for a happy union. The main reason for this is that one cannot generate a theory at the same time as one tests a theory. For example, with this 'combined approach' findings that serve to disconfirm the theory on the basis of the falsification of a proposed set of hypotheses can lead to a researcher formulating a theory to support the falsified results, which does not sit easily with the principle of falsification. Finally, the model has been criticized for being based or developed on successful performance and unsuccessful performance or failure, which are both qualitatively and quantitatively different, and therefore the model may not have efficacy in predicting anxiety–performance relationships across a range of intensity scores.

Other theoretical accounts of emotion in sport

Mood states in sport

Researchers in the field of emotion in sport have criticized the strong focus on competitive state anxiety in studies in sport and have called for the study of a broader range of emotional and feeling states in sport contexts (Hanin 2000). Research on mood states has provided insight into the effect of a more varied range of feeling states and their effects on sport performance. Mood states are, by definition, different from specific emotions like anxiety in that they are more enduring and less intense feeling states but their effect on sports performance is thought to be substantial. Due to the number of feeling states that constitute mood, much research has adopted a profile approach (McNair *et al.* 1971). The profile approach suggests that while individual mood or feeling dimensions can be distinguished at the subordinate level, it is the patterning or overall profile of the levels of these moods that gives rise to specific cognitive and emotional outcomes in sport performance.

Investigation into mood states in sport owes much to the work of Morgan and colleagues who adopted the profile of mood states to investigate performance levels in athletes (Morgan 1980; Morgan *et al.* 1988). They adopted the profile of mood states (POMS, McNair *et al.* 1971) inventory to distinguish between successful and unsuccessful performance in elite and non-elite performers. The POMS has 30 items that measure six subscales: tension, depression, anger, vigour, fatigue, and confusion. Morgan *et al.* found that elite athletes exhibited a characteristic profile of depressed levels of all of the POMS subscales with the exception of the vigour subscale which tended to be rated very highly prior to competition (see Figure 6.4). This characteristic 'spike' in the mood state pattern that distinguished elite performers was termed the *iceberg* profile.

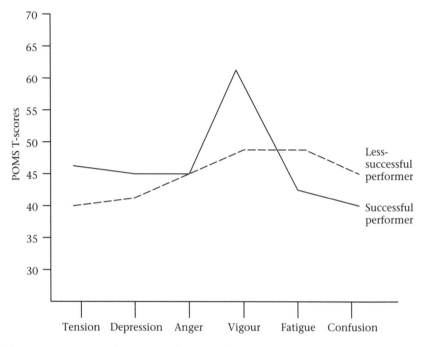

Figure 6.4   Morgan's (1980) iceberg profile

While Morgan's iceberg represented a neat and intuitively clear patterning of mood states that is predictive of performance, other researchers have been critical of its true value. Cockerill, Neville, and Lyons (1991) indicated that the POMS exhibits little or no variance in elite and non-elite performers in the hours prior to performance, while there is considerable variance in the days leading up to competition. They suggested that as an immediate predictor of performance, mood was relatively poor, but a better prediction could be made in longitudinal analyses of the POMS over the days leading up to competition. Analogously, Rowley *et al.* (1995) conducted a meta-analysis of 16 studies that had adopted the iceberg profile to predict sport performance. Findings indicated that although the mood profile significantly predicted sport performance, the effect size was small (Cohen's $d = 0.15$) and only accounted for less than 1 per cent of the variance in sport performance. It was concluded that despite a significant relationship, the explanatory value of the iceberg profile is questionable and explains a degree of variance in sport performance that is largely unsubstantial.

In addition, subsequent research adopting an alternative perspective to the explanation of elite sport performance has provided findings contrary to Morgan's original results. For example, studies in sport training have found that the POMS could not readily distinguish between elite and less successful athletes but it could readily distinguish between high-fit and low-fit athletes and was a useful tool for establishing the effects of overtraining in endurance athletes (Berglund and Safstrom 1994). In addition, mood states have been shown to be efficacious in predicting successful and unsuccessful perform-ances in fitness tests in adolescents (Lane and Lane 2002). This is in keeping with the clinical context in which the POMS was developed. Indeed, Prapaves-sis (2000) reviewed the conceptual issues and research associated with POMS and mood state investigation in sport and concluded that the POMS was an inappropriate model to apply to the study of pre-competitive mood states because of its lack of explanatory value, inconclusive findings, and limited theoretical underpinning.

Recent research in mood states has provided strong, psychometrically sound instruments to measure mood states in sport contexts and advanced research in the prediction of sport performance from mood states. For example, Terry and colleagues (2003) have developed a revised inventory that has been shown to have satisfactory construct, predictive, and concurrent reliability, and adequate reliability in a number of athletic populations. The advent of such inventories resolved some of the critiques of the methodology in mood state research (Cockerill *et al.* 1991; Berger and Motl 2000). Indeed, research with these mood state instruments has yielded successful explanation of perform-ance in a number of sport contexts (e.g. Lane and Lane 2002; Terry *et al.* 2003). In addition, Beedie, Terry, and Lane (2000) conducted a meta-analysis of the POMS in sport contexts, but, unlike Rowley *et al.*, made the distinction between studies in which the dependent variable was level of achievement and studies where the dependent variable was performance outcome. In this distinction, sport achievement was considered measures of *absolute* attain-ment in sport such as winning a gold medal while sport performance measures reflected *relative* attainment such as gaining a personal best time. In keeping with Rowley et al.'s findings, the effect size for the influence of mood on sport achievement was small (Cohen's $d = 0.10$). However, the effect of mood on sport performance outcomes yielded a moderate effect size (Cohen's $d = 0.31$). In addition, Beedie *et al.* examined the effects of the individual subscales from mood state measures and found a moderate and positive effect size for vigour, and moderate and negative effect sizes for tension and depression with sport performance outcomes, but small or no effect sizes for the other subscales. The authors concluded that these findings supported the model proposed by Mor-gan and co-workers (Morgan 1980; Morgan *et al.* 1988) and provided support for the importance of the vigour subscale in the prediction of performance outcomes.

Importantly, these findings have stressed the salience of examining and dif-ferentiating between the individual subscales from the POMS, and not the adoption of aggregate scales, a finding that has been corroborated elsewhere (Hanin 2000; Lane and Lane 2002). Terry and Slade (1995) also recommend that not only should individual mood subscales be the focus of research, but the mood subscales may interact in the prediction of sport performance. They indicated that depression, for example, might moderate the effects of other mood state subscales like anger and tension on sport performance. For example, Terry and Slade studied the influence of both competitive state anxiety and mood states on karate performance. Results indicated that the somatic, cognitive, and self-confidence components of competitive state anxiety and the individual mood states of vigour and anger were able to discriminate between successful and unsuccessful performers. Finally, Beedie et al.'s (2000) meta-analysis also illustrated the importance of the definition of the performance parameters and measures to be studied. Clearly, the prediction of athletic achievement may be too insensitive and crude a measure of sport performance, and the measurement of relevant performance outcomes is recommended when examining the efficacy of mood states in predicting performance.

Reversal theory

Reversal theory is a relatively new approach applied to the study of anxiety and emotion in sport performance, but recent applications have been promising and have received empirical support. Reversal theory provides a general framework for the understanding of the relationships between arousal and emotion, and how these influence motivational constructs and behaviour (Apter 1982). A key premise of reversal theory is that an individual can interpret his/her state of arousal as pleasant or unpleasant, and this is known as *hedonic tone*. Given that an individual may also experience high or low levels of arousal, this gives rise to a 2 × 2 formation of hedonic tone and arousal level. In this paradigm, high levels of arousal interpreted as pleasant result in an excited affective state, high levels of arousal interpreted as unpleasant produce an anxious state, low levels of arousal interpreted as pleasant generate a relaxed state, and low levels of arousal interpreted as unpleasant give rise to a boredom response (Figure 6.5).

Reversal theory predicts that an individual's *metamotivational state* will determine the relationship between their hedonic tone and arousal level. A metamotivational state is a person's interpretation of their motives or goals in a given context and at a given point in time. An individual can either be goal-focused or 'serious' in their pursuit of their outcomes, known as a *telic* metamotivational state or be activity-orientated or 'playful' in their approach, known as the *paratelic* metamotivational state. When in arousal-evoking situations, a person can switch between metamotivational states that will determine whether they will be on the relaxation–anxiety hedonic tone-arousal curve (solid line, Figure 6.5) or the excitement–boredom hedonic tone-arousal curve (broken line, Figure 6.5). This 'switch' is known as a reversal, and as metamotivational states are state-like constructs and subject to changes in the environment, reversals can happen at any time during an activity. A telic metamotivational state is often viewed as arousal-avoiding while a paratelic metamotivational state is often viewed as arousal-seeking or thrill-seeking.

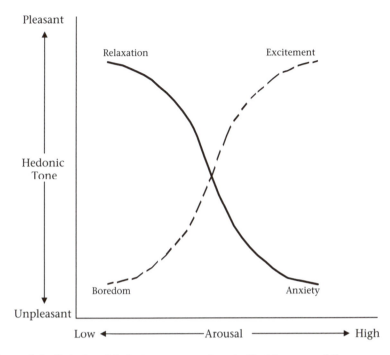

Figure 6.5 Relationship between arousal and affect in reversal theory
Source: Kerr (1985)

Evidence for this has been shown in the tendency for people who approach or participate in thrill-seeking activities (e.g. frightening funfair rides like rollercoasters) to exhibit a high paratelic state and increased preferred arousal with positive emotional states like excitement and positive emotions compared with individuals who perform 'safe' activities. Therefore, both situational factors and habituation (known as 'satiation') of the activity and metamotivational state may result in a reversal (Kerr 1997). Thus, reversal theory, like catastrophe theory, attempts to integrate affective states with activation or arousal states. The theory proposes that an individual's interpretation of arousal as pleasant or unpleasant is dependent on whether their metamotivational state is arousal-avoidant/telic or arousal-seeking/paratelic.

There have been numerous tests of reversal theory since Kerr's initial application of the theory in sport contexts, and many provide support for its hypotheses. Bellew and Thatcher (2002) tested the factors affecting reversals from telic to paratelic states in a naturalistic setting with rugby players and found that reversals generally occurred as a consequence of factors external to the athletes, or frustration caused by external factors. The authors concluded that internal factors such as satiation or feeling the same state for an extended period of time were not responsible for changes in metamotivational state. This finding is supported by previous research that has showed that unexpected environmental events like errors are an important influence on inducing reversals from telic to paratelic metamotivational states in athletes (Kerr and Tacon 2000). Research has also focused on the relationships between metamotivational states and motivation in sport. For example, Lindner and Kerr (2001) found that participation motivation was predicted by metamotivational states from general or life-oriented and contextual or sport-oriented sources.

Other studies have provided only limited support for some of the premises of reversal theory and questioned some of its predictions. For example, Legrand and LeScanff (2003) used an idiographic approach to the study of a javelin thrower's metamotivational states before competition. They found that hedonic tone did not distinguish between high and low achievement across the season, but did find that when individual mood components were considered rather than global emotional groupings, the mood states of placidity, anger, boredom, and provocativeness were found to fluctuate significantly between the thrower's best and worst performances of the season. Similarly, Kerr, Fujiyama, and Campano (2002) found that serious (telic) and hedonistic (paratelic) recreational tennis players did not differ on measures of tension and effort stress, but significant decreases in overall 'negative' emotions and tension stress was evident in both groups after the completion of a practice session, but especially so in the serious group. Taken together, the findings of reversal theory are not unequivocal. However, like catastrophe theory, research on reversal theory in sport has not been the subject of intensive research, unlike multidimensional anxiety theory, and thus support in terms of the number of findings is limited. Clearly, more investigation needs to be done, but laboratory- or field-based studies in particular are required to test the existence of reversals and whether they can be induced experimentally.

Suggested reading

Craft, L.L., Magyar, T.M., Becker, B.J. and Feltz, D.L. (2003) The relationship between the Competitive State Anxiety Inventory-2 and sport performance: a meta-analysis, *Journal of Sport and Exercise Psychology*, 25: 44–65. Very recent cumulative analysis of the impact of competitive state anxiety on sport performance.

Hanin, Y.L. (2000) *Emotions in Sport*. Champaign, IL: Human Kinetic. Hanin's detailed reader on his IZOF model with important contributions from Vallerand on the importance of emotions in models of social cognition in sport.

Jones, G. (1995) More than just a game: research developments and issues in competitive anxiety in sport, *British Journal of Psychology*, 86: 449–78. All about the control model of facilitative and debilitative anxiety in sport.

Summary

- Affect is an umbrella term that includes all 'feeling states', with emotion and mood as specific examples. Emotions are single, intense, and changeable 'feeling states' that tend to have 'action tendencies' while mood tends to be conceptualized as a profile of affective states that is considered more enduring, less intense, and with no action tendency.
- Competitive state anxiety is considered to be multidimensional comprising cognitive anxiety, somatic anxiety, and self-confidence (Martens *et al.* 1990). Cognitive anxiety, in particular, is consistently and negatively linked with sport performance (Craft *et al.* 2003), but may be positively related to performance if it is interpreted as facilitative (Jones 1995).
- Arousal may be an outcome of increased state anxiety, and is implicated in the anxiety-performance relationship in catastrophe theory (Hardy and Parfitt 1991). The theory states that the arousal–performance relationship will follow an inverted-U relationship under conditions of low cognitive anxiety, but a catastrophic drop in performance will occur under conditions of high cognitive state anxiety and high arousal.
- The individual zone of optimal functioning model (IZOF, Hanin 2000) and reversal theory (Kerr 1997) focus on an individual-based approach to emotional processes in sport. The IZOF identifies specific limits in which anxiety is 'optimal' and athletes within their zone exhibit better performance. Reversal theory charts how the interpretation of arousal and hedonic tone give rise to specific metamotivational states that are related to motivation and behaviour in sport.

Group processes in sport

'There is no I in team' and 'the whole is greater than the sum of its parts'; these oft-cited clichés provide a useful prologue to this chapter that aims to evaluate the salient group processes that occur among athletes in sport contexts. In team sports, success is often contingent on the team working effectively and collectively toward a common goal. Often this means accepting given roles and responsibilities within a team, foregoing personal ambitions, investing effort for the common good, having extensive knowledge of other team members' abilities, and providing support and feedback for the members of the team. Within sport teams, there is a wealth of information available to each member regarding the team's operation and effectiveness, as well as information regarding their own personal performance within the team. Therefore, individuals in a team behave on the basis of information from the group – about their membership and role in the group – as well as their own beliefs, personality, and other intrapersonal constructs. Social psychology has a lot to offer in terms of explaining how individuals respond and interact in groups and how they affect individual and group behaviour and performance. This section will examine some of the key processes that underlie group or team performance in sport and will examine the theoretical and empirical work that has attempted to explain these processes.

Definition of a group and a conceptual framework

A group is not a mere collection of two or more individuals. The mere presence of others is a necessary but not sufficient condition for a group to be established (Zajonc 1965). As we shall see in the next section, the presence of others when performing motor tasks like sports skills does have an influence on cognition, behaviour, and performance, but this form of social influence is different from that which operates in a group. Membership of a group gives rise to a specific set of social cognitions or beliefs among the group members brought on by the interaction between group members, the notion of a common goal or desired outcome, a specific structure within the group, and the presence of important group processes such as communication and cohesion (Carron and Hausenblas 1998). Therefore, a group comprises one or more people, involves interaction between people, demands an awareness of some form of common fate or goals – although this may not be clearly defined, has a specific structure known to all members such as the role and status of individuals within the group, and group norms.

Why group membership?

One of the key motives often cited for participation in exercise and sport is one of affiliation (Ashford *et al.* 1993), and this can be considered indicative of a basic human psychological need to form social bonds or relationships with others. For example, Baumeister and Leary (1995) cited the need to form attachments to others and form interpersonal relations as a fundamental human motive. These authors found that the motivation to form interpersonal relations satisfied a number of essential criteria to establish it as a fundamental motive; it operates across a wide variety of contexts; it influences a variety of important social cognitive and emotional constructs; it can predict behaviour in a variety of contexts; it is independent of other psychological and biological needs; it can affect psychological adjustment and well-being if absent; and it is essential for all humans. Organismic theories of motivation also share the view that the need for affiliation or relatedness is an essential human need. Deci and Ryan (1985, 2000) suggest that relatedness is a basic psychological need, and is complementary but independent of other psychological needs for competence and autonomy. Thus, membership of groups is something that is essential for psychological health and satisfies our innate needs. Sport is a social setting in which group affiliation processes abound and is a prime example of people satisfying their basic needs to form interpersonal relationships or relatedness. Further, not only does group affiliation assist in satisfying group needs, it is considered an essential part of the way in which we define ourselves. Often an individual's self-esteem is, in part, derived from the social groups to which he or she belongs (Tajfel and Turner 1986). It is therefore important when considering group behaviour in sport that such behaviour is determined by innate needs and that a person's sense of self is likely to be intrinsically tied in with group behaviour.

A conceptual framework

Carron and Hausenblas (1998) provide a conceptual framework to study the major factors that influence group behaviour in sport. The proposed model is given in Figure 7.1. The model outlines the major influences on group structure and formation, group processes, and group outcomes. Group structure

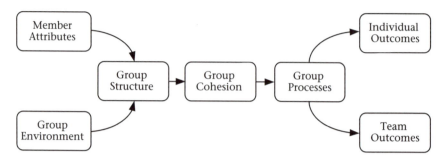

Figure 7.1   Carron and Hausenblas' (1998) conceptual framework for the study of sport teams
Source: Carron and Hausenblas (1998: 20)

comprises the norms within the team (i.e. what is acceptable and unacceptable behaviour) and the roles (e.g. leadership, status, and function) of the group members. Member attributes such as abilities and personalities and group environment such as size and territory contribute to the group structure. Group structure influences important group processes such as team goals, **collective efficacy**, and cooperation within the group. This is proposed to be mediated by the important variable of cohesion, or the degree to which the group members act in unison in the pursuit of common goals. Cohesion is considered to be an extremely important social psychological construct in the group dynamics in sport because it has a pervasive effect on a number of interpersonal variables at the group processes stage such as collective efficacy, cooperation, effort, and motivation. These group processes affect individual and personal outcomes such as performance and satisfaction.

The aim of this chapter is not to provide an extensive overview of Carron and Hausenblas' (1998) model. Indeed, Carron and Hausenblas have provided an excellent and lucid text on these elements. Instead, the chapter focuses on the social psychological processes that underlie the key elements of this model. It will examine the effect of a specific member attribute, namely *player ability*, on group structure. Factors relating to group environment will be visited in greater detail in the section on *social influence* and *home advantage*. The role that group norms have to play in determining group structure will be reviewed. Much emphasis will be placed on *group* or *team cohesion* as an essential influence on group processes and outcomes such as collective efficacy and sport performance respectively. This will provide an in-depth overview of some salient variables involved with group dynamics research and practice. Finally, some practical solutions in terms of team building will be presented, to provide some pragmatic solutions to enhancing team cohesion and team performance in sport.

Ability of team members

One assumption often made in sport is that the teams with the best individual players are often the most successful. To some extent, this is borne out by observation of the win–lose statistics of successful teams in a number of professional sports. However, this is juxtaposed by the reality that some teams perform very well with a collection of members whose individual ability may not be of the calibre of others, indeed, they may outperform teams that have individuals of high ability but perhaps do not function well as a unit. In such cases, the ability of a team of high-ability individuals may be limited by group-level variables like lack of cohesion, while the team of lower ability individuals performs above standard because their levels of group-oriented constructs like cohesion are optimal. The issue of cohesion will be visited in detail in subsequent sections, but this illustrates that individual ability is important but its relative contribution to team performance is moderated by group-level constructs.

Research in social psychology has focused on problem-solving tasks to study the effects of individual ability on group performance. Many researchers have shown that when solving problems at a group level, group performance can be heavily dependent on the individual resources at the disposal of the group, and in particular the relative abilities of the group members (e.g. Devine 1999). Reviews of studies on problem solving have found significant effects of individual cognitive ability on group performance (Devine 1999). However, there are occasions when the ability of the individual team members does not always result in optimal team performance. Studies on fine motor tasks found that individual team members did not perform as well in the group situation as they did alone, even though the overall team performance was superior to the individual team members' performance (Devine 1999). This was attributed to the lack of individual performance feedback and a subsequent **social loafing** effect. Research has suggested that other factors not related to ability may affect the relationship between individual ability on group performance such as the nature of the task, the clarity of the goal, and the size of the group. In addition, research has shown that tacit and task-related knowledge, skills, and abilities may be important in determining an individual's ability to work in a group situation (Miller 2001). These findings indicate that the ability of individual team members is an important artefact in team performance, but it does not account for all the variance in team performance.

In sport, a number of studies have examined the effect of individual skills and abilities on the effectiveness of team performance (Widmeyer 1990). In a review of these studies, Widmeyer (1990) concluded that the relationship between individual ability parameters and performance was consistently significant across all studies. Suggested moderators of this relationship included attributes of the sport that limit the productivity of the individuals in the team and team psychological characteristics. For example, in sports like basketball, where a great deal of coordination among players and greater cohesion is necessary for success, ability accounts for less variance in performance than in sports like baseball where success is less dependent upon coordination of resources (Carron and Hausenblas 1998). Team characteristics that are likely to affect the efficacy of individual team members' abilities in producing optimal performance are aspects of group cohesion such as task motivation and the presence of clearly defined performance goals and role structure within the team.

Gill (1984) suggests that given the consistent relationship between individual ability and team performance, there is no reason to select team members on the basis of any attribute other than their individual ability. However, to attain maximal productivity from the players at a coach's disposal, whose ability may be limited, the moderator variables relating to team effectiveness such as cohesion, team goals, and roles, particularly in sports that demand coordinated play and strategy, need to be maximized. Indeed, coaches' perceptions of players' ability are also significant in this regard. Clearly, the coach must make executive team decisions based on his/her players' ability but these will also be mitigated by the demands of the team, i.e. whether a player will be able to contribute to the cohesiveness of the team. Research suggests that coaches' efficacy expectations regarding their team, which included estimates of perceived ability as well as perceived opponents', ability and control over outcomes, were significantly related to performance indicators in basketball players (Chase *et al.* 1997).

Group norms

One of the key constructs in theory and research in group dynamics is group norm. Group norms describe which behaviours are acceptable and unacceptable, condoned and shunned, within a group. Group norms are a powerful influence on behaviour because, according to social identity theory, a player's self-esteem is intrinsically intertwined with their membership of the group and their acceptance by other group members (Tajfel and Turner 1986). Therefore, a group member who behaves in a manner that is contrary to the accepted norms within the group risks being vilified by the other group members. In addition, behaving contrary to the accepted norms will also violate the member's own self-stereotype as a member of the ingroup. As a consequence, their behaviour does not match up to their perceived expectations of what a prototypical group member would do, and this would create *cognitive dissonance* (Festinger and Carlsmith 1958). Dissonance is a feeling of cognitive discomfort when cognition is incongruent with behaviour. Festinger and Carlsmith state that individuals strive to reduce dissonance and create a state of consistency or *consonance* between their personal beliefs and social behaviours. As a result, non-conformity to group norms is often checked by the individual, and the dissonant action corrected in order to restore consonance within the dissenter between their role as a group member and the types of normative behaviours that are condoned within the group.

In sports teams, a number of group norms may be considered valuable for success. In interviews with team sports players, Colman and Carron (2001) identified the team norms perceived to exist in teams in different contexts. In competition, effort, support, and punctuality were considered important, while in training punctuality, productivity, and attendance were considered virtuous. This is hardly surprising since successful team performance is generally dependent upon attendance, and hard work is viewed as essential for success. However, while a team may endorse a team norm that is adaptive, the performance of the group is only likely to be successful if it is accompanied by adaptive group properties like group cohesion. Interestingly, a norm for productivity, a highly salient performance-related variable in team competition, has been found to interact with the degree of cohesion viewed among team members to produce optimal performance. Therefore, if a team norm of high productivity is prevalent in a cohesive team, their performance is likely to be optimal. But if the norm for productivity is low, then a dramatically poorer performance will prevail because a cohesive group is likely to endorse the prevailing group norm more vociferously (Colman and Carron 2000).

Coaches can use team norms to enhance and maintain unity and cohesion within a team. Means to instil long-term group norm in naturalistic settings like a sport teams may come from the attitude change (Eagly and Chaiken 1993) and elaboration-likelihood model (Petty and Cacioppo 1986) literature. Techniques of persuasive communication use information giving and persuasive messages to evoke dissonance and precipitate changes in attitudes. Social learning theory uses exemplars, modelling, and vicarious experience to change behaviour (Bandura 1977). Research has suggested that such messages may have an effect on both individuals and groups. Coaches should therefore focus on persuasive communication and use role model sports teams with effective group norms as examples in order to promote favourable group norms such as productivity (Carron and Hausenblas 1998).

Collective efficacy

Bandura's (1977, 1997) construct of self-efficacy, regarded as one of the most important interpersonal variables in social psychology (see Chapter 5), also operates at group level (Spink 1990). Just as self-efficacy is a set of beliefs regarding ability to produce outcomes in a given situation, collective efficacy reflects the beliefs shared by a group of individuals in their team's abilities to function as a unit and to successfully achieve outcomes in group behaviours (Carron and Hausenblas 1998). Importantly, measurement of collective efficacy not only involves measuring the belief in the ability of the team of each individual team member but also in the consensus of these beliefs shared by the team. Thus, a team is said to have high collective efficacy if the majority of team members cite high levels of beliefs in the team's ability. Zaccaro et al. (1995) draw on Bandura's (1977) work on self-efficacy and state that collective efficacy comprises two sets of beliefs: collective resources and coordinative capabilities. Collective resources are beliefs in the extent of the abilities (skills, knowledge, strategy etc.) of the team to produce salient outcomes (Spink 1990). Coordinative capabilities are beliefs in the team's ability to draw upon the resources in the collective or team and act cooperatively towards the common goal or outcome. Collective efficacy also has the property of situational specificity, that is, it reflects beliefs about team abilities in specific situations.

A number of antecedent variables of collective efficacy have been identified: verbal persuasion and leadership, group cohesion, group size, vicarious experience, and prior performance. Teams likely to have high collective efficacy are those that have effective leaders who provide active encouragement, positive reinforcement of group goals, and positive feedback on the abilities of the team. Widmeyer and Ducharme (1997) state that accomplishing team goals will foster collective efficacy, so it is important that team members have their goals reinforced through feedback from team leaders and coaches. Vicarious experiences, also a key influence on the social learning of competence in Bandura's conceptualization of self-efficacy, will also enhance collective efficacy. Thus watching and modelling successful teams can enhance collective efficacy. Prior experiences of success will also have a positive effect on collective efficacy. For example, Feltz and Lirgg (1998) found that perceived team efficacy was reduced after a loss and increased after a win, suggesting that collective efficacy fluctuates according to performance outcome. This does not mean that teams that always lose will have low collective efficacy. Rather, it means that there may be important mediators of this relationship. What is more important than match or game results is the way in which the outcome is perceived and portrayed by the team and the people around the team like coaches and parents. Success in team sports can be defined beyond the match or game result. It can be losing but playing well, or successfully completing a target number of passes or rebounds, or keeping a clean defensive record.

The role of group size as a positive or negative influence on collective efficacy is controversial, and yet to be fully investigated. While a larger group has more resources that can be made available, it may also lack cohesion because it opens up the possibility of sub-groups to form that undermines the superordinate group. Furthermore, larger groups may make individual performance and contribution more ambiguous and difficult to quantify; a performer's personal contribution may be 'lost' in the collective. This may result in reduced effort and motivation in these members when performing due to their perception that their performance is of reduced consequence to the team; a phenomenon known as social loafing. Finally, group cohesion exerts a powerful effect on collective efficacy. Teams that act like a unit, are coordinated, have a clear, shared notion of the collective goal, and are more likely to be efficacious. Research into the role of group cohesion as an antecedent of collective efficacy and other salient group performance-related variables will be reviewed in the next section.

While collective efficacy has been shown to be related to the performance of sports teams (Feltz and Lirgg 1998), studies have focused on establishing the mechanisms by which collective efficacy determines performance. In particular, studies have indicated that group goals are implicated in the effect of collective efficacy on performance. For example, Greenlees, Graydon, and Maynard (2000) found that athletes with high collective efficacy and appropriately set goals were able to maintain their personal performance. Bray (2004) found that collective efficacy significantly predicted group performance in a muscular endurance task and this influence was mediated by group goals. In summary, these results illustrated that collective efficacy regarding future team performance in sport was significantly related to team performance and this relationship was mediated by the nature of the goals set by the team.

Recent studies have examined the psychological processes that determine and induce collective efficacy in sports settings. Magyar, Feltz, and Simpson (2004) examined the effects of constructs from achievement goal theory and self-efficacy theory on the collective efficacy of competitive rowers. It was found that task self-efficacy predicted individual perceptions of collective efficacy and a mastery-oriented motivational climate determined collective efficacy at group level. Similarly, research has shown significant correlations between task self-efficacy and collective efficacy (Bray *et al.* 2002). It seems that individual perceptions of ability as well as the appropriate motivational climate that cultivates these senses of high ability and skill are contributory factors to the development of collective efficacy of the team. Therefore, just as the individual ability of team members is predictive of team performance, individual perceptions of task-related efficacy lead to high levels of collective efficacy.

Group cohesion

Previously we saw that the individual abilities of members in a sports team usually determined a successful sports team (Widmeyer 1990). However, it was also emphasized that while a team may have an abundance of resources to draw on and a productivity potential (possible performance level) that was very high, group-level variables may limit or even inhibit these. One construct that may serve to moderate the relationship between potential productivity and performance is **group cohesion** or team cohesion. It seems a given that more cohesive teams are more likely to be successful in attaining optimal performance, and there are many anecdotal examples of teams that have relatively low levels of individual ability but high cohesiveness outperforming teams with patently higher levels of potential productivity but low cohesiveness. This section will examine group cohesion in team sports by defining group cohesion, examining a proposed model of group cohesion, studying the effect of cohesion on performance and other psychological outcomes in sports teams, and the predictors and determinants of cohesion.

What is group cohesion?

The study of group cohesion in sport arose from the group dynamics literature in social psychology and is defined as the social forces that maintain the attraction between members of a group and the resistance of the group to disruptive forces. Carron and colleagues (Carron 1982; Carron *et al*. 1985; Carron and Hausenblas 1998) proposed a conceptual framework of group cohesion in sport that accounts for the factors that contribute to the formation of group cohesion and the effect that group cohesion has on team performance outcomes. The model is shown in Figure 7.2. Team cohesion is viewed as a function of personal, team, leadership, and situational or environmental factors. *Personal factors* reflect the shared personal psychological attributes of the team members such as shared goals and motivation to succeed. These can be a shared at a person level such as each member reporting high task self-efficacy or at a group level such as the collective efficacy levels of the team as a whole and the endorsement and maintenance of group norms such as productivity and performance norms. *Team factors* include psychological variables that operate at group level, such as group norms and collective efficacy. These are associated with cohesion but may act alongside or interact with personal factors such as task self-efficacy. Coaches have the potential to influence the cohesiveness of the group, and these *leadership factors* may influence cohesiveness directly and indirectly through the mediation of personal and team factors. Coaches are responsible for the pervading motivational climate and group norms operating in the team's training and competitive situations,

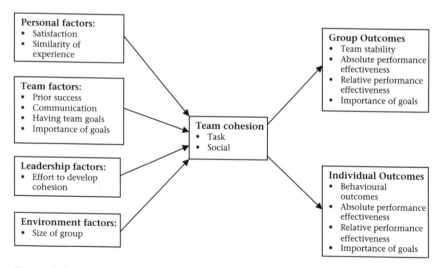

Figure 7.2   Carron's (1982) model of antecedents and outcomes of group cohesion in sport
Source: Carron (1982: 131)

which have been shown to affect personal variables like task self-efficacy and collective efficacy. Finally, *situational factors* include the physical and functional proximity of team members such as closeness on the pitch or field, but also in terms of living and socializing. Research has shown that teams spending more time together in residential training camps are more likely to be highly cohesive (Rainey and Schweickert 1988), and this is reflected in the popularity of mid-, end-, and pre-season training camps in which team players live, train, and socialize together in an environment they share.

Together, these factors, termed 'inputs' by Carron (1982), are viewed as influencing task cohesion, which mediates the influence of the input variables on group and individual outcomes or 'outputs'. These outputs include *group outcomes* such as actual performance and team-level variables such as stability, but are also likely to affect *individual performance outcomes* and *psychological outcomes* such as satisfaction. The next section will identify the properties of group cohesion in sports teams and examine the relationships between the key factors in Carron's (1982) framework of group cohesion.

A conceptual model of group cohesion and its measurement

Carron *et al.* (1985) identified two related but independent dimensions of cohesion, namely, *individual attraction to the group* or *group integration* and *task* or *social* reasons for involvement with the group. This gave rise to a 2 × 2 framework for group cohesion, shown in Figure 7.3, in which an individual's

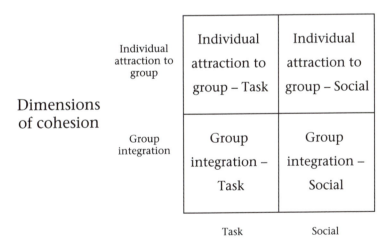

Figure 7.3   Carron et al.'s (1985) 2 × 2 framework for group cohesion
Source: Carron *et al.* (1985: 248)

perception of team cohesion could be characterized by a profile of scores giving rise to the individual attractions to group-social (ATG-S), individual attractions to the group-task (ATG-T), group integration-social (GI-S), and group integration-task (GI-T). These dimensions were measured on scales from the Group Environment Questionnaire (GEQ), a standardized psychometric instrument validated for the measurement of group cohesion in sports teams. This scale has demonstrated adequate construct validity and reliability (Carron *et al.* 1985). In the GEQ, the group integration items ask respondents about the general unity of the team with respect to task or social motives for involvement. The individual attractions to group items reflect personal motives to maintain affiliation to the team.

Cohesion–performance relationships

The hypothesis that cohesive teams will be more successful in accordance with Carron et al.'s (1985) conceptual model has been tested in a meta-analytic study of 46 studies that adopted the GEQ to measure cohesiveness in sport settings. A large average corrected effect size correlation was evident for the group cohesion-group performance relationship. In addition, group cohesion also predicted the performance of individuals in the team (Bray and Whaley 2001). Furthermore, ethnographic studies adopting a qualitative approach have also supported the perception that team cohesion will result in superior performance (Holt and Sparkes 2001). Overall, the weight of evidence from these studies seems to suggest that teams high on cohesiveness will exhibit better performance.

Research has also sought to examine the mechanisms that may explain the group cohesion-performance relationship. Using a simple manipulation, Grieve, Whelan, and Meyers (2000) found that they were able to change the level of cohesiveness in triadic basketball teams. The manipulation successfully created teams of high and low cohesion, but the cohesiveness of the team had little effect on performance. However, performance had strong effects on team cohesion, so that winning teams had higher cohesion. This is supported by studies that have examined the reciprocity of group cohesion on performance (e.g. Mullen and Copper 1994). These studies addressed the question: Does successful performance engender cohesiveness or does cohesiveness generate successful performance, or both? These studies adopted a cross-lagged correlation design in which cohesiveness and performance are measured simultaneously at one point in time and again at a second time point. Cross-lagged partial correlations are then calculated for the proposed reciprocal relationship while holding the effect of the time 1 variables on the dependant variables constant. This is illustrated in Figure 7.4. Reciprocity is supported if the cross-lagged correlations are equal, and the direction of causality is inferred if one correlation is significantly higher than the other. A meta-analysis of longitudinal studies on the group cohesion–performance

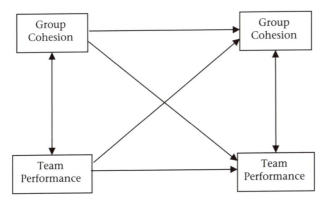

Figure 7.4   A cross-lagged model of the relationship between group cohesion and performance

relationship across many competitive situations supported a direction of causality from performance to cohesion (Mullen and Copper 1994). However, cross-lagged panel studies have found only weak support for the causal relationship between cohesion and performance in sport contexts (e.g. Slater and Sewell 1994). More studies are required to test this relationship using robust designs to examine the true nature of this relationship in the sport psychology literature.

Much of the research on the group cohesion–performance relationship has focused on team sports where the group environment involves constant interaction between the members of each team, and the opposing team. Some research has focused on the role that cohesiveness plays in team sports where there is little or no interaction between team members or that of the opposition. For example, Matheson, Mathes, and Murray (1996) compared changes in the levels of group cohesion of interacting (lacrosse, basketball) and co-acting (swimming, gymnastics) sports over pre-, mid-, and post-season time points. There was a significantly greater change in the attraction to group-task dimensions for the coacting group mid-season, suggesting that experience across the season for coacting sports tends to foster greater cohesion, while there is less scope for cohesion improvements in already well-functioning interactive sport teams. In a follow-up analysis, Matheson *et al.* (1997) examined the effects of outcomes (winning and losing) on cohesiveness throughout a season for interacting and coacting teams. Scores for the attraction to group-task scales were higher on all occasions in the coacting teams, and this was especially pronounced in losing situations. Together these results suggest that cohesiveness seems to be influential to performance in coacting sports, and levels may be higher than those in team sports for attraction to group-task dimension. This is perhaps because this aspect of cohesiveness is most relevant to sports participants who do not interact within the confines of their sport, so they characterize their relations with team mates on the attraction and task-related aspects of cohesiveness.

Cohesion–outcome relationships

Team cohesion has influenced a number of outcome variables other than individual and group performance. According to Carron et al.'s (1985) model, cohesion will have an impact on both performance-related and psychological outcomes. Teams high in cohesiveness often report elevated levels of motivational psychological constructs at the group level such as collective efficacy (Spink 1990), and at the personal level such as motivation (Williams and Widmeyer 1991). Thus, it seems that cohesion is motivationally adaptive and predicts constructs related to persistence in behaviours in interacting and coaching sports teams, and in non-competitive situations. Further, cohesion is also related to psychological well-being constructs in team members like goal and performance satisfaction (Carron 1982). Analogously, teams that are high in cohesion are also resistant to disruptive elements (Brawley *et al.* 1988) and have low levels of undesirable outcomes among team members such as drop-out (Robinson and Carron 1982), social loafing (Everett *et al.* 1992), and anxiety (Eys *et al.* 2003). In summary, it seems that group cohesion is consistent with adaptive outcomes and affective states among team members and minimizes disruptive elements.

Predictors of cohesion

In the conceptual framework for cohesion and group dynamics, Carron (1982) suggests that a number of influential factors will determine a team's level of cohesiveness: personal, team, leadership, and environmental/situational factors (see Figure 7.2). Focusing first on personal factors, research has shown that significant variance in group cohesion could be explained by perceptions of individual and team sacrifice (Prapavessis and Carron 1997), so it seems that knowledge that others are foregoing personal gain and resources contributes to the formation of a cohesive team. Turning next to team factors, prior success and team goals are proposed to have an effect on cohesion (Widmeyer and Ducharme 1997). Another team factor thought to influence team cohesion is communication. For example, Sullivan and Feltz (2003) identified that three dimensions of effective communication – acceptance, distinctiveness, and positive conflict – were positively related to all of the GEQ dimensions. This preliminary evidence suggests that the adaptive aspects of communication may be an antecedent of group cohesion.

In terms of leadership factors, perceptions of leadership and coaching behaviours have been shown to affect cohesion. Cohesive team members tend to rate their coaches as displaying high levels of democratic behaviour, positive feedback, social support, and training and instruction behaviours, and low in autocratic behaviours (Gardner *et al.* 1996). Turman (2003) identified the coaching behaviours that promoted team cohesion such as motivational speeches, athlete-directed techniques, team prayers and dedications, and behaviours that undermined cohesion such as ridiculing and embarrassing players. Finally, in terms of environmental factors, there is evidence that group size affects cohesiveness. Widmeyer, Brawley, and Carron (1990) found that there was a significant inverse relationship between team size and team cohesiveness. Together these findings provide a support for influential factors on group cohesion proposed by Carron's (1982) framework.

Team-building interventions and group cohesion

Interventions and programmes to improve levels of group cohesion in sports performers have been met with success. Team-building exercises usually adopt a number of strategies to increase the key variables thought to increase cohesiveness among teams such as collective efficacy, communication, cooperation, and acceptance. Widmeyer and McGuire (1996, cited in Carron and Hausenblas 1998) offer a season-long approach to team building, which begins in pre-season training and has four phases. The *educational phase* in which players' awareness of the key principles involved in goal setting is raised and the importance of setting team goals emphasized. The *goal-development phase* is essentially a planning phase in which players form the essential components of the team such as attack and defence and discuss strategies to address problematic areas in their game flagged by previous seasons statistics. These strategies then form the basis of five key team goals, which are agreed in a plenary session. During the *implementation phase*, a team attains feedback from match statistics to evaluate the effectiveness of their team goal pursuit over a period of six games or competitions. Finally, the *renewal phase* is an overall evaluation of the team's effectiveness in addressing the team goals for the six-game period against the statistics and an opportunity to produce a revised level for the next six games. The effectiveness of this team building programme has been supported with increases in team cohesiveness being noted after completion of the programme (e.g. Voight and Callaghan 2001).

Role ambiguity, role efficacy, and team performance

Role involvement is implicated in Carron's conceptual framework for the study of group processes as a team factor that has a pervasive and direct influence on group cohesion, team effectiveness, and performance. According to Carron and Hausenblas: 'A role is the pattern of behaviour expected of an individual in a social situation' (1998: 157). Theorists in group dynamics have identified two types of roles in sports teams: *formal* and *informal*. Formal roles are those assigned to players and team personnel within the team structure such as forward, full-back, marker, captain, and so on, and arise from team structure. Informal roles arise from social interactions among team members and emerge as the team develops. They have no functional purpose within a team's strategy for performance. Examples of informal roles are team policeman, spokesperson, social director, and team 'joker'. Team performance is dependent upon team personnel performing in accordance with their formal role in the team, and much of the literature has focused on the influence of formal roles in sport teams. This does not mean that informal roles should be discounted, and they may very well be significant determinants of other important group processes.

Formal roles in sports teams affect team characteristics such as group cohesion and team performance. An indirect property of team cohesion is the degree to which a player accepts, assumes, and performs in accordance with his or her role. Further, within teams there are likely to be roles that are more high-profile in terms of recognition and prestige. However, team cohesion and, indirectly, its effectiveness and productivity are dependent on all players performing in accordance with their role, even if it is at the expense of assuming a more prestigious role. Indeed, it is a property of group cohesion that sacrifices such as these are accepted and recognized by the team members.

Beauchamp *et al.* (2002) have identified three key role-related constructs which determine a team player's performance in their role. Role performance, a key outcome variable in the study of team player's roles and team performance, is the extent to which an individual behaves consistently with their assigned and expected role. Successful role performance is an important outcome because team performance and other team properties such as team cohesion are dependent on it. Role performance is influenced by **role conflict, role ambiguity**, and **role efficacy** (Figure 7.5). Role conflict refers to the degree to which a player experiences an inability to meet the demands of their established or assigned role. Role ambiguity reflects a lack of understanding in the player of the expected behavioural demands of the role, full role clarity is necessary for optimal role performance. Role efficacy is a player's estimate of their ability to perform the behaviours expected for successful role performance. It has similar sources and properties of other efficacy beliefs such as task self-efficacy and collective efficacy (Bandura 1997), but it has been found to be conceptually and empirically distinct from these efficacy beliefs (Bray and Brawley 2002). It is thought that high role ambiguity and low role efficacy may lead to role conflict. Put simply, if a player is unsure of the nature of his/her role in a team and they are not confident in their abilities to perform their role, they are likely to experience conflict between different behavioural demands related to their role. The effect of role conflict on role efficacy is mediated by role ambiguity (see Figure 7.5; Beauchamp and Bray, 2001).

Beauchamp *et al.* studied the effect of role ambiguity on role performance in rugby players, and proposed a triadic mediational model in which the effect of role ambiguity on performance was mediated by role efficacy (see Figure 7.5). Research has suggested that the effect of role ambiguity on role performance differs for offensive and defensive players, but the defensive model supported the mediational model. This suggested that an individual player's lack of

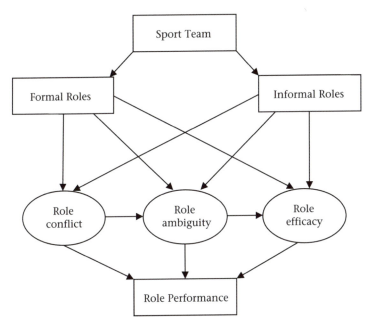

Figure 7.5   Beauchamp's model of role performance
Source: Beauchamp (2004)

clarity regarding his/her role in the team negatively influenced his/her role performance, but this relationship was extinguished by each player's belief in his or her own abilities to perform the role adequately. This emphasizes the need to promote high role efficacy, using similar strategies to promote self-efficacy proposed by Bandura (1977, 1997), as it mitigates any potential for role ambiguity to affect performance. In addition, role ambiguity is also related to other adaptive and maladaptive outcomes within team sport. Research in sport teams has shown that role ambiguity is positively related to both cognitive and somatic competitive state anxiety and that clarity of scope of responsibilities is related to satisfaction with team ability, strategy utilization, training and instruction, team task contribution, and group integration at both early and late season (Beauchamp *et al*. 2003; Eys *et al*. 2003). Together these results provide preliminary evidence to suggest that lack of clarity in individual players' roles in sport teams can have a disruptive effect, and is related to maladaptive outcomes and group processes like role conflict.

Several important practical guidelines arise from this research (Beauchamp and Bray 2001; Beauchamp *et al*. 2002). First, coaches would do well to foster role efficacy in team players. Mastery experiences in training are important in this regard, to provide players with practices designed to emphasize the importance of their role in the team. In addition, coaches should incorporate in their team building programmes educational and information sessions aimed at clarifying: (a) team players' scope of responsibilities; (b) their role behaviours; (c) their evaluative criteria; and (d) the consequences. Given the findings that different aspects of ambiguity affect role performance in offensive and defensive roles, coaches should also take into account the contexts in which roles are likely to be fulfilled. It is also recommended that coaches be explicit and clear in outlining why players have been given specific roles (emphasizing specialties and specific abilities) and how players' roles fit in with overall team strategy. Most of all, coaches should not keep their strategies as secret designs to add 'mystique' to their methods but should instead emphasize common goals and the fact that team success is dependent upon players fulfilling their roles.

Social influence

One of the earliest studies in social psychology was conducted in a sport context and examined the effect of the presence of other people on the performance of motor skills and cognitive tasks, a phenomenon that became known as **social facilitation** (Triplett 1898). Triplett's (1898) study examined the effects of the presence of others in cycling racing and in children participating in a fine motor skill ('turning fishing-line reels'). Triplett found that cyclists' times were faster when they raced in competition with others compared with paced and unpaced 'solo' races. Analogously, children were much faster when turning reels when in direct competition with another than when on their own. Triplett suggested that the presence of a competitor 'served to liberate latent energy not ordinarily available' (1898: 507) in pursuit of the task. This pioneering study stimulated much research on the effects of the presence of other in skills and tasks, including sports skills. However, research in the area was met with inconsistent findings, with some studies finding a significant effect of the presence of others on performance (e.g. Dashiell 1930) and some studies finding an inconsistent or significant effects at all (e.g. Allport 1920). These inconsistent results led to a lull in the theoretical and empirical advances in the area until Zajonc (1965) proposed a theoretical explanation of the effects of an audience on behaviour that rejuvenated and intensified research in social facilitation (Cottrell 1972).

Zajonc's (1965) theory of social facilitation

Zajonc's (1965) theory of social facilitation provided an explanation of the inconsistent findings in social facilitation research. Zajonc made a number of important observations regarding the nature of the audience and the way it was interpreted by the performer. The theory was based on findings that organisms have a set of behavioural tendencies or responses that are dominant and override all other responses. These *dominant responses* tend to be well-learned skills or response patterns that have been incorporated into an individual's repertoire through experience. These are opposed to non-dominant responses that usually delineate novel, difficult, or unpractised skills. Zajonc noted from studies in drive theory that high levels of arousal tended to result in an individual adopting on his or her 'dominant' response to a stimulus and the performance of the response was exacerbated, or 'facilitated', by the increased arousal (Yerkes and Dodson 1908). It was hypothesized that under conditions of coaction or in the presence of an audience an individual would experience increased arousal that would give rise to the dominant response being displayed when the individual engaged in a task. If the task was a simple or well-practised one, a social facilitation effect was observed because the dominant response was the successful execution of the skill. However, if the task was complex, novel, or unpractised, the dominant response tended to be one of failure, and therefore the opposite of a social facilitation effect was observed, or social inhibition. This theory was able to account for the observation of a social facilitation effect in tasks that were simple, well-learnt, or instinctive such as a basic motor skill or driving a car, while a negative social facilitation effect was found when participants were engaged in novel or complex tasks such as a complex motor skill or solving puzzles and mathematics problems.

Importantly, Zajonc's notion of social facilitation considered the presence of others as passive and that had no interaction with the performer. Thus, Zajonc's proposed social facilitation effect gave rise to the *mere presence* hypothesis. That is, observers of an individual performing a task will evoke arousal and the dominant response by virtue of fact that they are just in attendance and research in social facilitation using a passive audience corroborates the mere presence hypothesis. However, it must be noted that 'physical presence' may not be necessary to evoke a social facilitation effect, information that others are performing the task co-operatively but at a different location may be enough for a social facilitation effect to be observed in some individuals (Dashiell 1930). This finding has been corroborated in studies in which participants were told they were being monitored by 'electronic' surveillance (e.g. Aiello and Douthitt 2001).

Evaluation apprehension and social facilitation

Cottrell (1972) proposed that the mechanism behind the social facilitation effect did not lie in mere presence alone, but in whether the individual performing in front of the audience believed that the audience were judging or evaluating their performance. This **evaluation apprehension** was perceived to be the source of the increased arousal in the performer, and thus evoked the dominant response. The mediating effect of apprehension evaluation has been supported studies on individual and group and performers that have adopted passive or non-evaluative, evaluative, and no-audience conditions (e.g. Bray and Sugarman 1980). Although many of these studies have indicated that evaluation apprehension seems to explain a great deal of the variance in the social facilitation effect, it does not completely account for the effect and authors have suggested that mere presence has a unique effect on social facilitation (Bond and Titus 1983).

Bond and Titus conducted a meta-analysis of 241 studies that examined the social facilitation effect. A significant, albeit small, average corrected effect sizes for the influence of an audience on performance was found, accounting for between 0.3 and 3 per cent of the variance in the difference in performance in relation to non-audience conditions. Further analyses revealed that arousal was only heightened by the presence of an audience if the task was complex. The speed of a simple task was facilitated by the presence of an audience, while complex tasks showed a social inhibition effect. It was also found that the presence of an audience compromised the accuracy of a complex task, but had a small facilitative effect on the accuracy of a simple task. Importantly, the social facilitation effects were unique and were not affected by evaluation apprehension. These findings therefore suggest that evaluation apprehension may be a methodological artefact and cast some doubt on Cottrell's (1972) modification of Zajonc's theory.

In a sport context, social facilitation effects have been confirmed in a number of studies, with results tending to lend support to the evaluation apprehension hypothesis than mere presence (Strauss 2002). Strauss suggests that mere presence effects tend to be weak, and the effects of an audience of different types of motor task tend to be inconsistent. Several studies have supported the role of an evaluative audience or co-actor on sport performers. For example, Smith and Crabbe (1976) found that active experimenter participation increased the learning of a balancing motor task in participants compared with passive or no experimenter conditions, supporting the evaluation apprehension hypothesis. In a novel adaptation of the social facilitation experiment, Paulus et al. (1972) studied the performance of novice and experienced gymnasts in the presence of an audience. One group of gymnasts in each performance level were forewarned about the presence of an audience while others were not. Those who were not warned exhibited high quality performances compared to the forewarned gymnasts who incurred a decrement in performance. The authors suggested that the anticipated evaluation of the audience evaluation was responsible for the decrement in performance and undermined the dominant response in the skilled performers. In the presence of an evaluative audience, Bell and Yee (1989) found that karate experts' performance was unaffected in terms of the speed and accuracy of a kicking task relative to a solo condition. However, unskilled karate performers reduced the performance of their kicking to avoid errors, indicating that the presence of an audience has a slight social inhibitory effect causing a speed–accuracy trade-off. This supports the findings found in previous studies in which complex tasks for novice performers tend to incur an accuracy decrement (Allport 1920; Bond and Titus 1983).

While these studies found effects largely consistent with Zajonc's (1965) and Cottrell's (1972) hypotheses, Kozar (1973) found no difference in supportive, non-supportive, or no audience conditions in learning a gross motor skill. Kozar also found no differences in the learning performance of high- and low-anxious participants, negating the potential moderating effect of evaluation apprehension. However, it must be stressed that this study focused on learning rather than performance and used a gross, relatively simple motor task, not a complex task.

Role of cognition in social facilitation effects

Social cognitive constructs may also have important effects on social facilitation. Research examining cognitive variables on the social facilitation effect has given rise to explanations based on attention conflict in which the distraction of an audience competes for cognitive resources or attention from the individual (Baron 1986). For example, Hall and Bunker (1979) found a significant interaction between social facilitation and the social cognitive variable of locus of control. Participants engaged in a novel task that reported an internal locus of control did not exhibit a decrement in performance before an audience while those reporting an external locus did. Similarly, Forgas et al. (1980) found social inhibition effects for expert squash players and social facilitation effects for novice squash players when playing as a pair before an audience. To explain this, Forgas et al. suggested that under solo conditions the match was viewed as a straightforward competition, so it was acceptable for players to play to their ability. However, when playing before an audience, the expert players may have felt the need to curtail their performers as there was an increased need to be seen to be participating co-operatively. These results suggest that the social facilitation effect is more complex than the premises put forward by Zajonc (1965) and Cottrell (1972) over four decades ago. Future research on social facilitation will account cognitive and address hypotheses relating to the mechanisms involved in this complex phenomenon.

Social loafing

While the social facilitation literature provides a theoretical explanation for the conditions under which co-actors may facilitate or debilitate performance, researchers have identified an additional outcome of performance of a task in a co-acting or collective situation in which an individual exhibits a clear motivational decrement or performance loss. This process is called social loafing, and individual performance of a sport-related task in a team environment is an ideal naturalistic setting to examine this phenomenon. The social loafing effect was observed in early research in group influence on individual performance toward a collective task by Ringelmann (1927, cited in Latané et al. 1979) in which people exhibited worse performance when engaging in a task in co-operation with others than when they were working in solitude. In essence, these observations were the opposite of the social facilitation effects in co-acting conditions (working alongside others rather than in front of an audience) observed in the studies of Triplett (1898), Allport (1920), and Dashiell (1930), and this has since become known as the Ringelmann effect. Since, researchers have argued that this effect should be studied in conjunction with the social facilitation effect to provide a unified theory of social facilitation (Aiello and Douthitt 2001).

One of the first studies to integrate these findings and offer an explanation for the two seemingly contradictory social influence effects was conducted by Jackson and Williams (1985). Using the completion of computer mazes, the research indicated that individual performance was optimal when working collectively on difficult mazes and when working individually on simple mazes. Importantly, only when the performance of the group on the maze was readily identifiable and individual performance was not, were individual performances on the maze inhibited. When individual performance was distinguishable from that of the group, individual performance when working collectively was improved. Sanna (1992) provided evidence that high self-efficacy moderated the social loafing effect. Theorists have also suggested that the social loafing effect was observed when performers did not receive any feedback regarding their own performance or the group performance. In summary, social loafing seems to arise when high-self-efficacy individuals working toward the collective task are aware that they were not being evaluated and were not given feedback relating to this performance.

In sport, social loafing research has focused on identifying the factors responsible for the reduced motivation in individuals competing in team sports for which the collective rather than the individual is held responsible (C. J. Hardy 1990). In keeping with theory, identifiability, defined as the extent to which an athlete's performance is known to him or her and others, of an individual within a team, moderated the social loafing effect in collegiate swimmers (Everett *et al.* 1992). The sport ability of an individual performer in a team relative to his/her teammates has also been shown to magnify the social loafing effect, suggesting that perceptions of incompetence may account for motivational decrements probably because of the athlete's perception that they would have little impact on collective performance (Hardy and Crace 1991). This effect was also seen in collective team situations when faced with opposition that was vastly superior to themselves (Heuze and Brunel 2003).

Recent research has focused on group-centred social cognitive variables that may affect social loafing. Lichacz and Partington (1996) found that participants with high collective efficacy and with prior experience of the group exhibited fewer inhibition effects due to social loafing. Indeed, research has indicated that the cohesiveness of the team is negatively related to the social loafing effect (Everett *et al.* 1992), however, it must be noted that team cohesion and collective efficacy alone may not negate the social facilitation effect. For example, Hardy and Latané (1988) found that members of established teams performing intrinsically motivating (i.e. interesting) tasks exhibit social loafing, an effect that could be explained by complacency in the absence of evaluative feedback. Interestingly, when athletes were given information about the social loafing effect before group competition, there was still evidence of a decrement in motivation and performance in a team competition compared with a solo condition (Huddleston *et al.* 1985). This suggests that prior knowledge does not interfere with situational characteristics that may influence social loafing such as presence of evaluative performance feedback, collective efficacy, and competence levels.

Future directions in social facilitation research

Social facilitation research has met with considerable success in identifying the phenomenon, providing explanations for the effect, and identifying the different conditions and influences on performance under conditions of social facilitation. However, some have criticized the lack of an integrative or unified approach to the different explanations and facilitating conditions in the extant literature (Aiello and Douthitt 2001). Aiello and Douthitt claim that this lack of a framework limits research in the area due to a lack of clearly defined hypotheses. These authors suggest that theories of social facilitation could benefit from further clarification of some key tenets or features of the effect: (1) the definition of social facilitation; (2) identification of the salient dimensions of social facilitation; and (3) the predicted effects of the presence of other under a given set of situational and psychological conditions. Such an integrative approach may assist in directing future investigations toward the appropriate research hypotheses necessary to fill gaps in theory.

An integrative model was presented by Aiello and Douthitt in an attempt to draw together the various theoretical strands and research findings into a conceptual framework to explain social facilitation effects. The integrative model is presented in Figure 7.6. The model is presented with individual influences on social facilitation at its heart, indicating that intrapersonal variables mediate the effects of other, more extraneous, influences on performance factors and outcome variables portrayed at the base of Figure 7.6. Three main areas of extraneous influences on the individual or personal factors that are associated with social facilitation effects are identified: (1) situational factors; (2) presence factors; and (3) task factors. Situational factors represent the characteristics of the climate in which the audience is presented, whether they are seen or heard, how close they are, whether feedback on the situation is available, and the structure of the motivational climate. A set of presence factors map the features of the audience likely to have an effect on social facilitation, namely, the type of presence or make-up of the group, the role of the audience, how salient they are to the individual and their relationship to them (e.g. parents vs. strangers), and the length of the presence. Then the model accounts for the task factors that feature most prominently in social facilitation research: the difficulty (simple vs. complex) and type of task (cognitive vs. motor), and the time demand of the task.

These variables are proposed to affect the individual factors. Central to this are the perceptions and reactions of the individual to the extraneous factors.

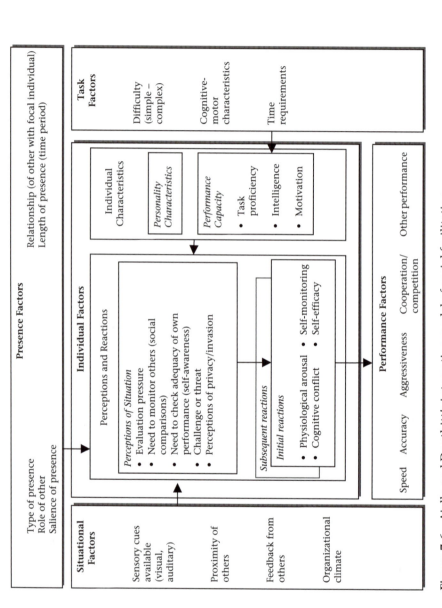

Figure 7.6 Aiello and Douthitt's integrative model of social facilitation
Source: Aiello and Douthitt (2001: 74)

These include evaluation pressure, social comparisons, self-awareness or self-presentation, whether the extraneous factors are a challenge or a threat, or invasive. These initial perceptions and reactions are envisaged to mediate the influence of the extraneous influences on subsequent reactions such as physiological arousal, cognitive conflict, self-monitoring, and self-efficacy. Personality and other individual characteristics such as motivation, intelligence and ability also play a moderating role in the effects of extraneous and situational perceptions and reactions on subsequent reactions and performance. It is proposed that subsequent reactions, especially physiological arousal, will affect the performance factors, many of which have been dependent variables in social facilitation research: speed and accuracy. Aiello and Douthitt (2001) claim that other responses to social facilitation such as aggressiveness, cooperation vs. competition, and effects of social facilitation of the performance of others need to be studied in greater depth. While a number of these aspects have been studied, increases in the sophistication of the methodology in social facilitation research may provide future studies that incorporate more elements of this proposed model. This is particularly pertinent in examining the effects of social facilitation in sport, as the findings to date have been inconsistent.

Home advantage

One of the most pervasive, consistent, and oft-cited social effects in sport psychology is the **home advantage**. The effect is so well observed that it has been elevated into the lore of sports statistics as a principle rather than mere theory. Further, the effects of home advantage have been the subject of intense research interest by statisticians, sport scientists, and sport psychologists. Sport psychologists' interests stem from the view that the home advantage is a largely psychological phenomenon, particularly if physical parameters between two teams are considered to be relatively equal and any differences largely insubstantial. Since competitive sport is often undertaken by competent individuals, both arousal and cognitive explanations of social facilitation lend credence to the expectation that team players at home will have their dominant response reinforced and enjoy a facilitative effect on performance. However, as the previous section testifies, situational, presence, task, and individual factors can alter these effects. The aim of this section is to provide an overview of the home advantage in sport and to examine the theories that have been put forward in applied social psychology to explain these effects. In particular, the premise that crowd influence will have the most pervasive effect on the home advantage in accordance with social facilitation theory will be addressed.

Prevalence, methods of investigation, and the home advantage

The home advantage effect has been noted in a variety of sports including American football (Schwartz and Barsky 1977), baseball (Schwartz and Barsky 1977; Courneya and Carron 1991), basketball (Schwartz and Barsky 1977; Silva and Andrew 1987; Varca 1980), cricket (Jones *et al.* 2001), cross-country running (McCutcheon 1984), field hockey (Russell 1983), ice-hockey (Schwartz and Barsky 1977; McGuire *et al.* 1992; Agnew and Carron 1994), soccer (Brown *et al.* 2002), alpine skiing (Bray and Martin 2003), and wrestling (Gayton and Langevin 1992). These studies have indicated that teams win between 52 per cent and 88 per cent of their home games (Schwartz and Barsky 1977; Courneya and Carron 1991; Gayton and Langevin 1992; Bray 1999). Studies have also indicated that teams in outdoor sports such as American football and baseball seem to have only a marginal home advantage, while teams in indoor sports such as ice-hockey and basketball seem to enjoy more of a home advantage (Schwartz and Barsky 1977). However, there has been debate as to whether the home advantage occurs all of the time. Some studies have shown that in championship series and play-off matches in baseball and basketball, the final games at the end of the season that decide championships, home teams won the majority of early games in the series, but lost the majority of the final games (Baumeister and Steinhilber 1984). As a consequence, the hypothesis has been disputed and is a topic of debate among researchers in the area (Baumeister 1995; Schlenker *et al.* 1995), suffice to say that on some occasions, perhaps in high pressure matches, a home advantage may be negated or even overturned. The next section will visit the methods and theories proposed to explain these inconclusive findings.

A number of methods have been adopted to examine the home advantage effect. Schwartz and Barsky were among the first to adopt formal statistical procedures and demographic information to explain the home advantage in indoor (ice-hockey and basketball) and outdoor (American football and baseball) sports. The authors used official published archival statistics from all league teams to explain the win and loss ratios on home compared to away grounds. Many studies have since adopted this methodology (e.g. Varca 1980; Gayton and Langevin 1992; McGuire *et al.* 1992; Agnew and Carron 1994). Other studies have examined the home advantage from the perspective of individual team statistics over the course of the season rather than league average (Bray 1999). Some studies have used observational techniques by trained observers to provide additional information regarding performance not based on published statistics, such as Greer's (1983) observation of crowd protest over the course of the season. Studies have also used these observational techniques to collect data from televised sports matches (Salminen 1993). Finally, the most challenging studies from an empirical point of view are those that collect additional data from players and participants in the competitions throughout the course of the season (Bray and Martin 2003; Neave and Wolfson 2003). These studies are usually data-rich, but are very expensive and time-consuming to conduct and are often plagued by the problems typically experienced in applied social psychological research such as small sample sizes and missing data due to participant drop-out. Together, these methods of investigation have provided converging evidence for the influential factors and consequences of home advantage in sport.

Explanations and theories of home advantage

The home advantage has been attributed to a number of factors, some demographic such as age, others situational such as size of crowd and distance to venue. More sophisticated theories have been proposed to explain the mechanisms behind the influence of these factors, and how they affect the social psychological processes that underlie performance. Of all these factors, it seems that the make-up of the crowd and its effects on the arousal levels and perceptions of the home team players are the most pervasive. This section will examine a variety of theories and factors thought to influence and explain the home advantage.

Territorial/ethological theories
One of the more controversial but compelling explanations for home advantage is based on ethological observations in organisms relating to marked territory and their defence of it. Russell (1983, 1993) argues that organisms are more fervent in their defence of their territory because it represents their livelihood for breeding and feeding. Therefore, organisms attach greater value in the defence of contested territory when it is their own because they have a lot to lose. Futhermore, this has an evolutionary advantage as organisms that cannot defend their territory successfully are selected out of the species and there is evidence in support of this 'home advantage' in animals (e.g. Rajecki *et al.* 1979). According to Russell (1993), the theoretically greater fervour exhibited in the defence of their home territory could be attributed to a greater display of aggressive behaviours by the home team and this has been supported in some studies (e.g. Varca 1980). Further, recent evidence has provided some additional evidence to support a territorial explanation of home advantage in 'human competitive encounters' like sports competition. Neave and Wolfson (2003) found that testosterone levels were higher in soccer players before their home games, and especially higher when facing 'extreme' rivals compared with 'moderate' rivals. The authors suggest that elevated hormone levels may be concomitant with a greater innate propensity to defend home territory and display aggressive behaviours. However, sport research has not conclusively supported increased aggressive behavioural displays in home teams. While ethological and territorial explanations may potentially account for the home advantage effect, Russell (1993) claims that these theories provide a more philosophical than empirical explanation for the home advantage.

Crowd size, density, and hostility

As proposed earlier, one of the key explanations offered for the home advantage is the presence of a partisan home audience or crowd during play. A number of studies have examined the effect of crowd size and density on performance of teams at home. As is almost exclusively the case in team sports particularly at elite level, the majority of home spectators support the home team, even in so-called derby games. Therefore it is reasonable to assume that the size of the home audience is a reflection of the number of home supporters present. Schwartz and Barsky (1977) were among the first to examine the effect of crowd size on home advantage in American football, basketball, baseball, and ice-hockey, and their results found that winning percentage of home teams increased in proportion to crowd size. In addition, Russell (1983) studied the effect of crowd size on indicators of performance (e.g. goals scored) in home teams in field hockey, and found no significant correlation between these for the home team. However, a significant negative correlation between crowd size and performance parameters of the away team was found. This suggests that the home advantage may be more due to the inhibitory effect of crowd size on away performers. This supported findings that suggested the home advantage was really an 'away disadvantage' (Silva and Andrew 1987). Some researchers have hypothesized that it may not be the size of the crowd *per se*, but its density. Agnew and Carron (1994) studied the effect of crowd density on home performance of junior ice-hockey teams and found that density was significantly related to the home advantage, but only accounted for a small percentage of the variance in winning percentage. These results lend some support to the hypothesis that the density rather than size of the crowd matters in home advantage, while the size of the crowd may be implicated in visitor disadvantage.

Given the finding that visitors may be adversely affected by the audience, researchers have sought to examine whether the nature of the support offered by the crowd has a detrimental effect on away teams. Greer (1983) examined the effect of spectator protest ('booing') on the performance parameters of home and away teams in college basketball games. Results indicated that the performance gap between the home and away teams increased dramatically during episodes of protest. However, although there were marginal increases in the performance of the home team, it was decreases in the performance of the away teams (greater number of fouls committed and reduced overall performance) that contributed to the increase in the performance advantage already enjoyed by the home team.

By way of explanation, Silva (1979) suggested that hostile and angry behaviours exhibited by the crowd towards players may disrupt concentration and inhibit execution of motor skills. This 'distraction' effect is consistent with the social facilitation and social loafing literature that suggests that the audience draws cognitive resources and attention that should be committed to the performance of the task (Baron 1986). However, other studies have not supported a negative effect of spectator protest on visiting team performance.

Salminen's (1993) study of basketball, ice-hockey, and soccer teams revealed that, contrary to hypotheses, when the home crowd supported the visiting team, the home team also scored more points/goals. These findings question the conclusion that away teams suffer a decrement in performance before a hostile crowd, and suggest that *any* display of support, regardless of direction, is likely to have a positive influence on home team performance. In sum, research examining the size, composition, and nature of the crowd on the home advantage makes intuitive and theoretical sense. A partisan home support, for example, that is spread out across a large stadium is less likely to facilitate the performance of the home team because support is likely to be diluted, compared with an audience of comparable size that is closely packed.

Explanation of the facilitative and inhibitory effects in home advantage research can be explained by social facilitation theories. However, the research suggests that the effects of the crowd on home advantage or visitor disadvantage demands a more complex explanation than Zajonc's (1965) theory of mere presence. Some researchers suggest that the arousal effect of the presence of a crowd may evoke more 'assertive behaviours' in athletes as suggested previously in ethological explanations of home advantage. Varca (1980) suggested that the home advantage evoked the types of behaviours consistent with aggressive but performance-enhancing play. Examining these 'functional assertive behaviours' in school basketball teams supported this hypothesis. Further, visiting teams exhibited a significantly greater number of 'dysfunctional assertive behaviours' such as fouls, a finding consistent with the visitor disadvantage. Varca supposed that the presence of these aggressive behaviours partly explained the home advantage effect. McGuire *et al.* (1992) corroborated these results in league ice-hockey players. They found that aggression was advantageous in home players but disadvantageous to away team players. One possible mechanism for this aggression is the increased arousal evoked by the partisan crowd (Sanna 1992).

Sport type
Schwartz and Barsky (1977) identified indoor sports like basketball and ice-hockey as being most influenced by home advantage, while outdoor sports had fewer effects. This may be due to the proximity and density of crowds in indoor arenas. However, there has been little research to investigate the parameters that might affect the extent of the home advantage across different sports. However, some interesting research has examined whether the home advantage is as pervasive in individual sports as it is in team sports. Studies have found a significant home advantage in individual sports like wrestling (Gayton and Langevin 1992). Results were attributed to increased feelings of security and dominance and attributed to a 'prior residence effect' in which an initial resident in a geographical area has a social dominance advantage over an intruder. However, others have found no home advantage was found in a study of individual downhill skiiers (Bray and Martin 2003). The studies of home advantage in individual sports are limited, and further research will

reveal further trends. It is possible that the extent of the home advantage will vary according to the sport itself as observed across different team sports.

Home venue familiarity

Competitor's familiarity with the site and facilities of the home venue may account for the variance in performance over home and away fixtures. In a novel study, Loughhead *et al.* (2003) investigated the effect of a change in home venue on home performances of professional basketball, hockey, and soccer teams. They found no differences in the teams' performance immediately after relocation and the games following relocation compared to before location. However, when the quality of the team was introduced as a moderator, it was found that high quality teams were unaffected by the move, while low quality teams benefited, in terms of performance, from the relocation. A possible reason for this may be that the improved quality of the facilities for the lower quality teams may outweigh the detrimental effects of unfamiliar surroundings, possibly because the gap in standard between the old and new facilities was greater for the lower quality teams. Jones *et al.* suggested that familiarity with facilities was a plausible explanation for a home advantage effect found in cricket teams, a sport in which audience influence was minimal. One possible explanation for the effect of familiarity on home advantage may be that athletes are more likely to perform better when performing the skills in the environment in which they originally learnt them, as opposed to a novel one (Russell 1993).

Distance and travel

One of the most well-researched factors thought to contribute to the home advantage is the distance travelled by the away team. Early research supported an effect of distance travelled on home advantage (Schwartz and Barsky 1977). However, the effect of distance travelled alone provides only a partial explanation for the effect of distance on home advantage, and there are a number of distance-related variables that may influence home advantage. Courneya and Carron (1991) found only a very small effect for distance travelled, presence of home travel for either the home or the away team, and time of season (number of games into season) on home advantage in baseball players. The effect of further distance-related parameters, including number of time zones crossed by the visiting team, on home advantage in professional ice-hockey players was investigated by Pace and Carron (1992). While the number of time zones crossed and preparation time were inversely related to visiting team performance, these factors also only accounted for a small amount of variance in the home advantage. Converging evidence from these studies suggests that there is a minimal, albeit significant effect of visiting team travel on home advantage, but the variance this artefact explains in performance is small.

Recently, an interesting new perspective on the effect of visiting teams travelling across time zones on home advantage has been proposed and has promise to account for inconsistencies in research on travel effects. Steenland

and Deddens (1997) used archival data from professional United States basketball (U.S. National Basketball Association) and American football (U.S. American Football League) teams to examine the effect of players' circadian times of day on home advantage. As hypothesized, they found that teams based on the West Coast of the United States playing away games at East Coast locations performed significantly better in the those particular away games because they were playing at a time of day closer to their theoretical physiological peak. These results suggest that the effect of distance and travel across time zones *per se* may not fully explain the effect of visitor team travel on home advantage. It is possible that these results could be extrapolated to travel of international visiting teams from west to east, and suggests that an adequate recovery period should be included for teams travelling from east to west.

Referee bias
Opposition supporters to successful teams often state, albeit slightly tongue-in-cheek, that their opponents seldom get sanctioned with penalties (e.g. fouls, free kicks) against them and often get penalties in their favour from match referees and officials when playing at home. Referee bias has therefore been cited as one factor that may contribute to home advantage. In his study on crowd protest, Greer (1983) did not attribute the significantly greater number of fouls incurred by visiting teams after protest episodes to referee bias, rather, this seemed to be due to an overall decline in performance not just increased incidence of fouls. Recently, however, Nevill *et al.* (2002) conducted an experimental study in which soccer officials assessed videotaped game situations with and without crowd noise. Results showed that the officials watching the games with crowd noise were more uncertain in their decision-making and awarded significantly fewer fouls to the home team. These results suggested that crowd noise had a pervasive effect on referee bias, but questions still remain over the ecological validity of the experiment and the partisan nature of the crowd noise. Interestingly, in a study on county cricket, a sport with virtually no crowd influence, Jones *et al.* (2001) found no evidence of match umpire decisions for home and away teams, which may lend further weight to the influence of the crowd in biasing decisions. Another factor that may affect match official or referee bias is the quality and profile of the team members. In a study on a professional basketball team, Lehman and Reifman (1987) also found that while officials awarded equal number of fouls to ordinary, 'nonstar' players in home and away teams, the well-known 'star' players on the home team incurred significantly fewer penalties than the away team players.

A number of explanations for referee bias have been put forward. One prominent effect observed in social psychology known as interpersonal bias, often referred to as the Pygmalion effect, may account for referee bias. Referees may unconsciously bias their decisions toward the home team and star players because they have an expectation that the home team and star players will perform better. Evidence for this is given by two studies on judging officials in gymnastics and figure skating respectively. Scheer and Ansorge (1979) studied the effect of prior expectation on gymnastics judges' decisions. In gymnastics, it is commonly known that coaches in each team always send their gymnasts out to the apparatus in reverse order of ability, as judges have an expectation that the best gymnasts will compete last in the rotation. Scheer and Ansorge required gymnastics judges to score videotaped Olympic qualifier routines, but reversed the order of presentation of the routines such that the first gymnast in each team appeared last, and so on. The judges' scoring was found to be biased to favour the last performer, even though they were the least skilled in each team. Interestingly, this effect was found to be moderated by the personality traits of the individual judges. Judges who reported having an external locus of control and thought that events were subject to extraneous factors and luck were more likely to be biased toward the order of the competitors than judges with an internal locus of control. This evidence suggests that biased decisions may therefore be a function of the psychological profile of the referee themselves rather than their expectations alone. In a study on figure skater judges, Findlay and Ste-Marie (2004) found that judges gave significantly better marks to skaters who were known to them, suggesting an influence of reputation bias. Together this evidence suggests that prior expectations and reputation are likely to bias decisions of referees and judges rather than audience effects *per se*.

Home disadvantage
In the introduction to this section, we visited Baumeister and Steinhilber's (1984) experiments on the paradox of the home advantage in high pressure, last-game situations. In situations of high audience expectation it seems that the home advantage is negated. A re-analysis of the findings and addition of new data suggested that the disadvantage effect was not as pervasive as previously cited (Schlenker *et al.* 1995). However, Baumeister (1995) insists that the effect still exists even though it may be weaker than previously stated. Explanations for these effects come from the social facilitation literature and the potential for the high-pressure, anxiety-provoking situation to interfere with the 'dominant response'. The increased expectations of the home crowd may inhibit performance for several reasons: (1) increased arousal due to the audience presence may cause a distraction or an inability to focus attention on the task at hand (Baron 1986); (2) a heightened self-awareness causes players to move their attention away from the appropriate cues for action (Baumeister 1984); or (3) the player may focus too greatly on the execution of well-learnt skills and this exertion of cognitive control results in disruption (Baumeister 1984); or (4) fearing failure, the competitor becomes self-aware and again experiences distraction from appropriate cues. It seems that the 'championship choke' is a phenomenon that is difficult to explain, but it likely to have a pervasive effect on the expectations of home teams in high pressure match situations. Home teams may therefore not assume or rely on any home advantage in last-game or championship series.

Future directions in home advantage research

The home advantage effect is found to be a robust and consistent effect across a number of sports. Investigations into the causes of this effect have mainly been centred on the influence that the audience has on the players of the home team, and theoretical explanations have been based on models of social facilitation, the arousing effects of an audience, and their effect on social cognitive variables like self-efficacy and self-confidence. Other explanations have been proposed including travel fatigue, home venue familiarity, referee bias, sport type, team quality, and age. However, much of the research for these effects has not led to consistent results, suggesting that one universal model or theory is unlikely to account for all of the variance in performance between home and away games. This is just an illustration of the complexity of the phenomenon and regression models to explain home advantage may exist for each different sport. One criticism that can be levelled at the home advantage research is their bias towards culturally-specific sport disciplines. American football, baseball, and, to a lesser extent, basketball and ice-hockey tend to be sport disciplines played predominantly in North America, and the majority of the studies have come from this region. Studies on European and international sporting disciplines are becoming more prevalent (e.g. Jones *et al.* 2001; Brown *et al.* 2002), but further research needs to be done in order to examine the extent of the home advantage in different cultures and sports disciplines. Further, future research needs to examine the effect of the home advantage on social cognitive variables in order to form a comprehensive theory for the home advantage.

Suggested reading

Aiello, J.R. and Douthitt, E.A. (2001) Social facilitation from Triplett to electronic performance monitoring, *Group Dynamics*, 5: 163–80. Recent review that charts the progress in social facilitation research and presents a new and exciting conceptual model.

Baumeister, R.F. and Steinhilber, A. (1984) Paradoxical effects of supportive audiences on performance under pressure: the home field disadvantage in sports championships, *Journal of Personality and Social Psychology*, 47: 85–93. Baumeister's fascinating classic paper on the paradox of the home disadvantage.

Carron, A.V. and Hausenblas, H.A. (1998) *Group Dynamics in Sport*, 2nd edn. Morgantown, WV: Fitness Information Technology. The leading text on the influence of group processes in sport.

Schwartz, B. and Barsky, S.F. (1977) The home advantage, *Social Forces*, 55: 641–61. The paper that started it all; the citation classic on home advantage in sports teams.

Summary

- Social psychologists define a group as a collection of people who interact with each other, have a common goal, have a clear structure, and have shared communication processes and behavioural outcomes. Sports teams are one example of a group and the interactions and other processes operating within the team have a pervasive effect on the behaviour of the individual members that make up the team.
- Carron and Hausenblas's (1998) conceptual model provides a framework for understanding group processes in sport. In the model, group structure is determined by team norms and the roles of the group members. Group structure influences important outcomes in sports teams such as team goals, collective efficacy, and cooperation. Group cohesion mediates these relationships.
- Group cohesion is an important construct in group processes and has profound effects on team outcomes and performance.
- Role ambiguity is a threat to cohesion and coaches should promote clarity and efficacy in sports performers regarding their role in a sport team.
- Social facilitation describes the effects of the mere presence and perceived evaluative apprehension of other people such as an audience or co-actors on sport performance. Social facilitation is moderated by degree of evaluation apprehension.
- The lack of personal agency, role clarity, self-efficacy, and clear feedback on individual performance can give rise to reduced effort and performance level in team members, known as social loafing.
- The home advantage for sports teams is influenced by the size, density, and hostility of the audience, reputation of performers in team, age of team members, and home facility familiarity. There is research to suggest that the home advantage effect is actually due to impaired performance by visiting teams, known as away disadvantage.
- Home advantage tends to be least affected by distance travelled to match and referee bias. Further, the home advantage seems to be overturned in matches that lead to athletes performing at their optimal time of day and in the later games of championship series matches.

Aggression and crowd violence

Aggression in sport

There is perhaps no more reprehensible and harrowing sight than groups of athletes fighting each other over an infraction, a point, a disputed tackle, or some other relatively minor penalty during a sports game or competition. To a neutral observer, the cause of the melee may seem trivial, almost insignificant, and therefore unjustified. However, move closer to the action, and the fans, crowd, or spectators can all be seen to hold strong views about the matter and may even endorse such aggressive action (Russell 1979). Further, coaches often side with their players in matters of dispute, invariably supporting their teams, the politician 'inside' them often the only thing preventing them from joining the fracas in defence of their players. The players themselves are often united in their aggravated feelings and provocative gestures towards the opposition, but are often observed stopping short in participating in actual aggressive behaviours. Alongside the players, the coaches, and the spectators, the media watches with morbid fascination, selecting, recording, and presenting the events that ensue and their intricate details prominently in their headlines often with a 'holier than thou' sense of moral outrage.

Why do players resort to such violent conduct when they know there are clear penalties for doing so? Why do coaches defend their players when they can clearly see that such **aggression** is counter-productive and morally dubious? And what role do the media play in perpetuating such aggression? Do the media present such hostilities in such sensationalist fashion through an exaggerated sense of moral obligation? Or is it because the consumers of such media are captivated by such aggression? This chapter will seek to address these questions and evaluate the social psychological research into aggression and crowd violence in sport. Definitions of aggression and key social psychological theories will be reviewed, and several important studies of aggression in sport will be visited. **Crowd violence** and a specific form of fan violence, **hooliganism**, will also be reviewed. The chapter will conclude that aggression and crowd violence are frequently occurring phenomena in sport and are affected by situational, interpersonal, and inter-group factors.

Definition of aggression

Aggression is an often misinterpreted construct in social psychology. It is commonly thought that non-descript violent shouting and other outbursts such as fist-shaking and provocative gestures at the opposition or equipment abuse such as throwing a tennis racket on the ground in disgust constitute aggression. However, in terms of a formal definition, these violent or aggravated behaviours are not aggression. Aggression is a set of *behaviours* that are likely to, or have the potential to, *cause harm* to others, and are *intended* to cause harm, and are therefore *goal-directed* (Berkowitz 1993). Just as gesture and equipment abuse tend to lie outside the realm of aggression, some behaviours in sport are often misinterpreted as aggression. Examples are *assertive* behaviours which are merely actions that enhance the competitiveness of a team by imposing dominance over the opponent, but without injuring him, her, or them. Often coaches want players to be more 'aggressive' in their approach to their opponents. What they mean is that they want their players to display more assertive behaviours such as hard tackling in soccer and rugby, or hitting or pitching the ball at the opponent in tennis and baseball respectively. Such behaviours are physically vociferous, but have a purely pragmatic goal toward being successful rather than deliberately injuring an opponent. The definition of aggression can also be considered relative to what is tolerated by rule-producing governing bodies and what is not. For example, apparently provocative, 'aggressive' behaviour such as the Haka performed by the New Zealand All Blacks rugby teams prior to matches is endorsed by the authorities of the game. However, other violent acts are punished, albeit leniently, but for other reasons other than their causing injury to others, such as racket or verbal abuse in tennis. These acts are not aggression, so while aggression is usually against the regulations of given sports, some violent infringements in sport cannot be defined as aggression unless they are coupled with the defining criteria listed previously. To summarize, aggression is a set of behaviours that are intended to harm others, but are not to be confused with nondescript verbal outbursts or violent conduct towards inanimate objects and assertive behaviours in sport.

A number of authors have identified two types of aggression that can operate in sport contexts, *hostile aggression* and *instrumental aggression* (Silva 1980; Berkowitz 1993). Hostile aggression has the primary goal of harming or injuring another person or player. It is often a response to provocation, coupled with high emotional arousal, and an accompanying negative emotion often appraised as sourced from the focus of the aggressive act (see Figure 8.1). In hostile aggression, aggressive acts supersede other goals of the sport such as scoring points and will distract from the aggressive players' role in the team (see Chapter 7, Beauchamp and Bray 2001). For example, in April 2001, Roy

Keane, mid-fielder for Manchester United soccer team, deliberately caused injury to Alf Inge Haaland from the opposition team, Manchester City. 'I'd waited long enough. I hit him hard. The ball was there (I think). Take that . . . I didn't wait for Mr Elleray [the match referee] to show the [red] card. I turned and walked to the dressing room', commented Keane of the incident in his autobiography, for which he was later censured. Keane had no goal other than to injure the opponent, and, in getting himself sent off, actually jeopardized the chances of his team's success. Thus, the probable cause of hostile aggression can be clearly traced and the goal of the resulting violent behaviours is clearly focused on bringing retaliatory harm to the perceived perpetrator and not on other instrumental outcomes.

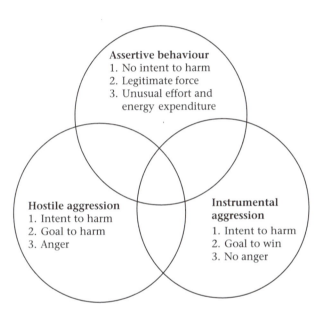

Figure 8.1 Silva's diagram of the different types of aggression in sport
Source: Silva (1980: 205)

Instrumental aggression, on the other hand, is intent to harm another but with a superordinate goal to achieve an outcome that is of benefit to the athlete, player, or his or her team. Thus, the effect of injuring the opponent or source of the aggression mediates the effect of the athletes' intention on their primary goal or outcome. Unlike hostile aggression, therefore, intent to harm is only peripheral to the overall goal (see Figure 8.1). Stories exist that in some team environments players are encouraged to deliberately injure opposing team players, at a risk to themselves in terms of personal safety or sanction from the match officials and governing bodies, in order to achieve a team goal. Instrumental aggression tends to be less spontaneous and is not necessarily provoked by elevated levels of arousal or anger, although it can be seen that hostile aggression can be calculated rather than spontaneously provoked, as in the Keane example previously. There are therefore 'grey' or ambiguous cases in the classification of assertive behaviours and hostile or instrumental aggression. The distinctions and overlap between these three behavioural types are conceptualized in Silva's (1980) taxonomy, illustrated in Figure 8.1.

Silva's conceptualization of the aggression and assertive behaviours not only illustrated the core features of the three behavioural types, but also indicates that there are ambiguities in all three. Thus, these definitions may not encapsulate all instances of such behaviours in sport, and some types of behaviours may share features with more than one definition. Examples of these types of behaviours are *gamesmanship* behaviours, where players perform actions that are not illegitimate by the rules of the game but are considered 'unsportsmanlike' in nature. For example, a tennis coach may actively instruct a player able to play powerful forehand volleys to hit the ball directly at their opponent's body at close range. The purpose of this tactic is to give them a winning advantage as it is clearly more difficult for an opponent to return a ball passed to the body and it is, strictly speaking, within the rules of the game. However, the underlying intention may be to injure, physically or psychologically, the opposing player. Thus, the intent to harm may exist, but it is difficult to overtly accuse someone of this, given that the behaviour is legitimate within the rules of the game. Therefore, in this case, the behaviour shares some properties of assertive behaviours, particularly legitimate force (see Figure 8.1), but also with instrumental aggression, particularly intent to harm.

Theories of aggression

Frustration–aggression hypothesis

One of the earliest social psychological explanations of aggression was put forward by Dollard *et al.* (1939), known as the frustration–aggression hypothesis. Aggression was supposedly the product of an anger response to the frustration of goals and desires of the individual. It predicted that frustration led an individual to select and direct their frustration towards the perceived source of that frustration in the form of aggression. Therefore, a highly skilled field hockey forward may become frustrated because she is not getting sufficient service in the form of cross and through balls from the mid-field players to score sufficient goals. However, she is also marked out of the game by an opposing team defender. According to the frustration–aggression hypothesis, the frustration felt by the hockey player will ultimately lead to aggression, and she may decide to take out that frustration by assaulting the defender. However, while this may happen occasionally, frustrated hockey players seldom assault their markers and often do little more than create some minor fouls or infringements. Indeed, there is little support for the frustration–aggression hypothesis in sport. Theorists have recognized that the competitive environment of sport does lend itself to frustration, but seldom aggression (Russell 1993). This was a major limitation of the frustration–aggression hypothesis because frustration did not lead inevitably to aggression. It was therefore ineffective in explaining the circumstances under which frustration did not lead to aggression. Recent revisions of the theory have incorporated hypotheses from social learning theory (Bandura 1977, 1997) to delineate the factors that affect the translation of frustration into aggression (Berkowitz 1993). Berkowitz proposed that the arousal induced in stressful situations gave rise to an emotional response such as frustration. However, frustration would only be manifested in aggression if previously learned patterns of behaviour linked frustrated emotions in that situation with an aggressive response.

Social learning theory

Bandura's (1977, 1997) social learning theory has already been considered in Chapters 2 and 5 as an influential theory of motivation. The observational learning aspects of social learning theory can also be applied to the genesis of aggressive behaviour in social situations. Bandura's seminal work on aggression as an imitation of modelled behaviour or vicarious experience by children serves as both an important but also controversial and distasteful comment on the development of human aggression. Bandura's seminal 'Bobo doll' experiments not only supported the hypothesis that aggressive behaviour is acquired through the observation of aggressive acts, but could also explain the circumstances most likely to result in their manifestation and their persistence or maintenance.

Social learning theory has had a profound effect on how aggression is portrayed in the media and its effects on children. However, Bandura outlined that there were moderating factors on the extent of imitation of aggressive behaviour. These factors included: (1) past experiences with the aggressive behaviour, both personally and the observation of others; (2) previous 'success' with aggressive behaviour in relation to personal goals; (3) the pattern of reinforcement expected on the display of aggression – is it likely to be rewarded or punished?; and (4) psychological, social, and environmental factors such as personality, verbal encouragement, and presence of significant others, respectively. Bandura's theory is therefore more comprehensive and far-reaching than the frustration–aggression hypothesis because it explains the development and conditions under which aggression occurs.

In sport, social learning theory has been used to explain the effects of overt aggression in professional sports on hero selection among fans. Using interviews and archival data, Russell (1979) found that goals scored and penalties incurred predicted ice-hockey fans' favourite player and team choice. In particular, teams were selected more on the basis of penalties conceded than goals scored, suggesting that aggressive behaviours have a more pervasive effect on attitudes than performance indicators. Russell attributed this to the media's disproportional focus on aggressive conduct, resulting in such acts becoming so ubiquitous in the coverage that they are considered an integral part of the game and are associated with success. The suggestion is that the participants learnt to associate success with aggressive behaviours in the professional game and used it as a criterion for their selection of their favourite team. However, Russell (1993) subsequently reported that there was no relation between the level of aggressive play in the favourite teams and the aggressive behaviours displayed in their own play. This suggests that the players may have learnt that success among professionals is concomitant with aggression, but this was not something that was necessary for success in their own play.

Social learning theory has also been applied to help drive interventions to promote assertive behaviours in sport, but to avoid the learning of aggressive behaviours. Connelly (1988) suggests that modelling of aggressive players' behaviours is an appropriate technique to modify non-assertive players' behaviour in competition towards being more intense. However, she claims it is important when making such modifications to clearly distinguish between increased intensity of sport behaviours that are legitimate and goal-directed and the features of the aggressive behaviours such as those outlined in Silva's (1980) model (see Figure 8.1). Therefore, it is important when using modelling and techniques to enhance assertive but not aggressive behaviours that an overt distinction is made between desired behaviours and overly aggressive play that may be penalized and result in injury to other players.

Personality and individual difference explanations

Some personality characteristics have been linked to aggression, although there is no evidence to suggest that there is one sole trait that characterizes those who engage in aggressive behaviours. Research examining the associations between personality and aggression has shown that one personality factor, *agreeableness*, is not only strongly and negatively associated with aggressive behaviour in adolescents, but also predicts the **social cognitions** that are hypothesized to give rise to aggression such as frustration. This is an important finding because agreeableness is the personality dimension that is most associated with maintaining positive and harmonious relationships with others. Recent research, however, has identified aggression as a distinct and unique personality factor (e.g. Zuckerman *et al.* 1993). Zuckerman *et al.* isolated an aggressiveness–hostility factor that was distinct from the other personality dimensions. Future research will further examine the predictive validity of the relationships between these personality dimensions and aggressive tendencies, particularly in sport contexts.

In addition to personality factors, researchers have also identified a stable behavioural pattern known as 'Type A' personality (Matthews *et al.* 1982). Type A personalities are highly-driven, competitive, and extrovert in their behaviour and interactions with others. There is some evidence to suggest that Type As display higher levels of aggression and hostility towards others in competitive situations. It is likely that the interaction between the situational climate, e.g. performance-oriented or competitive, is likely to interact with personality factors such as a Type A pattern in contributing to aggressive responses. There are few studies examining Type A personality in aggression in sport. Biasi (1999) found that Type A personalities are more than twice as prevalent in athletes and dancers than a normal comparison group. Despite their possible Type A personality, dancers were much less likely to express negative emotion and more likely to avoid interpersonal conflict. This seems to contradict the expected behavioural pattern of a Type A personality. However, it can be seen that emotional control and low interpersonal conflict are very important to dancers who have to act cooperatively for success and for whom emotionality is a sign of weakness and fragility, both undesirable behaviours in their profession. To speculate, it may be that social cognitive variables such as group cohesion and self-efficacy towards success may moderate the effect of Type A personality on aggressive behaviours.

A major criticism of personality theories of aggression is that they are limited because they ignore the influence of individual and group-level social cognitive constructs. While the effects of personality constructs such as agreeableness and Type A personality on aggression indicate that personality constructs account for a modest amount of variance in aggression, a large proportion of the variance goes unexplained. More sophisticated approaches would take into account situational and social cognitive influences on aggression that would identify the mediators and moderators of the personality constructs on aggressive behaviour. This may provide answers to the questions about the relative contribution, if any, that personality makes in the explanation of aggressive acts in sport performers.

Factors that influence aggression

The cathartic hypothesis

It is often said that aggression is instrumental in venting 'pent-up' frustration and unexpressed emotion. The act of expressing such emotions and the concomitant feeling state of release are known as catharsis, and the premise that this occurs in social situations where aggression serves this purpose is known as the *cathartic hypothesis*. The belief in this instrumental purpose of aggression is prevalent in sports, particularly among spectators and observers of sport. For example, Wann *et al.* (1999) found that participants believed in the cathartic function of watching aggressive sports and said that they were less likely to be aggressive themselves because of this effect. Further, the belief that participation in sports with aggressive characteristics is healthy for young people because of its cathartic function is prevalent among sports coaches and school teachers (Bennett 1991).

Despite these deep-seated beliefs, there is very little evidence to support the cathartic hypothesis, and research suggests that persistent exposure to aggression does not reduce the likelihood of it being expressed elsewhere but, paradoxically, such exposure increases it. For example, Bushman, Baumeister, and Stack (1999) gave experimental participants one of three ostensible newspaper articles written in support of the cathartic hypothesis (pro-catharsis), against the cathartic hypothesis (anti-catharsis), and neutral point of view. Participants were then asked to write an essay from the point of view expressed in the article they read, which was to be criticized by a student in another room. After hearing very harsh criticism of the essay, participants were asked to fill out an emotion questionnaire to measure anger and then given a choice of task, one of which was a punching bag exercise. Angry participants in the pro-cathartic condition were more likely to choose the punching bag exercise, indicating that media attention may propagate the belief that aggression has a cathartic effect. A follow-up study showed that participants in the pro-cathartic condition were more likely to administer a high level of punishment to their critic, even those who had spent time in the punching bag task. Therefore, while participants believed in the cathartic purpose of aggression, they were more likely to commit an aggressive act (administer punishment) when they punched the bag and received the cathartic essay. These data suggest that the cathartic hypothesis is a belief rather than an actual effect, although research suggests that the belief is as present as ever despite little empirical support (Bennett 1991).

Gender

It is often cited that men are more likely to engage in aggressive behaviours than women (Wrangham and Peterson 1996) and more likely to express aggressive attitudes and beliefs (Eagly and Chaiken 1993). These differences have been attributed to: (1) elevated levels of androgens (sex hormones) in males; (2) the notion that aggression has an evolutionary benefit in demonstrating dominance and status; and (3) the socialization of aggressive tendencies in men during development. In sport, the majority, but not all, of the aggressive acts seen in team competitions are committed by male athletes, and men seem more likely to endorse aggression in sport than women (Tucker and Parks 2001). Young girls have been shown to express high levels of moral behaviour in sports participation (Stephens and Bredemeier 1996), but studies suggest that females do endorse aggressive acts towards opponents if the group norm endorses it (Stephens and Bredemeier 1996; Tucker and Parks 2001). Interestingly, though, females engage in verbal assault as readily as men even though they do not engage in subsequent aggression, verbal or physical (Harris 1992).

Morality issues

Prosocial behaviours are representative of the general moral conduct and conformity observed towards others in everyday life. However, as mentioned previously, social identity theory suggests that personal moral behaviour can be rendered insignificant in contexts where group membership is salient and a **group norm** pervades. In such situations, people become 'deindividuated' and assume the social identity of the group members. In doing so, the individual internalizes the attitudes of the group and has a tendency to evaluate ingroup members positively and outgroup members negatively. Bredemeier and Shields (1986) suggest that assuming a group identity in sports teams could result in the prosocial moral attitudes normally pervasive in everyday life being suppressed and individuals undergoing a moral transformation towards a more egocentric view of morality. This results in a *bracketed morality* in which the 'usual moral obligation to equally consider the needs and desires of all persons' (1986: 257) is suspended. This bracketed morality can lead to a legitimization of injurious or aggressive acts in a sports setting. Bredemeier and Shields illustrated this by presenting moral dilemmas to establish the level of moral reasoning in basketball players and non-athletes. The moral dilemmas pictured situations in which aggressive acts in sport were legitimized and participants were asked to make a decision about what the correct choice would be and their reasons why. Findings indicated that basketballers cited more egocentric and less prosocial reasons in their resolutions to the dilemmas, indicating a clear egocentric bias in sports participants' moral reasoning. These findings illustrate a moral element to the acceptability of aggressive behaviours in sporting contexts and a legitimization of these acts in the eyes of athletes.

Arousal

Other factors that contribute to aggression in sport may be external physiological factors such as heightened physiological arousal. By the nature of intense effort, athletes tend to be in a state of heightened autonomic arousal during competition. Further, this heightened state of arousal may seem to abate after a short recovery period, but can be elevated for hours afterwards (Zillman et al. 1974). For example, there is evidence to suggest that heightened physiological arousal can be misinterpreted by an individual and expressed as an emotional response like anger or frustration. Further, a participant may not be aware that their heightened physiological state is responsible for their emotional response (Zillman et al. 1974). This was particularly pervasive in Zillman et al.'s experiment in which participants in an aroused state due to physical exertion expressed more hostility towards an actor who insulted them when they were still aroused from the exercise. Importantly, the hostility was exaggerated when their awareness of that arousal was negated by the introduction of a time gap between the insulting situation and the bout of exercise. In sport, particularly multiple sprint sports like hockey, rugby, soccer, and lacrosse that have periods of intense effort followed by periods or rest, players are likely to be in a physiologically aroused state that may contribute to feelings of anger and, in a group situation where a norm legitimizes it, result in aggression.

Hormones and steroid abuse

Other external factors that may play a role in influencing the tendency of individuals to display aggressive behaviour in sport may be the prevalence of substance abuse in players. While the level and type of substance abuse vary across sport type and level, this cannot be denied as a potential contributory factor to aggression. Pharmacological studies have reported a clear link between the abuse of anabolic steroids and aggressive behaviour (Pope and Katz 1994). The abuse of such substances by athletes changes the androgen profile of the athletes which results in behavioural changes due to increased levels of testosterone. Indeed, testosterone has been implicated in the higher incidence of aggressive behaviours expressed by male athletes when compared with females (van Goozen *et al.* 1994). Although the relatively low prevalence of drug abuse may mean that the overall effect of such hormonal changes on aggressive behaviours may be minimal, it is important to note that situational factors may interact with physiological changes caused by drug abuse and predispose such individuals to aggressive conduct.

Crowd violence, collective aggression, and hooliganism

The aggression between athletes in sport encompasses only a small part of the aggressive acts that occur in sporting contexts. Aggression and violence, particularly among spectators, crowds, and fans, have been a prevalent, notorious, and unpleasant occurrence at sports venues and events worldwide, particularly in Western Europe, and North and South America. It also seems that particular sports are plagued with crowd violence (e.g. soccer). Although its incidence seems to be abating in some areas, sports authorities, governments, and anti-hooliganism groups have yet to fully eradicate this scourge of sport. This section aims to outline the problem and get a measure of the scale of crowd violence in sport, introduce and critically analyse some of the major social psychological theories that have been proposed to explain these insurgencies, identify the influential factors that predispose crowds to be aggressive, and provide a balanced view regarding possible solutions to the problem.

In society, one should be under no illusion as to the popularity and importance that many members attach to sports and sport success. Sport is ingrained in our social fabric, and sports fans' moods, emotions, motivations, and personal relationships are sometimes fully ensconced in the fortunes of the local sports team. In addition, it is clear that professional sports teams are not only part of the 'fabric' of the local community and representative of its success, they also generate a vast amount of revenue and are integral to many local industries such as the service industry and tourism. Thus, sports teams have great responsibility, given their power to affect people at an individual and greater social level. It also means that when things go wrong and the team experiences failure, such as relegation from a league competition, it may be implicated in social ills such as violence and aggressive behaviour.

A neutral observer could cynically dismiss the influence of sport and sports teams on aggression and aggressive behaviour in everyday life, but research suggests that such a dismissal would be unwise, given some compelling preliminary evidence of the powerful effect sports teams can have on social behaviour. For example, Fernquist (2000) studied two indices of violent behaviour: (1) homicide, a direct measure of aggression toward others; and (2) suicide relative to the successes and failures of professional sports teams in 30 North American cities between 1971 and 1990. Making play-off tournaments (end of season championship matches) was significantly related to declines in both homicide and suicide rates, while championship wins were negatively correlated with suicide rates only. Fernquist (2000) cited Gabennesch's (1988) broken promises theory to explain the results. He suggested that the frustration and hopelessness created by the unfulfilled hopes presented by the sports teams may lead to social manifestations of those negative emotions in homicide and suicide. These findings suggest that sports teams may have a pervasive effect on social behaviour, and this must be considered when examining crowd violence and collective aggression. However, it must also be noted that crowd violence may not necessarily be a function of the outcome or fortunes of the supported team, there are numerous instances in the literature where the sport event itself and fortunes of the team are peripheral to the lived experience of those involved in a crowd of supporters.

Theoretically, this section shifts focus away from the individual athlete and aggression in sport contexts, and takes a broader view, examining aggression among teams, sports crowds, spectators, and sports fans. These explanations demand a different perspective from the approaches to individual violent conduct and aggression which tend to focus on micro-level explanations on situated behaviours and individual differences (Weed 2000). Instead, crowd violence needs to be studied at group level, identifying the broader social context as well as group-level perceptions held by individuals. However, it is important to note that many social psychological theories applied to the study of group interaction and conflict maintain an empirical, theory-testing, information-processing approach, and use the individual as the main unit of analysis. For example, social identity theorists, one of the major overarching social psychological paradigms that will be visited to explain collective violence, cite the necessity to examine the group attitudes and perceptions at an individual level (Marsh and Harré 1978; Stott 2001).

Definitions of group aggression, crowd violence, and hooliganism

Research on group processes has indicated that focusing on individual-based factors alone in group situations will result in a misleading and incomplete explanation of social behaviour. This is because many social psychological theories on group processes recognize that people behave differently in groups and tend to assume the psychological and behavioural characteristics of other group members. A sports crowd is one of the many clearly identifiable groups in society, and its members represent a common goal and share a common bond in their attributes as football fans and supporters of a particular team. One of the major social psychological frameworks adopted to explain crowd violence, social identity theory, predicts that the attributes of fellow crowd members, the way other group members are evaluated, the way members of rival teams fans are portrayed, and the importance of the crowd to individual members' self-esteem are all important elements of crowd behaviour.

Crowd violence is a form of collective aggression. Collective aggression can be defined as violent, unified behaviour with intent to cause injury or harm to another individual or group of people. In some cases, such unified aggression may occur even when the defining characteristics of the group are very weak and the individuals within the group may not know each other very well (Tajfel and Turner 1986). Much research on crowd violence has been centred about the behaviour of soccer fans in Europe, known as **hooliganism** (Marsh and Harré 1978). There is little consensus over the precise definition of a hooligan or hooliganism and the meaning of these terms depend on the source and academic approach to the hooligan events (Weed 2001). Although researchers tend to view hooliganism as the embodiment of a crowd of sports supporters displaying negative behaviours associated with collective aggression and violence, the definition also encompasses non-violent, extroverted behaviours displayed in a sports crowd such as singing, chanting, jeering, and shouting. These non-violent behaviours often constitute an alternative definition of 'hooligan' within a group of supporters, referring to a person performing extroverted or outrageous acts (Marsh and Harré 1978; Weed 2001). Such behaviours among sports supporters would be condoned and actively encouraged, such that the self-esteem and group identification of individuals making such behavioural displays would be enhanced and reinforced through the positive feedback given by other group members. On this basis, one could say that, in some groups of sports fans, the label 'hooligan' would be positively evaluated and worn like a 'badge of honour', rather than have the negative, violent connotations often associated with the term. Often the media are responsible for whipping up adverse public opinion regarding hooligans through a hyperbolic stereotype of a typical sports 'hooligan' and the behaviour of crowds of hooligans (Weed 2001).

Theoretical accounts of collective aggression

Numerous theoretical approaches from the social psychology literature have been put forward to explain **collective aggression** and crowd violence. Some of these theories focus on individual differences on group-level variables using an empirical, hypothesis-testing framework from an information-processing perspective to explain collective aggression. Prominent among these theories are social learning theory (Bandura 1977), reversal theory (Kerr 1997), and social identity theory (Tajfel and Turner 1986). Conversely, theories that stem from a more sociological tradition tend to examine the effects of broader social contexts on crowd violence (Ward 2002). These approaches include Dunning and co-worker's (Dunning *et al.* 1988), also known as the 'Leicester School', figurational approach to soccer hooliganism that focuses on cultural norms, conflict theory whose roots are in Marxism and tell of the working-class resistance to the *embourgeoisement* of football (Coakley 1981), and functionalist theory that outlines the purpose of institutions such as sport to maintain a well-functioning society (Marsh and Harré 1978). Other theoretical accounts come from innate biological bases for behaviour such as ethological theory or instinct theory and hooligan addiction theory (Ward 2002). The aim of this section is not to provide a comprehensive overview of these theories, readers interested in learning more about the various approaches are directed to the numerous lucid reviews available on the prevailing social psychological (e.g. Tajfel and Turner 1986; Kerr 1997) and sociological (e.g. Dunning *et al.* 1988; Weed 2001; Ward 2002) theories of crowd violence. Instead, the present section aims to provide a comprehensive overview of four key approaches from the psychological social psychology (social identity theory and reversal theory) and sociological social psychology (the figurational approach and conflict theory) traditions. The major premises of these approaches will be critically reviewed, the empirical research in these areas evaluated, and their effectiveness as accounts of crowd violence and group aggression examined.

Social identity theory

Social identity theory was first introduced in Chapter 7 as an explanation for inter-group processes and group cohesion. In this section we will outline how major premises of social identity theory serve to explain prejudice and collective aggression among sports spectators. The aim of social identity theory is to provide an explanation of the mechanisms behind social behaviour in a group context by studying how the influence of group membership affects the behaviour of individuals within the group. The theory supposes that individuals forego their own identity and assume the shared beliefs, attitudes, and expectations of the group. This leads to a number of processes that can result in complex group and individual patterns of behaviour such as prejudice and aggression towards other sports teams.

One of the key hypotheses of social identity theory is that individuals' personal attitudes are superseded by the attitudes shared by the group. An individual in a group will assume the beliefs, judgements, and behavioural patterns shared by other group members. They do this because their self-esteem is tied in with their membership of the group. Readers will recall in Chapter 4 that self-esteem statements form the basis of a self-concept. In the case of assuming a social identity, self-concept statements will, in part, reflect the attributes and values that person shares with the group(s) to which they belong. In order to maintain a positive sense of self, group members have to experience a feeling of belonging (identification) with the group, so common interests and attitudes are important, and they have a need to receive ongoing endorsement of their self-esteem and so view themselves as a proto-typical group member. This results in self-stereotyping where an individual in a group or crowd categorizes him or herself as part of group. This self-categorization process results in group members conforming to the norma-tive behaviours (what is acceptable to the group) and people look to the core group members for guidance or as models. This self-categorization process is met by a social comparison process in which the person forms judgements regarding members of his or her own group, the *ingroup*, relative to members of other groups to which they are not members, or *outgroups*. As we shall see later, these comparison processes form the basis of inter-group prejudice. The net effect of assuming the shared attitudes of the group and the investment of self-esteem within the group is a deindividuation of the person. Deindi-viduation, proposed by Festinger (1954), supposes that the individual no longer views themselves in individual terms and this results in anonymity and a loss of individual identity. Clearly, the person does not lack identity, instead they assume a social identity that they share with the other group members.

Deindividuation, as an isolated process, has provided an explanation for group members' expression of behaviours that they would not normally dis-play in an individual context (Reicher *et al.* 1995). In a group situation, each group member's relative anonymity within the group means that their indi-vidual responsibility is reduced as they are no longer readily identifiable for repercussions and there is a lack of the personal control that is normally exer-cised in individual situations (Mann 1981). As a result, behaviour of group members can become more disinhibited, extrovert, instinctive, and irrational. A number of experimental studies have used uniforms and other means to create an artificial group environment and deindividuate participants. These studies found that deindividuated participants tended to display more divisive behaviours than easily identifiable participants. For example, deindividuated participants were more critical of their parents and were more likely to steal when given the opportunity than identifiable participants (e.g. Diener 1976). Most compelling and relevant to the study of crowd violence in sport are Zimbardo's (1970) studies that showed deindividuated participants to have a greater propensity to act aggressively.

The processes of self-categorization, group identification, and self-stereotyping, and deindividuation result in conformity to group norms and group members assuming the prevailing attitudes of the other group members. Under these circumstances, a social identity is created that is separate from personal identity and personal self-esteem. As a result, ingroup members are more positively evaluated than members of outgroups. Even though the ingroup is viewed in a largely stereotypical way, their salient features are more relevant to the ingroup members while outgroup members are viewed in a relatively homogenous way. This creates an 'us' and a 'them' distinction. In groups whose group membership is perceived to be under threat or leads them to question their group membership, prejudice against the outgroup members can result. This prejudice is likely to take the form of exaggerating differences between the ingroup and the outgroup, such as stygmatizing the membership of the outgroup through arbitrary surface features such as race and religion. Such prejudice may be manifested in aggressive behaviours.

Although sports crowds very seldom resort to actual aggression, the threats are often displays of solidarity more for the benefit of galvanizing the ingroup members than to bring harm to the outgroup. The act of stigmatizing others maintains the positive sense of self or social identity that the group members glean from their membership of the ingroup. Interestingly, Tajfel and Turner (1986) argue that group prejudice can occur even in groups that share the most minimal of characteristics, as outlined by their minimal group experiments, which may explain why often crowds of sports spectators often seem like a coherent group with a coordinated set of behaviours. Indeed, studies of crowd violence such as rioting and looting have shown surprisingly orderly patterns of aggressive behaviours that are directed towards specific targets representative of outgroups.

Despite the large body of literature on social identity theory examining collective aggression and crowd violence in the context of riots between social groups, there have been relatively few studies examining the role of social identity theory on crowd violence among opposing supporters and between sports crowds and police in a sport context. Stott and colleagues (Stott 2001) have conducted one of the most in-depth and comprehensive analysis of collective aggression adopting a social identity theory approach. Stott used ethnographic and qualitative methods to develop an extended social identity model that examined the effects of contextually defined social identity on the display of aggressive behaviour in collective 'disorder' among soccer fans. Reicher's (1987) original theory of self-identity indicated, after Tajfel and Turner (1986), that collective behaviour is determined by the social identity acquired by group members that is, partly contextually defined (e.g. soccer game context when confronted by opposing fans) and partly determined by collective norms (e.g. shared attitudes towards outgroups) rather than the personal identities and beliefs of the individuals in the group. In the extended model, Stott argues that the effects of collective identity on group behaviours and intergroup conflict is reciprocal rather than one-way. Therefore, not only does collective identity determine the purpose and nature of sport crowd behaviour, but the group behaviour affects and changes the situation. Given that the collective identity is defined, in part by the context, changes in the environment will therefore affect and change social identity.

In summary, social identity theory has provided a unique and comprehensive explanation of the mechanisms and processes that underlie violent behaviour in sport crowds. Adopting theoretical perspectives from Festinger (1954) and self-esteem theorists, Tajfel and Turner (1986) highlighted the importance of group-level individual difference constructs like social identity that supersede personal constructs like attitudes and self-identity in social contexts. Importantly, self-esteem is considered a primary reason why prejudice develops between groups. This is because group members' self-esteem is tied in with their group membership, and when the group is threatened by others, this threat is viewed as a threat to self-esteem. In order to maintain a positive sense of self-esteem, group members are likely to vigorously defend their group in the interest of maintaining a positive sense of self through the group. This can result in an escalation of aggression and violent displays toward outgroup members and, without proper moderation, may result in scenes of confrontation and violence between opposing sets of fans and/or police seen at soccer venues throughout Europe.

Reversal theory

Kerr (1997) adapted Apter's (1982) reversal theory to the study of sport aggression and crowd violence in soccer. Reversal theory is described in detail in Chapter 6 with respect to motivation and emotional experiences in sport. Recall that reversal theory outlines the metamotivational states – psychological evaluations of the direction of a person's motives in that given context – that underpin motivation to engage in a behaviour. The context is important as it will determine which metamotivational state operates and can instigate a 'reversal', i.e. a switch from one metamotivational state to another. The external contingencies that lead to these reversals are frustration and satiation of goals. In Chapter 6, the telic and paratelic metamotivational states were introduced. A telic state orientates a person toward being directed and serious in the pursuit of their goals, while a paratelic state reflects a playful, activity-oriented approach. The telic–paratelic motivational states are considered to be bipolar, so in any given context, a person can be in either state. This is why it is possible for a person to have a goal-directed motivational orientation at one occasion or point in time, but to hold an opposite motivational orientation at another according to the effect of the context to frustrate or satiate goals. Apter introduced several other bipolar metamotivational states that operate alongside the telic–paratelic states, *conformity–negativism*, *mastery–sympathy*, and *autic–alloic*. The autic state represents a concern or focus on oneself while an alloic state reflects a concern for others. The interpretation of arousal as pleasant or unpleasant, or its hedonic tone, interacts with the metamotivational states to give rise to specific emotional experiences. While metamotivational states are changeable according to situations, personality factors can determine the dominant or prevalent metamotivational state and dictate how long a person remains in that state.

Applied to soccer hooliganism and crowd violence, reversal theory makes predictions regarding the events that lead to violence at soccer matches. Members of 'hooligan' crowds are proposed to be paratelic dominant, that is, they seek activity and excitement and, coupled with low arousal and an unpleasant hedonic tone, are likely to become bored at football matches. In this case their expected aroused state and pleasant hedonic tone from the football has been frustrated and they have experienced reversal. This results in a desire to seek satiation by pursuing arousal-giving, exciting actions elsewhere in the context. According to Kerr, the excitement-seeking traits of the soccer hooligan are similar to others who engage in thrill-seeking behaviour such as bungee-jumping. Therefore, the unfulfilled satiation of anticipated excitement in those fans who have a predominantly paratelic metamotivational state leads to compensatory behaviour and this manifests itself in aggressive behaviours. Critics of the theory claim that Kerr does not offer any explanation why certain people become hooligans in the first place and why paratelic dominant fans do not seek other non-violent compensatory behaviours.

The figurational approach

One of the most influential sociological theories of crowd violence was proposed by Dunning and the 'Leicester School' of researchers (e.g. Dunning *et al.* 1988). Their theory was developed in the ethnographic study of soccer supporter violence. As a starting point, the **figurational approach** to soccer hooliganism adopts an individualist perspective and is at odds with the 'group mind' and 'submergence' theories of collective behaviour that were pervasive in early explanations of collective behaviour. The theory therefore focuses on an individualist perspective because dispositions within the individual are hypothesized to give rise to violent behaviour. Dunning and co-workers draw on Elias' (1978) theory of civilization that proposes that members of society expect a 'civilizing' process to occur over time. This civilizing process is hypothesized to occur in a top-down fashion from the privileged to the working classes. It is proposed that in this civilizing process, the unstructured and unexpected periods of aggression displayed by groups in the past would be replaced by ritualized, socially constructed types of aggression. Therefore, individuals in society experience anxiety and anger at the prospect of the expression of such aggression, and guilt and shame for experiencing aggressive tendencies. Dunning *et al.* support Elias' proposition, but argue that the civilizing process has not yet filtered down entirely to the working classes. However, Dunning *et al.* state that violent crowds in soccer are dominated by the 'rough' working class, a premise that is supported by statistics which indicate that sports crowds comprise predominantly of partly skilled or unskilled workers (Murphy 1990).

It is the disproportionately high presence of individuals of a 'rough' working-class background in the sports crowd that is thought to lead to displays of collective aggression. Dunning *et al.* proposed that these elements are likely to display aggression because of internalized cultural values that are inherently masculine in nature and a propensity to resolve issues with aggression. These values suggest that among the 'rough' working class, violent conduct is both legitimized and respected as a means of addressing perceived injustice. As a result, the figurational approach to soccer hooliganism explains why incidents of hooliganism arise in the context of soccer fans, due to the civilization process and presence of working-class elements, but focuses on individual dispositions rooted in cultural norms as causes of violent behaviour in group contexts.

Conflict theory

Steeped in Marxist ideology, **conflict theory** suggests that violence in sports contexts is connected to underlying social, political, and economic grievances held by the working-class element of the crowd. Therefore, sport contexts in which fans share these common resentments serve as a hotbed for the expression of aggression directed at the perceived perpetrators of the inequalities. Leading proponents of this theory suggest that sport is an ideal conduit for the expression of dissent through aggression because elements of modern professional sport are perceived as economically exploitative of the 'average' working-class fan (Levine and Vinten-Johansen 1981). Collective aggression is therefore explained in terms of perceived economic and social injustices specific to the sport. Taylor (1971) and Clarke (1978) talk of crowd violence in soccer as an attempt to wrestle the honest, working-class values underpinning the game from middle-class elements who seek to claim it for themselves. These working-class elements feel marginalized by an increasingly bourgeois society controlled by the *nouveau riche*.

On the surface it seems that conflict theory and the figurational approach to soccer hooliganism share common explanations in that sport violence is viewed as emanating from the working class and their grievances. However, they fundamentally differ in the proposed direction of the aggressive displays. Conflict theory suggests aggression is a reflection of the grievances and injustice felt by the working-class elements in sports crowds and an attempt to show dissent, defiance, and redress the balance, while figurational theory explains the violence as tendencies arising from cultural values that legitimize violence as a means to resolve conflict. While conflict theory appeals, particularly in light of the economic rise of elite professional sports leagues owned by super-rich benefactors such as Premier League soccer in England (Weed 2001), Taylor (1971) proposes that its premises are speculative and have yet to receive empirical support. Furthermore, Weed (2001) views this approach as having limited explanatory power as much sports crowd aggression occurs between supporters of rival teams and not toward the authority figures of sport.

Influential factors in crowd aggression

There are numerous environmental and social factors that can affect the incidence and public perception of crowd violence and collective aggression. Some of these have been reviewed previously such as crowd size and drug abuse. This section will briefly outline two of the important contributory factors that may serve to moderate collective aggression, and also affect the perception and evaluation of members of sports spectators by those outside these groups.

The media

As mentioned previously, social learning theory predicts that the observation of violence may have a pervasive influence on others (Bandura 1977, 1997). Television and newspapers are prompt in their condemnation of collective aggression when these events are portrayed in the media. However, the coverage is usually a thin, diluted, and one-sided view of the events, which can have damaging effects on the sport and those not involved in the violence but whose livelihood is tied in with their involvement in the sport. Moreover, despite the bias in the coverage, such events are often given a huge profile within the media, and such prominence, if not coupled with a sense of perspective or explanations of contingency, may result in such events being perceived as the norm. As we shall see later, this may have the effect of damaging the reputation of the sport or even create a hyperbolic response and moral outrage. Further, it may have an effect on young players and fans in sport. If crowd violence and violence between players is given such prominence and is observed by young people over long periods, it may be viewed as the accepted norm and legitimized in those contexts. The social learning of aggressive acts may then be internalized and re-enacted by young players and fans, habits which could perpetuate such behaviours. There is evidence to support this such as the tendency for players to select their heroes on the basis of their aggressive play rather than other performance indicators (Russell 1979). Furthermore, research has shown that similar behaviours, including infringements, are viewed in the same sports team across generations, suggesting that younger players mimic the behaviours of other older players and these are passed on (Russell 1993).

Recently, Weed (2001) has indicated that media coverage of crowd violence in sport tends to be portrayed disproportionately by the media, a fact that may perpetuate hooligan stereotypes among the general public, but also by the authorities such as the government and police forces involved. Weed uses the example of media portrayal of crowd violence among English and German fans at the 2000 European Championship soccer tournament in Charleroi, Belgium. The English tabloid press tended to portray the violence as caused by English soccer fans and on a wider scale, while broadsheet and television coverage provided a greater sense of perspective: very little violence or hand-to-hand fighting was observed with the crowds mostly reacting to a small hard-core minority of hooligans that tried to drum up support for the violence. It was argued that past reputation plus the culture of English soccer fans in Europe may have resulted in the judgmental treatment of the evidence. To explain this limited, small-scale violence, Weed cites Marsh and Harré's (1978) meso-level approach in which individuals in a group gain status through the display of aggressive behaviour, but rely on the support of the other crowd members to prevent any real harm coming to them. Overall, the research suggests that some elements of the media produced biased and sensationalist portrayals of the crowd violence in Charleroi. This misrepresented view had the potential to evoke an unwarranted moral outrage among the general public and at the same time sold a lot of newspapers.

The pervading sense of moral outrage that may be incurred by the exaggeration of the scale of events in hooligan contexts such as those outlined by Weed (2001), may filter through to policy-makers, resulting in increasingly stringent and heavy-handed measures towards even the most innocuous of non-violent behaviours, such as singing, chanting, and shouting. Such measures are less likely to bring the potential for violence in check than to provoke increased violence among fans and police, where fans are seen as protecting their rights to perform non-violent forms of support for their team (Stott 2001). Ward (2002) suggests that governments and other institutions like newspapers can use such events for positive public relations to restore public faith in their desire to deal with unwanted social elements and to keep their citizens safe. It is therefore important that authorities as well as the public view the portrayal of collective aggression in sport from a number of sources and adopt a considered approach to the role of the media and its tendency to misrepresent such incidents and manipulate public opinion.

Alcohol abuse

Misuse of alcohol is commonly implicated in a great deal of social violence, particularly aggressive behaviours in the home and in public places. In the case of crowd violence and collective aggression, excessive use of alcohol is often considered a contributory factor. This is particularly true of fans of particular sports such as soccer, but again such a reputation may be one that is perpetuated by the media. In the social psychological literature meta-analytic studies have suggested that there is a link between alcohol consumption and aggression (Bushman and Cooper 1990), and explanations for this lie in the disinhibition effect, that is, under the influence of alcohol intrapersonal controls that may mitigate the expression of behaviours such as aggression are suspended. However, the causal link between aggression and use of alcohol may be moderated by contextual factors such as threat and encouragement. In terms of threat, Taylor and Gammon (1976) found that participants intoxicated with alcohol were prepared to give an electric shock of much higher intensity to a confederate learner when they were told prior to the experiment that the learner was prepared to give the highest levels of shocks when their roles were reversed. In terms of encouragement, Taylor and Sears (1988) showed that goading by the experimenter persuaded participants intoxicated with alcohol to give much higher shocks to a confederate compared with control participants. Without threat or goading, the participants behaved in a manner consistent with the responses of non-intoxicated participants. These studies suggest that the social context is important when considering the effects of alcohol on aggressive behaviour, but if those social conditions are present, then crowd members may be more likely to be aggressive. Alcohol should not be made a scapegoat for collective aggression but this research suggests that it has the potential to exacerbate behaviour, should the situational contingencies arise. With respect to solutions, it seems that calming statements can reduce aggressive tendencies in intoxicated people, and so telling people to calm down may be a simple and effective course of action (Taylor and Gammon 1976). However, this may have less effect in a crowd situation, especially if there are others goading and baiting the intoxicated persons.

Suggested reading

Stott, C. (2001) 'Hooligans' abroad? Inter-group dynamics, social identity and participation in collective 'disorder' at the 1998 World Cup finals, *British Journal of Social Psychology*, 40: 359–84. A detailed account of a social identity theory approach to football hooliganism.

Ward, R.E. (2002) Fan violence: Social problem or moral panic? *Aggression and Violent Behavior*, 7: 453–75. A brief yet comprehensive review of the theoretical approaches to crowd violence in sport.

Weed, M. (2001) Ing-ger-land at Euro 2000: how 'handbags at 20 paces' was portrayed as a full-scale riot, *International Review for the Sociology of Sport*, 36: 407–24. An interesting insight into the role of media portrayal and sports crowd violence.

Summary

- Aggression is any behaviour or verbal comment that has intent to injure or harm another person.
- Theoretical explanations of aggression among sports performers come from the frustration–aggression hypothesis, social learning theory, and personality theories. Modern views of aggression have combined hypotheses from social learning, frustration–aggression, and personality theories to explain aggressive behaviours among athletes.

- Aggression is affected by drug and alcohol abuse, moral norms, and physiological arousal.
- Collective aggression is unified violent behaviour with the intent to harm other individuals or groups, and crowd violence is one form of collective aggression.
- Hooliganism is a term that descries a set of aggressive tendencies in sports fans, but can also refer to extroverted, boisterous, rowdy, and outrageous non-violent behaviours.
- Theoretical explanations of crowd violence and collective aggression include psychological social psychology (e.g. social identity theory and reversal theory) and sociological social psychology (e.g. the figurational approach and conflict theory) traditions.
- Two of the most pervasive influential factors on collective aggression are the media and alcohol consumption.

9

Conclusion

Applied social psychology research aimed at understanding the processes, mechanisms, and behaviours in the exercise and sport domains have tended to treat each domain separately. This chapter will focus on some of the common ground shared by the social psychological research in the two domains. The chapter will identify commonalities in the research covered in the two parts of this book and draw conclusions about these common aspects in terms of themes, methods, and theories, and contrasts. The themes common to exercise and sport research covered in this book are the prediction of behaviour, the prediction and role of affect and other outcomes, and the prediction and role of social influences. Common methodological approaches include cross-sectional studies, longitudinal, cross-lagged panel designs, experimental designs, and qualitative enquiry in exercise and sport. Theories of intention and motivation are common across both disciplines, and these will be compared and contrasted. Finally, the contrasts between the two approaches, particularly within the specific context of physical education will be covered and recommendations for practice reviewed.

Themes

The prediction of behaviour

One of the recurrent themes in this book is the prediction of behaviour. This is not surprising given that the overarching aim of psychology is the explanation of human behaviour and one of the primary aims of social psychology is the understanding of behaviour in social contexts. In the first part of this book, social psychology was applied to the understanding of exercise behaviour, and in particular, leisure time exercise associated with health. The main focus was understanding the social psychological antecedents that underpinned exercise behaviour particularly the social psychological constructs such as attitudes, social pressures, self-efficacy and perceived behavioural control, anticipated affect and regret, self-esteem, perceived susceptibility, and, of course, desires and intentions. Central to the purpose of understanding exercise behaviour is the development of social psychological models that not only identified *what* constructs were important in explaining exercise behaviour, but also *why* they were important. Therefore social psychological models that examined the network of relationships that gave rise to exercise behaviour were covered, such as the health belief model, the theory of planned behaviour, and the model of goal-directed behaviour. In addition, the chapter also concerned itself with the antecedent variables of exercise behaviour and how the various antecedent and determinant variables were formed. Integrated models like the transcontextual model aimed to explain the formation of variables like attitudes and subjective norms on the basis of motivational styles such as identified external regulation from self-determination theory that were said to arise from fundamental psychological needs. Together, these belief-based constructs formed the distal bases for the proximal predictors of exercise behaviour.

The second part of this book, in contrast, dealt with a very different set of behaviours, namely sports performance. Generally, sports performance was measured in terms of absolute success such as runs, points, or goals scored or awarded, times recorded, distances thrown, and so on. However, on occasion, sports performance was measured in terms of improvement relative to personal best performance. The important aspect here was that a valid, objective, and reliable means of establishing performance was recorded. In order to explain sports performance, the research focused on the motivational (Chapter 5), emotional (Chapter 6), and social (Chapters 7 and 8) influences on sports performance. The research examined a number of theoretical models that aimed to understand sports performance from these different perspectives, and identified key antecedent variables that were motivational (e.g. achievement goal orientations and intrinsic motivation), emotional (e.g. self-confidence and facilitative state anxiety), and social (e.g. group cohesion) in nature. However, unlike the attempts to unify the antecedent variables in cogent, comprehensive, and parsimonious models such as the transcontextual model in the exercise domain, there are few models that have attempted such integration in the domain of sport performance. One of the reasons for this might be the diversity in performance parameters and methods responsible for sports performance, but the other may be a lack of a clear framework to incorporate these influences. Some of these models have attempted such a union, such as Hanin's (1995, 2000) IZOF model and the application of Apter's (1982) reversal theory by Kerr (1997). However, these theories tend to focus on the affective and emotional aspects and less on the cognitive aspects relating to sports performance. In addition, these theories lack parsimony and the ability to have their hypotheses tested simultaneously. Future research would do well to integrate findings from the affective, social cognitive and motivational, and social influence on sports performance using an integrated or multi-theory approach. Such a model may provide a more complete explanation of sports performance. A good starting point may be more complete tests of Hanin's and Apter's models, but researchers should also turn their attention to integrate the findings of mainstream social psychological models applied to sport such as Jones's (1995) control model of facilitative and debilitative anxiety and Deci and Ryan's (1985) self-determination theory.

The prediction and role of affect and other outcomes

In addition to behaviour, one of the major themes of this text is the prediction of outcomes such as emotion and self-esteem. Such outcomes are considered adaptive and desirable alongside the explanation of behaviour exercise and sport domains. One of the reasons why such outcomes are desirable is the link that such outcomes have with behaviour itself, and also the importance of salient outcomes to positive well-being and general psychological as well as physical health. Indeed, well-being itself can be considered a salient outcome of both exercise and sport, and is cited as a reason for participation in exercise and sport (Ashford et al. 1993). In addition, affective variables are integral to models in the prediction of behaviour. Therefore, such affective variables can mediate and moderate the relationships between cognition and exercise and sport behaviour.

In the exercise domain, affective processes play an important role in the prediction of behaviour such as affective attitudes in the theory of planned behaviour (Ajzen 1985) and desires, that represent the affective aspects of intention, in the model of goal-directed behaviour (Perugini and Conner 2000). Indeed, in the latter case, the affective component of the model serves to mediate the effect that intention, a cognitive construct, has on behaviour. Thus, emotion is an important antecedent of behaviour in such models. However, research has also indicated that motivation also leads to concomitant positive affective states. For example, high levels of intrinsic motivation in self-determination theory often lead to increased satisfaction when engaging in a given behaviour, while external regulation and regulatory styles on the perceived locus of causality reflect close to external regulation are accompanied by maladaptive affective states like feelings of guilt and shame (Deci and Ryan 1985). Thus, the motivational processes that underlie behaviour can also affect emotional states in exercisers.

In sport, the prediction of affective states and emotion plays an important role in explaining the mechanisms underlying sport performance. However, the focus is not on the prediction of positive affective states *per se*, but on the control of negative affective states such as anxiety. For example, Jones's (1995) control model of facilitative and debilitative anxiety suggests that performance is best predicted from cognitive anxiety direction and self-confidence levels. Catastrophe theory views the level of cognitive anxiety as controlling the debilitating effect that high levels of arousal has on performance (L. Hardy 1990). These examples illustrate that it is not emotion *per se*, but the interpretive aspects of emotion that affect sports performance.

In addition to affective states, behaviour and motivation in both the exercise and sport domains are also linked to self-esteem in exercisers. Self-esteem tends to be viewed as a positive outcome of exercise, and research suggests that self-esteem may be enhanced by the demonstration of competence in the physical domain, such as Sonstroem and Morgan's (1989) model of self-esteem. Self-esteem in athletes is also regarded as an important outcome. Athletes tend to report higher levels of physical self-esteem than the general population and those who participate in recreational exercise (Marsh *et al.* 1995). This is generally attributable to the higher levels of competence in sport and athletic situations. Importantly, self-esteem is also a predictor of sports performance and exercise behaviour, and as a result the prediction of self-esteem is an adaptive outcome in this regard.

The prediction and role of social influences

Social influences are also an important theme that straddles the theories in both the exercise and sport domains. In the exercise domain, all theories of intention have some element of social influence (see Chapter 2). The theory of planned behaviour, for example, has subjective norms as a direct predictor of exercise intentions, but has also been expanded to include other aspects of social influence such as social support (Courneya *et al.* 2000) and descriptive norm (Rivis and Sheeran 2003). Other theories such as self-determination theory incorporate the need for relatedness with others that has a pervasive effect on a person's motivation to engage in exercise and sport. Indeed, research has suggested that a primary motive for exercise participation is for social benefits and affiliation (Ashford *et al.* 1993). Thus, while personal constructs such as intentions, attitudes, autonomy, and competence may have strong influences on exercise motivation and behaviour, motives linked with social participation also make an important contribution.

Social factors are also core to athletes' participation and performance. The motives for affiliation are similar among exercisers for recreation and competitive athletes, but theories relating social factors to sports performance often raise different questions, such as the impact of performing in a socially supportive environment (Colman and Carron 2000) or in front of a crowd of sports fans (Varca 1980). An example of the importance of social factors is illustrated in the impact of the strength of social bonds, or group cohesion, on sports performers in sports (Carron and Hausenblas 1998). The effect that an audience has on sports performance is also noteworthy, and the social facilitation effect has illustrated that the social environment can be both supportive (Strauss 2002) and detrimental to performance (Baumeister and Steinhilber 1984). In particular, it seems that home teams that have high levels of cohesion and are familiar with their teammates' style of play tend to provide excellent results in terms of performance and persistence (see Chapter 7). In summary, social factors cannot be ignored in the examination of motivation and behaviour in exercise and sport psychology.

Methods

Cross-sectional studies

Perhaps the most often adopted methodology in the exercise and sport disciplines is the usage of cross-sectional, questionnaire-based studies to confirm measurement validity, test theoretical hypotheses, and establish patterns of prediction such as mediation and moderation. In exercise psychology, the majority of the theories of intention lend themselves to being tested using this approach. There is large number of studies examining relationship among the key antecedent variables in the health belief model, protection motivation theory, the theories of reasoned action and planned behaviour, the transcontextual model, and the model of goal-directed behaviour, a conclusion corroborated by the number of meta-analyses conducted in these areas (e.g. Hausenblas *et al.* 1997; Hagger *et al.* 2002b). This is also true for sport. Meta-analytic and narrative review studies have used evidence from cross-sectional studies of the key relationships among variables in theories of emotion like multidimensional anxiety theory (Kliene 1990; Craft *et al.* 2003), theories of motivation such as achievement goal theory (Ntoumanis and Biddle 1999) and attribution theory (Biddle *et al.* 2001), and theories of group influence such as group cohesion (Carron and Hausenblas 1998). In addition, there is a great deal of converging evidence to be gleaned from a large body of cross-sectional research on theories such as self-efficacy theory and social cognitive theory (Feltz and Chase 1998; McAuley and Blissmer 2002). The cross-sectional or prospective approach is attractive because it represents an economical manner to test theoretical hypotheses within a given population and contemporary multivariate statistical procedures such as factor analysis provide robust tests of such relationships while accounting for artefacts like measurement error.

Such studies are also efficacious in revealing important mechanisms like mediation and moderation. For example, the theory of planned behaviour in the exercise domain consistently illustrates the mediating role of intentions on the relationships between attitudes and exercise behaviour. Analogously, in a sports context, such cross-sectional studies have supported the mediation of the self-efficacy–performance relationship by goal setting (Theodorakis 1995). Furthermore, moderators of important relationships in theories of exercise behaviour such as the moderation of the relationship between attitudes towards success and intentions to try by expectations of success in the theory of trying, and the moderation of the self-efficacy–performance relationship by goal setting in a sport context have been indicated (Theodorakis 1995). The latter example being one where the same variable is implicated in the moderation and mediation of the same relationship. These results indicate the importance of the cross-sectional approach in explaining proposed mechanisms within the theories.

Longitudinal, cross-lagged panel designs

Cross-sectional studies are limited in terms of their ability to infer causality. One of the reasons for this is that they measure the social psychological independent and dependent variables simultaneously and therefore any theoretical directional relationship cannot be tested unequivocally when alternative hypotheses such as the opposite relationship or reciprocity cannot be ruled out and are tenable in an empirical sense (see Introduction). Furthermore, the researcher cannot control for the stability of the constructs. A cross-lagged panel design is more powerful because the cross-lagged relationships permit alternative hypotheses to be tested and control for the stability of the constructs. Examples of these models are rife in the exercise and sport literature. In an exercise context, such designs have been used to test the hierarchical nature of Fox and Corbin's self-esteem model (Kowalski *et al.* 2003) and Vallerand's hierarchical model of motivation (Guay *et al.* 2003). In sport, the exact same model has been proposed to test the effect of group cohesion on sport performance (Slater and Sewell 1994). These designs are powerful and have been able to assist researchers in resolving the nature of a set of relationships observed in cross-sectional studies.

Experimental designs

In comparison to studies in other areas of social psychology, there is a relative dearth of experimental studies examining the effects of key independent variables on exercise and sport behaviour. Perhaps one of the reasons for this is that exercise and sport behaviour is difficult to assess unequivocally in a laboratory environment, and those that do frequently involve novel tasks that do not necessarily reflect real-life sport situations. In other words, they lack *ecological validity*. However, some experimental social psychologists would view this as an advantage of experimental approach because it allows the unequivocal focus on the mechanism alone while any extraneous variables with the potential to disrupt the effects are negated. Nevertheless several ingenious social psychological experimental designs have been adopted to examine key processes in exercise and sport. For example, in the exercise domain, experimental field studies have examined the effects of interventions to alter the intention–behaviour relationship in favour of doing more exercise (Milne *et al.* 2002; Prestwich *et al.* 2003). Such field studies are useful because they involve more naturalistic, ecologically valid settings, suggesting the effects of such manipulations are powerful in context that are more akin with real life than the laboratory. In the domain of sport, the provision of false performance feedback to athletes performing novel sports tasks in a laboratory setting has been used to manipulate self-efficacy and such experiments have provided evidence for the effect of self-efficacy on sports performance and persistence of effort (e.g. Weinberg 1986). In sum, the experimental approach has provided important data to support cross-sectional studies on intention and motivation in exercise and sport respectively and is an important method to confirm both direction of effects and mechanisms.

Qualitative approaches

Some studies have adopted qualitative approaches to the study of exercise and sport phenomena. Such approaches have been found to co-exist and comple-ment other quantitative approaches. For example, the theories of reasoned action and planned behaviour have frequently relied upon the content analy-sis of open-ended interviews and questionnaires to inform the development of belief-based questionnaires for exercise behaviour (Ajzen 1991). In sport, Holt and Sparkes (2001) used a qualitative ethnographic study to identify the fac-tors that influenced group cohesion in sports teams over a competitive season. This study was innovative in that it used a number of different means such as participant observation, formal and informal interviews, documentary sources, field diaries, and reflexive journals to generate the rich set of data for subsequent content and interpretive analysis. There are other examples in sport such as the numerous approaches to the study of crowd violence and football hooliganism in sport (Ward 2002). Importantly, it needs to be recog-nized that qualitative inquiry does not necessarily imply a non-theoretical approach. Some studies adopting this method do, but other qualitative inquir-ies can adopt a theoretical basis that has equal rigour with quantitative inquiry. Therefore, although less prevalent, the adoption of qualitative approaches provides rich, informative data and has also been shown to augment and extend the meaning of data collected by quantitative means.

Theories

As illustrated earlier, a common theme running through this text is that of intention and motivation, and it is therefore not surprising that social psycho-logical inquiry into the exercise and sport domains has adopted similar theor-etical approaches. For example, theories of intention such as the theory of planned behaviour have been adopted to examine the social psychological influences on exercise behaviour and some aspects of sport, such as training adherence. The theory of planned behaviour and its variants and extensions have been a primary theoretical framework which is both flexible and parsi-monious in accounting for exercise intentions and behaviour (Hausenblas *et al.* 1997; Hagger *et al.* 2002b). However, there are also numerous studies that have applied the theory of planned behaviour to account for behaviours rele-vant to facilitating sports performance. For example, studies have found that the theory variables can account for significant variance in sports training participation (e.g. Theodorakis *et al.* 1991b) suggesting that coaches and those involved with promoting continued adherence to training regimes in athletes would do well to adopt the intervention techniques offered by planned behaviour theorists. Indeed, few differences have been noted between the predictors of intention in regular exercisers and athletes attending training programmes. This suggests, as Ajzen (1985) states, that the theory of planned behaviour is a general theory of intention and can be applied across many contexts. Ajzen does concede that the relative contribution that each theory variable makes in the prediction of intention may differ, a hypothesis that has been supported empirically. However, since exercise and sport are similar contexts and the behaviours involved are similar in terms of the pressures and constraints involved such as the amount of relative control a person perceives they can have over the behaviour, their antecedents are likely to exhibit congruence.

In addition to theories of intention, self-determination theory has been adopted to explain the effect of the motivational styles and the contextual contingencies under which an individual operates on intrinsic motivation and behaviour. In exercise, the primary focus of this work has been in the adoption of motivational styles delineated by the perceived locus of causality and organismic integration sub-theory to predict exercise behaviour. Intrinsic motivation and intrinsic forms of external regulation such as identification have been found to influence the proximal psychological determinants of exercise behaviour such as attitudes and intentions (Chatzisarantis *et al.* 2002; Hagger *et al.* 2002a; Standage *et al.* 2003), as well as exercise behaviour itself (Chatzisarantis *et al.* 1997; Chatzisarantis *et al.* 2002). In addition, contexts that support intrinsic motivation and identification have been shown to give rise to intrinsic motivation and have a positive, indirect effect on leisure-time exercise behaviour (Chatzisarantis *et al.* 2002; Hagger *et al.* 2003b). In addition, self-determination theory, particularly intrinsic motivation and an autonomy-supported motivational climate, has been shown to predict intentions to participate in sports training (Escarti and Gutierrez 2001) and actual sports participation (Robinson and Carron 1982). Such evidence corroborates the adoption of the theory of planned behaviour to account for the underlying influences on exercise and sports training participation (Theodorakis *et al.* 1991b). However, self-determination theory has also been adopted to explain motivation to participate and persist in sports tasks. For example, intrinsic motivation has been shown to be related to motivational variables like goal orientations (Seifriz *et al.* 1992; Duda *et al.* 1995; Newton and Duda 1999). In addition, intrinsic motivation has been shown to be associated with sport performance (Ryan *et al.* 1984). Autonomy support has also been linked with positive affect intrinsic motivation in athletes (Gagné *et al.* 2003). Together, this evidence suggests that the fostering of intrinsic motivation or at least an identified regulation by highlighting the importance of the goal to exercisers and athletes, providing non-contingent positive feedback, and providing activities and practices that enhance competence will positively influence exercise behaviour.

One of the overarching themes among social psychological theories in exercise and sport is the notion of generality of constructs. Throughout this book, the distinction has been made between generalized, stable, and distal predictors of motivation and behaviour in theories of sport and exercise and specific, changeable, and proximal influences. Examples of state-like constructs covered in this text are attitudes and intentions (Ajzen 1985, 1991) and competitive state anxiety (Jones *et al.* 1993), while trait-like influences include global intrinsic motivation (Vallerand 1997) and personality constructs (Rhodes *et al.* 2002a). Theories that incorporate both types of construct often arrange them hierarchically. Models that make this distinction explicitly are the physical self-esteem models (e.g. Fox and Corbin 1989; Marsh and Redmayne 1994) presented in Chapter 4 and Vallerand's (1997) hierarchical model of motivation presented in Chapters 3 and 5. These models have provided some evidence to suggest that there are proximal and distal forms of motivation, some of which are changeable and alterable and others that are less open to change and may serve as inter-individual covariates to be accounted for in intervention studies aimed at promoting exercise behaviour and sports performance. However, there is some recent evidence that such arrangements may misrepresent the actual structure of these constructs. For example, using cross-lagged panel designs Kowalski *et al.* (2003) and Guay *et al.* (2003) have questioned the hierarchical nature of the physical self-esteem and Vallerand's (1997) model of motivation respectively. These studies were, however, conducted over long time periods and more short-term panel designs may shed more light on such arrangements.

Contrasts

In the introduction to this chapter, the contrasts between social psychological approaches to exercise and sport have been made all too apparent and the reasons for this, in some cases, are obvious. The objectives of sport and competition are generally perceived to be at odds with those of exercise for health reasons. This because sport, particularly high-level competitive sport, places considerable motivational and physical demands on the participants. For those whom participation in exercise is primarily for weight loss and the benefits outlined in Chapter 1, such high demands are not only unrealistic, but also likely to undermine motivation to participate and persist. However, it must also be recognized that not all sport involves the competition and pressure as found in elite sport, and for some individuals whose goals are to lose weight or gain fitness, sport of the appropriate level, intensity, and type can be instrumental in maintaining interest and persistence in exercise. In essence, this relates to self-determination theory in that people with autonomous motives are more likely to persist, and given that interest is one of the characteristic features of autonomous forms of motivation, interesting activities like sports that satisfy psychological needs are likely to foster autonomous motives. Given that the role of sport, a specific subtype of physical activity, can be implicated in the process of fostering greater levels of exercise behaviour among sedentary individuals because of the inherent interest it may hold for such individuals, those involved with the promotion of active lifestyles must be aware of the role of sport in leisure-time exercise promotion. They must also, however, be aware of the conflicting messages that may arise from the promotion of competitive sport to those who are not interested in high-level competition.

This has been illustrated by the policy of promotion of sport and health-related exercise in schools. Schools are recognized by health professionals, sports promoters, and national governing bodies for sport as an important existing network to promote exercise and sport among young people. In particular, health professionals are increasingly recognizing school physical education as an opportunity to encourage an active lifestyle and regular exercise for health benefits to young people, because they have a captive audience. However, government organizations responsible for the development of sport excellence also see schools as a hotbed of talent to be harnessed for future success at national and international level. In addition, education policy-makers often cite sport in physical education as an important conduit to promote the ideals of moral development and a productive work ethic in young people. Such a view assumes that lessons learnt in sport participation can generate positive behavioural traits in other domains such as academic work and social maturity.

In a recent paper, Hagger and Weed (2000) have suggested that these three roles for physical education can result in policies and curricula that lack direction and convey conflicting messages for young people. Drawing on policy documents put forward by UK Department of Education for the National Curriculum in physical education and the UK government's overall strategy for sport, Hagger and Weed ask whether the ideals for sport promotion such as talent identification and excellence and moral development can co-exist with the promotion of health-related activity in school physical education. They argue that the application of a model of sport performance in physical education often ignores and undermines the competence and desire for participation among children who do not display sport talent of the highest level. They conclude that the challenge for physical education is to provide alternative routes within physical education that permit the talented to flourish while providing fun, interesting, and exciting opportunities for the majority to participate in sport and exercise for a healthy and active lifestyle. Such opportunities may then track into increased exercise outside normal school hours and perhaps lead to persistence in later life (Hagger *et al.* 2003b).

Interventions and practice

Drawing on the theories of motivation presented in this book, this section highlights the commonality in the practical guidelines offered to exercisers and athletes on the basis of research. The focus of this book has been on applying social psychological research to exercise and sport behaviour, and, as a result, practical guidelines across both disciplines are theory-based. Given that there is considerable commonality in the theories and methods used to explain phenomena in both the exercise and sport disciplines, it follows that there will be some commonality in the strategies adopted by practitioners to intervene. This section will briefly outline the practical recommendations highlighted from the theoretical investigations in this book and demonstrate that they share many of the techniques involved.

Exercise psychology practical guidelines

In an exercise context, research suggests that interventions to alter exercise behaviour should focus on three specific aspects: (1) the antecedents of intentions and motivation; (2) the factors that convert intentions into behaviour; (3) and the underlying beliefs and motives that give rise to these antecedents. Given the pervasive effects that attitudes and perceived behavioural control, particularly self-efficacy, have on exercise behaviour from various theoretical models (e.g. theory of planned behaviour), practitioners would do well to target these antecedent variables (Hardeman *et al.* 2002). In particular, interventions need to provide information about the advantages of exercise, how people can overcome salient barriers, and the means available to them to participate in regular exercise. Practitioners should also avoid an approach that uses scare tactics or a controlling, authoritarian approach. This is because intervention approaches such as motivational interviewing and research on self-determination theory that focus on supporting people's psychological needs suggest that a controlling approach will undermine intrinsic motivation and inhibit the formation of intentions to exercise. Such approaches advocate the creation of a motivational climate that supports intrinsic and identified motives for action. These autonomy-supportive environments can be fostered by providing individuals with sensible, personally relevant goals that are suggested by the individual, providing informational feedback, and encouraging the choice and selection of activities that are interesting and satisfying.

Sports psychology practical guidelines

In sport, a number of practical guidelines for practitioners such as coaches, trainers, and sports psychologists working with athletes have been adopted. These are based on empirical studies examining the antecedents of sports performance from theoretical perspectives such as social cognitive theory, achievement goal theory, and self-determination theory. The focus of these guidelines is on pragmatic recommendations that aim to increase athletes' levels of motivation and adaptive outcomes such as self-esteem and competence. Coaches should avoid making comparisons with others, not equate performance outcomes with self-esteem, and handle and correct errors constructively and in an autonomy-supportive way. In addition, creating a task-oriented motivational climate by providing challenges and handling failures, setbacks, and mistakes constructively and avoiding language that undermines autonomous motivation (e.g. using words like 'should' and 'must'), being positive in approach, and communicating and listening to athletes are cornerstones of recommendations that theory states will generate interest, persistence, and positive affective and psychological outcomes. In team sports, research suggests that the coaches can foster greater team cohesion by being relationship-oriented and trying to satisfy innate needs for relatedness. Specific behaviours that can assist in this are the forging of better relationships with athletes by helping to solve problems, being empathic, and knowing the team members as individuals. These comprehensive, theory-based guidelines can result in improving intrinsic motivation, promoting a mastery-involved goal orientation, and increase self-esteem in athletes.

Summary

- The application of social psychology to social processes and behaviour in exercise and sport adopts similar perspectives in both disciplines. These similarities can be classified in terms of themes, methods, theories, contrasts, and practical guidelines.
- Common themes include the prediction of behaviour, the role and prediction of affective outcomes, and the role and prediction of social influences.
- Methods adopted across both disciplines include cross-sectional studies, longitudinal, cross-lagged panel designs, experimental designs, and qualitative approaches.
- The theories common to the exercise and sport disciplines include theories of intention and motivation, and, in particular, self-determination theory.
- In terms of contrasts, the purposes of exercise for health and sport can sometimes co-exist in that sports participants also have motives that are health-related, but these may also conflict as in cases where competition may undermine intrinsic motivation.
- Common to the interventions are the importance of an autonomy-supportive context and the setting of appropriate goals.

Glossary

Achievement goal theory: Proposes that motivation is determined by an individual's global orientations regarding their perceived ability. Two orientations influence motivation: a task orientation that represents a perception of ability as self-referenced, and an ego orientation in which ability is perceived as other-referenced.

Activity disorder: Psychological condition in which individuals develop disordered patterns of exercise characterized by extreme levels of physical activity; tends to be accompanied by compromised psychological well-being and self-esteem.

Affect: Umbrella term referring to all types of 'feeling states'. See *emotion* and *mood*.

Affective attitudes: Attitudes based on affective (emotional) beliefs about attitude objects. See *attitude*.

Aggression: A set of behaviours that are likely to, or have the potential to, cause harm to others, and are intended to cause harm.

Anticipated regret: Feelings and emotions that an individual would expect to experience as a consequence of rejecting alternative behavioural decisions.

Anxiety: A negative affective state characterized by an inability to cope with the stress placed on an individual by environmental demands.

Applied research: Empirical studies that examine the effects of social psychological models and interventions in ecologically valid (everyday) contexts.

Arousal: A heightened sense of psychological and physiological awareness and readiness.

Attitude: A general orientation, positive or negative, toward an attitude object. See *affective attitudes* and *cognitive attitudes*.

Attitude strength: The strength of the association between a set of beliefs about an attitude object and a target behaviour.

Attitudinal ambivalence: The holding of two potentially conflicting attitudinal beliefs simultaneously.

Attribution theory: Weiner's (Weiner *et al.* 1972) theory proposes that future sport engagement and salient outcomes are determined by people's attribution of the cause of their behaviour to various sources that are perceived to be internal, stable, or controllable.

Behavioural belief: Beliefs that engaging in a target behaviour will result in certain salient outcomes. Along with *outcome evaluation*, this forms an *expectancy-value model* of beliefs that underpins the *attitude* component of the *theory of planned behaviour*.

Belief: A learned personal orientation regarding a person, object, or behaviour. See *attitude*.

Catastrophe theory: Hardy's (1990) theory of anxiety in sport that predicts non-linear changes in the relationship between anxiety and performance with different levels of arousal.

Choke: Term used to describe a catastrophic drop in sport performance in high-pressure competition.

Cognitive attitudes: Attitudes based on instrumental beliefs about the utility of an attitude object. See *attitude* and *affective attitudes*.

Cognitive evaluation theory: Sub-theory of self-determination theory that hypothesizes that environmental contingencies such as rewards have a pervasive effect on level of intrinsic motivation.

Collective aggression: Aggressive and violent behaviour of a group of people with intent to cause injury or harm to another individual or group.

Collective efficacy: Beliefs in the ability of a group or team to produce certain desirable outcomes such as win a point or execute an effective defence.

Conflict theory: Theory that suggests that violence in sports contexts reflects underlying social, political, and economic grievances held by the working-class element of the sport crowd.

Continuation intention: A stated plan to engage in a behaviour like exercise even after salient behavioural outcomes have been achieved.

Control beliefs: Beliefs that external factors will facilitate or inhibit behavioural engagement. Along with *perceived power*, this forms the *expectancy-value model* of the *perceived behavioural control* component of the *theory of planned behaviour*.

Correspondence rule: Boundary condition of the *theory of planned behaviour* dictating that social cognitive predictors like *attitudes* and *intentions* must agree in terms of action, target, context, and time.

Crowd violence: A form of collective aggression and violence between crowds of sports spectators. See *collective aggression*.

Descriptive norms: Beliefs regarding the extent to which significant others engage in a target behaviour. Normative construct included in augmented versions of the *theory of planned behaviour*.

Desire: Reflects the motivational content of *attitudes*. See *model of goal-directed behaviour*.

Emotion: A specific feeling state often thought to have physiological (somatic) and cognitive (interpretive) components.

Evaluation apprehension: An individual's belief that an audience or crowd of spectators are critically evaluating his/her performance of a behaviour.

Exercise: Formal form of *physical activity* encompassing all type of energy-expending movement usually for health reasons.

Expectancy-value model: Model in which the effect of a social cognitive construct on a behavioural or outcome variable (e.g. intention) is determined by the product of the expectancy (e.g. behavioural belief) and the personal value attached to that belief (e.g. outcome evaluation). Ajzen (1985) proposed that this model reflects the nature of the belief systems that underpin the *theory of planned behaviour* and *theory of reasoned action* constructs.

Figurational approach: Theory of crowd violence that proposes that aggression among sport supporters arises because of violence is an acceptable means to resolve conflict among the working classes. However, the violence seen among sports fans is ritualistic and ordered and reflects a civilizing process.

Formative research: Empirical research that focuses on the origins of social cognitive constructs and behaviour.

Group cohesion: The social forces that maintain the attraction between members of a group and the resistance of the group to disruptive forces.

Group dynamics: The study of the effect of group membership on group members' perceptions and behaviour.

Group norm: The accepted roles and ways of behaving endorsed by group members.

Health belief model: A social cognitive theory of health behaviour that hypothesizes that an individual's readiness or intention to perform a health behaviour is function of his/her perceived vulnerability to a health condition and the probable severity of that condition.

Hierarchical model: Refers to a hierarchical organization of a psychological construct from different levels of generality and implies both bottom-up and top-down patterns of influence. Vallerand's (1997) hierarchical models of self-determined motivation and Fox and Corbin's (1989) hierarchical model of physical self-perceptions are examples.

Home advantage: Phenomenon in which a sport team has a significantly better chance of winning when playing at their home ground or venue, although some argue this may be indicative of an 'away disadvantage'.

Hooliganism: A brand of sport violence usually reserved for conflict among soccer fans in Europe, although some argue that this term also refers to non-violent extrovert and outrageous behaviours.

Hostile aggression: Aggression for which the primary purpose is injurious to others and coupled with high emotional arousal. Should be contrasted to *instrumental aggression*.

Implementation intention: Volitional strategy in which the link between *intention* and behaviour is enhanced by the creation of cues (e.g. when and where to perform the behaviour) that permit the automatic enactment of the behaviour once they are encountered.

Individualized zones of optimal functioning (IZOF): Hanin's (2000) eclectic theory that has been primarily described as a theory of *anxiety* and hypothesizes that athletes have an individual level of anxiety at which they will exhibit optimal performance.

Instrumental aggression: Aggressive acts that may result in injury, but the intent to injure is peripheral to the performance advantage the aggressive act yields.

Intention: Stated plans to act and the most proximal predictor of behaviour in the theory of planned behaviour. See *theory of planned behaviour*.

Intention stability: Consistency in *intentions* over time, thought to moderate the intention–behaviour relationship in the *theory of planned behaviour*.

Intervention: A strategy implemented to change a number of (usually) psychological variables and examine their effect of perceptions and behaviour.

Intrinsic motivation: Motivation to participate in social behaviours with no discernible external reinforcement. Intrinsic motivation is often characterized as behaviours that are done out of enjoyment, fun, interest, a sense of choice, and personal autonomy.

Inverted-U hypothesis: Hypothesis that athletes have an 'optimal' level of arousal at which performance is maximized, while lower or higher levels of arousal lead to progressively inferior performance.

Meta-analysis: Statistical technique that aims to find the average effect size (relationship or difference) between key variables from tests of the effect across a number of empirical studies while correcting for sampling (e.g. sample size) and measurement (e.g. reliability) error.

Model of goal-directed behaviour: Social cognitive theory of volitional behaviour that hypothesizes desires to be the most proximal determinant of goal intentions. In the model, intentions are viewed as intentions to perform a target behaviour to achieve a specific goal and are the most proximal predictor of behaviour. Attitudes, subjective norms, perceived behavioural control, and anticipated positive and negative affect all influence intentions via the mediation of desires.

Mood: A feeling state that is longer lasting and less intense than emotion, often viewed from a 'profile' perspective.

Motivation: A social cognitive construct that activates, energizes, or drives behaviour and determines its intensity, direction, and persistence of a behaviour.

Motivation to comply: Individuals' beliefs that they will generally comply with the wishes of their significant others. With *normative beliefs*, this construct forms the *expectancy-value* belief system that underpins the subjective norm component of the *theory of planned behaviour.*

Motivational climate: The environmental context operating in achievement settings. A mastery motivational climate tends to engender a task-oriented motivational orientation while performance motivational climate tends to foster an ego-oriented motivational orientation.

Motivational interviewing: Intervention technique that aims to change exercise behaviour by focusing on client-centred reasons for change, reducing ambivalence, increasing self-efficacy, and reducing resistance to change.

Normative Beliefs: Individuals' beliefs that significant others would want them to participate in the target behaviour. With *motivation to comply*, this construct forms the *expectancy-value* belief system that underpins the subjective norm component of the *theory of planned behaviour.*

Organismic integration theory: A sub-theory of self-determination theory that hypothesizes that externally regulated behaviours can be integrated into an individual's repertoire of behaviours that service personally salient goals or outcomes. This integration is met with a shift in the perceived locus of causality from external to internal.

Outcome evaluation: Individuals' beliefs that certain behavioural outcomes are positive or negative. With *behavioural belief*, this construct forms the *expectancy-value* belief system that underpins the attitude component of the *theory of planned behaviour.*

Past behaviour: Frequency or recency of past behaviour is considered to reflect the influence of unmeasured constructs in social cognitive models like the theory of planned behaviour and the model of goal-directed behaviour. Controversially, it is also said to reflect more automatic routes to behavioural engagement.

Perceived autonomy support: An individual's evaluation of the extent to which their environment supports their intrinsic motivation.

Perceived behavioural control: Social cognitive construct that reflects an individual's degree of subjective control over a target behaviour in the *theory of planned behaviour.* Hypothesized to affect behaviour directly and indirectly via the mediation of intention.

Perceived locus of causality: Continuum that reflects the source of the reason for doing behaviour in a given context. Intrinsic motivation and external regulation lie at the extremes of the continuum with identified regulation and introjected regulation reflecting intermediate levels of autonomous and controlling regulation respectively. See *organismic integration theory.*

Perceived power: The extent that external factors affect behavioural engagement. Along with *control beliefs*, this forms the *expectancy-value model* of the *perceived behavioural control* component of the *theory of planned behaviour*.

Personality: Trait or trait-like constructs that are general and stable in nature and are hypothesized to affect a variety of behaviours across a number of contexts.

Physical activity: Umbrella term that encompasses all energy-expending body movement.

Physical self-esteem: An individual's evaluation of their self in physical contexts.

Protection motivation theory: A social cognitive theory that hypothesizes that engagement in health behaviour is function of threat and coping appraisals.

Psychological social psychology: Approach to social psychological investigation that adopts an empirical, hypothesis-testing framework based on the principles of falsification and converging evidence.

Reversal theory: Theory of motivation and emotion that states that an individual's behaviour is determined by a series of metamotivational states. These states dictate whether the individual experiences a positive or negative affective state or hedonic tone and the level of arousal associated with the behaviour.

Role ambiguity: The degree of clarity that an individual has regarding his role in a sport team or group.

Role conflict: The degree to which an individual perceives they are unable to meet the demands of their established or assigned role in a sport team or group.

Role efficacy: An individual's estimate of their ability to perform the behaviours expected to successfully fulfil their role in the sport team or group.

Self-determination theory: Influential theory of motivation that hypothesizes that human motivation is determined by the goal of satisfying the basic psychological needs of autonomy (see *intrinsic motivation*), competence, and relatedness. Self-determination theory concerns itself with the environmental conditions that give rise to intrinsically motivated behaviour (see *cognitive evaluation theory*) and the way in which extrinsically motivated behaviours (see *perceived locus of causality*) become integrated into an individual's repertoire of behaviours that satisfy psychological needs (see *organismic integration theory*).

Self-efficacy: Situation-specific self-confidence.

Social cognition: Approach to social psychology that assumes individuals are rational decision-makers who process information from their social environment and past experience prior to making decisions to act.

Social cognitive theory: Bandura's (1977) theory that proposed that behaviour was a function of environmental reinforcements (presence of models) and internal factors (such as observational learning).

Social facilitation: The study of the effects of audiences and coaction on individual performance, particularly audiences and other competitors on sport performance.

Social identity theory: Tajfel and Turner's (1986) theory that hypothesizes individual group members' behaviour to be affected by their own categorization of themselves as stereotypical group members and their associated attributes.

Social learning theory: Branch of Bandura's (1986) *social cognitive theory* that focuses on how individuals' observation of others' behaviour can reinforce their own behaviours.

Social loafing: Phenomenon in which an individual in a group exhibits a decrement in their personal performance due to the perception that they are unable to contribute to the group effort and their individual contribution is not being evaluated.

Sociological social psychology: Approach to social psychology that focuses on theory building rather than theory testing through phenomenological accounts from individuals regarding behaviour.

Sport: Competitive endeavours that usually have a system of governing rules. Many sports have a physical element to them that may yield benefits similar to exercise.

Subjective norm: Social cognitive construct that reflects an individual's perceived belief that significant others want them to engage in a target behaviour like exercise. In the *theory of planned behaviour*, subjective norm is hypothesized to influence behaviour via the mediation of *intentions*.

Theory of planned behaviour: Often cited theory of intentional behaviour that hypothesizes that *intention* is the most proximal predictor of volitional behaviour and mediates the influence of a set of personal (see *attitude*), social (see *subjective norms*), and control-related (see *perceived behavioural control*) beliefs on behaviour. Ajzen (1985) hypothesizes that perceived behavioural control also influences behaviour directly.

Theory of reasoned action: Precursor to the theory of planned behaviour. Hypothesizes that volitional behaviour is influenced by the indirect effect of attitudes and subjective norms via the mediation of intentions (Ajzen & Fishbein 1980).

Trans-contextual model: Multi-theory model that hypothesizes that an adolescent's *perceived autonomy support* in a physical education context influences his/her attitudes, perceived behavioural control, and intention from the *theory of planned behaviour* and exercise behaviour via the mediation of autonomous motives in physical education and leisure-time contexts.

Volitional theories: Theories that aim to examine the processes by which intentions are translated into actions.

Bibliography

Abraham, C., Clift, S. and Grabowski, P. (1999) Cognitive predictors of adherence to malaria prophylaxis regimens on return from a malarious region: a prospective study. *Social Science and Medicine*, 48: 1641–54.

Abraham, C. and Sheeran, P. (2003) Acting on intentions: the role of anticipated regret. *British Journal of Social Psychology*, 42: 495–511.

Abraham, C. and Sheeran, P. (2004) Deciding to exercise: the role of anticipated regret. *British Journal of Health Psychology*, 9: 269–78.

Ackard, D.M., Croll, J.K. and Kearney-Cooke, A. (2002) Dieting frequency among college females: association with disordered eating, body image and related psychological problems. *Journal of Psychosomatic Research*, 52: 129–36.

Adams, J.M., Miller, T.W. and Kraus, R.F. (2003) Exercise dependence: diagnostic and therapeutic issues for patients in psychotherapy. *Journal of Contemporary Psychotherapy*, 33: 93–107.

Agnew, G.A. and Carron, A.V. (1994) Crowd effects and the home advantage. *International Journal of Sport Psychology*, 25: 53–62.

Aiello, J.R. and Douthitt, E.A. (2001) Social facilitation from Triplett to electronic performance monitoring. *Group Dynamics*, 5, 163–80.

Ajzen, I. (1985) From intentions to actions: a theory of planned behavior. In J. Kuhl and J. Beckmann (eds), *Action – control: From Cognition to Behavior* (pp. 11–39). Heidelberg: Springer.

Ajzen, I. (1991) The theory of planned behavior. *Organizational Behavior and Human Decision Processes*, 50: 179–211.

Ajzen, I. (2002a) Perceived behavioral control, self-efficacy, locus of control, and the theory of planned behavior. *Journal of Applied Social Psychology*, 32: 1–20.

Ajzen, I. (2002b) Residual effects of past on later behavior: habituation and reasoned action perspectives. *Personality and Social Psychology Review*, 6: 107–22.

Ajzen, I. and Fishbein, M. (1980) *Understanding Attitudes and Predicting Social Behavior*. Englewood Cliffs, NJ: Prentice Hall.

Allen, J.B. (2003) Social motivation in youth sport. *Journal of Sport and Exercise Psychology*, 25: 551–67.

Allport, F.H. (1920) The influence of the group upon association and thought. *Lancet*, 60: 159–82.

American College of Sports Medicine. (1998) ACSM Position stand: exercise and physical activity for older adults. *Medicine and Science in Sports and Exercise*, 30: 992–1008.

American Heart Association. (1999) AHA/ACC scientific statement: assessment of cardiovascular risk by use of multiple-risk-factor assessment equations. *Circulation*, 100: 1481–92.

American Psychiatric Association. (1994) *Diagnostic and Statistical Manual of Mental Disorders* (revised 4th edn). Washington, DC: American Psychiatric Association.

American Psychiatric Association Work Group on Eating Disorders. (2000) Practice guideline for the treatment of patients with eating disorders (revision) *American Journal of Psychiatry*, 157 (Suppl.): S1 – S39.

Ames, C. (1992) Classrooms: goals, structures, and student motivation. *Journal of Educational Psychology*, 84: 261–71.

Andersen, A.E. (1995) Eating disorders in males. In K.D. Brownell and C.G. Fairburn (eds), *Eating Disorders and Obesity: A Comprehensive Handbook* (pp. 177–87). New York: Guilford Press.

Apter, M. (1982) *The Experience of Motivation: The Theory of Psychological Reversals*. New York: Academic Press.

Armitage, C. and Arden, M.A. (2002) Exploring discontinuity patterns in the transtheoretical model: an application of the theory of planned behaviour. *British Journal of Health Psychology*, 7: 89–103.

Armitage, C.J. and Conner, M. (1999a) Predictive validity of the theory of planned behaviour: the role of questionnaire format and social desirability. *Journal of Community and Applied Social Psychology*, 9: 261–72.

Armitage, C.J. and Conner, M. (1999b) The theory of planned behavior: assessment of predictive validity and 'perceived control'. *British Journal of Social Psychology*, 38: 35–54.

Armitage, C.J. and Conner, M. (2000) Attitudinal ambivalence: a test of three key hypotheses. *Personality and Social Psychology Bulletin*, 26: 1421–32.

Armitage, C.J. and Conner, M. (2001) Efficacy of the theory of planned behaviour: a meta-analytic review. *British Journal of Social Psychology*, 40: 471–99.

Armitage, C.J., Povey, R. and Arden, M.A. (2003) Evidence for discontinuity patterns across the stages of change: a role for attitudinal ambivalence. *Psychology and Health*, 18: 373–86.

Asçi, F.H., Asçi, A. and Zorba, E. (1999) Cross-cultural validity and reliability of the physical self-perception profile. *International Journal of Sport Psychology*, 30,:399–406.

Ashford, B., Biddle, S. and Goudas, M. (1993) Participation in community sports centres: motives and predictors of enjoyment. *Journal of Sport Sciences*, 11: 249–56.

Bagozzi, R.P., Gürhan-Canli, Z. and Priester, J.R. (2002) *The Social Psychology of Consumer Behaviour*. Buckingham: Open University Press.

Bagozzi, R.P. and Yi, Y. (1989) The degree of intention formation as a moderator of the attitude-behavior relationship. *Social Psychology Quarterly*, 52: 266–79.

Baker, C.W., Little, T.D. and Brownell, K.D. (2003) Predicting adolescent eating and activity behaviors: the role of social norms and personal agency. *Health Psychology*, 22: 189–98.

Bandura, A. (1977) Self-efficacy: toward a unifying theory of behavioral change. *Psychological Review*, 84: 191–215.

Bandura, A. (1994) Self-efficacy. In V.S. Ramachaudran (ed.), *Encyclopedia of Human Behavior* (Vol. 4, pp. 71–81). New York: Academic Press.

Bandura, A. (1997) *Self-efficacy: The Exercise of Control*. New York: Freeman.

Bargh, J.A. (1994) The Four Horsemen of automaticity: awareness, efficiency, intention, and control in social cognition. In R.S. Wyer and T.K. Srull (eds), *Handbook of Social Cognition* (Vol. 2, pp. 1–40). Hillsdale, NJ: Erlbaum.

Baron, R.S. (1986) Distraction-conflict theory: progress and problems. *Advances in Experimental Social Psychology*, 19: 1–36.

Baumeister, R.F. (1984) Choking under pressure: self-consciousness and paradoxical effects of incentives on skillful performance. *Journal of Personality and Social Psychology*, 46: 610–20.

Baumeister, R.F. (1995) Disputing the effects of championship pressures and home audiences. *Journal of Personality and Social Psychology*, 68: 644–8.

Baumeister, R.F. and Leary, M.R. (1995) The need to belong: desire for interpersonal attachments as a fundamental human motivation. *Psychological Bulletin*, 117: 497–529.

Baumeister, R.F. and Steinhilber, A. (1984) Paradoxical effects of supportive audiences on performance under pressure: the home field disadvantage in sports championships. *Journal of Personality and Social Psychology*, 47: 85–93.

Beauchamp, M.R. and Bray, S.R. (2001) Role ambiguity and role conflict within interdependent teams. *Small Group Research*, 32: 133–57.

Beauchamp, M.R., Bray, S.R., Eys, M.A. and Carron, A.V. (2002) Role ambiguity, role efficacy, and role performance: multidimensional and mediational relationships within interdependent sport teams. *Group Dynamics: Theory, Research and Practice*, 6: 229–42.

Beauchamp, M.R., Bray, S.R., Eys, M.A. and Carron, A.V. (2003) Effect of role ambiguity on competitive state anxiety. *Journal of Sport and Exercise Psychology*, 25: 77–92.

Becker, A.E., Grinspoon, S.K., Klibanski, A. and Herzog, D.B. (1999) Eating disorders. *New England Journal of Medicine*, 340: 1092–8.

Beedie, C.J., Terry, P.C. and Lane, A.M. (2000) The profile of mood states and athletic performance: two meta – analyses. *Journal of Applied Sport Psychology*, 12: 49–68.

Bell, P.A. and Yee, LA. (1989) Skill level and audience effects on performance of a karate drill. *Journal of Social Psychology*, 129: 191–200.

Bellew, E. and Thatcher, J. (2002) Metamotivational state reversals in competitive sport. *Social Behavior and Personality*, 30: 613–23.

Bennett, J.C. (1991) The irrationality of catharsis theory of aggression as a justification for educators' support for interscholastic football. *Perceptual and Motor Skills*, 72: 415–18.

Berger, B.G. and Motl, R.W. (2000) Exercise and mood: a selective review and synthesis of research employing the profile of mood states. *Journal of Applied Sport Psychology*, 12: 69–92.

Berglund, B. and Safstrom, H. (1994) Psychological monitoring and modulation of training load of world-class canoeists. *Medicine and Science in Sports and Exercise*, 26: 1036–40.

Berkowitz, L. (1993) *Aggression: Its Causes, Consequences, and Control*. Philadelphia, PA: Temple University Press.

Biasi, V. (1999) Personological studies on dancers: motivations, conflicts and defense mechanisms. *Empirical Studies of the Arts*, 17: 171–86.

Biddle, S.J.H. (1997) Cognitive theories of motivation and the physical self. In K. R. Fox (ed.), *The Physical Self* (pp. 59–82). Champaign, IL: Human Kinetics.

Biddle, S.J.H. (1999) Motivation and perceptions of control: tracing its development and plotting its future in exercise and sport psychology. *Journal of Sport and Exercise Psychology*, 21: 1–23.

Biddle, S.J.H., Akande, D., Armstrong, N., Ashcroft, M., Brooke, R. and Goudas, M. (1996) The self-motivation inventory modified for children: evidence on psychometric properties and its use in physical exercise. *International Journal Sport Psychology*, 27: 237–50.

Biddle, S.J.H., Hanrahan, S.J. and Sellars, C.N. (2001) Attributions: past, present, and future. In R.N. Singer, H.A. Hausenblas and C.M. Janelle (eds), *Handbook of Sport Psychology* (pp. 444–71). New York: Wiley.

Bond, C.F. and Titus, L.J. (1983) Social facilitation: a meta-analysis of 241 studies. *Psychological Bulletin*, 94: 265–92.

Bond, K.A., Biddle, S.J.H. and Ntoumanis, N. (2001) Self-efficacy and causal attribution in female golfers. *International Journal of Sport Psychology*, 32: 243–56.

Bornstein, R.F. (2001) A meta-analysis of the dependency eating-disorders relationship: strength, specificity, and temporal stability. *Journal of Psychopathology and Behavioral Assessment*, 23: 151–62.

Boyd, M.P., Weinmann, C. and Yin, Z. (2002) The relationship of physical self-perceptions and goal orientations to intrinsic motivation for exercise. *Journal of Sport Behavior*, 25: 1–18.

Boyd, M.P., Yin, Z., Ellis, D. and French, K. (1995) Perceived motivational climate, socialization influences, and affective responses in Little League Baseball. *Journal of Sport and Exercise Psychology*, 17 (Suppl.): S30.

Bozionelos, G. and Bennett, P. (1999) The theory of planned behaviour as predictor of exercise: the moderating influence of beliefs and personality variables. *Journal of Health Psychology*, 4: 517–29.

Branca, F. (1999) Physical activity, diet and skeletal health. *Public Health Nutrition*, 2 (Suppl.): S391 – S396.

Brawley, L.R. (1993) The practicality of using psychological theories for exercise and health research and intervention. *Journal of Applied Sport Psychology*, 5: 99–115.

Brawley, L.R., Carron, A.V. and Widmeyer, W.M. (1988) Exploring the relationship between cohesion and group resistance to disruption. *Journal of Sport and Exercise Psychology*, 10: 199–213.

Bray, C.D. and Whaley, D.E. (2001) Team cohesion, effort, and objective individual performance of high school basketball players. *The Sport Psychologist*, 15: 260–75.

Bray, R.M. and Sugarman, R. (1980) Social facilitation among interacting groups: Evidence for the evaluation-apprehension hypothesis. *Personality and Social Psychology Bulletin*, 6: 137–42.

Bray, S.R. (1999) The home advantage from an individual team perspective. *Journal of Applied Sport Psychology*, 11: 116–25.

Bray, S.R. (2004) Collective efficacy, group goals, and group performance of a muscular endurance task. *Small Group Research*, 35: 230–8.

Bray, S.R. and Brawley, L.R. (2002) Role efficacy, role clarity, and role performance effectiveness. *Small Group Research*, 33: 233–53.

Bray, S.R., Brawley, L.R. and Carron, A.V. (2002) Efficacy for interdependent role functions: evidence from the sport domain. *Small Group Research*, 33: 644–66.

Bray, S.R. and Martin, KA. (2003) The effect of competition location on individual athlete performance and psychological states. *Psychology of Sport and Exercise*, 4: 117–23.

Breaux, C.A. and Moreno, J.K. (1994) Comparing anorectics and bulimics on measures of depression, anxiety, and anger. *Eating Disorders: The Journal of Treatment and Prevention*, 2: 158–67.

Bredemeier, B.J.L. and Shields, D.L. (1986) Moral growth among athletes and non-athletes: a comparative analysis. *Journal of Genetic Psychology*, 147: 7–18.

Brown, T.D., van Raalte, J.L., Brewer, B.W., Winter, C.R., Cornelius, A.E. and Andersen, M.B. (2002) World cup soccer home advantage. *Journal of Sport Behavior*, 25: 134–44.

Bundred, P., Kitchiner, D. and Buchan, I. (2001) Prevalence of overweight and obese children between 1989 and 1998: population-based series of cross-sectional studies. *British Medical Journal*, 322: 326–8.

Burton, D. (1988) Do anxious swimmers swim slower? Reexamining the elusive anxiety-performance relationship. *Journal of Sport and Exercise Psychology*, 10: 45–61.

Burton, D. (1998) Measuring competitive state anxiety. In J.L. Duda (ed.), *Advances in Sport and Exercise Psychology Measurement* (pp. 129–48). Morgantown, WV: Fitness Information Technology.

Bushman, B.J., Baumeister, R.F. and Stack, A.D. (1999) Catharsis, aggression, and persuasive influence: self-fulfilling or self-defeating prophecies? *Journal of Personality and Social Psychology*, 76: 367–76.

Bushman, B.J. and Cooper, H.M. (1990) Effects of alcohol on human aggression: an integrative research review. *Psychological Bulletin*, 107: 341–54.

Butler, R. (1987) Task-involving and ego-involving properties of evaluation: effects of different feedback conditions on motivational perceptions, interest, and performance. *Journal of Educational Psychology*, 79: 474–82.

Byers, T., Nestle, M., McTiernan, A., Doyle, C., Currie-Williams, A., Gansler, T. and Thun, M. (2002) American Cancer Society Guidelines on Nutrition and Physical Activity for cancer prevention: reducing the risk of cancer with healthy food choices and physical activity. *CA – Cancer Journal of Clinicians*, 52: 92–119.

Cale, L. and Almond, L. (1992) Children's physical activity levels: a review of studies conducted on British children. *Physical Education Review*, 15: 111–18.

Cameron, J. and Pierce, W.D. (1994) Reinforcement, reward, and intrinsic motivation: a meta-analysis. *Review of Educational Research*, 64: 363–423.

Carnahan, B.J., Shea, J.B. and Davis, G.S. (1990) Motivational cue effects on bench-press performance and self-efficacy. *Journal of Sport Behavior*, 13: 240–54.

Carnes, M. and Sachs, M. (2002, October 9–12) Too much of a good thing. Paper presented at the Addiction Medicine Review Course 2002, Newport Beach, California.

Carron, A.V. (1982) Cohesiveness in sport groups: interpretations and considerations. *Journal of Sport Psychology*, 4: 123–38.

Carron, A.V. and Hausenblas, H.A. (1998) *Group Dynamics in Sport* (2nd edn). Morgantown, WV: Fitness Information Technology.

Carron, A.V., Widmeyer, W.M. and Brawley, L.R. (1985) The development of an instrument to assess cohesion in sport teams: the group environment questionnaire. *Journal of Sport Psychology*, 7: 244–6.

CDC/NCHS (2001) *National Health and Nutrition Examination Survey*. Atlanta, GA: National Center for Disease Control and Prevention and National Center for Health Statistics.

Centers for Disease Control and Prevention. (2002) *2002 BRFSS Summary Prevalence Report*. Atlanta, GA: US Department of Health and Human Services, Public Health Service, Centers for Disease Control and Prevention, National Center for Chronic Disease Prevention and Health Promotion.

Centers for Disease Control and Prevention. (2003) Physical activity levels among children aged 9–13 years: United States, 2002. *Mortality and Morbidity Weekly*, 52: 785–8.

Chaiken, S. (1980) Heuristic versus systematic information processing and the use of source versus message cues in persuasion. *Journal of Personality and Social Psychology*, 39: 752–66.

Chase, M.A., Lirgg, C.D. and Feltz, D.L. (1997) Do coaches' efficacy expectations for their teams predict team performance? *The Sport Psychologist*, 11: 8–23.

Chatzisarantis, N.L.D. and Biddle, S.J.H. (1998) Functional significance of psychological variables that are included in the theory of planned behaviour: a self-determination theory approach to the study of attitudes, subjective norms, perceptions of control and intentions. *European Journal of Social Psychology*, 28: 303–22.

Chatzisarantis, N.L.D., Biddle, S.J H. and Meek, G.A. (1997) A self-determination theory approach to the study of intentions and the intention-behaviour relationship in children's physical activity. *British Journal of Health Psychology*, 2: 343–60.

Chatzisarantis, N.L.D., Hagger, M.S., Biddle, S.J.H. and Karageorghis, C. (2002) The cognitive processes by which perceived locus of causality predicts participation in physical activity. *Journal of Health Psychology*, 7: 685–99.

Chatzisarantis, N.L.D., Hagger, M.S., Biddle, S.J.H. and Smith, B. (in press a) The stability of the attitude-intention relationship in the context of physical activity. *Journal of Sport Sciences*.

Chatzisarantis, N.L.D., Hagger, M.S., Biddle, S.J.H., Smith, B.M. and Sage, L. (in press b) The influences of perceived autonomy support on physical activity within the theory of planned behaviour. *Journal of Sport and Exercise Psychology*.

Chatzisarantis, N.L.D., Hagger, M.S., Biddle, S.J.H., Smith, B. and Wang, J.C.K. (2003) A meta-analysis of perceived locus of causality in exercise, sport, and physical education contexts. *Journal of Sport and Exercise Psychology*, 25: 284–306.

Chatzisarantis, N.L.D., Hagger, M., Smith, B. and Phoenix, C. (in press c) The influences of continuation intentions on the execution of social behaviour within the theory of planned behaviour. *British Journal of Social Psychology*.

Chatzisarantis, N.L.D., Hagger, M.S., Smith, B. and Sage, L.D. (in press d) The influences of intrinsic motivation on execution of social behaviour within the theory of planned behaviour. *European Journal of Social Psychology*.

Clarke, J. (1978) Football and the working class fans: tradition and change. In R. Ingham (ed.), *Football Hooliganism: The Wider Context*. London: Interaction.

Coakley, J.J. (1981) The sociological perspective: alternate causations of violence in sport. *Arena*, 5: 44–56.

Cockerill, I.M., Neville, A.M. and Lyons, N. (1991) Modelling mood states in athletic performance. *Journal of Sports Sciences*, 9: 205–12.

Cockerill, I.M. and Riddington, M.E. (1996) Exercise dependence and associated disorders: a review. *Counselling Psychology Quarterly*, 9: 119–29.

Colman, M.M. and Carron, A.V. (2000) The group norm for productivity in individual sport teams. *Journal of Sport and Exercise Psychology*, 22 (Suppl.): S27 – S28.

Colman, M.M. and Carron, A.V. (2001) The nature of norms in individual sport teams. *Small Group Research*, 32: 206–22.

Connelly, D. (1988) Increasing intensity of play of nonassertive athletes. *The Sport Psychologist*, 2: 255–65.

Conner, M. and Abraham, C. (2001) Conscientiousness and the theory of planned behavior: toward a more complete model of the antecedents of intentions and behavior. *Personality and Social Psychology Bulletin*, 27: 1547–61.

Conner, M. and Armitage, C.J. (1998) Extending the Theory of Planned Behavior: a review and avenues for further research. *Journal of Applied Social Psychology*, 28: 1429–64.

Conner, M., Povey, R., Sparks, P., James, R. and Shepherd, R. (2003) Moderating role of attitudinal ambivalence within the theory of planned behaviour. *British Journal of Social Psychology*, 42: 75–94.

Conner, M., Sheeran, P., Norman, P. and Armitage, C. (2000) Temporal stability as a moderator of relationships in the theory of planned behaviour. *British Journal of Social Psychology*, 39: 469–93.

Conner, M., Sherlock, K. and Orbell, S. (1998) Psychosocial determinants of ecstasy use in young people in the UK. *British Journal of Social Psychology*, 3: 295–317.

Cottrell, N.B. (1972) Social facilitation. In C.G. McClintock (ed.), *Experimental Social Psychology* (pp. 185–236). New York: Holt, Rinehart and Winston.

Courneya, K.S. (1995) Understanding readiness for regular physical activity in older individuals: an application of the Theory of Planned Behavior. *Health Psychology*, 14: 80–7.

Courneya, K.S. and Carron, A.V. (1991) Effects of travel and length of home stand/road trip on the home advantage. *Journal of Sport and Exercise Psychology*, 13: 42–9.

Courneya, K.S. and Friedenreich, C.M. (1997) Relationship between exercise pattern across the cancer experience and current quality of life in colorectal cancer survivors. *Journal of Alternative and Complementary Medicine*, 3: 215–26.

Courneya, K.S., Friedenreich, C.M., Sela, R.A., Quinney, H.A. and Rhodes, R.E. (2002) Correlates of adherence and contamination in a randomized controlled trial of exercise in cancer survivors: an application of the theory of planned behavior and the five factor model of personality. *Annals of Behavioral Medicine*, 24: 257–68.

Courneya, K.S. and McAuley, E. (1994) Factors affecting the intention-physical activity relationship: intention versus expectation and scale correspondence. *Research Quarterly for Exercise and Sport*, 65: 280–5.

Courneya, K.S., Plotnikoff, R.C., Hotz, S.B. and Birkett, N.J. (2000) Social support and the theory of planned behavior in the exercise domain. *American Journal of Health Behavior*, 24: 300–8.

Cox, R.H., Martens, M.P. and Russell, W.D. (2003) Measuring anxiety in athletics: The Revised Competitive State Anxiety Inventory-2. *Journal of Sport and Exercise Psychology*, 25: 519–33.

Craft, L.L., Magyar, T.M., Becker, B.J. and Feltz, D.L. (2003) The relationship between the Competitive State Anxiety Inventory-2 and sport performance: a meta-analysis. *Journal of Sport and Exercise Psychology*, 25: 44–65.

Crocker, J. and Luhtanen, R.K. (2003) Level of self-esteem and contingencies of self-worth: unique effects on academic, social, and financial problems in college students. *Personality and Social Psychology Bulletin*, 29: 710–12.

Crocker, P.R.E., Alderman, R.B. and Smith, F.M.R. (1988) Cognitive-affective stress management training with high performance youth volleyball players: effects on affect, cognition, and performance. *Journal of Sport and Exercise Psychology*, 10: 448–60.

Dashiell, J.F. (1930) An experimental analysis of some group effects. *Journal of Abnormal and Social Psychology*, 25: 190–9.

Davidson, R. (1992) Prochaska and DiClemente's model of change: a case study? *British Journal of Addiction*, 87: 1–2.

Davis, C. (1999) Excessive exercise and anorexia nervosa: addictive and compulsive behaviors. *Psychiatric Annals*, 29: 221–4.

Deci, E.L., Betley, G., Kahle, J., Abrams, L. and Porac, J. (1981) When trying to win: competition and intrinsic motivation. *Personality and Social Psychology Bulletin*, 7: 79–83.

Deci, E.L., Eghrari, H., Patrick, B.C. and Leone, D.R. (1994) Facilitating internalization: the self-determination theory perspective. *Journal of Personality*, 62: 119–42.

Deci, E.L., Koestner, R. and Ryan, R.M. (1999a) A meta-analytic review of experiments examining the effects of extrinsic rewards on intrinsic motivation. *Psychological Bulletin*, 125: 627–68.

Deci, E.L., Koestner, R. and Ryan, R.M. (1999b) The undermining effect is a reality after all: extrinsic rewards, task interest, and self-determination: Reply to Eisenberger, Pierce and Cameron (1999) and Lepper, Henderlong and Gingras (1999). *Psychological Bulletin*, 125: 692–700.

Deci, E.L. and Ryan, R.M. (1985) *Intrinsic Motivation and Self-determination in Human Behavior*. New York: Plenum Press.

Deci, E.L. and Ryan, R.M. (2000) The 'what' and 'why' of goal pursuits: human needs and the self-determination of behavior. *Psychological Inquiry*, 11: 227–68.

Department of Health (1996) *Strategy Statement on Physical Activity*. London: Department of Health.

Devine, D.J. (1999) Effects of cognitive ability, task knowledge, information sharing, and conflict on group decision-making effectiveness. *Small Group Research*, 30: 608–34.

Diener, E. (1976) Effects of prior destructive behavior, anonymity, and group presence on deindividuation and aggression. *Journal of Personality and Social Psychology*, 33: 497–507.

Dollard, J., Doob, L., Miller, N., Mowrer, O.W. and Sears, R.R. (1939) *Frustration and Aggression*. New Haven, CT: Yale University Press.

Duda, J.L. (1993) Goals: a social cognitive approach to the study of achievement motivation in sport. In R.N. Singer, M. Murphey and L.K. Tennant (eds), *Handbook of Research on Sport Psychology* (pp. 421–36). New York: Macmillan.

Duda, J.L. (2001) Achievement goal research in sport: pushing the boundaries and clarifying some misunderstandings. In G.C. Roberts (ed.), *Advances in Motivation in Sport and Exercise* (pp. 129–82). Champaign, IL: Human Kinetics.

Duda, J.L., Chi, L., Newton, M.L., Walling, M.D. and Catley, D. (1995) Task and ego orientation and intrinsic motivation in sport. *International Journal of Sport Psychology*, 26: 40–63.

Duda, J.L. and Nicholls, J.G. (1992) Dimensions of achievement motivation in schoolwork and sport. *Journal of Educational Psychology*, 84: 290–9.

Duncan, T. and McAuley, E. (1987) Efficacy expectations and perceptions of causality in motor performance. *Journal of Sport Psychology*, 9: 385–93.

Dunning, E., Murphy, P. and Williams, J. (1988) *The Roots of Football Hooliganism*. London: Routledge.

Dweck, C.S. (1992) The study of goals in psychology. *Psychological Science*, 3: 165–7.

Eagly, A.H. and Chaiken, S. (1993) *The Psychology of Attitudes*. San Diego, CA: Harcourt, Brace and Jovanovich.

Edwards, T. and Hardy, L. (1996) The interactive effects of intensity and direction of cognitive and somatic anxiety and self-confidence upon performance. *Journal of Sport and Exercise Psychology*, 18: 296–312.

Edwards, T., Kingston, K., Hardy, L. and Gould, D. (2002) A qualitative analysis of catastrophic performances and the associated thoughts, feelings, and emotions. *The Sport Psychologist*, 16: 1–19.

Ekman, P. (1992) Facial expression of emotion: new findings, new questions. *Psychological Science*, 3: 34–8.

Elias, N. (1978) *The Civilising Process*. Oxford: Blackwell.

Escarti, A. and Gutierrez, M. (2001) Influence of motivational climate in physical education on the intention to practice physical activity or sport. *European Journal of Sport Science*, 1: 1–12.

Everett, J.J., Smith, R.E. and Williams, K.D. (1992) Effects of team cohesion and identifiability on social loafing in relay swimming performance. *International Journal of Sport Psychology*, 23: 311–24.

Eys, M.A., Carron, A.V., Bray, S.R. and Beauchamp, M.R. (2003) Role ambiguity and athlete satisfaction. *Journal of Sports Sciences*, 21: 391–401.

Eys, M.A., Hardy, J., Carron, A.V. and Beauchamp, M.R. (2003) The relationship between task cohesion and competitive state anxiety. *Journal of Sport and Exercise Psychology*, 25: 66–76.

Fazio, R.H. (1990) Multiple processes by which attitudes guide behavior: the MODE model as an integrative framework. In M.P. Zanna (ed.), *Advances in Experimental Social Psychology* (Vol. 23, pp. 75–109). San Diego, CA: Academic Press.

Feltz, D.L. and Chase, M.A. (1998) The measurement of self-efficacy and confidence in sport. In J.L. Duda (ed.), *Advances in Sport and Exercise Psychology Measurement* (pp. 65–80). Morgantown, WV: Fitness Information Technology.

Feltz, D.L. and Lirgg, C.D. (1998) Perceived team and player efficacy in hockey. *Journal of Applied Psychology*, 83: 557–64.

Fernquist, R.M. (2000) An aggregate analysis of professional sports, suicide, and homicide rates: 30 U.S. metropolitan areas, 1971–1990. *Aggression and Violent Behavior*, 5: 329–41.

Festinger, L. (1954) A theory of social comparison processes. *Human Relations*, 7: 117–40.

Festinger, L. and Carlsmith, J.M. (1958) Cognitive consequences of forced compliance. *Journal of Abnormal and Social Psychology*, 58: 203–10.

Findlay, L.C. and Ste-Marie, D.M. (2004) A reputation bias in figure skating judging. *Journal of Sport and Exercise Psychology*, 26: 154–66.

Finlay, K.A., Trafimow, D. and Villarreal, A. (2002) Predicting exercise and health behavioral intentions: attitudes, subjective norms, and other behavioral determinants. *Journal of Applied Social Psychology*, 32: 342–58.

Flegal, K.M. (1999) The obesity epidemic in children and adults: current evidence and research issues. *Medicine and Science in Sports and Exercise*, 31 (Suppl.): S509–S514.

Fonseca, A. and Balague, G. (1996) Measuring goal orientations in youth competitive soccer: a comparison of TEOSQ and POSQ measures. *Journal of Applied Sport Psychology*, 8 (Suppl.): S143.

Forgas, J.P., Brennan, G., Howe, S., Kane, J.F. and Sweet, S. (1980) Audience effects on squash players' performance. *Journal of Social Psychology*, 111: 41–7.

Fox, K.R. (1999) The influence of physical activity on mental well-being. *Public Health Nutrition*, 2 (Suppl.): 411–18.

Fox, K.R. (2000) The effects of exercise on self-perceptions and self-esteem. In S.J.H. Biddle, K.R. Fox and S.H. Boutcher (eds), *Physical Activity and Psychological Well-being* (Vol. 13, pp. 81–118). London: Routledge.

Fox, K.R. and Biddle, S. (1989) The child's perspective in P.E. Part IV: psychology and professional issues. *British Journal of Physical Education*, 20: 35–38.

Fox, K.R. and Corbin, C. (1989) Physical self-perception profile: development and preliminary validation. *Journal of Sport and Exercise Psychology*, 11: 408–30.

Frijda, N.H. (1994) Varieties of emotions: emotions and episodes, moods and sentiments. In P. Ekman and R.J. Davidson (eds), *The Nature of Emotion: Fundamental Questions* (pp. 59–67). New York: Oxford University Press.

Gabennesch, H. (1988) When promises fail: a theory of temporal fluctuations in suicide. *Social Forces*, 67: 129–45.

Gagné, M., Ryan, R.M. and Bargmann, K. (2003) Autonomy support and need satisfaction in the motivation and well-being of gymnasts. *Journal of Applied Sport Psychology*, 15: 372–90.

Gardner, D.E., Shields, D.L.L., Bredemeier, B.J.L. and Bostrom, A. (1996) The relationship between perceived coaching behaviors and team cohesion among baseball and softball players. *The Sport Psychologist*, 10: 367–81.

Gaudreau, P., Blondin, J.P. and Lapierre, A.M. (2002) Athletes' coping during a competition: relationship of coping strategies with positive affect, negative affect, and performance-goal discrepancy. *Psychology of Sport and Exercise*, 3: 125–50.

Gayton, W.F. and Langevin, G. (1992) Home advantage: does it exist in individual sports? *Perceptual and Motor Skills*, 74: 706.

George, T.R. (1994) Self-confidence and baseball performance: A causal examination of self-efficacy theory. *Journal of Sport and Exercise Psychology*, 16: 381–99.

Gernigon, C. and Delloye, J.B. (2003) Self-efficacy, causal attribution, and track athletic performance following unexpected success or failure among elite sprinters. *The Sport Psychologist*, 17: 55–76.

Gill, D.L. (1984) Individual and group performance in sport. In J.M. Silva and R.S. Weinberg (eds), *Psychological Foundations of Sport* (pp. 315–28). Champaign, IL: Human Kinetics.

Gill, D.L. and Deeter, T.E. (1988) Development of the sport orientation questionnaire. *Research Quarterly for Exercise and Sport*, 59: 191–202.

Godin, G., Valois, R., Jobin, J. and Ross, A. (1991) Prediction of intention to exercise of individuals who have suffered from coronary heart disease. *Journal of Clinical Psychology*, 47: 762–72.

Golden, N.H. (2002) A review of the female athlete triad (amenorrhea, osteoporosis and disordered eating). *International Journal of Adolescent Medicine and Health*, 14: 9–17.

Gollwitzer, P.M. (1999) Implementation intentions: strong effects of simple plans. *American Psychologist*, 54: 493–503.

Goudas, M., Biddle, S.J.H. and Fox, K.R. (1994) Perceived locus of causality, goal orientations, and perceived competence in school physical education classes. *British Journal of Educational Psychology*, 64: 453–563.

Gould, D., Greenleaf, C. and Krane, V. (2002) Arousal-anxiety and sport behavior. In T.S. Horn (ed.), *Advances in Sport Psychology* (pp. 207–41). Champaign, Il: Human Kinetics.

Gould, D., Petlichkoff, L., Hodge, K. and Simons, J. (1990) Evaluating the effectiveness of a psychological skills educational workshop. *The Sport Psychologist*, 4: 249–60.

Gould, D., Petlichkoff, L. and Weinberg, R.S. (1984) Antecedents of, temporal changes in, and relationships between CSAI-2 components. *Journal of Sport Psychology*, 6: 289–304.

Gould, D. and Tuffey, S. (1996) Zones of optimal functioning research: a review and critique. *Anxiety, Stress and Coping*, 9: 53–68.

Gould, D., Tuffey, S., Hardy, L. and Lockbaum, M. (1993) Multidimensional state anxiety and middle distance running performance: an exploratory analysis of Hanin's (1980) zones of optimal functioning hypothesis. *Journal of Applied Sport Psychology*, 5: 85–95.

Gould, D. and Weiss, M.R. (1981) The effects of model similarity and model talk on self-efficacy and muscular endurance. *Journal of Sport Psychology*, 3: 17–29.

Greenlees, I., Graydon, J. and Maynard, I.W. (2000) The impact of individual efficacy beliefs on group goal selection and group goal commitment. *Journal of Sport Sciences*, 18: 451–59.

Greer, D.L. (1983) Spectator booing and the home advantage: a study of social influence in the basketball arena. *Social Psychology Quarterly*, 46: 252–61.

Grieve, F.G., Whelan, J.P. and Meyers, A.W. (2000) An experimental examination of the cohesion-performance relationship in an interactive team sport. *Journal of Applied Sport Psychology*, 12: 219–35.

Griffin, J. and Harris, J. (1996) Coaches' attitudes, knowledge, experiences, and recommendations regarding weight control. *The Sport Psychologist*, 10: 180–94.

Griffiths, M. (1999) Exercise addiction: a case study. *Addiction Research*, 5 161–8.

Grove, J.R. and Pargman, D. (1986) Relationships among success/failure, attributions, and performance expectancies in competitive situations. In L.V. Velden and J.H. Humphrey (eds), *Psychology and Sociology of Sport: Current Selected Research* (Vol. 1, pp. 85–95). New York: AMS Press.

Guay, F., Boggiano, A.K. and Vallerand, R.J. (2001) Autonomy support, motivation, and perceived competence: conceptual and empirical linkages. *Personality and Social Psychology Bulletin*, 27: 643–50.

Guay, F., Mageau, G.A. and Vallerand, R.J. (2003) On the hierarchical structure of self-determined motivation: a test of top-down, bottom-up, reciprocal, and horizontal effects. *Personality and Social Psychology Bulletin*, 29: 992–1004.

Hagbloom, S.J., Warnick, R., Warnick, J.E., Jones, V.K., Yarbrough, G.L., Russell, T.M., Borecky, C.M., McGahhey, R., Powell, J.L., Beavers, J. and Monte, E. (2002) The 100 most eminent psychologists of the 20th century. *Review of General Psychology*, 6: 139–52.

Hagger, M.S., Ashford, B. and Stambulova, N. (1998) Russian and British children's physical self-perceptions and physical activity participation. *Pediatric Exercise Science*, 10: 137–52.

Hagger, M.S., Biddle, S.J.H., Chow, E.W., Stambulova, N. and Kavussanu, M. (2003a) Physical self-perceptions in adolescence: generalizability of a hierarchical multidimensional model across three cultures. *Journal of Cross-Cultural Psychology*, 34: 611–28.

Hagger, M.S., Biddle, S.J.H. and Wang, C.K.J. (in press a) Physical self-perceptions in adolescence: generalizability of a multidimensional, hierarchical model across gender and grade. *Educational and Psychological Measurement*.

Hagger, M.S. and Chatzisarantis, N.L.D. (in press) First- and higher-order models of attitudes, normative influence, and perceived behavioural control in the Theory of Planned Behaviour. *British Journal of Social Psychology*.

Hagger, M.S., Chatzisarantis, N.L.D., Barkoukis, V., Wang, C.K.J. and Baranowski, J. (in press b) Perceived autonomy support in physical education and leisure-time physical activity: a cross-cultural evaluation of the trans-contextual model. *Journal of Educational Psychology*.

Hagger, M.S., Chatzisarantis, N. and Biddle, S.J.H. (2002a) The influence of autonomous and controlling motives on physical activity intentions within the Theory of Planned Behaviour. *British Journal of Health Psychology*, 7: 283–97.

Hagger, M.S., Chatzisarantis, N. and Biddle, S.J.H. (2002b) A meta-analytic review of the theories of reasoned action and planned behavior in physical activity: predictive validity and the contribution of additional variables. *Journal of Sport and Exercise Psychology*, 24 3–32.

Hagger, M.S., Chatzisarantis, N., Biddle, S.J.H. and Orbell, S. (2001) Antecedents of children's physical activity intentions and behaviour: predictive validity and longitudinal effects. *Psychology and Health*, 16 391–407.

Hagger, M.S., Chatzisarantis, N., Culverhouse, T. and Biddle, S.J.H. (2003b) The processes by which perceived autonomy support in physical education promotes leisure-time physical activity intentions and behavior: a trans-contextual model. *Journal of Educational Psychology*, 95: 784–95.

Hagger, M.S., Lindwall, M. and Asçi, F.H. (2004) A cross-cultural evaluation of a multidimensional and hierarchical model of physical self-perceptions in three national samples. *Journal of Applied Social Psychology*, 34: 1075–1107.

Hagger, M.S. and Weed, M.E. (2000) Developing physical activity in children: The relationship between P.E. and sport. Paper presented at the Annual Congress of the European College of Sports Science, University of Jyaväskylä, Jyaväskylä, Finland, 19–24 July.

Hall, E.G. and Bunker, L.K. (1979) Locus of control as a mediator of social facilitation effects during motor skill learning. *Journal of Sport Psychology*, 1: 332–5.

Hall, H.K. and Kerr, A.W. (1998) Predicting achievement anxiety: a social-cognitive perspective. *Journal of Sport and Exercise Psychology*, 20: 98–111.

Halliburton, A.L. and Weiss, M.R. (2002) Sources of competence information and perceived motivational climate among adolescent female gymnasts varying in skill level. *Journal of Sport and Exercise Psychology*, 24: 396–418.

Hanin, Y.L. (1995) Individual zones of optimal functioning (IZOF) model: an idiographic approach to performance anxiety. In K. Henschen and W. Straub (eds), *Sport Psychology: An Analysis of Athlete Behavior* (pp. 103–99). Longmeadow, NY: Mouvement.

Hanin, Y.L. (2000) Successful and poor performance and emotions. In Y.L. Hanin (ed.), *Emotions in Sport* (pp. 157–88). Champaign, IL: Human Kinetics.

Hanton, S. and Jones, G. (1999a) The acquisition and development of cognitive skills and strategies: I. Making the butterflies fly in formation. *The Sport Psychologist*, 13: 1–21.

Hanton, S. and Jones, G. (1999b) The effects of a multimodal intervention program on performers: II. Training the butterflies to fly in formation. *The Sport Psychologist*, 13: 22–41.

Hardeman, W., Johnston, M., Johnston, D.W., Bonetti, D., Wareham, N.J. and Kinmonth, A.L. (2002) Application of the theory of planned behaviour change interventions: a systematic review. *Psychology and Health*, 17: 123–58.

Hardy, C.J. (1990) Social loafing: motivational losses in collective performance. *International Journal of Sport Psychology*, 21: 305–27.

Hardy, C.J. and Crace, R.K. (1991) The effects of task structure and teammate competence on social loafing. *Journal of Sport and Exercise Psychology*, 13: 372–81.

Hardy, C.J. and Latané, B. (1988) Social loafing in cheerleaders: effects of team membership and competition. *Journal of Sport and Exercise Psychology*, 1988, 10: 109–14.

Hardy, L. (1990) A catastrophe model of performance in sport. In J.G. Jones and L. Hardy (eds), *Stress and Performance in Sport* (pp. 81–106). New York: Wiley.

Hardy, L. (1996) Testing the predictions of the Cusp Catastrophe Model of anxiety and performance. *The Sport Psychologist*, 10: 140–56.

Hardy, L. and Parfitt, C.G. (1991) A catastrophe model of anxiety and performance. *British Journal of Psychology*, 82: 163–78.

Harland, J., White, M., Drinkwater, C., Chinn, D., Farr, L. and Howel, D. (1999) The Newcastle exercise project: a randomised controlled trial of methods to promote physical activity in primary care. *British Medical Journal*, 319: 828–32.

Harris, N.B. (1992) Sex, race, and experiences of aggression. *Aggressive Behavior*, 18: 201–17.

Harrison, J., Mullen, P. and Green, L. (1992) A meta analysis of studies of the health belief model with adults. *Health Education Research*, 7,:107–16.

Harter, S. (1988) *Manual for the Self-Perception Profile for Adolescents*. Denver, CO: University of Denver.

Harter, S. (1996) Historical roots and contemporary issues involving self-concept. In B.A. Bracken (ed.), *Handbook of Self-concept: Developmental, Social, and Clinical Considerations* (pp. 1–37). New York: Wiley.

Harwood, C.G. (2002) Assessing achievement goals in sport: caveats for consultants and a case for contextualization. *Journal of Applied Sport Psychology*, 14: 106–19.

Hausenblas, H.A., Carron, A.V. and Mack, D.E. (1997) Application of the Theories of Reasoned Action and Planned Behavior to exercise behavior: a meta analysis. *Journal of Sport and Exercise Psychology*, 19: 36–41.

Hausenblas, H.A. and Giacobbi, P.R., Jr. (2004) Relationship between exercise dependence symptoms and personality. *Personality and Individual Differences*, 36: 1265–73.

Hausenblas, H.A. and Symons-Downs, D. (2002a) Exercise dependence: a systematic review. *Psychology of Sport and Exercise*, 3: 89–123.

Hausenblas, H.A. and Symons-Downs, D. (2002b) How much is too much? The development and validation of the exercise dependence scale. *Psychology and Health*, 17: 387–404.

Heider, F. (1958) *The Psychology of Interpersonal Relations*. New York: John Wiley.

Heuze, J.P. and Brunel, P.C. (2003) Social loafing in a competitive context. *International Journal of Sport and Exercise Psychology*, 1: 246–63.

Hinrichsen, H., Wright, F., Waller, G. and Meyer, C. (2003) Social anxiety and coping strategies in the eating disorders. *Eating Behaviors*, 4: 117–26.

Hodge, K. and Petlichkoff, L. (2000) Goal profiles in sport motivation: a cluster analysis. *Journal of Sport and Exercise Psychology*, 22: 256–72.

Hodgkins, S. and Orbell, S. (1998) Can protection motivation theory predict behaviour? A longitudinal test exploring the role of previous behaviour. *Psychology and Health*, 13: 237–50.

Holt, N.L. and Sparkes, A.C. (2001) An ethnographic study of cohesiveness in a college soccer team over a season. *The Sport Psychologist*, 15: 237–59.

Huddleston, S., Doody, S.G. and Ruder, M.K. (1985) The effect of prior knowledge of the social loafing phenomenon on performance in a group. *International Journal of Sport Psychology*, 16: 176–82.

Hulley, A.J. and Hill, A.J. (2001) Eating disorders and health in elite women distance runners. *International Journal of Eating Disorders*, 30: 312–17.

Institute of European Food Studies (1999) *Pan EU Survey on Consumer Attitudes to Physical Activity, Body Weight and Health*. Brussels: European Commission Directorate V/F.3.

Institute of Psychiatry (2004) *Illness Prevalence in Society: Is There an Increase of Eating Disorder Cases in General Population?* London: Institute of Psychiatry.

Iso-Ahola, S. (1977) Immediate attributional effects of success and failure in the field: Testing some laboratory hypotheses. *European Journal of Social Psychology*, 7: 275–96.

Iyengar, S.S. and DeVoe, S.E. (2003) Rethinking the value of choice: considering cultural mediators of intrinsic motivation. In V. Murphy-Berman and J.J. Berman (eds), *Cross-cultural Differences in Perspectives on the Self* (Vol. 49, pp. 129–74). Lincoln, NE: University of Nebraska Press.

Jackson, J.M. and Williams, K.D. (1985) Social loafing on difficult tasks: working collectively can improve performance. *Journal of Personality and Social Psychology*, 49: 937–42.

Joint Surveys Unit (1999) *Health Survey for England, 1998*. London: The Stationery Office.

Jokela, M. and Hanin, Y.L. (1999) Does the individual zones of optimal functioning model discriminate between successful and less successful athletes? A meta-analysis. *Journal of Sports Sciences*, 17: 873–87.

Jones, G. (1995) More than just a game: research developments and issues in competitive anxiety in sport. *British Journal of Psychology*, 86: 449–78.

Jones, G., Hanton, S. and Swain, A. (1994) Intensity and interpretation of anxiety symptoms in elite and nonelite performers. *Personality and Individual Differences*, 17: 657–63.

Jones, G. and Swain, A. (1995) Predispositions to experience debilitative and facilitative anxiety in elite and nonelite performers. *The Sport Psychologist*, 9: 201–11.

Jones, G., Swain, A. and Hardy, L. (1993) Intensity and direction dimensions of competitive state anxiety and relationships with performance. *Journal of Sport Sciences*, 11: 525–32.

Jones, G., Swain, A. and Harwood, C. (1996) Positive and negative affect as predictors of competitive anxiety. *Personality and Individual Differences*, 20: 109–14.

Jones, J.G. (1990) A cognitive perspective on the processes underlying the relationship between stress and performance in sport. In J.G. Jones and L. Hardy (eds), *Stress and Performance in Sport* (pp. 17–42). New York: Wiley.

Jones, J.G. and Hanton, S. (1996) Interpretation of competitive anxiety symptoms and goal attainment expectancies. *Journal of Sport and Exercise Psychology*, 18: 144–57.

Jones, J.G. and Hardy, L. (1990) The academic study of stress in sport. In J.G. Jones and L. Hardy (eds), *Stress and Performance in Sport* (pp. 3–16). New York: Wiley.

Jones, M.V., Bray, S.R. and Bolton, L. (2001) Game location and officiating bias in English club cricket. *Perceptual and Motor Skills*, 93: 359–62.

Jones, M.V., Mace, R.D., Bray, S.R., MacRae, A.W. and Stockbridge, C. (2002) The impact of motivational imagery on the emotional state and self-efficacy levels of novice climbers. *Journal of Sport Behavior*, 25: 57–73.

Kalodner, C.R. and DeLucia-Waack, J.L. (2003) Theory and research on eating disorders and disturbances in women: suggestions for practice. In M. Kopala and M.A. Keitel (eds), *Handbook of Counseling Women* (pp. 506–34). Thousand Oaks, CA: Sage.

Kane, T.D., Marks, M.A., Zaccaro, S.J. and Blair, V. (1996) Self-efficacy, personal goals, and wrestlers' self-regulation. *Journal of Sport and Exercise Psychology*, 18: 36–48.

Kavussanu, M., Crews, D.J. and Gill, D.L. (1998) The effects of single versus multiple measures of biofeedback on basketball free throw shooting performance. *International Journal of Sport Psychology*, 29: 132–44.

Kavussanu, M. and Roberts, G.C. (1996) Motivation in physical activity contexts: The relationship of perceived motivational climate to intrinsic motivation and self-efficacy. *Journal of Sport and Exercise Psychology*, 18: 264–80.

Kavussanu, M. and Roberts, G.C. (2001) Moral functioning in sport: An achievement goal perspective. *Journal of Sport and Exercise Psychology*, 23: 37–54.

Kerr, J.H. (1997) *Motivation and Emotion in Sport: Reversal Theory*. Hove: Psychology Press.

Kerr, J.H., Fujiyama, H. and Campano, J. (2002) Emotion and stress in serious and hedonistic leisure sport activities. *Journal of Leisure Research*, 34: 272–89.

Kerr, J.H. and Tacon, P. (2000) Environmental events and induction of metamotivational reversals. *Perceptual and Motor Skills*, 91: 337–8.

Keski-Rahkonen, A. (2001) Exercise dependence: a myth or a real issue? *European Eating Disorders Review*, 9: 279–83.

Kliene, D. (1990) Anxiety and sport performance: a meta-analysis. *Anxiety Research*, 2: 113–31.

Koestner, R., Lekes, N., Powers, T.A. and Chicoine, E. (2002) Attaining personal goals: self-concordance plus implementation intentions equals success. *Journal of Personality and Social Psychology*, 83: 231–44.

Koestner, R., Ryan, R.M., Bernieri, F. and Holt, K. (1984) Setting limits on children's behavior: the differential effects of controlling versus informational styles on intrinsic motivation and creativity. *Journal of Personality*, 52: 233–48.

Koka, A. and Hein, V. (in press) The effect of perceived teacher's feedback on intrinsic motivation in physical education. *Psychology of Sport and Exercise.*

Kowalski, N.P., Crocker, P.R.E. and Kowalski, K.C. (2001) Physical self and physical anxiety relationships in college women: does social physique anxiety moderate effects? *Research Quarterly for Exercise and Sport*, 72: 55–62.

Kowalski, K.C., Crocker, P.R.E., Kowalski, N.P., Chad, K.E. and Humbert, M.L. (2003) Examining the physical self in adolescent girls over time: further evidence against the hierarchical model. *Journal of Sport and Exercise Psychology*, 25: 5–18.

Kozar, B. (1973) The effects of a supportive and nonsupportive audience upon learning a gross motor skill. *International Journal of Sport Psychology*, 3: 27–38.

Landers, D.M. (1980) The arousal-performance relationship revisited. *Research Quarterly for Exercise and Sport*, 51: 77–90.

Lane, A.M. and Lane, H.J. (2002) Predictive effectiveness of mood measures. *Perceptual and Motor Skills*, 94: 785–91.

Latané, B., Williams, K. and Harkins, S. (1979) Many hands make light the work: the causes and consequences of social loafing. *Journal of Personality and Social Psychology*, 37: 822–32.

Legrand, F.D. and LeScanff, C. (2003) Tension-stress, effort-stress and mood profiling with an elite javelin performer. *Psychology of Sport and Exercise*, 4: 429–36.

Lehman, D.R. and Reifman, A. (1987) Spectator influence on basketball officiating. *Journal of Social Psychology*, 127: 673–5.

Lehoux, P.M., Steiger, H. and Jabalpurlawa, S. (2000) State/trait distinctions in bulimic syndromes. *International Journal of Eating Disorders*, 27: 36–42.

Levine, P. and Vinten-Johansen, P. (1981) The historical perspective: violence and sport. *Arena Review, Journal of Sport and Social Issues*, 5: 583–95.

Lichacz, F.M. and Partington, J.T. (1996) Collective efficacy and true group performance, 27: 146–58.

Lindner, K.J. and Kerr, J.H. (2001) Predictability of sport participation motivation from metamotivational dominances and orientations. *Personality and Individual Differences*, 30: 759–73.

Liu, J.L.Y., Maniadakis, N., Gray, A. and Rayner, M. (2002) The economic burden of coronary heart disease in the UK. *Heart*, 88: 597–603.

Lohasz, P.G. and Leith, L.M. (1997) The effect of three mental preparation strategies on the performance of a complex response time task. *International Journal of Sport Psychology*, 28: 25–34.

Loomes, G. and Sugden, R. (1982) Regret theory: an alternative theory of rational choice under uncertainty. *Economic Journal*, 92: 805–24.

Loughead, T.M., Carron, A.V., Bray, S.R. and Kim, A.J. (2003) Facility familiarity and the home advantage in professional sports. *International Journal of Sport and Exercise Psychology*, 1: 264–74.

Lowe, R., Eves, F. and Carroll, D. (2002) The influence of affective and instrumental beliefs on exercise intentions and behavior: a longitudinal analysis. *Journal of Applied Social Psychology*, 32: 1241–52.

Madison, J.K. and Ruma, S.L. (2003) Exercise and athletic involvement as moderators of severity in adolescents with eating disorders. *Journal of Applied Sport Psychology*, 15: 213–22.

Magyar, T.M., Feltz, D.L. and Simpson, I.P. (2004) Individual and crew level determinants of collective efficacy in rowing. *Journal of Sport and Exercise Psychology*, 26: 136–53.

Mann, L. (1981) The baiting crowd in episodes of threatened suicide. *Journal of Personality and Social Psychology*, 41: 703–9.

Markland, D. (2004) Motivational interviewing and self-determination theory. Retrieved August 1, 2004, from University of Wales, Bangor, School of Sport, Health, and Exercise Sciences Exercise Psychology Web site: *http://www.bangor.ac.uk/%7Epes004/exercise_psych/misdt.htm:* University of Wales, Bangor.

Markland, D. and Tobin, V. (2004) A modification to the Behavioural Regulation in Exercise Questionnaire to include an assessment of amotivation. *Journal of Sport and Exercise Psychology*, 26: 191–6.

Marsh, H.W. (1989) Age and sex effects in multiple dimensions of self-concept: Preadolescence to early adulthood. *Journal of Educational Psychology*, 81: 417–30.

Marsh, H.W. (1990) A multidimensional, hierarchical model of self-concept: theoretical and empirical justification. *Educational Psychology Review*, 2: 77–172.

Marsh, H.W., Marco, I.T. and Asçi, F.H. (2002) Cross-cultural validity of the physical self-description questionnaire: comparison of factor structures in Australia, Spain and Turkey. *Research Quarterly for Exercise and Sport*, 73: 257–70.

Marsh, H.W. and O'Niell, R. (1984) Self-description questionnaire III (SDQ III): the construct validity of multidimensional self-concept ratings by late-adolescents. *Journal of Educational Measurement*, 21: 153–74.

Marsh, H.W., Perry, C., Horsely, C. and Roche, L. (1995) Multidimensional self-concept of elite athletes: how do they differ from the general population? *Journal of Sport and Exercise Psychology*, 17: 70–83.

Marsh, H.W. and Redmayne, R.S. (1994) A multidimensional physical self-concept and its relations to multiple components of physical fitness. *Journal of Sport and Exercise Psychology*, 16: 43–55.

Marsh, H.W., Richards, G.E., Johnson, S., Roche, S. and Tremayne, P. (1994) Physical self description questionnaire: psychometric properties and a multitrait-multimethod analysis of relations to existing instruments. *Journal of Sport and Exercise Psychology*, 16: 270–305.

Marsh, H.W. and Shavelson, R. (1985) Self-concept: its multifaceted hierarchical structure. *Educational Psychologist*, 20: 107–23.

Marsh, H.W. and Yeung, A.S. (1998) Top-down, bottom-up, and horizontal models: the direction of causality in multidimensional, hierarchical self-concept models. *Journal of Personality and Social Psychology*, 75: 509–27.

Marsh, P. and Harré, R. (1978) The world of football hooliganism. *Human Nature*, 1: 62–9.

Marshall, S.J. and Biddle, S.J.H. (2001) The transtheoretical model of behavior change: a meta-analysis of applications to physical activity and exercise. *Annals of Behavioral Medicine*, 23: 229–46.

Martens, R., Vealey, R.S. and Burton, D. (1990) *Competitive Anxiety in Sport*. Champaign, IL: Human Kinetics.

Martin, J.J. and Gill, D.L. (1991) The relationship among competitive orientation, sport-confidence, self-efficacy, anxiety, and performance. *Journal of Sport and Exercise Psychology*, 13: 149–59.

Martin, J.J. and Gill, D.L. (1995) The relationships of competitive orientations and self-efficacy to goal importance, thoughts, and performance in high school distance runners. *Journal of Applied Sport Psychology*, 7: 50–62.

Martin, K.A. and Hausenblas, H.A. (1998) Psychological commitment to exercise and eating disorder symptomology among female aerobic instructors. *The Sport Psychologist*, 12: 180–90.

Maslow, A. (1943) A theory of human motivation. *Psychological Reports*, 50: 370–96.

Matheson, H., Mathes, S. and Murray, M. (1996) Group cohesion of female intercollegiate coacting and interacting team across a competitive season. *International Journal of Sport Psychology*, 27: 37–49.

Matheson, H., Mathes, S. and Murray, M. (1997) The effect of winning and losing on female interactive and coactive team cohesion. *Journal of Sport Behavior*, 20: 284–98.

Matthews, K.A., Krantz, D.S., Dembroski, T.M. and MacDougall, J.M. (1982) Unique and common variance in Structured Interview and Jenkins Activity Survey measures of Type A behavior pattern. *Journal of Personality and Social Psychology*, 42: 303–13.

McAuley, E. (1985) Modeling and self-efficacy: a test of Bandura's model. *Journal of Sport Psychology*, 7: 283–95.

McAuley, E. and Blissmer, B. (2002) Self-efficacy and attributional processes in physical activity. In T.S. Horn (ed.), *Advances in Sport Psychology* (pp. 185–206). Champaign, IL: Human Kinetics.

McAuley, E. and Tammen, V.V. (1989) The effects of subjective and objective competitive outcomes on intrinsic motivation. *Journal of Sport and Exercise Psychology*, 11: 84–93.

McAuliffe, B.J., Jetten, J., Hornsey, M.J. and Hogg, M.A. (2003) Individualist and collectivist norms: when it's ok to go your own way. *European Journal of Social Psychology*, 33: 57–70.

McCrae, R.R. and Costa, P.T. (1996) Toward a new generation of personality theories: theoretical contexts for the five-factor model. In J.S. Wiggins (ed.), *The Five-factor Model of Personality: Theoretical Perspectives* (pp. 51–87). New York: Guilford Press.

McCutcheon, L.E. (1984) The home advantage in high school athletics. *Journal of Sport Behavior*, 7: 135–8.

McGuire, E.J., Courneya, K.S., Widmeyer, W.N. and Carron, A.V. (1992) Aggression as a potential mediator of the home advantage in professional ice hockey. *Journal of Sport and Exercise Psychology*, 14: 148–58.

McNair, D., Lorr, M. and Droppleman, L. (1971) *Profile of Mood States*. San Diego: Education and Industrial Testing Service.

McNamara, J.J., Molot, M.A., Stremple, J.F. and Cutting, R.T. (1971) Coronary artery disease in combat casualties in Vietnam. *Journal of the American Medical Association*, 216(7): 1185–7.

Meiland, J. W. (1970) *The Nature of Intention*. London: Methuen.

Mellalieu, S.D., Hanton, S. and Jones, G. (2003) Emotional labeling and competitive anxiety in preparation and competition. *The Sport Psychologist*, 17: 157–74.

Meyers, A.W., Schleser, R. and Okwumabua, T.M. (1982) A cognitive behavioral intervention for improving basketball performance. *Research Quarterly for Exercise and Sport*, 53: 344–7.

Miller, C.T. and Downey, K.T. (1999) A meta-analysis of heavy weight and self-esteem. *Personality and Social Psychology Review*, 3: 68–84.

Miller, D.L. (2001) Reexamining teamwork KSAs and team performance. *Small Group Research*, 32: 745–66.

Miller, J.T. and McAuley, E. (1987) Effects of a goal-setting training program on basketball free-throw self-efficacy and performance. *The Sport Psychologist*, 1: 103–13.

Miller, W.R. (1999) Toward a theory of motivational interviewing. *Motivational Interviewing Newsletter: Updates, Education and Training*, 6: 2–4.

Milne, S., Sheeran, P. and Orbell, S. (2000) Prediction and intervention in health-related behavior: a meta-analytic review of protection motivation theory. *Journal of Applied Social Psychology*, 30: 106–43.

Milne, S.E., Orbell, S. and Sheeran, P. (2002) Combining motivational and volitional interventions to promote exercise participation: protection motivation theory and implementation intentions. *British Journal of Health Psychology*, 7: 163–84.

Morgan, W.P. (1980) Test of a champion: the iceberg profile. *Psychology Today*, 14: 92–108.

Morgan, W.P., O'Connor, P.J.O., Ellickson, K.A. and Bradley, P.W. (1988) Personality structure, mood states, and performance in elite male distance runners. *International Journal of Sport Psychology*, 19: 247–63.

Mullen, B. and Copper, C. (1994) The relation between group cohesiveness and performance: an integration. *Psychological Bulletin*, 115: 210–27.

Mullen, B. and Riordan, C. (1988) Self-serving attributions for performance in naturalistic settings: a meta-analytic review. *Journal of Applied Social Psychology*, 18: 3–22.

Murphy, P. (1990) Why there are no equivalents of soccer hooliganism in the United States. In P. Murphy, J. Williams and E. Dunning (eds), *Football on Trial: Spectator Violence and Development in the Football World* (pp. 194–212). London: Routledge.

National Centre for Social Research (1999) *Health Survey for England*. London: Department of Health.

National Health Service Health Development Agency (1996) *Active For Life*. London: Health Development Agency.

National Institute of Mental Health (1993) *Eating Disorders (NIH Publication No. 94–3477)* Bethesda, MD: Office of Communications and Public Liaison, National Institute of Mental Health (NIMH).

Neave, N. and Wolfson, S. (2003) Testosterone, territoriality, and the 'home advantage'. *Physiology and Behavior*, 78, 269–75.

Nederhof, A. (1989) Self-involvement, intention certainty and attitude-intention consistency. *British Journal of Social Psychology*, 28: 123–33.

Nevill, A.M., Balmer, N.J. and Williams, A.M. (2002) The influence of crowd noise and experience upon refereeing decisions in football. *Psychology of Sport and Exercise*, 3: 261–72.

Newton, M.L. and Duda, J.L. (1995) Relations of goal orientations and expectations on multidimensional state anxiety. *Perceptual and Motor Skills*, 81: 1107–12.

Newton, M.L. and Duda, J.L. (1999) The interaction of motivational climate, dispositional goal orientations, and perceived ability in predicting indices of motivation. *International Journal of Sport Psychology*, 30: 63–82.

Nicholls, J.G. (1989) *The Competitive Ethos and Democratic Education*. Cambridge, MA: Harvard University Press.

Notani, A.S. (1998) Moderators of perceived behavioral control's predictiveness in the theory of planned behavior: a meta-analysis. *Journal of Consumer Psychology*, 7: 247–71.

Ntoumanis, N. (2001) A self-determination approach to the understanding of motivation in physical education. *British Journal of Educational Psychology*, 71: 225–42.

Ntoumanis, N. and Biddle, S. (1998) The relationship between competitive anxiety, achievement goals and motivational climates. *Research Quarterly for Exercise and Sport*, 69: 176–87.

Ntoumanis, N. and Biddle, S.J.H. (1999) A review of motivational climate in physical activity. *Journal of Sports Sciences*, 17: 543–665.

Ntoumanis, N., Biddle, S.J.H. and Haddock, G. (1999) The mediating role of coping strategies on the relationship between achievement motivation and affect in sport. *Anxiety, Stress and Coping*, 12: 299–327.

Ntoumanis, N., Pensgaard, M., Martin, C. and Pipe, K. (in press) An idiographic analysis of amotivation in compulsory school physical education. *Journal of Sport and Exercise Psychology*.

Ogden, J., Veale, D. and Summers, Z. (1997) The development and validation of the Exercise Dependence Questionnaire. *Addiction Research*, 5: 343–55.

Ommundsen, Y. and Pedersen, B.H. (1999) The role of achievement goal orientations and perceived ability upon somatic and cognitive indices of sport competition trait anxiety: a study of young athletes. *Scandinavian Journal of Medicine and Science in Sports*, 9: 333–43.

Orbell, S. (2003) Personality systems interactions theory and the theory of planned behaviour: evidence that self-regulatory volitional components enhance enactment of studying behaviour. *British Journal of Social Psychology*, 42: 95–112.

Orbell, S., Hodgkins, S. and Sheeran, P. (1997) Implementation intentions and the Theory of Planned Behavior. *Personality and Social Psychology Bulletin*, 23: 945–54.

Orbell, S. and Sheeran, P. (1998) 'Inclined abstainers': a problem for predicting health related behaviour. *British Journal of Social Psychology*, 37: 151–65.

Oxendine, J.B. (1970) Emotional arousal and motor performance. *Quest*, 13: 23–32.

Oyserman, D. (2004) Self-concept and identity. In M.B. Brewer and M. Hewstone (eds), *Self and Social Identity* (pp. 5–24). Oxford: Blackwell.

Pace, A. and Carron, A.V. (1992) Travel and the home advantage. *Canadian Journal of Sport Sciences*, 17: 60–4.

Paffenbarger, R.S. and Hale, W.E. (1975) Work activity and coronary heart mortality. *New England Journal of Medicine*, 292: 545–50.

Parker, D. and Bar-Or, O. (1991) Juvenile obesity: the importance of exercise. *The Physician and Sports Medicine*, 19: 113–16.

Parker, D., Manstead, A.S.R. and Stradling, S.G. (1995) Extending the theory of planned behaviour: the role of personal norm. *British Journal of Social Psychology*, 34: 127–37.

Pate, R.R., Pratt, M., Blair, S.N., Haskell, W.L., Macera, C.A., Bouchard, C., Buchner, D., Ettiger, W., Heath, G.W., King, A.C., Kriska, A., Leon, A.S., Marcus, B., Morris, J., Paffenbarger, R.S., Patrick, K., Pollock, M.L., Rippe, J.M., Sallis, J. and Wilmore, J.H. (1995) Physical activity and public health: a recommendation from the Centers for Disease Control and Prevention and the American College of Sports Medicine. *Journal of the American Medical Association*, 273: 402–7.

Paulus, P.B., Shannon, J.C., Wilson, D.L. and Boone, T.D. (1972) The effect of spectator presence on gymnastic performance in a field situation. *Psychonomic Science*, 29: 88–90.

Pelletier, L.G., Fortier, M.S., Vallerand, R.J., Tuson, K.M., Briere, N.M. and Blais, M.R. (1995) Toward a new measure of intrinsic motivation, extrinsic motivation and amotivation in sport: the sport motivation scale (SMS). *Journal of Sport and Exercise Psychology*, 17: 35–53.

Pensgaard, A.M. (1999) The dynamics of motivation and perceptions of control when competing in the Olympic Games. *Perceptual and Motor Skills*, 89: 116–25.

Pensgaard, A.M. and Roberts, G.C. (1995) Perceived motivational climate and sources of stress for winter Olympic athletes. *Journal of Applied Sport Psychology*, 7(Suppl.): S9.

Perugini, M. and Bagozzi, R.P. (2001) The role of desires and anticipated emotions in goal-directed behaviours: broadening and deepening the theory of planned behavior. *British Journal of Social Psychology*, 40: 79–98.

Perugini, M. and Conner, M. (2000) Predicting and understanding behavioral volitions: the interplay between goals and behaviors. *European Journal of Social Psychology*, 30: 705–31.

Petersen, S., Peto, V. and Rayner, M. (2004) *Coronary Heart Disease Statistics*. London: British Heart Foundation.

Petherick, C.M. and Weigand, D.A. (2002) The relationship of dispositional goal orientations and perceived motivational climates on indices of motivation in male and female swimmers. *International Journal of Sport Psychology*, 33: 218–37.

Petty, R.E. and Cacioppo, J. (1986) *Communication and Persuasion: Central and Peripheral Routes to Attitude Change*. New York: Springer-Verlag.

Pierce, E.F., Eastman, N.W., Tripathi, H.L. and Olson, K.G. (1993) B-Endorphin response to endurance exercise: relationship to exercise dependence. *Perceptual and Motor Skills*, 77: 767–70.

Pope, H.G. and Katz, D.L. (1994) Psychiatric and medical effects of anabolic-androgenic steroid use: a controlled study of 160 athletes. *Archives of General Psychiatry*, 51: 375–82.

Povey, R., Conner, M., Sparks, P., James, R. and Shepherd, R. (2000) Application of the Theory of Planned Behaviour to two dietary behaviours: roles of perceived control and self-efficacy. *British Journal of Health Psychology*, 5: 121–39.

Prapavessis, H. (2000) The POMS and sports performance: a review. *Journal of Applied Sport Psychology*, 12: 34–48.

Prapavessis, H. and Carron, A.V. (1997) Sacrifice, cohesion, and conformity to norms in sport teams. *Group Dynamics*, 1: 231–40.

Prestwich, A., Lawton, R. and Conner, M. (2003) The use of implementation intentions and the decision balance sheet in promoting exercise behaviour. *Psychology and Health*, 10: 707–21.

Prichard, R.D., Campbell, K.M. and Campbell, D.J. (1977) Effects of extrinsic financial rewards on intrinsic motivation. *Journal of Applied Psychology*, 62: 9–15.

Prochaska, J.O. and DiClemente, C.C. (1982) Trans-theoretical theory: Towards a more integrated model of change. *Journal of Consultative Clinical Psychology*, 19: 276–88.

Prochaska, J.O., Velicer, W.F., Rossie, J.S., Goldstein, M.G., Marcus, B.H., Rakowski, W., Fiore, C., Harlow, L.L., Redding, C.A., Rosenbloom, D.A. and Rossi, S.R. (1994) Stages of change and decisional balance for 12 problem behaviors. *Health Psychology*, 13: 39–46.

Quine, L., Rutter, D.R. and Arnold, L. (1998) Predicting and understanding safety helmet use among schoolboy cyclists: a comparison of the theory of planned behaviour and the health belief model. *Psychology and Health*, 13: 251–69.

Quine, L., Rutter, D. and Arnold, L. (2001) Persuading school-age cyclists to use safety helmets: effectiveness of an intervention based on the Theory of Planned Behaviour. *British Journal of Health Psychology*, 6: 327–45.

Rainey, D.W. and Schweickert, G.J. (1988) An exploratory study of team cohesion before and after a spring trip. *The Sport Psychologist*, 2: 314–17.

Raitakari, O.T., Porkka, K.V., Taimela, S., Telama, R., Rasanen, L. and Viikari, J.S. (1994) Effects of persistent physical activity and inactivity on coronary risk factors in children and young adults. *American Journal of Epidemiology*, 140: 195–205.

Rajecki, D.W., Nerenz, D.R., Freedenberg, T.G. and McCarthy, P.J. (1979) Components of aggression in chickens and conceptualizations of aggression in general. *Journal of Personality and Social Psychology*, 37: 1902–14.

Raudsepp, L., Liblik, R. and Hannus, A. (2002) Children's and adolescents' physical self-perceptions as related to moderate to vigorous physical activity and fitness. *Pediatric Exercise Science*, 14: 97–106.

Reeve, J. (2002) Self-determination theory applied to educational settings. In E.L. Deci and R.M. Ryan (eds), *Handbook of Self-determination Research* (pp. 183–203). Rochester, NY: University of Rochester Press.

Reeve, J., Bolt, E. and Cai, Y. (1999) Autonomy-supportive teachers: how they teach and motivate students. *Journal of Educational Psychology*, 91: 537–48.

Reeve, J. and Deci, E.L. (1996) Elements of the competitive situation that affect intrinsic motivation. *Personality and Social Psychology Bulletin*, 22: 24–33.

Reeve, J., Olson, B.C. and Cole, S.G. (1985) Motivation and performance: two consequences of winning and losing a competition. *Motivation and Emotion*, 9: 291–8.

Reicher, S.D. (1987) Crowd behaviour and social action. In J.C. Turner, M.A. Hogg, P.J. Oakes, S.D. Reicher and M.S. Wetherell (eds), *Rediscovering the Social Group: A Self-categorisation Theory* (pp. 171–202). Oxford: Blackwell.

Reicher, S.D., Spears, R. and Postmes, T. (1995) A social identity model of deindividuation phenomena. In M. Hewstone and W. Stroebe (eds), *European Review of Social Psychology* (Vol. 6). Chichester: Wiley.

Rhodes, R.E., Courneya, K.S. and Jones, L.W. (2002a) Personality, the theory of planned behavior and exercise: a unique role for extroversion's activity facet. *Journal of Applied Social Psychology*, 32: 1721–36.

Rhodes, R.E., Jones, L.W. and Courneya, K.S. (2002b) Extending the theory of planned behavior in the exercise domain: a comparison of social support and subjective norm. *Research Quarterly for Exercise and Sport*, 73: 193–9.

Richards, G.E. (1988) *Physical Self-concept Scale*. Sydney: Australian Outward Bound Foundation.

Rivis, A. and Sheeran, P. (2003) Descriptive norms as an additional predictor in the theory of planned behaviour: a meta-analysis. *Current Psychology*, 22: 218–33.

Roberts, G.C. and Pascuzzi, D. (1979) Causal attributions in sport: some theoretical implications. *Journal of Sport Psychology*, 1: 203–11.

Roberts, G.C., Treasure, D.C. and Balague, G. (1998) Achievement goals in sport: the development and validation of the perception of success questionnaire. *Journal of Sports Sciences*, 16: 337–47.

Robinson, T.T. and Carron, A.V. (1982) Personal and situational factors associated with dropping out versus maintaining participation in competitive sport. *Journal of Sport Psychology*, 4: 364–78.

Rodgers, W.M. and Brawley, L.R. (1993) Using both self-efficacy theory and the theory of planned behavior to discriminate adherers and dropouts from structured programs. *Journal of Applied Sport Psychology*, 5: 195–206.

Rogers, R.W. (1975) A protection motivation theory of fear appeals and attitude change. *Journal of Psychology*, 91: 93–114.

Rogers, R.W. (1983) Cognitive and physiological processes in fear appraisals and attitude change: a revised theory of protection motivation. In J.T. Cacioppo and R.E. Petty (eds), *Social Psychology: A Source Book* (pp. 153–76). New York: Guilford Press.

Rollnick, S. and Miller, W.R. (1995) What is Motivational Interviewing? *Behavioural and Cognitive Psychotherapy*, 23: 325–34.

Rosenberg, M. (1979) *Conceiving the Self*. New York: Basic Books.

Rosenstock, I.M. (1974) Historical origins of the health belief model. *Health Education Monographs*, 2: 328–35.

Rowley, A.J., Landers, D.M., Kyllo, L.B. and Etnier, J.L. (1995) Does the Iceberg Profile discriminate between successful and less successful athletes? A meta-analysis. *Journal of Sport and Exercise Psychology*, 17: 185–99.

Rudisill, M. (1989) Influence of perceived competence and causal dimension orientations on expectations, persistence and performance during perceived failure. *Research Quarterly for Exercise and Sport*, 60: 166–75.

Russell, G.W. (1979) Hero selection by Canadian ice hockey players: Skill or aggression? *Canadian Journal of Applied Sport Sciences*, 4: 309–13.

Russell, G.W. (1983) Crowd size and density in relation to athletic aggression and performance. *Social Behavior and Personality*, 11: 9–15.

Russell, G.W. (1993) *The Social Psychology of Sport*. New York: Springer-Verlag.

Ryan, R. (1992) Management of eating problems in athletic settings. In K.D. Brownell, J. Rodin and J.H. Wilmore (eds), *Eating, Body Weight, and Performance in Athletes: Disorders of Modern Society* (pp. 344–62). Philadelphia, PA: Lea and Febiger.

Ryan, R.M. and Connell, J.P. (1989) Perceived locus of causality and internalization: examining reasons for acting in two domains. *Journal of Personality and Social Psychology*, 57: 749–61.

Ryan, R.M. and Deci, E.L. (1989) Bridging the research traditions of task/ego involvement and intrinsic/extrinsic motivation: comment on Butler (1987). *Journal of Educational Psychology*, 81: 265–8.

Ryan, R.M., Vallerand, R.J. and Deci, E.L. (1984) Intrinsic motivation in sport: a cognitive evaluation theory interpretation. In W.F. Straub and J.M. Williams (eds), *Cognitive Sport Psychology* (pp. 231–42). Lansing, NY: Sport Science Associates.

Sallis, J.F. and Patrick, K. (1994) Physical activity guidelines for adolescents: consensus statement. *Pediatric Exercise Science*, 6: 302–14.

Salminen, S. (1993) The effect of the audience on the home advantage. *Perceptual and Motor Skills*, 76: 1123–8.

Sanna, L.J. (1992) Self-efficacy theory: Implications for social facilitation and social loafing. *Journal of Personality and Social Psychology*, 62: 774–86.

Sarason, S.B., Davidson, K.S., Lighthall, F.F., Waite, R.R. and Ruebush, B.K. (1960) *Anxiety in Elementary School Children*. New York: Wiley.

Sarrazin, P., Biddle, S., Famose, J. P., Cury, F., Fox, K. and Durand, M. (1996) Goal orientations and conceptions of the nature of sport ability in children: a social cognitive approach. *British Journal of Psychological Society*, 35: 399–414.

Sarrazin, P., Vallerand, R.J., Guillet, E., Pelletier, L.G. and Cury, F. (2002) Motivation and dropout in female handballers: a 21-month prospective study. *European Journal of Social Psychology*, 32: 395–418.

Schacter, S. and Singer, J.E. (1962) Cognitive, social, and physiological determinants of emotional state. *Psychological Review*, 69: 379–399.

Scheer, J.K. and Ansorge, C.J. (1979) Influence due to expectations of judges. *Journal of Sport Psychology*, 1: 53–8.

Schlenker, B.R., Phillips, S.T., Boniecki, K.A. and Schlenker, D.R. (1995) Championship pressures: choking or triumphing in one's own territory? *Journal of Personality and Social Psychology*, 68: 632–43.

Schwartz, B. and Barsky, S.F. (1977) The home advantage. *Social Forces*, 55: 641–61.

Schwenkmezger, P. and Steffgen, G. (1989) Anxiety and motor performance. In B. Kirkcaldy (ed.), *Normalities and Abnormalities in Human Movement* (Vol. 29, pp. 78–99). Basle, Switzerland: S. Karger AG.

Sedikides, C. and Gregg, A.P. (2003) Portraits of the self. In M.A. Hogg and J. Cooper (eds), *Sage Handbook of Social Psychology* (pp. 110–38). London: Sage.

Seifriz, J.J., Duda, J.L. and Chi, L. (1992) The relationship of perceived motivational climate to intrinsic motivation and beliefs about success in basketball. *Journal of Sport and Exercise Psychology*, 14: 375–91.

Shavelson, R.J., Hubner, J.J. and Stanton, G.C. (1976) Self-concept: validation of construct interpretations. *Review of Educational Research*, 46: 407–41.

Sheeran, P. (2002) Intention-behavior relations: a conceptual and empirical review. In W. Stroebe and M. Hewstone (eds), *European Review of Social Psychology* (pp. 1–36). London: Wiley.

Sheeran, P., Norman, P. and Orbell, S. (1999a) Evidence that intentions based on attitudes better predict behaviour than intentions based on subjective norms. *European Journal of Social Psychology*, 29: 403–6.

Sheeran, P. and Orbell, S. (1999) Implementation intentions and repeated behaviour: augmenting the predictive validity of the theory of planned behaviour. *European Journal of Social Psychology*, 29: 349–69.

Sheeran, P. and Orbell, S. (2000) Self schemas and the theory of planned behaviour. *European Journal of Social Psychology*, 30: 533–50.

Sheeran, P., Orbell, S. and Trafimow, D. (1999b) Does the temporal stability of behavioral intentions moderate intention-behavior and past behavior-future behavior relations? *Personality and Social Psychology Bulletin*, 25: 721–30.

Sheeran, P. and Silverman, M. (2003) Evaluation of three interventions to promote workplace health and safety: evidence for the utility of implementation intentions. *Social Science and Medicine*, 56: 2153–63.

Sheldon, K.M., Elliot, A.J., Kim, Y. and Kasser, T. (2001) What is satisfying about satisfying events? Testing 10 candidate psychological needs. *Journal of Personality and Social Psychology*, 80: 325–39.

Sheppard, B.H., Hartwick, J. and Warshaw, P.R. (1988) The theory of reasoned action: a meta-analysis of past research with recommendation and future research. *Journal of Consumer Research*, 15: 325–43.

Sherman, S. and Fazio, R. (1983) Parallels between attitudes and traits as predictors of behavior. *Journal of Personality*, 51: 308–45.

Short, S.E., Bruggeman, J.M., Engel, S.G., Marback, T.L., Wang, L J., Willadsen, A. and Short, M.W. (2002) The effect of imagery function and imagery direction on self-efficacy and performance on a golf-putting task. *The Sport Psychologist*, 16: 48–67.

Silva, J.M. (1979) Behavioral and situational factors affecting concentration and skill performance. *Journal of Sport Psychology*, 1: 221–7.

Silva, J.M. (1980) Assertive and aggressive behavior in sport: a definitional clarification. In C.H. Nadeau, W R. Halliwell, K.M. Newell and G.C. Roberts (eds), *Psychology of Motor Behavior and Sport, 1979* (pp. 199–208). Champaign, IL: Human Kinetics.

Silva, J.M. and Andrew, A. (1987) An analysis of game location and basketball performance in the Atlantic Coast Conference. *International Journal of Sport Psychology*, 18: 188–204.

Singer, R.N. and McCaughan, L. (1978) Motivational effects of attributions expectancy, and achievement motivation during the learning of a novel motor task. *Journal of Motor Behavior*, 10: 245–53.

Slater, M.R. and Sewell, D.F. (1994) An examination of the cohesion-performance relationship in university hockey teams. *Journal of Sport Sciences*, 12: 423–31.

Smith, C.A., Kelly, N.H., Lazarus, R.S. and Pope, L.K. (1993) In search of the 'Hot' cognitions: attributes, appraisals, and their relation to emotion. *Journal of Personality and Social Psychology*, 65: 916–29.

Smith, L.E. and Crabbe, J. (1976) Experimenter role relative to social facilitation and motor learning. *International Journal of Sport Psychology*, 7: 158–68.

Smith, R.A. and Biddle, S.J.H. (1999) Attitudes and exercise adherence: test of the Theories of Reasoned Action and Planned Behaviour. *Journal of Sports Sciences*, 17: 269–81.

Sonstroem, R.J., Harlow, L.L., Gemma, L.M. and Osborne, S. (1991) Test of structural relationships within a proposed exercise and self-esteem model. *Journal of Personality Assessment*, 56: 348–64.

Sonstroem, R.J., Harlow, L.L. and Josephs, L. (1994) Exercise and self-esteem: validity of model expansion and exercise associations. *Journal of Sport and Exercise Psychology*, 16: 29–42.

Sonstroem, R.J., Harlow, L.L. and Salisbury, K.S. (1993) Path analysis of a self-esteem model across a competitive swim season. *Research Quarterly for Exercise and Sport*, 64(3): 335–42.

Sonstroem, R.J. and Morgan, W.P. (1989) Exercise and self-esteem: rationale and model. *Medicine and Science in Sports and Exercise*, 21: 329–37.

Spano, L. (2001) The relationship between exercise and anxiety, obsessive-compulsiveness, and narcissism. *Personality and Individual Differences*, 30: 87–93.

Spielberger, C.D., Gorusch, R.L. and Lushene, R.E. (1970) *Manual for the State Trait Anxiety Inventory*. Palo Alto, CA: Consulting Psychologists Press.

Spink, K.S. (1990) Collective efficacy in the sport setting. *International Journal of Sport Psychology*, 21: 380–95.

Stajkovic, A.D. and Luthans, F. (1998) Self-efficacy and work-related performance: a meta-analysis. *Psychological Bulletin*, 124: 240–61.

Standage, M., Duda, J.L. and Ntoumanis, N. (2003) A model of contextual motivation in physical education: using constructs from self-determination and achievement goal theories to predict physical activity intentions. *Journal of Educational Psychology*, 95: 97–110.

Starek, J. and McCullagh, P. (1999) The effect of self-modeling on the performance of beginning swimmers. *The Sport Psychologist*, 13: 269–87.

Steenland, K. and Deddens, J.A. (1997) Effect of travel and rest on performance of professional basketball players. *Sleep: Journal of Sleep Research and Sleep Medicine*, 20: 366–9.

Stephens, D.E. and Bredemeier, B.J.L. (1996) Moral atmosphere and judgments about aggression in girls' soccer: relationships among moral and motivational variables. *Journal of Sport and Exercise Psychology*, 18: 158–73.

Stott, C. (2001) 'Hooligans' abroad? Inter-group dynamics, social identity and participation in collective 'disorder' at the 1998 World Cup finals. *British Journal of Social Psychology*, 40: 359–84.

Strauss, B. (2002) Social facilitation in motor tasks: a review of research and theory. *Psychology of Sport and Exercise*, 3: 237–56.

Sullivan, P. and Feltz, D.L. (2003) The preliminary development of the Scale for Effective Communication in Team Sports (SECTS). *Journal of Applied Social Psychology*, 33: 1693–715.

Sundgot-Borgen, J. (2000) Eating disorders in athletes. In R.J. Maughan (ed.), *Nutrition in Sport* (pp. 510–22). Oxford: Blackwell.

Sutton, S. (2000) Interpreting cross-sectional data on stages of change. *Psychology and Health*, 15: 163–71.

Swain, A. and Jones, G. (1992) Relationships between sport achievement orientation and competitive state anxiety. *The Sport Psychologist*, 6: 42–54.

Swain, A.B.J. and Harwood, C.G. (1996) Antecedents of state goals in age-group swimmers: an interactionist perspective. *Journal of Sport Sciences*, 14: 111–24.

Tajfel, H. and Turner, J.C. (1986) The social identity theory of intergroup behaviour. In S.G. Worchel and W. Austin (eds), *Psychology of Intergroup Relations* (2nd edn, pp. 7–24). Chicago, IL: Nelson-Hall.

Taylor, I. (1971) Football mad: a speculative sociology of soccer hooliganism. In E. Dunning (ed.), *The Sociology of Sport*. London: Routledge.

Taylor, S.P. and Gammon, C.B. (1976) Aggressive behavior of intoxicated subjects: the effects of third-party intervention. *Journal of Studies on Alcohol*, 37: 917–30.

Taylor, S.P. and Sears, J.D. (1988) The effects of alcohol and persuasive social pressure on human physical aggression. *Aggressive Behavior*, 14: 237–43.

Terry, D.J. and O'Leary, J.E. (1995) The Theory of Planned Behaviour: the effects of perceived behavioural control and self-efficacy. *British Journal of Social Psychology*, 34: 199–220.

Terry, P.C., Lane, A.M. and Fogarty, G.J. (2003) Construct validity of the Profile of Mood States: adolescents for use with adults. *Psychology of Sport and Exercise*, 4: 125–39.

Terry, P.C. and Slade, A. (1995) Discriminant effectiveness of psychological state measures in predicting performance outcome in karate competition. *Perceptual and Motor Skills*, 81: 275–86.

Terry, P.C. and Youngs, E.L. (1996) Discriminant effectiveness of psychological state measures in predicting selection during field hockey trials. *Perceptual and Motor Skills*, 82: 371–7.

Theodorakis, Y. (1994) Planned behavior, attitude strength, role identity, and the prediction of exercise behavior. *The Sport Psychologist*, 8: 149–65.

Theodorakis, Y. (1995) Effects of self-efficacy, satisfaction, and personal goals on swimming performance. *The Sport Psychologist*, 9: 245–53.

Theodorakis, Y., Doganis, G., Bagiatis, K. and Gouthas, M. (1991a) Preliminary study of the ability of Reasoned Action Model in predicting exercise behavior in young children. *Perceptual and Motor Skills*, 72: 51–8.

Theodorakis, Y., Goudas, M., Bagiatis, K. and Doganis, G. (1991b) Reasoned action theory and the prediction of training participation in young swimmers. *British Journal of Physical Education*, 10: 10–13.

Thompson, R.A. and Sherman, R.T. (1999) 'Good athlete' traits and characteristics of anorexia nervosa: are they similar? *Eating Disorders: The Journal of Treatment and Prevention*, 7: 181–90.

Toro, J., Salamero, M. and Martinez, E. (1994) Assessment of sociocultural influences on the aesthetic body shape model in anorexia nervosa. *Acta Psychiatrica Scandinavica*, 89: 147–51.

Trafimow, D. and Finlay, K.A. (1996) The importance of subjective norms for a minority of people: between-subjects and within-subjects effects. *Personality and Social Psychology Bulletin*, 22: 820–8.

Trafimow, D. and Sheeran, P. (1998) Some tests of the distinction between cognitive and affective beliefs. *Journal of Experimental Social Psychology*, 34: 378–97.

Trafimow, D., Sheeran, P., Conner, M. and Finlay, K.A. (2002) Evidence that perceived behavioral control is a multidimensional construct: perceived control and perceived difficulty. *Journal of Applied Social Psychology*, 41: 101–21.

Trafimow, D., Triandis, H.C. and Goto, S.G. (1991) Some tests of the distinction between the private self and the collective self. *Personality and Social Psychology Bulletin*, 60: 649–55.

Treasure, D.C. and Roberts, G.C. (1998) Relationship between female adolescents' achievement goal orientations, perceptions of the motivational climate, belief about success and sources of satisfaction in basketball. *International Journal of Sport Psychology*, 29: 211–30.

Triandis, H.C. (1995) *Individualism and Collectivism*. Boulder, CO: Westview Press.

Triplett, N. (1898) The dynamogenic factors in pacemaking and competition. *American Journal of Psychology*, 9: 507–33.

Tucker, L.W. and Parks, J.B. (2001) Effects of gender and sport type on intercollegiate athletes' perceptions of the legitimacy of aggressive behaviors in sport. *Sociology of Sport Journal*, 18: 403–13.

Turman, P.D. (2003) Coaches and cohesion: The impact of coaching techniques on team cohesion in the small group sport setting. *Journal of Sport Behavior*, 26: 86–103.

UK Health Education Authority and Sports Council. (1992) *Allied Dunbar National Fitness Survey*. London: UK Sports Council.

Vallerand, R.J. (1997) Towards a hierarchical model of intrinsic and extrinsic motivation. In M.P. Zanna (ed.), *Advances in Experimental Social Psychology* (pp. 271–359). New York: Academic Press.

Vallerand, R.J., Gauvin, L.I. and Halliwell, W.R. (1986) Effects of zero-sum competition on children's perceived competence and intrinsic motivation. *Journal of Social Psychology*, 126: 465–72.

Vallerand, R. J. and Reid, G. (1984) On the causal effects of perceived competence on intrinsic motivation: a test of cognitive evaluation theory. *Journal of Sport Psychology*, 6: 94–102.

van Goozen, S., Frijda, N. and Van de Poll, N. (1994) Anger and aggression in women: influence of sports choice and testosterone administration. *Aggressive Behavior*, 20: 213–22.

Vansteenkiste, M. and Deci, E.L. (2003) Competitively contingent rewards and intrinsic motivation: can losers remain motivated? *Motivation and Emotion*, 27: 273–99.

Varca, P. (1980) An analysis of home and away game performance of male college basketball teams. *Journal of Sport Psychology*, 2: 245–57.

Veale, D. (1995) Does primary exercise dependence really exist? In J. Annett, B. Cripps and H. Steinberg (eds), *Exercise Addiction: Motivation for Participation in Sport and Exercise* (pp. 1–5). Leicester: British Psychological Society.

Vealey, R.S. (1986) Conceptualization of sport-confidence and competitive orientation: preliminary investigation and instrument validation. *Journal of Sport Psychology*, 8: 221–46.

Verplanken, B. and Faes, S. (1999) Good intentions, bad habits, and effects of forming implementation intentions on healthy eating. *European Journal of Social Psychology*, 29: 591–604.

Verplanken, B. and Orbell, S. (2003) Reflections on past behavior: a self-report index of habit strength. *Journal of Applied Social Psychology*, 33: 1313–30.

Vlachopoulos, S. and Biddle, S.J.H. (1997) Modeling the relation of goal orientations to achievement-related affect in physical activity: does perceived ability matter? *Journal of Sport and Exercise Psychology*, 19: 169–87.

Vlachopoulos, S., Biddle, S.J.H. and Fox, K.R. (1997) Determinants of emotion in children's physical activity: a test of goal perspectives and attribution theories. *Pediatric Exercise Science*, 9: 65–79.

Voight, M. and Callaghan, J. (2001) A team building intervention program: application and evaluation with two university soccer teams. *Journal of Sport Behavior*, 24: 420–31.

Walters, E.E. and Kendler, K.S. (1995) Anorexia nervosa and anorexic-like syndromes in a population-based female twin sample. *American Journal of Psychiatry*, 152: 64–71.

Wann, D.L., Carlson, J.D., Holland, L.C., Jacob, B.E., Owens, D.A. and Wells, D.D. (1999) Beliefs in symbolic catharsis: the important of involvement in aggressive sports. *Social Behavior and Personality*, 27: 155–64.

Wannamethee, S.G. and Shaper, A.G. (2001) Physical activity and the prevention of cardiovascular disease. *Sports Medicine*, 31: 101–14.

Ward, R.E. (2002) Fan violence: social problem or moral panic. *Aggression and Violent Behavior*, 7: 453–75.

Webber, L.S., Baugh, J.G., Cresanta, J.L. and Berenson, G.S. (1983) Transition of cardiovascular disease risk factors from adolescence to young adulthood: the Bogalusa post-high school study. *Circulation*, 68(Suppl.)(3): 160.

Weed, M. (2000) The social dynamics of sports groups: arguments for a meso-level analysis. In J. Avela, P.V. Komi and J. Komulainen (eds), *Proceedings of the 5th Annual Congress of the European College of Sport Science*. Javaskyla, Finland: LIKES Research Centre.

Weed, M. (2001) Ing-ger-land at Euro 2000: how 'handbags at 20 paces' was portrayed as a full-scale riot. *International Review for the Sociology of Sport*, 36: 407–24.

Weinberg, R.S. (1986) Relationship between self-efficacy and cognitive strategies in enhancing endurance performance. *International Journal of Sport Psychology*, 17: 280–92.

Weinberg, R.S., Yukelson, D. and Jackson, A. (1980) Effect of public and private efficacy expectations on competitive performance. *Journal of Sport Psychology*, 2: 340–9.

Weiner, B., Heckhausen, H., Meyer, W.U. and Cook, R.E. (1972) Causal ascriptions and achievement motivation: a conceptual analysis and reanalysis of locus of control. *Journal of Personality and Social Psychology*, 21: 239–48.

Weiss, M.R., Wiese, D.M. and Klint, K.A. (1989) Head over heels with success: the relationship between self-efficacy and performance in competitive youth gymnastics. *Journal of Sport and Exercise Psychology*, 11: 444–51.

White, R.W. (1959) Motivation reconsidered: the concept of competence. *Psychological Review*, 66: 297–333.

White, S.A. (1998) Adolescent goal profiles, perceptions of the parent-initiated motivational climate, and competitive trait anxiety. *The Sport Psychologist*, 12: 16–28.

Whitehead, J.R. (1995) A study of children's physical self-perceptions using an adapted physical self-perception profile questionnaire. *Pediatric Exercise Science*, 7: 132–51.

Whitehead, J.R. and Corbin, C.B. (1991) Youth fitness testing: the effect of percentile-based evaluative feedback on intrinsic motivation. *Research Quarterly for Exercise and Sport*, 62: 225–31.

Whitehead, J.R. and Corbin, C.B. (1997) Self-esteem in children and youth: the role of sport and physical education. In K.R. Fox (ed.), *The Physical Self*. Champaign, IL: Human Kinetics.

Widmeyer, W.N. (1990) Group composition in sport. *International Journal of Sport Psychology*, 21: 264–85.

Widmeyer, W.N., Brawley, L.R. and Carron, A.V. (1990) The effects of group size in sport. *Journal of Sport and Exercise Psychology*, 12: 177–90.

Widmeyer, W.N. and Ducharme, K. (1997) Team building through team goal setting. *Journal of Applied Sport Psychology*, 9: 97–113.

Wild, T.C. and Enzle, M.E. (2002) Social contagion of motivational orientations. In E.L.

Deci and R.M. Ryan (eds), *Handbook of Self-determination Research* (pp. 141–57). Rochester, NY: University of Rochester Press.

Williams, G.C., Gagne, M., Ryan, R.M. and Deci, E.L. (2002) Facilitating autonomous motivation for smoking cessation. *Health Psychology*, 21: 40–50.

Williams, G.C., Rodin, G.C., Ryan, R.M., Grolnick, W.S. and Deci, E.L. (1998) Autonomous regulation and long-term medication adherence in adult outpatients. *Health Psychology*, 17: 269–76.

Williams, J.M. and Widmeyer, W.N. (1991) The cohesion-performance outcome relationship in a coaching sport. *Journal of Sport and Exercise Psychology*, 13: 364–71.

Williams, K.E. and Bond, M.J. (2002) The roles of self-efficacy, outcome expectancies and social support in the self-care behaviours of diabetics. *Psychology, Health and Medicine*, 7: 127–41.

Williams, L. (1994) Goal orientations and athlete's preference for competence information sources. *Journal of Sport and Exercise Psychology*, 16: 416–30.

Williams, L. and Gill, D.L. (1995) The role of perceived competence in the motivation of physical activity. *Journal of Sport and Exercise Psychology*, 17: 363–78.

Wise, J.B. and Trunnell, E.P. (2001) The influence of sources of self-efficacy upon efficacy strength. *Journal of Sport and Exercise Psychology*, 23: 268–80.

Wrangham, R. and Peterson, D. (1996) *Demonic Males*. New York: Houghton Mifflin.

Yan Lan, L. and Gill, D.L. (1984) The relationship among self-efficacy, stress responses, and a cognitive feedback manipulation. *Journal of Sport Psychology*, 6: 227–38.

Yates, A.B. (1991) *Compulsive Exercise and the Eating Disorders*. New York: Brunner/Mazel.

Yates, W.R. (1999) Medical problems of the athlete with an eating disorder. In P.S. Mehler and A.E. Andersen (eds), *Eating Disorders: A Guide to Medical Care and Complications* (pp. 153–66). Baltimore, MD: Johns Hopkins University Press.

Yerkes, R.M. and Dodson, J.D. (1908) The relation of strength of stimulus to rapidity of habit formation. *Journal of Comparative Neurology and Psychology*, 18: 459–82.

Yoo, J. (2003) Motivational climate and perceived competence in anxiety and tennis performance. *Perceptual and Motor Skills*, 96: 403–13.

Zaccaro, S.J., Blair, V., Peterson, C. and Zazanis, M. (1995) Collective efficacy. In J.E. Maddux (ed.), *Self-efficacy, Adaptation, and Adjustment: Theory, Research, and Application* (pp. 305–28). New York: Plenum Press.

Zajonc, R.B. (1965) Social facilitation. *Science*, 149: 269–74.

Zeeman, E.C. (1976) Catastrophe theory. *Scientific American*, 234: 65–82.

Zillman, D., Johnson, R.C. and Day, K.D. (1974) Attribution of apparent arousal and proficiency of recovery from sympathetic activation affecting excitation transfer to aggressive behavior. *Journal of Experimental Social Psychology*, 10: 503–15.

Zimbardo, P. (1970) The human choice: individuation, reason, and order versus individuation, impulse, and chaos. In W.J. Arnold and D. Levine (eds), *Nebraska Symposium on Motivation* (Vol. 17, pp. 237–307). Lincoln, NE: University of Nebraska Press.

Zuckerman, M., Kuhlman, D.M., Joireman, J., Teta, P. and Kraft, M. (1993) A comparison of three structural models for personality: the Big Three, the Big Five, and the Alternative Five. *Journal of Personality and Social Psychology*, 65: 757–68.

Author index

Subject index